Blair Worden is one of Britain's pre-eminent historians of the seventeenth century. His books include *The Sound of Virtue: Politics in Philip Sidney's 'Arcadia'*; *Roundhead Reputations: The English Civil Wars and the Passions of Posterity*; *Literature and Politics in Cromwellian England: John Milton, Andrew Marvell, Marchamont Nedham*; *The English Civil Wars 1640–1660*; and *God's Instruments: Political Conduct in the England of Oliver Cromwell*. From 1974 to 1995 he taught at Oxford University, where he has subsequently been Visiting Professor of History and Emeritus Fellow of St Edmund Hall. He has also held professorships at the University of Sussex and at Royal Holloway, University of London.

Trevor-Roper at Peterhouse, Cambridge, 1980 (© Peter Lofts)

HUGH
TREVOR-ROPER

THE HISTORIAN

Edited by BLAIR WORDEN

I.B. TAURIS

LONDON · NEW YORK

MIX
Paper from responsible sources
FSC® C007584
www.fsc.org

Published in 2016 by
I.B.Tauris & Co. Ltd
London • New York
www.ibtauris.com

ISBN: 978 1 78453 124 9
eISBN: 978 0 85772 988 0

A full CIP record for this book is available from the British Library
A full CIP record is available from the Library of Congress
Library of Congress Catalog Card Number: available

Typeset by JCS Publishing Services Ltd, www.jcs-publishing.co.uk

Printed and bound in Sweden by Scandbook AB

Contents

Acknowledgements

Most of the contributions to this volume have drawn on material in Trevor-Roper's papers – the Dacre Papers – in Christ Church, Oxford. Their authors are indebted to the archivist, Judith Curthoys, without whose boundless helpfulness not only this book but the publication of many other writings on or by Trevor-Roper since his death would have been barely conceivable.

I thank the Harry Ransom Center, Austin, Texas, for allowing me to quote material from the papers of Gerald Brenan and A.D. Peters, and the Warburg Institute Library for permitting me to use material from the correspondence of Dame Frances Yates. I am grateful to the following for permission to reprint, in adjusted forms, essays first published in learned journals: Oxford University Press for Chapter 5, which appeared in the *English Historical Review*; Edinburgh University Press for Chapter 6, which appeared in the *Scottish Historical Review*; and Cambridge University Press for Chapter 11, which appeared in the *Cambridge Classical Journal*. Other acknowledgements are made in the notes to individual chapters.

Contributors

Rory Allan read for a BA (Hons) and MSt in Modern History at Christ Church, Oxford, where he is now completing his DPhil thesis on late nineteenth- and early twentieth-century historiography.

John Banville's novels include *The Book of Evidence* (1989), *The Sea* (2005), which won the 2005 Man Booker Prize, *Ancient Light* (2012) and most recently *The Blue Guitar* (2015). He has been awarded the Kafka Prize, the Austrian State Prize for Literature and the Prince of Asturias Award.

Sir John Elliott was Regius Professor of Modern History at Oxford University from 1990 to 1997. An early modern historian with a special interest in the Hispanic world, his books include *Imperial Spain* (1963), *The Revolt of the Catalans* (1963), *The Count-Duke of Olivares* (1986) and *Empires of the Atlantic World: Britain and Spain in America, 1492 to 1830* (2006). His most recent book, based on his experiences as a historian, is *History in the Making* (2012).

Mark Greengrass is Emeritus Professor at the University of Sheffield and Membre Associé of the Centre Roland Mousnier, Université de Paris-IV (Sorbonne). He is author of *Christendom Destroyed (1517–1648)* (2014). He co-directed the British Academy/Leverhulme Trust co-funded Hartlib Papers Project from 1988 to 1995.

E.D.R. Harrison specialises in the study of Nazi Germany and British Intelligence. He is the author of *The Young Kim Philby* (2012) and editor of Trevor-Roper's posthumous book *The Secret World* (2014).

Colin Kidd is Wardlaw Professor of Modern History at the University of St Andrews and a Fellow of All Souls College, Oxford. His thesis on eighteenth-century Scottish Whig historians, awarded in 1992, was the last doctorate to be examined by Trevor-Roper. Kidd is the author of *Subverting Scotland's Past*

(1993), *British Identities before Nationalism* (1999), *The Forging of Races* (2006) and *Union and Unionisms* (2008).

Sir Noel Malcolm is Senior Research Fellow at All Souls College, Oxford. His most recent books are an edition of Thomas Hobbes's *Leviathan* (3 vols, 2012) and *Agents of Empire: Knights, Corsairs, Jesuits and Spies in the Sixteenth-Century Mediterranean World* (2015).

S.J.V. Malloch is Associate Professor in Classics in the University of Nottingham. He works on early imperial Roman history, Latin historiography and the history of classical scholarship.

Richard Overy is Professor of History at the University of Exeter. He is the author of more than 25 books on the Second World War, the Hitler and Stalin dictatorships and the history of air power. His most recent book, *The Bombing War: Europe, 1939–1945* (2014), won a Cundill Award for Historical Literature.

John Robertson is Professor of the History of Political Thought at Cambridge, and a Fellow of Clare College. He was formerly a teaching Fellow and is now an Honorary Fellow at St Hugh's College, Oxford. His doctoral thesis on militia debates in the Scottish Enlightenment was supervised by Hugh Trevor-Roper. More recently he is the author of *The Case for the Enlightenment: Scotland and Naples, 1680–1760* (2005) and *The Enlightenment: A Very Short Introduction* (2015).

Gina Thomas has been London cultural correspondent of *Frankfurter Allgemeine Zeitung* since 1986. She edited the volume *The Unresolved Past: A Debate in German History* (1990), about the dispute among historians over the singularity of Nazi crimes, and is preparing an edition of Hugh Trevor-Roper's writings on the Hitler regime, *The Third Reich*.

Blair Worden was a pupil of Trevor-Roper, is his literary executor and has edited his posthumous book *Europe's Physician: The Various Life of Sir Theodore de Mayerne* (2006). He writes on political, religious, intellectual and literary history of the sixteenth and seventeenth centuries. His most recent books are *The English Civil Wars, 1640–1660* (2009) and *God's Instruments: Political Conduct in the England of Oliver Cromwell* (2012).

B.W. Young is University Lecturer and Charles Stuart Student and Tutor in Modern History at Christ Church, Oxford. He is the author of *Religion and Enlightenment in Eighteenth-Century England* (1998) and *The Victorian Eighteenth Century* (2007), and has written widely on the intellectual and religious history of Britain from the eighteenth into the twentieth centuries. He is currently at work on a study on relations between Christians and unbelievers in eighteenth-century England, and on an intellectual history of Britain during the eighteenth century.

The Life

Hugh Trevor-Roper was born in 1914, the son of a doctor in Northumberland. He went to Charterhouse, a public school, and from 1932 to 1936 was an undergraduate at Christ Church, Oxford, where he read for a degree in Classics before changing to History in his second year. He stayed in Oxford and in 1939 completed his first book, *Archbishop Laud*, which was published the following year. He served in intelligence during the war and conducted the investigation into the death of Adolf Hitler that produced *The Last Days of Hitler* (1947). After the war he returned to Oxford, where he was first a tutor at Christ Church and then, from 1957, Regius Professor of Modern History, a post he held until 1980, when he became Master of the Cambridge college Peterhouse. He retired in 1987 and died in 2003. He was raised to the peerage as Baron Dacre of Glanton in 1979.

Trevor-Roper's life is recounted in Adam Sisman, *Hugh Trevor-Roper: The Biography* (2010; published in the United States – with different pagination – as *An Honourable Englishman*). For other biographical accounts, see the memoir by Blair Worden published in *Proceedings of the British Academy: Biographical Memoirs of Fellows*, VI (2008) and available at www.britac. ac.uk, and the entry by Richard Davenport-Hines in the *Oxford Dictionary of National Biography*.

The Writings

A bibliography of Trevor-Roper's publications can be found at www.hughtrevorroper.co.uk or www.history.ox.ac.uk/research/project/hugh-trevor-roper/bibliography.htm. Those listed below are the ones published in book form, with their dates of first publication:

Archbishop Laud (1940)

The Last Days of Hitler (1947). There have been seven editions. Substantial prefatory material was added to the third edition (1956) and the seventh (1971)

Historical Essays (1957; published in the United States as *Men and Events*)

The Rise of Christian Europe (1965)

Religion, the Reformation and Social Change, and Other Essays (1967; published in the United States as *The Crisis of the Seventeenth Century*; one of its chapters was also published separately in 1969 as *The European Witch-Craze of the Sixteenth and Seventeenth Centuries*)

The Philby Affair (1968)

The Letters of Mercurius (1970; a pseudonymous publication)

The Plunder of the Arts in the Seventeenth Century (1970)

A Hidden Life: The Enigma of Sir Edmund Backhouse (1976; published in the United States, and subsequently in paperback in Britain, as *Hermit of Peking*)

Princes and Artists: Patronage and Ideology at Four Habsburg Courts, 1517–1633 (1976)

Renaissance Essays (1985)

Catholics, Anglicans and Puritans: Seventeenth-Century Essays (1987)

From Counter-Reformation to Glorious Revolution (1992)

Posthumous Books

Europe's Physician: The Various Life of Sir Theodore de Mayerne, ed. Blair Worden (2006)

Letters from Oxford: Hugh Trevor-Roper to Bernard Berenson, ed. Richard
  Davenport-Hines (2006)
The Invention of Scotland: Myth and History, ed. Jeremy J. Cater (2008)
History and the Enlightenment, ed. John Robertson (2010)
The Wartime Journals, ed. Richard Davenport-Hines (2010)
*The Secret World: Behind the Curtain of British Intelligence in World War II and the
  Cold War*, ed. E.D.R. Harrison (2014)
One Hundred Letters from Hugh Trevor-Roper, ed. Richard Davenport-Hines and
  Adam Sisman (2014)

Introduction

Blair Worden

No leading British historian of his generation has commanded so enduring a public readership as Hugh Trevor-Roper. The origin of this volume was a day of lectures delivered, under the auspices of the Dacre Trust and the Oxford University History Faculty, to a crowded audience in the university's Examination Schools in January 2014 to mark the centenary of Trevor-Roper's birth. The audience, like the readership he envisaged, was a mixture of professional historians and participants from a wider world. Centenaries are not perfect moments – if there are such – for the assessment of historians. A hundred years from their births, scholars may be caught between past and present, their personalities familiar to older people but strangers to the young, their writings and outlooks distant from the current historiographical scene but not yet foreign to it. Nevertheless, the perseverance of Trevor-Roper's impact since his death in 2003 is cause for reflection. In the area in which he wrote most, the sixteenth and seventeenth centuries, other British historians among his contemporaries – J.H. Plumb, Geoffrey Elton, Lawrence Stone, Christopher Hill – continue to hold respect or attention, but on the whole for their past achievements rather than any present instructiveness. The same is true, in the other period in which he was most prolific, the twentieth century, of his friend and antagonist A.J.P. Taylor.

There is admittedly a particular reason for the interest in Trevor-Roper's writings since his death. He wrote a great deal which he did not publish and which has demanded to be published posthumously. So far there have been seven posthumous volumes, consisting of books he had not completed, or of collections of essays first published in scattered places, or of private letters or journals.[1] The interest has been intensified by the appearance in 2010 of Adam Sisman's masterly study, *Hugh Trevor-Roper: The Biography*, a work of meticulous research and permanent achievement which, even if it is stronger on its subject's life than on his mind and principles (and for that reason will prompt occasional disagreement in these pages), recreates a vivid career and character in compelling terms. Yet if the posthumous volumes and Sisman's biography have enlarged the appetite for Trevor-Roper's writings, they have not created it.

Most historians are read because readers want to learn about the subjects of their books. Trevor-Roper is of the rare breed whom people want to read on matters to which they might not otherwise be drawn. An essential element of his appeal is literary. His compulsion to exercise his gifts of the pen preceded his choices of genre and subject. The novelist John Banville, who salutes Trevor-Roper's prose in this volume, has elsewhere placed him among the great prose stylists in the English language.[2] Readers acquainted with the lapidary purity of Banville's fiction will recognise the stature of the tribute. Though Banville has written remarkable historical novels, set in the sixteenth and seventeenth centuries, it is in Trevor-Roper's literary artistry rather than his scholarly perceptions that he rejoices. He made his assessment in reviewing the work published in 2010 as *The Wartime Journals*, where the 'faith in literary style' which Trevor-Roper felt he had 'somewhat neglected during the period of research' that produced his first book, *Archbishop Laud*, in 1940, 'took root again and blossomed in the cracks and rocky experiences of the war'.[3] In moments free from the drab routine and dispiriting wrangles of his work in intelligence, Trevor-Roper confided to notebooks which in his lifetime seem to have been known only to himself a series of reflections that are sometimes historical but more often – and at least as memorably – on literature, the natural world, religion or the social world around him. Joyously exploring the nuances of language and the range of its rhythms and tones and colours, they are experiments in the formation of an original style. A reader of the *Journals* who did not know their author's future would have seen that he had high historical talents and ambitions, but might have expected his career to lie elsewhere, perhaps as a twentieth-century parallel to those baroque prose writers of the seventeenth century whom he revered, Sir Thomas Browne at their head. In Trevor-Roper's historical writings, which the war interrupted, the demands of factual exposition and fidelity reduced his artistic freedom. As he aged, his prose became less ebullient, less excited, more measured, more reflective. Yet the stylistic imperative would persist, even in his most coolly forensic writings.

His addiction to language and his delight in its amplitude were formed early. He was trained not as a historian but as a classicist, a legacy explored by S.J.V. Malloch in Chapter 11. Even after his change of undergraduate course to History, classical poetry remained his most intimate mental love. He had great stretches of it by heart, and of poetry in other languages too. Late in Trevor-Roper's life, when he lived alone and was almost blind, a visitor made conversation, which was not always easy, by mentioning a production he had just seen of Shakespeare's rarely performed play *Timon of Athens*. Most people outside professional literary studies would be pressed to quote a single line of the text, but Trevor-Roper responded by reciting a long speech from it. Had he made a study of the play, the surprised visitor asked? No, but he had read it in a vacant evening in the war and been struck by the lines. They had lain in his memory for more than 50 years. Poetry ever pressed on his mind and imagination. He wrote comic and other verse, of which specimens survive of no mean quality. Though he had no time for modern literary criticism, he was an eloquent expositor of the 'alembicated style' of C.M. Doughty's *Arabia Deserta* and, in a spirit that recalls Dr Johnson's, an incisive guide to the properties of the ballad-form or to the rules for reading *Don Quixote* or the novels of Walter Scott.[4]

No word was inanimate to his ear. In the war, encouraged by his elderly friend the writer Logan Pearsall Smith, he made an erudite and enthralled study of the expressive capacities of adverbs. In the same period he lovingly listed 51 'hypnotic polysyllables' which, for all the damage done to the world by organised religion, would have been missed without it: 'Anchorite, Baptistery, Basilica, Canonical, Cardinal, Carmelite, Catacomb, Catechumen, Chasuble, Cloister [...] Septuagint, Seraphim, Supererogatory, Tympanum, Ultramontane'.[5] The misuse of language he detested. Throughout his life he had 'a moral hatred' of 'slovenly language, ambiguity, emotive obscurity'.[6] The oppression and artificial categories of bureaucratic prose dismayed him too. Asked by a colleague, in accordance with new administrative directions, to state whether the case of a candidate for promotion to a professorship was 'strong', 'very strong' or 'exceptionally strong', he dryly answered: 'To someone as fastidious and scrupulous about shades of language as I am, this is a very difficult question.'[7] He pounced on mixed metaphors, which cannot be seen, as a true metaphor must, in the eye of the writer's mind – though he supposed mixed metaphors might be better than no metaphors, that signal of imaginative timidity[8] – and on dead ones, brought not from observation of the world but from numbed tropes, or from books instead of life. 'Try', he enjoined a young friend and scholar who had sought literary advice, 'the letters of Samuel Rutherford', the seventeenth-century Scottish divine:

There is a metaphor in every sentence, and every one is stone-dead. He never draws his images from the peel-tower or the yew-tree, the oatmeal or the salt beef, the gannet or the grouse: it is always from the fish-pools of Hebron, the cedar and the cypress, the gourd and the hyssop, the flamingo and the quail.[9]

'I find more pleasure in good literature', he told his friend Gerald Brenan, the writer on Spanish history and literature, 'than in dull (even if true) history.'[10] Yet historians cannot read literature all day. In 1950, while doing the research in the Public Record Office in Chancery Lane that would spark the historical controversy known as the 'storm over the gentry', he lamented to another friend, the art-connoisseur Bernard Berenson, that 'I have read no books – only dry and dusty sixteenth-century leases and records of debt and bills and docquets of inconceivable philistinism. What a price one pays to write history! But I hope to get back to literature soon.'[11] He balked at the 'prolix and ungrammatical' sources for his long study of the Renaissance Huguenot physician Sir Theodore de Mayerne.[12] Not only dreary documents, but also his own expositions of them, cast him down. He found the chapters he had written of an unfinished book on the Elizabethan moneylender Thomas Sutton 'infinitely dull';[13] pronounced his long and intricate textual study of the Renaissance Scottish historian George Buchanan 'boring';[14] and described his principal contribution to the gentry controversy as a 'dusty', 'dry little work', 'a piece of specialization which can give no pleasure'.[15] 'I wish I could be reading literature,' he wrote to his wife, instead of his own draft of a long book on the Puritan Revolution, 'which is so dull'.[16]

The fact remains that he chose to spend most of his career working on historical sources or writing on historical subjects. He renounced a highly promising future as a classical scholar in favour of history, a less prestigious subject, because the linguistic challenges of classical study had come to seem thin intellectual fare. During the war he never seems to have contemplated any other long-term career than a historical one. In the postwar years he focused on economic history, the branch of historical study which is least friendly to literary display. Only amid the cheerlessness and pressures of war did he exult in style for style's sake, and even then it was not an encompassing gospel. When he wrote about style later, he always regarded it as an instrument, not an end in itself. On first acquaintance with the writings of Desiderius Erasmus, the late fifteenth- and early sixteenth-century thinker whom he would come to venerate, he was charmed by the wit and irony of his Latin prose, but in time he came to admire those qualities less for themselves than as the apt vehicle of a profound message.[17] He adored the style of another of his intellectual heroes, Gibbon, but declared the imputation 'that the foundation of Gibbon's work was his style' to be 'rubbish'.[18] Style, the image of character, was also the mirror of thought and of values. He found the debt of Cardinal Newman's style to Gibbon's 'one of the paradoxes of literature' because of the contrast, as he saw it, between Gibbon's timeless wisdom and Newman's inhuman postulations.[19] The dead metaphors of the 'detestable' Samuel Rutherford betrayed the mental equipment of a 'bigot'.[20] It was because of its political results rather than its aesthetic dereliction that slovenly language earned his 'moral' hatred.

Trevor-Roper's readers are drawn to what he says, not just the way he says it. The characteristics of his prose serve intellectual principles and purposes. Its vitality implements his urge to make history a living subject, a dimension of contemporary thought and debate. Its lucidity honours his insistence on clarity of thinking and on its inseparability from clarity of expression. Its irony and subtlety give voice to the complexity of life and indicate his resistance to dogmas which impoverish or threaten the variety of thought or experience. Its wit mocks the solemnities of enclosed or parochial attitudes. Behind those positions there lie a set of premises which constitute – to adopt the noun he favoured – a historical 'philosophy'. It is not the sole animator of his writing. Gratification in the discovery and communication of historical patterns or facts, the occupational pleasure of the historian, plays its inevitable part. Yet we can identify principles which give unity to the exceptional diversity of his writings. There were changes of preoccupation over his career, two overlapping ones above all, both of them roughly centring on the early 1960s, though they were not abrupt. First there was a shift in the balance of his interests, from economic and social to intellectual history. He told Brenan in 1968, 'I used [...] to think that I was interested in economic history; but then I realized that the only thing that raises humanity above the other animals, and makes its history worth studying, is its independence of mere conditioning' and its capacity for achievements of the mind and spirit.[21] In reality his interest in 'conditioning' was ineradicable and was brought to bear on intellectual history as on material history before it, though the shift did narrow the gap between his historical and literary inclinations. Secondly he moved from the beaten tracks and principal battlegrounds of current historical writing to new questions and horizons, where he found more scope for the individuality of his thought. Intellectual history, today a large academic presence, was then a marginal one. Neither of those developments, however, transformed an approach to the past which in its outlines had been formed at an early age.

It is the expression of a 'philosophy', he always maintained, that distinguishes a historian from an 'antiquarian'. His own philosophy is not easily pinned down or summarised. Intellectually a loner, not a member or founder of a school, he did not situate himself in relation to current historiographical programmes. The philosophy was not straightforward, and he drew back from straightforward summaries of it.[22] It is less often defined in general statements than woven into, or indicated in asides from, its particular illustrations. Although his approach conformed in principle to the classical view of history as 'philosophy teaching by examples', he judged that view superficial if it led historians to overlook the contexts within which the examples occurred, and without which they are liable to misinterpretation. His insistence on the particularities of contexts, and on the accumulated or momentary moods and pressures that distinguish one event, or the experience and outlook of one generation, from another, forbade the simple extraction of universal formulae.

The 'rules' of history, he declared, 'are not "scientific": they are tentative and conditional, like the rules of life'.[23] He did not build a system of thought or expound novel theoretical insights. He was not drawn to philosophical 'abstractions' or to forms of learning that were 'isolated from common sense and the world'.[24] He tended to choose his subject matter not from intellectual first principles but in reaction against the misconceptions or misrepresentations of other historians or in response to chance discoveries or commissions. Many of his arguments were, or anyway began life as, inversions of existing orthodoxies or theories. There are other obstacles. The pervasive irony of his writing, his capacity for self-mockery, the frequent carapace of frivolity, and the playful exaggerations of his private letters – where some of his historical thinking is most uninhibitedly stated, but where it is tailored to the tastes and enjoyment of his correspondents – all impede the definition of his views, not least by quotation, which, as the reader may already have sensed, can in his case be as reductive as it is necessary. Then there are the apparent contradictions between what he asserts at one time and says at another. They generally arise not from inconsistency but because episodes or persons looked different according to the angles from which he viewed them, and because any intelligent view of the world carries its ambivalences. Sympathy and antipathy – towards religious saints; towards Quakers; towards Oxford, which 'I love [...] and I hate';[25] to St Augustine, 'loved' by Trevor-Roper at one moment and a 'bigot' at another[26] – contended in his mind.

Complex as the identification of his historical premises is, they can be recovered. Lenin famously said that everything is connected to everything else. In other respects Trevor-Roper was hardly Lenin's kindred-spirit, but a serviceable starting point is the devotion of so much of Trevor-Roper's writing to the reconnection of subjects which specialist divisions of the past had divided by periods, by national boundaries, or by academic disciplines or subdisciplines. 'A historical philosophy', he argued, 'must apply to humanity in any period.' It 'is incompatible with' the 'narrow frontiers' within which 'most professional historians specialize',[27] for specialist studies can illuminate nothing beyond themselves. They can supply valuable material to historians but are not to be confused with their function. A historical philosophy requires comparisons over time and place, a method to which his capacity for lateral thinking – the analogical instinct which inspired not only so many metaphors but so many historical parallels – was ideally suited. All historical parallels, he knew, are 'imperfect and therefore dangerous',[28] but if treated cautiously, and with alertness to the surrounding divergences, they can illuminate general rather than merely particular truths.

Comparisons were for him an essential component of historical thought, whether they were made explicit on the page or whether they merely informed a historian's mind. Comparative history needs matter for comparison, which Trevor-Roper's inclinations forever impelled him to gather. What he noted of Gibbon he practised himself: 'Always, as his eye was fixed on one event, or one situation in history Gibbon's mind was ranging over distant horizons, thinking of analogies, contrasts, possibilities, to envisage, or correct, a generalization.'[29] Trevor-Roper's historical training was the undergraduate essay, which required its writer to get to the gist of a subject in one week before moving to another in the next. The essay, which in that era was still an accustomed literary form, was his instinctive mode. It took his publications across eras, and across geographical boundaries, as he 'swished through' the 'long series of jealously tended and strongly fenced small-holdings' of the specialists.[30] It was in the 'very variety' of his historical essays, he suggested, and in the 'general' questions that ran through them, that his own 'philosophy' was 'best illustrated'.[31]

The forestalling of comparisons was to his mind not the only drawback of specialisation. Its complementary fault is the separation of segments of the past from the 'continuum' or 'process' of history,[32] a practice that limits the specialists to short-term and thus shallow explanations. He admired beyond measure Gerald Brenan's 'astonishing book', *The Spanish Labyrinth*,[33] a study of the origins of the Spanish Civil War published in 1943, where Brenan broke ranks with historians who, as Trevor-Roper complained, 'conveniently break up Spanish history into centuries' and so 'do violence to its continuity'.[34] Brenan set his subject within the broad range of Spanish history, his pen moving back and forth across its periods. Trevor-Roper made his own 'best undergraduates studying sixteenth- and seventeenth-century Spain' read the book, for, as he told Berenson in 1954, 'there is more profound analysis' of the period between its lines 'than in the explicit statements of any work written directly on the subject'.[35]

The continuum of history links not only past eras with their neighbours but the past with the present. The historical dimension of the present – its evolution from the past, and its affinities or parallels to it – is part of the historian's necessary scope. Brenan, Trevor-Roper told him, was 'my ideal historian', for 'you *see* the past in the present'.[36] Trevor-Roper rejected the unhistorical terms of modern ideological conflict which others had brought to the interpretation of Spanish history, and which 'often ascribe a spurious novelty to ideas or experiments which are really old'.[37] He likewise took issue with the 'static' models of non-historical sociology, a cult subject in the late 1950s and the 1960s, which segregated the present and eliminated what should have been the third dimension of the discipline, movement over time.[38] His mind moved, as Gibbon's did, between past and present illustrations of recurrent phenomena. For example Eric Hobsbawm's thesis, announced in 1954, of a 'general crisis' of the seventeenth century gave Trevor-Roper a transferable phrase, at least after he had adjusted its use, to depict challenges, past and present and across national frontiers, to the whole order and mentality of society. Probably he already had a concept close to it from Burckhardt, but it seems to have been Hobsbawm's article which gave the term to his mind. As well as using it for an alternative explanation of seventeenth-century revolutions, he deduced, from observations about China and Europe in the fifteenth century, a 'general conclusion' about the ways societies respond 'when hit by a general crisis';[39] assessed Burckhardt's response to the 'general crisis' of and after 1848;[40] and meditated on 'the general crisis which – at least since 1945 – we all feel in the West'.[41]

The compartmentalisation of the past and of its study provoked many of his habitual aquatic metaphors, which might interest a Freudian by the frequency of their protests against freezing or blocking or stagnation. In the war he waxed metaphorical when exclaiming against the self-protective refusal of the various branches of the intelligence service to share their findings. After the war he applied the same principle of convergency to intellectual life. In the years after 1945 he was exhilarated by the work of Fernand Braudel and the *Annales* school in Paris, now 'the capital of historical studies'.[42] Under that inspiration he adopted the principle of 'what the French call *interhistoire*',[43] the crossing of disciplinary frontiers. It was a goal he pursued with almost evangelical commitment long after the achievements of the *Annales* school, and his own attention to it, had faded. History itself was dependent on refreshment by other disciplines:

> Conceive, if you can, modern history without the contributions of economists like Adam Smith, Simiand and Keynes, sociologists like Marx, Weber and Sombart, philosophers like Hume and Hegel, scholars of culture and art-history like Burckhardt and Mâle, even anthropologists and psychologists like Frazer and Freud. None of these were professional historians. And yet but for their work the study of history would have perished and dried up long ago.[44]

Sometimes he dwelt on the errors of those authors, in Hegel's case contemptuously,[45] in Marx's, especially after the rise of Soviet power,[46] ferociously. Even so, the speculative mistakes of thinkers who asked 'new questions' were 'more fruitful' than the search for 'finality', which in intellectual matters can be left to 'time and mediocrity'.[47]

If history needed to engage with other subjects, its internal frontiers must likewise be traversed. He was long exercised by the challenge of bringing together social and economic history with political history, both of which had been impoverished by their separation. He was excited by the recent evolution of social history. In the light of its advances he took it for granted that all good history would now have a sociological aspect,[48] though to him sociology was the historical subject founded in the century of Montesquieu and Hume and Adam Smith, not the modern claimant to the noun. In his younger years he revered, and often applied in his own work, the contribution of R.H. Tawney to the study of social and economic history. Time brought disenchantment. Once Trevor-Roper had discovered Braudel and other continental historians, Tawney's approach seemed insular. As Trevor-Roper explored the Puritan Revolution, a more fundamental objection emerged: Tawney's failure to establish the connections which he postulated between social and political history. One of Trevor-Roper's complaints about modern sociology was 'the divorce [...] so often made' by it 'between politics and society'.[49]

His book on the Puritan Revolution was an attempt to demonstrate their inseparability. Yet his most innovative contributions to the crossing of subdisciplinary boundaries lay elsewhere, in intellectual and cultural history. To most of today's historians it is axiomatic that the ideas or literature of earlier times, or their science or art or historical writing or medical practices, were to some degree shaped by the happenings and mental frameworks of their time and place, to which they need to be related. Half a century ago that was a suspect notion, resisted by specialists who explained past developments as processes of internal evolution in thought or art, and who only superficially referred to the wider movements of society. A number of historians, it is true, were achieving social or political contextualisation or were feeling their way towards it. Trevor-Roper's pioneering achievement was to make the approach a general principle, to be applied not just in particular cases or particular subdisciplines but across them. The constituent features of intellectual and cultural history, he believed, needed to be related not only to the events of a larger world but to each other, for beneath them there lay the mental infrastructure of a particular age and, within it, assumptions and premises which affected them all.

In his *Renaissance Essays*, published in 1985, his 'principal interest' was in 'intellectual and cultural history, which I have tried to see not in isolation but in its relation to, and expression in, society and politics'.[50] The five long essays that constitute his *Catholics, Anglicans and Puritans*, which appeared in 1987, 'are all concerned, in one way or another, with [...] intellectual history', which 'can never be studied in isolation. It is conditioned by its social and political context, quickened and distorted by events.'[51] Equipped with that principle he would spot, in the findings of a monograph of limited horizons, wider implications that had not occurred to its author. What other reader of the writings of G.H. Turnbull or W.A.L. Vincent on the group of seventeenth-century social reformers now known as the Hartlib circle would have glimpsed the significance of the interest taken by the parliamentary leaders of the English Civil Wars in the millenarian framework of the circle's ideas – ideas which by the light of modern thinking looked off-beam, not to say crazed, but which, once their roots in the thought and mood and experience of the age were recognised, could be seen to illuminate mainstream events? Historians of the Civil Wars, keeping to the political surface, had ignored so apparently eccentric a subject. Trevor-Roper's conclusions about the circle have their problems, as Mark Greengrass argues in Chapter 3, but historians of the seventeenth century now take the political potency of millenarian beliefs as read.

A much larger enterprise of interconnection and a still more remarkable feat of conception was his long study, based on sources in six countries and eight languages, of Sir Theodore de Mayerne, physician at the court of Henri IV of France and then of James I and Charles I of England. Mayerne's varied career, in medicine and art history and scientific experiment and diplomacy, had been shared out among the modern specialists, so that no one had begun to see him whole. The problem was compounded by the insularity of English historians and by the 'ignorance' of French historians in Anglo-Saxon matters,[52] for Mayerne's life and concerns ran back and forth across the Channel and could not be reconstructed from one side of it. Just as historical study should know no divisions of 'time', so must it cross the boundaries of 'space', most of all perhaps in intellectual history, which, because 'ideas overflow national boundaries', 'cannot be localized'.[53] The European dimension of English history was a recurrent theme of his studies. It is found, for example, in his account of mid-seventeenth-century British and European revolutions in his essay on 'The General Crisis of the Seventeenth Century', discussed by Sir John Elliott in Chapter 1; or in his recreations of the foreign connections of seventeenth-century English thinkers;[54] or in his exploration of the French and Swiss contributions to Gibbon's historical thinking.[55] Trevor-Roper placed Mayerne's career within the wide political and mental setting of Europe's wars of religion. He also related it to the intellectual suppositions that linked the physician's diverse activities. Here as elsewhere he paid special attention to the medical doctrine of Paracelsianism, which prospered and then dissolved in Mayerne's lifetime. This act of rescue was linked, across a subdisciplinary divide, to Trevor-Roper's study of the Hartlib circle, for Hartlib's ally John Amos Comenius 'has too often been seen as a merely educational reformer, just as Paracelsus has been seen as a merely medical reformer. In fact they were both total philosophers, presenting, with different emphasis, a continuous, comprehensive, Neoplatonic ideology,'[56] an ideology visited by Trevor-Roper in other contexts too.[57]

He furthered the inter-historical cause in his teaching and as a professor. In Oxford he ran a university class in 1961 on 'Intellectual Movements of the Sixteenth and Seventeenth Centuries', and recurrently held such classes over the next decade. One of the speakers in 1970 was the young Quentin Skinner, whose early work linked the political thought of the Civil Wars to political events, a practice now commonplace but then innovative. He addressed the seminar on the relationship of Hobbes's *Leviathan* to the political debates that followed the execution of Charles I. Trevor-Roper thanked him for his paper: 'I began this course with an allocution urging the class to treat intellectual history in its context and not merely as a kind of antiquarianism or genealogy of ideas. You gave a marvellous practical application of my general thesis.'[58] In the month before he wrote to Skinner he was arguing for 'a history of science in its intellectual and social context'. He took steps to advance the careers of two young scholars who shared that approach, Charles Webster and Piyo Rattansi. At Trevor-Roper's invitation Webster, whom he had been instrumental in bringing to Oxford, joined him in chairing the seminar series to which Skinner's paper belonged.[59] In a reference written, also in 1970, on behalf of an American candidate for a post, Trevor-Roper commended the candidate as 'one of those scholars who study history and literature together; who see literature in its historical context and history illustrated by literature'.[60] Historians now habitually make use of such literary evidence as ballads. Writing on Walter Scott nearly half a century ago, Trevor-Roper had to explain that Scott's interest in collecting ballads was not a frivolous pursuit, for

> ballad literature, to the student of it, is inseparable from history: it is the direct expression of a historical form of society which often has no other documents. In collecting the ballads of the past, Scott was re-creating and illustrating a vanished or vanishing society, and thereby, indirectly, becoming its historian.[61]

Trevor-Roper situated other historical writing within the mainstream of thought and politics, where nowadays its place is as familiar as it was then peripheral. That endeavour was a large strand of his writing from the mid-1960s. He also commissioned a series of volumes, edited by leading scholars, to introduce the works of major historians of the past to the public and to place them among the political and intellectual pressures of their time.[62]

Art history was another focus of his inter-historical commitment. In 1968 he helped find a post at Oxford for Robert Evans, who nearly 30 years later would join the list of Trevor-Roper's successors as Regius Professor. Evans's book on the Holy Roman Emperor Rudolf II, published in 1973 and based on a doctoral thesis that Trevor-Roper called 'the most interesting work that I have read for a long time',[63] had recreated the seemingly bizarre late sixteenth- and early seventeenth-century mental world of Rudolf's court, where, as in the

Stuart court attended by Mayerne, politics and art and science came together. 'The intermixture of art and politics' had long fascinated Trevor-Roper.[64] He had been inspired by the writings of Burckhardt on the Renaissance and of Emile Mâle, 'whose works were a revelation to me', on medieval religious art and by the company and library at Berenson's home at I Tatti outside Florence. 'What a revolution in the study of history', he reflected to Berenson in 1955, 'the development of art history *as a branch of history* has caused.'[65]

Trevor-Roper never imagined that historians could 'explain' the greatness of art. He was impressed by Whistler's dictum: 'Art happens.'[66] But the restoration of contexts could illuminate the character and subject matter of painting, especially through the study of artistic patronage. In his book *Princes and Artists*, published in 1976, he explored – amid the 'bristling poleaxes and flickering stilettos' of the specialist art historians – the patronage of four Habsburg rulers from the early sixteenth century to the early seventeenth. One of them was the obsessive collector Rudolf II, who, when viewed 'within the enclosed category of pure art history', had been taken to be 'a mere eccentric, or a mere aesthete, pursuing art for art's sake: the first collector who "freed himself entirely from every non-artistic criterion"'. But 'if we follow Mr Evans and try to see Rudolf's intellectual world as a whole, in its own right and its own context', we find the Emperor to have been 'the patron of that secular, ecumenical world of Renaissance humanism which still resisted both Reformation and Counter-Reformation' and which distanced not only Rudolf but the art he collected from the court of his fellow Habsburg Philip II of Spain, 'the patron of unyielding Catholicism throughout Europe'. Again Trevor-Roper was essaying connections, and drawing contrasts, beyond the scope of specialists. Again he was seeking out the unifying suppositions that supply the mental equipment of an era, for 'the Rudolfine age, like the Elizabethan age, is an age in itself; it had its own philosophy, its own inner springs.'[67] It was for the recovery of such inner springs that Trevor-Roper revered the studies of Renaissance intellectual history by Frances Yates.[68]

In Chapter 3 of this volume Sir Noel Malcolm chides Trevor-Roper for adopting, in his insistence on the posthumous influence of Erasmus in the field covered by Malcolm's essay, the 'approach which goes through the past identifying friends and allies' of a historian's own views. Trevor-Roper deplored that method and would have been troubled by Malcolm's criticism. But he would also have repudiated the modern supposition that historians should – or could – leave their human preferences at the entrance of their studies. They must, of course, avoid crude or partisan judgements, which reinforce prejudices instead of enlarging views, but unless they are machines – or ' antiquarians' – their writings will unavoidably incorporate their sense of moral or civic health. In 1969 Geoffrey Elton amiably pointed out to Trevor-Roper that, although the two men stood 'side by side' against the fashionable sociological theories of the time, 'we are poles apart on this question of lessons from history and studying the past for its own sake.'[69] Elton, like the great nineteenth-century advocate of scientific history Leopold von Ranke, believed in the separation of past and present. He thought that the discipline of professional study could insulate historians from the interpretative distortions brought by pressures of current thinking. Yet, as Trevor-Roper observed in his valedictory lecture at Oxford, 'Even the most "objective" of historians [...] are imprisoned, though they may not know it, in a philosophy, which is conditioned by human experience.'[70] Elton's reputation was built on the thesis that there was a 'Tudor Revolution in Government', which now sounds a twentieth-century rather than sixteenth-century concept.

To meet a historian, in Trevor-Roper's perspective, is to encounter not only views but also a personality with feelings and values, which likewise cannot and should not be left at the entrance. Trevor-Roper's style is the medium of personality as well as of thought. Many historians now appear to mistrust style, as if it were a distraction or mere decoration. They favour a species of prose which, if a computer resourceful enough were devised, could be written by it. One cannot imagine Trevor-Roper composing a sentence interrupted, as the house style of some academic publishers now requires, by brackets containing, as it might be, the words 'Smith, 2007, p. 443'. Implicit in his writing is the assumption that a historian's personality, no less than a historian's philosophy, should know no frontiers between the business of study and the business of living and thinking and feeling. The past and the present mingle freely in Trevor-Roper's letters to his friends or in his descriptions of his travels. In both cases the documents, though relaxations from historical labour, are permeated by historical reflection, often of a kind it would have been imprudent to print. Being handwritten, they convey personality as print never can. In the 1960s he was dismayed to learn that undergraduates had started typing their essays. Teaching was an act of personality too. His advice to his pupils was as likely to be given outside as within the formal context of a tutorial or the syllabus. It was for a way of thinking that rose above particular historical subjects that a number of his undergraduates gratefully remembered him. His graduate students would never have finished their theses if they had followed all his extracurricular advice: if they had read all the books, learned all the languages or visited all the cities and pastoral landscapes that he urged on them.

It was axiomatic to Trevor-Roper that history must be 'useful', as it can only be if it has 'some lay appeal'.[71] It must address the concerns not only of fellow scholars but also of readers for whom it cannot be a primary occupation, and who look to it for a comprehension of their daily world and for a broadening of its mental horizons. It is scarcely too much to say that he took the foremost purpose of historical writing to be the understanding of the present through investigation and reflection beyond it. Of course, a historical philosophy that is tied to the preoccupations and attitudes of its author's time will date. Enduring historical writing will be of contemporary use to the future too. Even so, 'the great historians', knowing the continuity of past and present, 'have [...] always been conscious of the problems of their own times' and have 'responded to some extent to the demands of their age'.[72] In reflecting on his own career he observed that 'historians of every generation, unless they are pure antiquaries, see history against the background – the controlling background – of current events. They call upon it to explain the problems of their own time' and 'to give to those problems a philosophical context'.[73]

He made it his business to ponder those problems and illuminate them. He set aside studies of past periods that were crowding upon him in order to bring a historical dimension to matters of public agitation: the exposure of the Soviet spy Kim Philby in 1968,[74] or the debate over Scottish devolution in the 1970s.[75] His book on Scottish mythopoeia was meant as a contribution to the devolution debate and was dropped when the debate receded.[76] His seminal essay on the Scottish Enlightenment, discussed by Colin Kidd in Chapter 6, was among other things a provocative challenge to the present-day intellectual scene in Scotland, which suffered by the comparison.[77] To scholars committed to specialisation, his diversions into the present may have seemed derelictions of duty. To him they were a discharge of responsibility. So were his frequent combats with historians who, wilfully or inadvertently, misrepresented the past, for to get the past wrong is to misinform the present, which takes its bearings from its perceptions of it. Moral judgements explicitly or implicitly inform his assessments of past as well as present historians, among them Thomas Carlyle, whose historical philosophy is set beside Trevor-Roper's by B.W. Young in Chapter 10.

Carlyle's appeal to Nazis gave his writing a disturbing modern pertinence in Trevor-Roper's mind. Trevor-Roper's own studies of Hitler again brought a historical dimension to concrete modern questions. During the war he knew himself to be living through momentous history, and thought of the conflict as Europe's Peloponnesian War.[78] His involvement in the living history of wartime intelligence, and then in the hunt for Hitler in 1945 that is the subject of the chapters by E.D.R Harrison and Richard Overy, coloured all his subsequent historical thinking. So did his alertness to the practical implications and consequences of his wartime work. His report on the Führer's death, from which *The Last Days of Hitler* would grow, was written 'to prevent the growth of a myth'.[79] It was submitted at a time when the legend of a living Hitler could have had terrible consequences, and when even General Eisenhower had accepted mendacious Soviet claims that the Führer had survived.[80] In the decade or two after the war Trevor-Roper understood the power of public perceptions and memories of the conflict to influence its aftermath. 'Two opposite errors' about Hitler were current, both of them obscuring the lessons of the war and capable of nourishing fresh horrors. First there was the perception of him as a 'mere charlatan, only accidentally placed in a position of absolute power', a view 'not only wrong but, by its almost inevitable political consequences, disastrous'. In reality Hitler, in the early days of Nazism, 'showed a political genius' which, warns *The Last Days*, 'we are in danger of forgetting, but which it is very important that we should remember'. 'His ultimate purpose', 'the destruction of European civilization by a barbarian empire in central Europe', had been 'clear to those who did not willingly deceive themselves', but would be missed by self-deceivers now. Secondly there was 'the error of tomorrow (and yesterday)', 'that he really could have solved the crisis of our century'. It was the need to 'correct' those misconceptions that gave birth to his transformative and lasting essay 'Hitler's War Aims'.[81]

Not all his writing had such direct or practical modern application. But even in his work on distant pasts the present is never far away. Two contemporary shadows hung over his writing and affected his choices and management of subjects. There was the 'crisis of civilization' – a concept so pervasive in public consciousness in the earlier part of his life[82] – that had been wrought by ideological fanaticism and two world wars, especially the barbarities of the second of them; and there was the subsequent ideological polarisation of the Cold War. Under the first grave shadow people 'look to history not for detail or for diversion but for serious lessons'. If professional specialism and introversion withhold them, the public will turn to the nonsense of 'the prophets of woe' or of 'change', Spengler, Toynbee, Marx.[83] A number of Trevor-Roper's attacks on bad postwar history summon the adjectives 'dangerous' and 'disastrous'. In 1960 he warned that the separation of sociology from the study of politics 'can lead to political disaster'.[84]

He was sure that there was such a thing as 'civilization', the opposite of barbarism, and that its strengths and weaknesses, its movements forwards or backwards, were the historian's proper subject. As he said in response to the new demand, based on the claim that 'all history is equal' and therefore equally worth studying, for the inclusion of African history in syllabuses of the early 1960s, there was no historical light to be drawn from studies of 'the unrewarding gyrations of barbarous tribes [...] whose chief function in history' – like the function of Afro-Asian or of Anglo-Saxon history to writers of the Enlightenment – 'is to show the present an image of the past from which, by its history, it has escaped'.[85] He believed that the Renaissance had begun a long period of what in general could be called 'progress'.[86] Until the end of the nineteenth century that development had bred a new human confidence. 'Serene' historians and thinkers 'in the happy years before 1914 [...] could look back on the continuous progress, since the seventeenth century, of "reason", toleration, and humanity, and see the constant improvement of society as the effect of the constant progress of liberal ideas'. The ideas were fundamental to Trevor-Roper, but they had become neither impregnable nor absolute, for now 'we recognize that even rationalism is relative.' Now, too, 'we have been forced [...] to devalue the power of mere thought.' His alertness to that development informed his inter-historical mission, for it showed that 'intellectual history is relative and cannot be disassociated from the wider, social context with which it is in constant interaction.'[87]

The destruction and savagery of the twentieth century had blighted the perspective of its predecessor, so that 'we no longer feel that history is the history of progress, or that our civilization is unique.'[88] In that mental climate the 'Dark Ages' which had followed the fall of the Roman Empire, when 'an imperial civilization, as mature as our own, by a seemingly organic mortality declined and crumbled', acquired a new relevance.[89] So did a subject on which he wrote much more: the religious fanaticism of Europe's wars of religion of the sixteenth and seventeenth centuries. For in the twentieth century the power of the irrational had reasserted itself. A historian could and should aid the understanding of it. The challenge is undertaken in his study, published in 1967 in his book *Religion, the Reformation and Social*

Change and subsequently printed on its own, of the European witch-craze of the sixteenth and seventeenth centuries. Since the 1960s the witch-craze has become an academic obsession, but at that time Trevor-Roper felt obliged to anticipate the imputation that the persecution of witches was 'a disgusting subject, below the dignity of history'.[90] In the nineteenth century, he reflected, it had been

> natural to see the witch-craze of the past, like the persecution of Moors and Jews, or the rise of torture, or the censorship of books, as a residue of mere obscurantism which growing enlightenment had gradually dispelled, and which would never now return. Unfortunately we have seen them return [...]. We have seen the darkest forms of superstitious belief and superstitious cruelty springing again ...

This time they had emerged 'not out of half-purged religious systems, but out of new, secular roots'.[91] The 'climate of fear' that fostered the persecution of witches had its 'parallel' in 'the McCarthyite experience' of the United States in the 1950s, which at least had been brief but which 'may yet recur'.[92]

Myth, the irrational, fantasy, the limitlessness of human credulity,[93] 'the haunted chambers of the human mind',[94] were recurrent preoccupations of Trevor-Roper, from Nazi mythology to the less nocuous mythopoeia of the Scots, who had 'domesticated a dangerous process' which had taken such hideous forms in Germany,[95] and to the 'hidden' imaginary life of the Sinologist Sir Edmund Backhouse. 'Fascinated by certain general problems raised by' Backhouse's career, Trevor-Roper reflected again on the witch-craze and felt he could better understand 'the psychology of the Desert Fathers'.[96] Alarmed as he could be by the irrational, and contemptuous as he frequently was of it, he was no cold rationalist. There was a characteristic ambivalence in his attitude to mythology, as to religion. They were permanent characteristics of humanity, with power for good as well as ill. Though 'theological doctrine and clerical discipline are both repellent to me', 'a world without devotion seems to me arrogant and vulgar, a world without mythology mean and threadbare.'[97]

The second shadow, the Cold War, animated his interest in Erasmus and Erasmianism, a theme explored by John Robertson in Chapter 5. In Trevor-Roper's mind Erasmus, the resister of ideological polarisation between Catholic and Protestant, was 'the intellectual hero of the sixteenth century, and his failure was Europe's tragedy'.[98] Whatever the shortcomings of Trevor-Roper's postulation of an 'Erasmian' third way – an adjective he knew to have its difficulties[99] – it gave him a shorthand term for a body of sixteenth- and seventeenth-century opinion which declined to submit to either the polarisation or the clerical authoritarianism of the wars of religion. The opinion, and the variety of the forms it took, are much better known to historians now, and are more easily understood by them, than they were at the height of the Cold War. Behind his essay on Erasmus in 1955 there lay the dispiriting experience of the 'Congress for Cultural Freedom' in Berlin five years earlier, which, as he recalled, 'mobilized the intellectuals of the West and invited them to howl in unison against the rival intellectuals similarly mobilized in an opposite "Intellectual Congress" in Breslau'.[100] The same event underlay an essay he wrote in the previous year on the pragmatic coexistence, and the capacity to learn from each other, of those ostensibly implacable sixteenth-century enemies, the Christian lands and the Turkish Empire.[101] Setting the two sixteenth-century subjects beside his experience in Berlin, he drew two lessons for the present day: that 'opposite sides in an ideological struggle, for all their high-sounding abstract slogans, are not so opposite as they think they are'; and that 'the theory that the world cannot live "half slave and half free", that a frontal struggle between opposing systems' – a prospect that was awaited now as it had been in the wars of religion – 'is sooner or later inevitable and might as well be hastened by an ideological crusade' is erroneous.[102]

It was because 'the age of rational, tolerant piety now seems to be closing' that he thought his essay on Erasmus might be 'useful'.[103] He kept a portrait of Erasmus above his desk, and surely drew inspiration from his example. He, like Erasmus, took on not only ideologues but also specialists, a class who declared the scholarship of both men to be lightweight and took offence at the more colloquial venues of its expression. Is there an autobiographical scent to Trevor-Roper's observation, in his inaugural lecture, that Erasmus's enemies 'accused him of levity, flippancy, irreverence (today they would accuse him of "journalism")'?[104] Is there another to his question, posed in the passage on the Berlin Congress in the same essay on Erasmus, 'What does a humanist do when bigotries swell, black and red, on either side?'[105] He would hardly have compared his gifts or achievements to Erasmus's, but Erasmus's ideals, while belonging to a doctrinal and spiritual make-up remote from his own thinking, spoke to him across the differences. Though Erasmus was defeated in his own time, his writings would outlive the tomes of the specialised theologians who denounced him. Like Trevor-Roper he appealed beyond the specialists and ideologues and addressed a laity unimpressed by both. The scholarship of both men was for use. Erasmus's philosophy was 'not merely a middle way of reform', a compromise: 'It was also a positive philosophy', directed towards intellectual and spiritual transformation.[106] In difficulties Erasmus was 'sustained by' the 'sense of mission' that inspired his struggle to recover, from so many centuries of theological accretion, the ideals of the New Testament. By bringing to his readers the lessons his own scholarship taught him, Erasmus strove to 'rescue Christianity from its "Jewish" inheritance and set out the "philosophy of Christ" in its irresistible simplicity'.[107] In reaching the laity and permeating the conflicting ideologies which outwardly rejected it, his teaching demonstrated the power of scholarship, and of historical reconstruction, to alter the world.

In Trevor-Roper's mind Erasmus's philosophy and impact mocked a practice not only of modern ideological historians but of those modern scholars – a much larger number – who were influenced by their categories. The ideas of the past, which are divisible no more by political than by geographical boundaries, were allocated between left and right, terms which 'have no meaning in intellectual history',[108] or were artificially split between progressive and reactionary concepts. It was when Erasmus was viewed in such lights that he seemed merely 'a civilized moderate scholar snuffed out by orthodoxies'.[109] Trevor-Roper made the same complaints about modern perceptions of figures whom he saw as heirs of Erasmus's thinking, the Arminians or Socinians of 'the Great Tew Circle', the subject of a long essay in *Catholics, Anglicans and Puritans*. The circle had gathered in the 1630s at the Oxfordshire house of Lord Falkland in the village of that name. Historians condescendingly thought of its members as either 'moderates' or 'dilettanti',[110] and as men remote from political and religious realities. In fact they were deeply engaged in those realities, which some of them would come to shape in later life. To Christopher Hill, the Marxist historian who had the wave of historiographical fashion behind him in the 1960s and early 1970s, and whom Trevor-Roper often has in his eye, the circle was 'a collection of intellectuals who discussed liberal ideas together in that depopulated parish. But while they were talking', the future Leveller William Walwyn and others 'were walking the streets of London, discussing, organizing, canvassing'.[111] Trevor-Roper protested against such characterisations: 'ideas cannot be ranged, like political parties, [...] according to the energy or violence with which men are prepared to go in one of two directions.'[112]

Current events, which helped shape his historical thinking during and after the Second World War, had already had a decisive impact on it before war broke out. The failure of Marxist history, to which in some of its aspects he had been drawn, to predict or explain the rise of Nazism propelled him towards a repudiation of historical determinism and towards 'the strongest conviction that I hold as a historian', in 'historical free-will'.[113] Sometimes the conviction seems to merge in his mind with another anti-determinist position, his insistence on the role of the contingent, in events great as well as small. In the postwar years Marxist determinism was a minority position. Again, however, a loose and diluted version of it, which concurred with it in presenting events as the mere surface of politics, was a powerful historiographical force, which Trevor-Roper was unusual in resisting.

Once more his stance was pertinent to the present – and the future – as well as to the past. If the past were held to show that politics were at the mercy of irresistible events, the inference could foster cowardice and defeatism. It was the 'doctrine of messianic defeatism' that provoked his attack in 1957 on the historical theories of Arnold Toynbee, an essay which concludes with the statement that, 'as some sage philosopher once observed, the irresistible is very often merely that which has not been resisted.'[114] Trevor-Roper was horrified by the pre-war policy of appeasement and by Neville Chamberlain's conduct in the Munich Crisis of 1938, a seminal moment, as he would frequently recall, in the evolution of his thinking. Always he was dismayed by disrespect both for the responsibilities and for the capacities of politics. In the war he expressed 'contempt for muddled thinking, especially in politics, where it affects men's lives and happiness'.[115] Here as elsewhere he drew unexpected parallels between Marxism and positions in other respects distant from it. The belittlement of the political arena by Marxists, who held that 'all politics are but an immaterial reflection of social relations', was shared by 'the technocrat', to whom, 'as to the Marxist, politics are irrelevant'. He had in mind Albert Speer, who, alone at Hitler's court, 'had the capacity to understand the forces of politics, and the courage to resist the master whom all others have declared irresistible', but who, 'supposing politics to be irrelevant', 'turned aside, and built roads and bridges and factories'. His choice, declares the concluding passage of *The Last Days of Hitler*, made Speer, 'in a political sense, the real criminal of Nazi Germany'.[116]

Twentieth-century evasions of political responsibility belonged to another pattern recognisable across the ages. Just as *The Last Days* describes the fatal separation of Nazi power from 'political skill' and the consequent entrenchment of 'irresponsible' power,[117] so elsewhere Trevor-Roper attributed the breakdown of the government of the Stuarts in 1642, which determinist history ascribed to the rise of a new political class seeking power proportionate to its wealth, to the dynasty's 'fatal lack of political skill',[118] especially under the 'irresponsible, unpolitical' Charles I – though the parliamentarian leaders, too, lacked the necessary 'political intelligence' and 'political skill' to prevent a needless civil war.[119] In contrast to historians who 'suppose that the crisis' of seventeenth-century England 'was caused entirely by political and economic changes which no political action could have corrected',[120] he maintained that 'there are no social contradictions which cannot be kept quiet by good politics.'[121] Indeed, it had been a high achievement of Macaulay's *History of England* to demonstrate 'the primacy of politics [...] as the essential motor even of social change'.[122] If Trevor-Roper had ever taken an interest in the preoccupation of a younger generation of historians with private lives, gender relations and patterns of material consumption he would have objected to the separation of those subjects from the political history which enables or destroys social conditions.

His sense of the historian's responsibility to the political present explains his outrage at A.J.P. Taylor's book *The Origins of the Second World War* in 1961. Trevor-Roper assailed its 'utterly erroneous' premise, which he believed Taylor to have made applicable to Hitler by wilful distortion of the evidence, that 'statesmen are too absorbed by events to follow a preconceived plan.' He warned against 'the lessons which might logically be deduced' if Taylor's argument were 'accepted [...] uncritically by the public'. Taylor's misrepresentation of the Führer stood – as did Toynbee's – alongside the errors about Hitler that Trevor-Roper had earlier sought to correct. The general historical problem raised in Trevor-Roper's mind by Taylor's book was 'the outbreak of world wars'.[123] Later Trevor-Roper wrote an essay on the outbreak of the Thirty Years War. There, his mind again crossing the centuries, he compared the episode to the events of 1914 and 1939, which had likewise led to general war, and to the confrontations between the two power blocs since 1945, which, so far, had not done so. Again a general conclusion emerges. Big wars break out, he argued, not by accident but because there are politicians who want war to happen.[124]

The adjectives most commonly applied to Trevor-Roper's historical thinking have placed him in one or other of two rival English political traditions. The fact that, as he wryly noted, the terms Whig and Tory were both applied to him[125] suggests the imperfection of the labels. They can mean too many things. In both cases some of the meanings fit him, and for that reason the terms are rightly if diversely deployed in this book. But as keys to his thought they will get us only so far. It is true that in youthful statements he called himself 'a Whig in politics'[126] and decided there was 'no getting away from the fact' that 'the Whig historians [...] were right.'[127] It is also true that when he became a peer in 1979 he took the Tory whip in the House of Lords, though he was no slave to it. In one sense – though it is a matter of words – he was perhaps both Whig and Tory, for he shared the respect for the organs of society defended by Edmund Burke,[128] a Whig politician with a Tory afterlife. Yet he mentioned Burke only rarely and preferred the humane simplicity of the prose of his adversary Tom Paine to the rotundities of Burke's.[129]

The labels falter as indications of political partisanship. 'It is a vain and desperate supposition', he wrote, to think that the seventeenth-century Whigs were 'the party of liberty and national resistance', or that the Revolution of 1688, which he thought 'on the whole, in its time, a good thing',[130] was the achievement of the Whig Party. 'Such liberties as were then attained were the direct achievement of neither Whigs nor Tories, but the consequence of their often deadlocks, their rare agreements.'[131] He was repelled by blind Tory loyalty to Anthony Eden during the Suez Crisis and detected 'fascist' or at least 'semi-fascist' undertones to it.[132] If Toryism was the party of empire or monarchy or aristocracy he was not in its ranks. He was 'ashamed', and 'felt a hatred of the British Empire', when he witnessed 'the dreadful contrast between wealth and poverty' created by imperial rule in Hong Kong.[133] He was 'nauseated' by the record of 'spoliation, blackmail, and fraud' in the English occupation of Ireland, where, he wrote, 'all English qualities reveal themselves in their most disagreeable form.'[134] Though, with Erasmus, he believed in polite conformity to the institutions of one's country, which provide the framework of stability that is essential to order and civility and improvement, his own instincts chimed with the 'basic republicanism' beneath Erasmus's outward complaisance.[135] Trevor-Roper shrank at the luxury and servility of Renaissance courts and admired writers of the period who contrived to retain at least a measure of independence from the moral and political pressure of royal entourages: Erasmus himself, who like so many others of the century thought of court service as 'gilded misery', and the historian William Camden, who in his 'magnificently uncourtly' account of Elizabeth I's reign resisted her successor's attempts to influence its content.[136] Trevor-Roper described sympathetically the attitude of backwoods English gentry 'nauseated by the unlimited grossness' of the Jacobean court, 'its vulgar ostentation of wealth, its fecklessness'.[137] Likewise sympathetically he portrayed Gibbon as the critic, and not, as Gibbon's readers usually suppose, the admirer, of the superficially benign despotism of the Emperor Augustus.[138] Trevor-Roper's feelings about the upper classes were among his ambivalences, for part of him aspired to join them. Yet he also wearied, especially in his younger days, of the 'vulgarity' and ignorance and triviality[139] of the lives of grand households which had become separated from the means of economic production.[140]

Perhaps there is Toryism, or anyway toryism, in his perennial scepticism and his mistrust of what the eighteenth century called 'enthusiasm'. He often disparaged the comfortable and self-deluding Whig or liberal optimism of the nineteenth century. The best historians, he declared, were pessimists. He concurred with Gibbon's depiction of history as 'little more than the register of the crimes, follies, and misfortunes of mankind'. When told that revolutions release creative and constructive forces, he would remember the account in Tocqueville's *Memoirs*, a work he absorbed in his younger years[141] and long remembered, of the Revolution of 1848 in Paris and of the madness it brought to the surface of society.[142]

Even so, the terms in which he thought of himself, during the war, as 'instinctively a British Whig' are instructive.[143] Mistrustful of concentrations of power, he favoured not only constitutional but also social balances which could withstand it, of the kind a prosperous and intelligent aristocracy could supply, though it would have to be a different class from the indolent and perhaps doomed aristocracy of modern Britain. He was no egalitarian. Many a Whig grandee might have endorsed his wartime statement that 'a fluid, mercantile ruling class, with dissimilar interests and dependent on adaptability, not privilege, for survival [...] is the best guarantee of sound politics, high material standards and the possibility of cultural achievement. The liberal virtues I regard as both absolutely good and empirically most serviceable.'[144] It was the commitment of Whig history to those virtues that led him to champion it against neo-tory history in his youth. The virtues served because they fostered pluralism. He craved 'variety and sophistication', a favourite phrase. The trends of his own time, not least the enlargement of trading areas and the postwar confidence in the capacity of science and social planning to eliminate the world's inconsistencies, seemed to be moving against those virtues. 'I like a various world,' he wrote to Brenan in 1968, 'full of social, political, intellectual differences: the "progressive" view of the world dispirits me. Must we have an identical pattern of thought and behaviour, of food, habits, speech, political totems, value-judgements, cant, from China to Peru?'[145] 'I sometimes feel', he told another correspondent in 1970, 'that the ultimate good in a modern scientifically dominated world' is a 'uniform, mindless, termite humanity'.[146] He sympathised with, but was troubled by, the movement towards Jewish assimilation: 'I do not *want* to see the Jews assimilated. I do not like the idea of "one world". I like variety and a plurality of ideas and social systems: it is out of such variety (it seems to me) that change and progress has come.'[147] In 1968 he sighed for 'European variety and sophistication' in the face 'of those two vast, blank, faceless, uniform continents' and of the crude Cold War ideologies they harboured.[148] While the Cold War lasted he longed for Europe to come together politically, as a counterweight to those rival powers. Later, when the European Community became an instrument of bureaucratic expansion and uniformity, he wanted Britain to withdraw from it.[149]

His inclination to variety came not only from taste, though the taste was decided,[150] but also from the conviction that without it societies tend towards a sameness that inhibits adaptability. One of the 'general conclusions' which emerge when history is 'seen [...] as a continuous process' was that

> any society, so long as it is, or feels itself to be, a working society, tends to invest in itself: a military society tends to become more military, a bureaucratic society more bureaucratic, a commercial society more commercial, as the status and profits of war or office or commerce are enhanced by success, and institutions are framed to forward it.

So when 'a general crisis' arises it may 'find itself partly paralyzed by the structural weight of increased social investment'. Adaptability is easier in 'a complex elastic society – what today we would call a liberal society – in which different interests have separate, competing institutions'.[151] In writing on the Puritan Revolution he compared the vulnerable condition of the *'ancien régime'* of pre-Civil War England to the social and political flexibility that enabled the nation to overcome what seemed to him comparable problems in the 1830s.[152]

Variety was an intellectual as well as a social or political necessity. In scholarship, as in religion, heresy 'is a sure sign of intellectual vitality just as

[...] uniformity is a sure sign of intellectual stagnation'.[153] 'Settled intellectual traditions' can 'inhibit the free thought of even the best of scholars',[154] which is one reason for his belief, which he pursued so fearlessly, that living history is always 'controversial' history.[155] The traditions are perpetuated by the intellectual monopolies commanded by churches and also by professions, such as the 'rigid social caste' of the medical fraternity which, until Paracelsus challenged it, had 'perpetuated the inveterate errors of a millennium'.[156] They are perpetuated too by dogmas. He linked Marxism and Catholicism, again very different creeds but both having a prominent place in the postwar intellectual scene, as fellow opponents of intellectual dissent and diversity. They betrayed their common craving for unthinking uniformity by joining hands in an interpretation of medieval English history which alleged that 'Protestant individualism', 'the ideology of capitalism', had 'broken up the social solidarity of Merry England'[157] – though in youth he had held not too dissimilar a view himself.[158]

In assailing the protective walls of clerisies Trevor-Roper was once more the follower of Erasmus, that champion of lay religion. Again across the periods, again including his own time, Trevor-Roper identified outlooks which distinguished lay from clerical and professional interests. In 1957 his inaugural lecture, 'History Professional and Lay', was a manifesto for the laity's entitlement to the historical instruction which the professionals, writing for each other, were denying them. In the same year he began the writing of his book on the Puritan Revolution, where he described the resentment of the English gentry at professional monopolies of wealth and expertise. 'For in spite of the Reformation', which had ostensibly emancipated the laity,

> it now seemed to them that religion, education and the law had all been professionalized. They had fallen, or fallen back, into the hands of complacent corporations which were converting them [...] into private monopolies with mysterious, private rules, the means of perpetuation.[159]

It was while writing the same book that he managed the successful campaign to elect Harold Macmillan as Chancellor of Oxford University, in preference to the candidate of the university's establishment. He viewed that outcome as the defeat of the 'professionals' and 'experts' by 'the educated laity who do not see why they should be excluded from politics because they are not politicians, nor from intellectual matters because they are not scholars, nor from the university because they are not academics'.[160] In 1962 he wished that in his book on Laud he had 'more positively' studied 'that elusive, still neglected force in our religious history, the English laity',[161] which in a later essay on Laud he called 'the measure of the Church'.[162]

A charge often was and is levelled at Trevor-Roper: that he failed to write, as great historians do write, a magnum opus. He described the book he attempted on the Puritan Revolution as 'my *magnum opus*',[163] and hoped that that 'huge book, in three volumes', would 'disperse my critics'.[164] In January 1957 Sir Lewis Namier, sympathising with Trevor-Roper's feeling that the Oxford professoriate was keeping him down, advised him to 'snap your fingers' at the university and 'write a *magnum opus*, as you can; and the outside world will set right the wrongs of a very small circle'.[165] Trevor-Roper worked intently on the project in the initial period of his tenure as Regius Professor. Though aged only 43 on his appointment, he was open to the charge of under-achievement. He had written famous controversial articles on the sixteenth and seventeenth centuries. A high proportion of the chapters (most of them book reviews) of his *Historical Essays* in 1957 were on the same era. Yet *Archbishop Laud* remained his only book on the period. Namier was not the only senior historian to urge him to improve the record. Also in 1957 Trevor-Roper's retired senior colleague at Christ Church Sir Keith Feiling hoped that he would write 'a long book on the seventeenth century'.[166] In 1968, when Trevor-Roper had abandoned the book on the Puritan Revolution, his friend the nonagenarian American historian of seventeenth-century England Wallace Notestein, unaware of that decision, admonished him: 'It will be a sin against the gods if you go down to the shades' without having written a multivolume work on the Cromwellian period. 'I shall haunt you from Hades.'[167]

Because he did not produce the book, Trevor-Roper has been said to have 'squandered his marvellous gifts'.[168] He had offered a hostage to fortune by confiding to his wartime journals his 'fond ambition to write a book that someone, one day, will mention in the same breath as Gibbon', an aspiration which, it has been stated, 'would never be fulfilled'.[169] It might be objected that in alluding to Gibbon, whom he anyway took to be on a level unreachably above his own, he is unlikely to have been thinking of the scale of *The Decline and Fall*; after all, it is the cast of Gibbon's mind, not the length of his book, that the adjective 'Gibbonian' customarily signals. It might also be answered that the prose of *The Last Days of Hitler*, and of other writings of Trevor-Roper, has often been compared to Gibbon's. *The Last*

Days has established an enduring claim to greatness, though not of course to the length which the term magnum opus conventionally indicates. Then there is the long, albeit single-volume, posthumous book on Mayerne, an extraordinary scholarly achievement. 'Great history books are few and far between,' declared the *Times Literary Supplement*. 'This is one.'[170] Even so, it is not quite the book it would have been had he completed it and, as he surely would have done, refreshed it by rewriting. It does not quite have his customary sparkle of presentation, so that only the more penetrating or persevering of non-specialist readers are likely to be drawn into the complexities of Mayerne's life and thought. And though Mayerne was an ideal subject through which to recreate many aspects of the mental world of the Renaissance, as the book formidably does, his career was too rarely at the centre of events or of influence to allow full scope to Trevor-Roper's panoramic perspective on the age.

There has been a common explanation of Trevor-Roper's failure to publish a monograph of weighty erudition: he spent too much time writing journalism. His friends feared that danger. As early as 1948 one of them urged him, 'seriously', to resist the 'temptations of contemporary journalism'.[171] Twenty years later Notestein told him: 'I wish you did not have to spend energy on journalism [...] you cannot ride two horses indefinitely and you may be one of the greatest of English historians.'[172] Trevor-Roper sometimes complained to his wife that the financing of her expensive tastes by writing for money was diverting him from scholarship. Yet no one was more insistent than she that he should be 'a *serious* writer' and not 'waste his energies' on 'writing for the press'.[173] In February 1954, when they were planning to marry and he was planning a book, a 'major work' – likewise destined to non-fulfilment – on late Elizabethan and Jacobean England, she told him that if they were together she would 'make it my aim in life' to

> get you to write your book [...]. After all, you must admit that you do not have very much output to show, so far [...]. It is not enough. As soon as your sabbatical year starts, *you* are to start writing – and *I* am going to force you.

Three weeks later, when she repeated the instruction, the subject 'worried' her 'beyond words'.[174] The sabbatical came and went, with great industry but, as he had been terrified to think might happen,[175] no book to show for it. In 1957 he raised the stakes by committing himself, not merely to the writing of another book, but to the production of a very big one. The project became widely known, and by the early 1960s stories about a huge unfinished work lying in the attic, which had a long life ahead of them, were commonplaces of academic gossip. His failure to complete the book was unmentionable in his presence (though he was in any case always secretive about his literary plans). Adverse public comments became ceaseless, and by early 1964, according to his wife, were 'having a disastrous effect on him'.[176] The attacks of others may in reality have been a less heavy burden than self-reproach. 'My greatest fear', he had written during the war, 'is that in the end I shall have achieved nothing which will have made my life worthwhile; my deepest depression is when I realize that I am achieving nothing.'[177] In 1953 he was 'very determined' to 'write another book', and 'fearful' lest he should fail.[178] What went wrong?

It is quite true that he wrote a great deal of journalism, and that – long before his marriage as well as after it – he was alert to its financial returns.[179] He always thought the labourer worthy of his hire. It is also quite true that the writing of a big book requires undivided attention, which he achieved only in spurts. Yet journalism is both an insufficient and a misdirected explanation. Whatever his shortcomings, a shortage of scholarly activity was not among them. He failed, not to write books, but to complete them. His work on the Puritan Revolution, though much the most ambitious of his projected books of the 1950s, succeeded to a series of others, all of them substantial, as he tried to find the right focus for the intellectual and nervous energy, and the prodigious range of reading and reflection, that he brought to the sixteenth and seventeenth centuries. First there was Thomas Sutton; then – Sutton proving too 'dull' a 'dog' to hold together a book well advanced[180] – a collection of studies of the use of great wealth in and around his time; then the succession crisis of late Elizabethan England and the social bases of the parties of those rivals for the Queen's favour, Robert Cecil and the Earl of Essex; then the policy of Cecil himself, under Elizabeth and James I; then Anglo-Spanish relations from 1604 to 1660; then – another extensively drafted project – the Weber thesis of the relationship of Protestantism to capitalism. In the midst of all this he wrote an unfinished book, of around 55,000 words, on the Catholic Revival of the nineteenth century.[181]

Almost everything that he published in newspapers, even when it rests on thin reading, expresses his search for historical instruction and invites the reader to thought and intellectual curiosity. 'Pandering to the taste of the public, or the level of the market', he avowed during the war, is 'disgusting, a sin against the light'.[182] As Rory Allan points out in his discussion of Trevor-Roper's role as a public intellectual in Chapter 12, he never pandered. The term 'journalism' covers many kinds of outlets, and he wrote in many of them. But the less deep the forms which journalism takes, the less time the writing of it occupies. What divided his attention was not departures from serious thought but the width and diversity of it. Even on the subjects of brief essays, published in venues which we think of as journalism but only in a loose sense as 'the press', evidence of abundant and patient investigation is often to be found behind the writing. The overweening assurance of the volume of 1957, *Historical Essays*, which were mostly republished from the weekly journal the *New Statesman*, in that time a leading light of the literary scene, can give them an initial appearance of flashiness. The impression conceals an intimidating breadth of study.

The variety of his exertions, a high proportion of them strenuous, can be dizzying to behold. The quantity of his production challenges the power of belief, the more so since he supposed himself to write 'so slowly, so painfully slowly',[183] and since he never appeared hurried. Belief is further strained by the bulk of the scholarly correspondence which he undertook with no eye to publication. There are his long private communications with historians, answering their questions or discussing their or his arguments. There are his painstaking examinations of scholarly questions and documents on behalf of graduate students or archivists or publishers or learned societies.

Somehow the torrents of composition and publication were achieved. Thus in 1959–61, when he was writing hundreds of thousands of words on the Puritan Revolution, he also produced his essay on 'The General Crisis of the Seventeenth Century' and a reply to critics of its thesis;[184] wrote his seminal analysis of Hitler's war aims; did battle with A.J.P. Taylor on the origins of the Second World War; wrote a carefully prepared series of undergraduate lectures on Spanish history and another series on Gibbon and Macaulay; delivered seminar papers on the mid-seventeenth century in Paris and Rome (the latter written in his own Italian);[185] visited Israel to write on the trial of Adolf Eichmann and again to give the Herbert Samuel Memorial Lecture on 'Jewish and Other Nationalisms';[186] wrote introductions or prefaces to works by Burckhardt and Gibbon and Lord Acton, as well as an introduction to a biography of the subject of Gina Thomas's chapter in this volume, Himmler's masseur Felix Kersten; wrote an essay on Alexander von Humboldt, in whom he was developing a warm interest;[187] wrote the essay on the Venetian doge Francesco Foscari that would reappear as the opening chapter of *Renaissance Essays*; wrote his essay on the Hartlib circle; wrote on David Hume; wrote on witch-craft. Even then the list of publications is not complete. There were many other lectures too. He addressed the Oxford University Sociology Society on the shortcomings of modern sociology;[188] addressed the Norfolk branch of the Oxford Society;[189] and delivered in Galway the lecture on Protestantism and capitalism that in 1967 would be the opening essay of his *Religion, the Reformation and Social Change*. In the same period he reviewed more than 60 books and involved himself in a series of minor public controversies. When we move into 1962 we find him writing on the authorship of Shakespeare's plays and giving a lecture on medieval Greece, which he intended to write up as an essay.[190] Somehow he contrived, amid so much intellectual activity, to lead a life. In 1959 he moved into the house in Scotland where he would spend the university vacations. In 1960 he devoted an academic term to the election of Macmillan as chancellor. Meanwhile he wrote, as always, innumerable long letters. No doubt he also found moments for the vacant truancy that he believed necessary to a sense of intellectual proportion.

To have yielded all or even some of those historical subjects to the demands of a single project he would have had to be a different person. As he wrote to Brenan in 1968, 'I find so many people and persons interest me that I am unable to choose, but go constantly from one thing to another.'[191] 'The trouble', he told Notestein four months later in response to the older man's exhortations, is that 'I am interested in too many things; and [...] by the time I have written a chapter I have got interested in something else.'[192] Restlessness of mind ever summoned him to pastures new. Never does he look like a man destined to write a single, towering work. Temperament, talent and conviction all drove him towards variety. For all the immensity of his industry he lacked the evenness of keel and the prosaic persistence demanded by the completion of immense undertakings. To write 'in such a way that will satisfy me' he needed to feel 'buoyant and resilient',[193] a frame of mind frequently halted by depression or exhaustion or a 'private disease',[194] which was apparently a form of sinusitis with attendant complications, and in which nervous stress, invisible to the colleagues and audiences to whom he was so imposing a presence, played its part. Sometimes, in his letters to his future wife, written from his lonely Oxford rooms in 1953–4, he seems close to breakdown. His belligerence in controversy can look like a refuge from unhappiness. In the depths of the long vacation of 1953, a time of year when solitariness could be most oppressive, he told his wife that he was 'enjoying hugely' the '*particularly* malicious' passages he was writing for his work on nineteenth-century Catholicism,[195] which was taking him away from his multiple projects on the sixteenth and seventeenth centuries. The ploughing of a lengthy furrow cast him down. It also induced doubts about the validity of the project. As the drafts of the Mayerne book piled beside him he would ask himself whether the subject and effort were 'worth it'.[196] The drudgery that always attends the completion of a book and the checking of facts and references excludes the sense of fresh exploration on which he thrived. What was it, after all, but a search for the 'finality' that could not inspire him? He would take his explorations for his projected books a long way, but wilted when they began merely to confirm a pattern he had already identified, and thus to illustrate the law of diminishing returns.

If there is such a thing as a nervous artistic sensibility, he possessed it, even if his exterior, at once worldly and emotionally buttoned, allowed few signs either of his inner strains or of the sharpness and delicacy of his antennae. There is his intense alertness, perhaps heightened by the weakness of his eyesight, to mood and atmosphere around him: for example, to 'the quality of the air', 'a thing I am very sensitive to' and a recurrent theme of his letters. Clarity or transparency of air made him 'so well and so gay'. He delighted in it in his native Northumberland or on the coast at Dunbar, where he was a schoolboy.[197] He exulted in 'that air, that sky', which 'make Greece, to me, so infinitely more beautiful than Italy, that touch of cloud and mist that carries the outlines of mountains and seas out of clarity and into mystery, a kind of divine mystery!'[198] He delighted in the air of Nazareth, where he found 'a delicate wildness', 'a sudden changing of atmosphere and colour, that I thought existed nowhere other than in Greece'.[199] The 'transparency of the air' delighted him on his solitary journeys in the 'infinite volcanic wastes' of Iceland.[200] But in the 'dank', 'dreadful', 'unhealthy' Thames Valley, where at least until 1959 most of his writing was done, 'black moods' of 'deepest depression' would overwhelm him, though again he would conceal them from the world.[201]

Other atmospheric sensations took their toll. Flying over the glutinous, 'vulgar' Mediterranean Ocean during the war, he was downcast by the sight of that 'vain, purposeless' sea 'throwing its waves wearily, eternally, upon the long, empty desert shore. It was a symbol of futility, of the purposelessness that so perplexes and dismays me.'[202] 'A feeling of hot spiritual claustrophobia' visited him amid the 'learned sawdust' on the shelves of Blackwell's university bookshop in Oxford, where 'all the accumulated mundungus of all the centuries of man' seemed to be gathered, while next door in the Bodleian Library there lay 'the unseen, oppressive, brooding presence of myriads of musty tomes, hundreds of tons of them weighing me down with their stifling, persecuting bulk'.[203] Not many scholars feel stifled or persecuted by the tools of their trade.

His defeat by the book on the Puritan Revolution must figure in any assessment of his career and is recounted in Chapter 2 of this book. Yet if we concentrate not on what he did not finish but on what he did, his restlessness and the range of curiosity that propelled it may seem not his weakness but his strength. If Trevor-Roper, who took all history for his province, was right to think that his philosophy was 'best illustrated' by the 'variety' of subjects from which he learned it, might not his writings have been less instructive had he curbed their scope? In a long and powerful article on Trevor-Roper's oeuvre Peter Ghosh has argued that 'it is the essays he wrote, and not the books that he failed to complete, which supply the best guide to his identity' as a historian.[204] The distinction should not be over-pressed, for Trevor-Roper's philosophical premises inform his writings in both genres. The essays themselves are of many kinds. The shorter ones, the great majority, implement his principle that a historian should be prepared 'to write essays even on subjects on which he may be ill-qualified to write books'.[205] Most of them are on topics on which Trevor-Roper had undertaken no independent research. They offer not new information but new thought, prompted by the subject at hand and centring on it but drawn from the experience of reflection on so many other ones.

Other essays, mainly long ones, are on subjects on which he did write extensively researched books, finished or unfinished. They were boiled down or extracted from the books, or else contributed to them. The unpublished books on the Puritan Revolution and the Weber thesis supply the core of the collection *Religion, the Reformation and Social Change*. Most of *The Invention of Scotland*, which brought together studies of medieval, Renaissance and eighteenth- and nineteenth-century history, was published in constituent parts. One would guess that a number of essays which did not become books – the long ones, say, on the Great Tew Circle in *Catholics, Anglicans and Puritans* or on Conyers Middleton in the posthumous collection *History and the Enlightenment* – would have been books, finished or not, had he had enough lifetimes for them. The chapters on Paracelsianism and Robert Burton in *Renaissance Essays* are among many other extended exercises. The marvel is the spread of the subjects on which he probed so far. Even if we confine ourselves to the subjects covered by the chapters of this book, we wonder how any one historian could acquire such authority on such a range of themes.

Religion, the Reformation and Social Change, published in 1967, was in effect his substitute for the book on the Puritan Revolution. Thereafter, except for two books of 1976 – one, *Princes and Artists*, a published version of a lecture-series, the other, *A Hidden Life*, his exquisite but, even by his standards, diversionary biography of Backhouse – the only volumes he published were collections of essays (and even then he did not complete all the collections he planned). It was in *Religion, the Reformation and Social Change* that he discovered the full possibilities of the long scholarly essay. *Catholics, Anglicans and Puritans* would repeat the formula. Though many other essays based on scholarly research in the later part of his career were less long, we can watch in them, as in the lengthier ones, a deepening of meditation and a ripening of insight. The achievement grows with his confidence in managing the proportions of the scholarly essay and in sifting, as the form requires of any author with more information than space to communicate it, the essential from the inessential. The more ambitious or reflective of the chapters of his *Renaissance Essays*, and of the posthumous collection, which he had planned, *History and the Enlightenment*, join the volumes of longer essays in supplying some of his most considered and original writing.

How was he able to write so penetratingly on so many different subjects? Alongside the versatility of a writer who could move so easily among diverse subjects, from poetry to economics or, during the war, from the measured analytical prose of his daytime compositions to the literary experiments of the evenings, we must place two other gifts. There is his power of imaginative identification, which enabled him to find his way so quickly in unfamiliar historical territory. Secondly there are his accomplishments as a reader. Swift but rarely hasty, he would cut immediately to the quick of a document or argument and was blessed with exceptional powers of retention and classification. He instantly mastered the demanding technicalities of the sources in the Public Record Office that he used in his contest with Lawrence Stone over the financial fortunes of the Elizabethan aristocracy. Still more imposing, and beyond the range of any of his contemporaries, was his command of the records, medical, artistic, political, diplomatic, that he collated for his study of Mayerne. The achievement is especially impressive given the loss of the physician's personal papers, for which Trevor-Roper conducted a vain search over the quarter of a century during which he worked on the book.[206] Had he at any point found them, his volume would doubtless have had to be recast. His projected book on Scotland was likewise held up by one of those archival hunts which Trevor-Roper, with a sleuth's gifts for the nosing out of records, relished, but which in this case was seen off by the uncooperative holder of the papers.[207]

If intellectual strengths assisted his endless switches of subject and his speed in controlling them, so did features of his character which might be regarded as necessary flaws. His resolve to illuminate subjects on which experts were beavering away, and about which they often knew far more than he, would have been incompatible with intellectual modesty. His facility brought its temptations. One of them, heightened by his alertness to historical analogies, was to fit people of the past – and the present – too briskly, and in his derogatory moments unfairly, into patterns or categories that had settled in his mind. Metaphors, too, carried hazards for a writer with so vivid an imagination, one who had 'such a visual mind that I am intellectually incapable of understanding things that cannot be visually represented'.[208] The instinct of surely the wittiest historian of his time for satire and caricature, who in youth had Aristophanes for his 'patron saint',[209] sometimes strained his prose against the leash of the evidence, or even detached it. Irrepressible high spirits alternated with his depressions. He never lost an undergraduate zest for comic depiction and elaboration. A comic view of the universe can bring powerful insights, but it can be better at spotting truths of human nature than at accurately reporting their manifestations.

Some of his most arresting analogical surveys were communicated in private letters. Who would exchange their mischievous accentuations for more sober assessments? There is his comic turn, for the enjoyment of his stepson, on the 'tiresome' characteristics of bluestockings, from the sixteenth century to the nineteenth.[210] Or there is his fascination with – and doubtless exaggeration of – continuities, across the changes over time, in the characters of institutions, especially Oxford and Cambridge colleges. His taste for the theme surfaces in his saucy index entries on Peterhouse, the Cambridge college of which he became a controversial Master.[211] It also inspires, in a letter, a disquisition – prompted by 'a rare flash of blinding historical illumination' – on George Abbot, James I's archbishop of Canterbury, as

the archetypal Balliol man: so pretentiously international and yet so parochial; so ostensibly progressive and yet so stuck in rigid and predictable postures; so apparently radical and yet so elitist: talking of grass-roots reform when he had never been in a parish but spent his time lobbying at court and hunting (not very successfully) with Lord Zouche. And then there is that sour-puss smug grumpiness about lesser breeds: Greek and Italian Protestants, liberal Huguenots, Grotius, Critopoulos.[212]

In another letter we watch Trevor-Roper in the Master's stall in Peterhouse Chapel, where he 'placed' himself

by versatile imaginative effort, as the various parts of the service succeed one another, among the fanatical Bedouin of ancient Judaea, the hooligan clergy of Byzantium or the Roman Maghreb, the scholarly Anglican bishops of the seventeenth and the snivelling Methodist hymnologists of the nineteenth century.[213]

*

Trevor-Roper liked to echo to historians the recommendation of Lord Acton to pupils to 'study problems, not periods'.[214] He wrote essays or lectures on universal themes – 'Jewish and Other Nationalisms' was one; 'Medicine in Politics' another[215] – or contemplated, for example, a study of 'the social and historical function of [...] utopias'.[216] In the war he planned a book on religious revivals across the eras, an intention from which, in the 1950s, there would emerge the book he half finished on the nineteenth-century Catholic Revival. It was written with an eye to the whole history of Catholicism – past and present.[217] Also in the war he planned a volume on the history of the English ruling classes, which would likewise have examined recurrent themes across the centuries.[218] His book on Scotland did the same, by bringing together subjects far apart in time which no specialist could have conceived of linking. The volume begins with general reflections on the power of myth in history, just as the book on Thomas Sutton opens with thoughts on the historical role of millionaires, of which the book offered a particular illustration.[219] Other writings were placed in comparable frames of generalisation.

Yet his preference for problems over periods was not absolute. He knew that history cannot thrive mainly on books which cover many periods but are rooted in none. To 'scholarship confined in one rut', he acknowledged, there 'was the opposite danger of dilettantism', so that 'one needs to be a disciplined specialist in one area to have a corrective standard outside that area.'[220] His own area was the sixteenth and (still more) seventeenth centuries, though in the later part of his career it extended into the eighteenth, principally its intellectual history. He never left other periods alone. Medieval history was one recurrent enjoyment, discovered even before he changed from Classics to History, and finding a provocative outlet in the televised lecture-series he published in 1965 as *The Rise of Christian Europe*. In 1951 an intelligent publisher feared that Trevor-Roper was about to abandon the Renaissance and seventeenth century for the Crusades.[221] Another frequent focus was the nineteenth century, where he developed interests in two themes above all: Catholicism; and the historiographical background to the formation of the Weber thesis. But he always came back to the intervening eras.

For all his attacks on specialisation and professionalisation, he had an unstinting respect for scholarship. History could never capture a lay audience unless 'perpetually refreshed [...] by research', which 'is not the same as professionalism'.[222] 'The kind of work that I most enjoy reading', he told one of his graduate pupils, was 'delicate scholarship gradually and irresistibly creating a new problem, or set of problems'.[223] He had his doubts about the doctoral system, which makes graduate students specialists from the start, but acknowledged that it had raised scholarly standards,[224] which he was ready to defend. 'Though I deplore the professionalism that loses sight of its purpose,' he wrote in a letter of 1986, 'I believe that it is professional standards and methods and discipline that have saved history from the far worse fate of Eng. Lit.',[225] in that era a subject in a wilfully disreputable phase.

As Regius Professor he enjoyed nothing more – at times, nothing other – than the supervision of graduate students and the discussion of their work. Earlier, when he was a college tutor, he had been exasperated by the refusal of the then-professoriate, who had a way of keeping graduate students for themselves, to allocate pupils to his supervision.[226] It was while still a tutor that, despairing of what he saw as the scholarly inactivity and backwardness of the History Faculty's leaders, he tried to promote plans for a research institute in England which would emulate that centre of avant-garde scholarship in Paris, the Ecole Pratique des Hautes Etudes, on whose achievements Oxford, and Britain, were missing out. When he became Regius Professor he made scholarly vitality his goal. In 1973 he tried, unsuccessfully, to secure the election of Peter Brown, the historian of late antiquity, to an Oxford professorship, and so to have as his two professorial colleagues at Oxford, in Brown and the holder of a sister-chair, the historian of the French Revolution

Richard Cobb, 'two historians of eccentric genius, who really make history live'.[227] Brown, replying to Trevor-Roper's feeling letter of condolence, wrote of his own disappointment: 'Most of all I appreciated the authentic touch of your enthusiasm for history as a living subject, and was convinced that I could be swept up into it.'[228]

When, in the 1950s, Trevor-Roper explained the rise of specialisation, he attributed it to the opening of the archives in the nineteenth century, which had so increased the volume of evidence available to historians and had prevented any of them from mastering much of it. Frightened of being caught out by colleagues who had read more or other documents, historians had 'drawn in their horns' and shied away from instructive generalisation.[229] He did not at that time remark on the force which in the decades ahead would drive specialisation ahead at an ever faster pace: the expansion of the historical profession and consequently of secondary rather than primary material – that is, of publication by historians rather than of the evidence available to them. No one can hope to keep up with that process. In the 1950s most historians already had a 'period' of study, but the periods normally had some breadth to them. And at least, within any one of them, there was a common stock of secondary reading. Indeed the stock often extended beyond the periods, for historians, who nowadays increasingly teach their specialisms or subjects near to them, then more frequently taught far away from them. Undergraduates, too, studied over a much wider range. The syllabus studied by Trevor-Roper required a 'continuous' knowledge of English history, from Anglo-Saxon times to recent ones. Examination questions bore less stamp of professional self-consciousness than they do now, paying little attention to the latest theory or article and concerned to test only the capacity to marshal information into thought. They were also more worldly, requiring a grasp of past problems of statesmanship or foreign policy that might have their modern counterparts in the outside world which the candidates would join – not least the diplomatic service, on which for a time Trevor-Roper set his sights.

The pace of specialist reassessment has been nowhere faster than in work on the Puritan Revolution, where the hypotheses of the gentry controversy were devoured by the investigations it provoked. It was with new research and new publications in mind that when, within a few years of his abandonment of his huge book, he was urged to return to it, he replied, 'It's too late now.'[230] In this volume Mark Greengrass finds it impressive that Trevor-Roper's essay on the Hartlib circle 'had a shelf-life of as long as a quarter of a century'. The books on Mayerne and Scotland, written in the 1970s, would have seemed more revolutionary, and made a greater impact, had they been published at the time rather than 30 years or so later. Getting work swiftly into print is a new pressure. Gibbon or Macaulay or Tocqueville or even S.R. Gardiner, who laid the scholarly foundations on which twentieth-century studies of the Puritan Revolution have been built, had no army of specialists breathing down his neck or challenging his command of his subject.

Not all dons are moles. Trevor-Roper's writing retains the interest and admiration of professional historians, as the composition of the audience on the day of the centenary conference showed. His scholarly findings are still cited and addressed. Yet most of the attention from academics comes from those of them – and there are many – who continue to think, even if they do not write, beyond their specialisms and who communicate something of that wider perspective to their pupils, who will have a place in tomorrow's public readership. On that front there is no real boundary between 'professional' and 'lay'. Nonetheless, specialist advances have placed his writing in a setting remote from his own. Specialization is always complication. It demonstrates labyrinthine patterns which few outside the field will have the time or prior knowledge to grasp, and before which successive generalizations tumble. It also characteristically highlights the uniqueness of any subject, and thus forestallls analogy with others. Yet it is easy to bemoan specialization, harder to see how to stop it or to want to rein in the curiosity that drives it. It has its own vitality. Far from achieving 'finality', it has created a permanent flux of uncertainty. If you do not like a current historical interpretation, then, as they say of the weather in seaboard Massachusetts, wait ten minutes. The religious conflicts of earlier seventeenth-century England, a recurrent subject of Trevor-Roper's writings, have been examined in a rapid series of specialist studies of distinguished scholarship and great subtlety. If their authors cannot match – as who can? – his powers of intellect and style, they have revealed a complexity of political and theological pattern which brings its own intellectual rewards and which it would be both dishonest and stultifying to deny.

At a number of points in this book its contributors propose modifications of statements by Trevor-Roper or explain that his subjects have moved on. Given his indifference to 'finality', and his greater interest in opening questions than in settling them, that might not have disheartened him. In any case, not a high proportion of what he wrote has been disproved.

When his work is set beside current specialist productions he looks less often wrong than different. Specialists feed off each other even as they disagree. Trevor-Roper read only sparingly the secondary literature that swelled in the later part of his career. Though as alert as anyone to the complexities of the past, he grew impatient with expositions of them when they obscured large questions or diverted attention from them. He followed his own nose among the primary sources and took his own directions among them. His choices were determined not by the pressures of current interpretative developments – let alone by the now-compulsory careerism of academic life – but by the comparative framework that was always in his mind. Was the religious policy of Charles I, and was the opposition that destroyed it, at heart political or religious? That question, to which he often returned, surfaces in a great deal of recent specialist writing. Though he glanced at the writing and was characteristically prompted by disagreement with it into the formulation of alternative hypotheses,[231] his dissent was not over details, or, if it was, it was over the selection of the significant ones. His choices of detail are informed, as those of the specialists are not, by reflection on perennial features, in societies where faith has political power, of the relationship between political and religious motive. That preoccupation does not impede the normal empirical tests of any generalisation. Nor, in the long essays on the seventeenth century which bear on the theme, does it preclude density of investigation. But he is always concerned with 'general' lessons, and always eager to convey them to the laity whom the specialists forget. For the educated laity, or for professionals thinking outside specialist boxes, his writing remains the place to start.

In a rash moment in 1983, in his seventieth year, he was duped into accepting the authenticity of the forged diaries of Adolf Hitler. It was a humiliating episode, tragic or comic according to one's sympathies. Since he was so often publicly critical of errors by others, he could hardly complain when his own were assailed. And since his public life was so coloured by his personality, the exposure of a flaw of personality was of proper public interest. Yet the episode has acquired a preposterously disproportionate place in public perceptions of him, at least outside the range of his readers. It became a calamity not because of the mistake itself – which though puzzlingly naive was intelligible in its context and was no more reprehensible than gaffes by other famous historians whose reputations have barely been affected by them – but because it was conducted in the glare of media publicity, which had, and retains, a hypnotic effect on public consciousness. Writers in the media refer to the episode, by reflex action, whenever his name arises. Yet when they encounter other aspects of his life they voice surprise that 'the Hitler diaries historian' should be known not for his writings, which were the endeavour and achievement of his life, but for the momentary aberration which the media have unrelentingly megaphoned. It is time, after a third of a century, to gain some sense of proportion.

The preface to Trevor-Roper's *Historical Essays* speaks of the 'underlying unity' beneath contents 'various in time, depth and subject' – and, he might have added, in length. The chapters of this book similarly vary, but have their unity in their assessments, from diverse angles, of aspects of his mind and writing. No book or conference on Trevor-Roper could encompass the range of a historian who wrote more widely than most of us read. The event in Oxford from which the volume arises concentrated on the two areas he illuminated most extensively: the era following the Renaissance, and the Second World War. Chapters 1–4, 8–9 and 13 are published versions of lectures delivered on that day. The other chapters enlarge the scope of the enterprise by giving fuller weight to his interest in the history of ideas, especially those of the Enlightenment, or by attending to general characteristics of his thought and prose. Chapters 5, 6, 7 and 11 are reproduced, in slightly amended forms, from learned journals. Chapters 10 and 12 have been newly written for this volume. Because the contributors do not always agree, and because their subjects sometimes overlap, there are occasional moments both of contradiction and of repetition, which it would have been intrusive to eliminate or disguise. The last chapter offers a flavour of his conversation and of the voicing – in this case in summary manner – of his intellectual and literary preferences.

PART ONE

Seventeenth-Century
Revolutions

1

The 'General Crisis of the Seventeenth Century'

John Elliott

Hugh Trevor-Roper's article on 'The General Crisis of the Seventeenth Century', which first appeared in *Past and Present* in 1959,[1] had an enormous impact at the time of its publication and stands as one of the most scintillating in that array of scintillating pieces which, when taken together, entitle him to be regarded as the greatest historical essayist of the twentieth century. Even though more than half a century has passed since the publication of that article, the controversy to which it gave rise never quite died away, and indeed is now showing new signs of life, thanks to the current enthusiasm for global and environmental history, neither of which impinged on the first stages of the debate.[2]

The immediate context of the debate was the publication by Eric Hobsbawm five years earlier, in 1954, of a seminal article which first appeared under the title 'The General Crisis of the European Economy in the Seventeenth Century',[3] and was reprinted in Trevor Aston's 1965 anthology of contributions to the debate, *Crisis in Europe, 1560–1660*, under the crisper title 'The Crisis of the Seventeenth Century'.[4] In that article, which formed part of an internal Marxist debate on the transition from feudalism to capitalism, Hobsbawm posed what, from the perspective of the debate, appeared to be a vital question: why did the expansion of the European economy in the late fifteenth and sixteenth centuries 'not lead straight into the epoch of the eighteenth-and nineteenth-century Industrial Revolution. What, in other words, were the obstacles in the way of capitalist expansion?'[5] His answer pointed to limitations in the market possibilities of feudal society, which eventually, in spite of the sixteenth-century advances, led in the 1620s to a general crisis of the European economy. But he went on to argue that the crisis itself 'created the conditions which were to make industrial revolution possible'.[6] The Dutch, and then the English, were to show the way forward, and, in Hobsbawm's words, 'the triumph of the English Revolution hastened the social transformation of England, and thereby the formation of an active home market.'[7]

In an article which was essentially concerned with economic developments, that seems to have been the only reference to any of the great political upheavals of the mid-seventeenth century which would later, and in large part because of Trevor-Roper's contribution, take centre stage in the debate. These upheavals included the revolts of Catalonia and Portugal in 1640, and of Naples in 1647, against the government of Philip IV of Spain; the English Civil Wars of the 1640s; the Fronde in France against the government headed by Cardinal Mazarin during the minority of Louis XIV; and the displacement in 1650 of the monarchical stadtholderate in the Netherlands by a republican regime under the leadership of the brothers de Witt. The story of these revolts was chronicled by the American historian Roger B. Merriman in a volume published in 1938 which drew particular attention to their contemporaneity and explored the cross-currents between them.[8]

As Blair Worden tells us in his memoir of Trevor-Roper, although he was 'always averse to Marxist determinism and to Marxist prophecy [...] in his younger writings he [Trevor-Roper] accepted the Marxist interpretation of the early modern period as a clash between declining feudalism and emerging capitalism.'[9] Towards the end of the 1930s, however, he became disillusioned with Marxism,[10] and any lingering respect for the Marxist theory of history had long since disappeared by the time of his 1956 essay on 'Karl Marx and the Study of History'.[11] But he remained strongly interested in economic history, partly no doubt under the influence of Fernand Braudel, whose *La Méditerranée et le monde méditerranéen à l'époque de Philippe II*[12] he admired enormously; and he became fascinated with the Weber thesis and the question of the alleged relationship between Protestantism and the rise of capitalism. As a result, he was well versed in the works of the major economic historians of the late nineteenth and early twentieth centuries, and when I first met him – I think in 1954 – he talked with animation about Werner Sombart, whose writings on the rise of capitalism he encouraged me to read, and about François Simiand's Phases A and B of the European economy, with an expansionist sixteenth century as a Phase A, followed by a Phase B of seventeenth-century recession.

He would, therefore, have read Hobsbawm's article with care, since it dealt with a subject in which he was at that time deeply interested, but a growing body of evidence makes it clear that Hobsbawm's piece was not the prime trigger for Trevor-Roper's 'General Crisis' essay. In the early 1950s he was engaged with R.H. Tawney and Lawrence Stone over the rise or fall of the gentry and with Christopher Hill over the Marxist interpretation of the English Civil Wars. He was at that time searching for evidence to support his view that the gentry were a declining and not a rising class – a view that would obviously scupper the thesis of the English rebellion as a bourgeois revolution leading by inexorable stages to economic and social transformation and industrial revolution.

There was nothing parochial, however, about Trevor-Roper as a historian, and although at that moment his primary focus was on English history and the origins of the Civil Wars, his wide-ranging curiosity led him to delve into general European history and encouraged his natural inclination to think comparatively. Spain was to form part of this extension into continental history. He paid his first visit to Spain in 1951, and soon afterwards had a meeting with Gerald Brenan, the student of Spanish history and literature whose book on the Spanish Civil War, *The Spanish Labyrinth* (1943), had made a deep impression on him.

In a letter dated 23 November 1952 he asked whether Brenan could advise him on a point of Spanish history which he saw as having possible European implications. 'It seems to me', he wrote,

> that in the 16th and 17th centuries there is, in Western Europe, on the one hand, a general cult of 'the court', represented socially by the great scramble for offices, the competition for titles, the character of education, the waste and display of official life [...] the tone set by such writers as Castiglione, Gracián, etc. etc., and, on the other hand, an opposite cult which can conveniently be called of 'the country': a cult (often also nurtured among failed courtiers or officials) of self-respecting parsimony and idealisation of an aristocratic attitude. The more I study the social background in England before the Great Rebellion, the more I become aware of this as the fundamental antithesis of society – far more fundamental than religious opposition.[13]

He believed that in the Spain of Philip III the same phenomenon was to be observed as in the England of James I, and he wanted Brenan to point him towards any work that might have been done on the attitude and behaviour of Spain's equivalent of the English gentry, the *hidalgos* of Castile.

He was therefore developing his concept of the court–country antithesis two or three years before the publication of Hobsbawm's article. In fact, two days before writing his letter to Brenan, he gave a talk to the Stubbs Society in Oxford under the title 'Court and Country in the Later Renaissance'. The principal themes of his 1959 essay were already present in embryo seven years earlier: the absorption of urban republics by the monarchical states of the sixteenth century; the expansion of jobs as a result of the administrative changes of the century and the growing pressures imposed on society by increasingly extravagant and profligate courts; and the response to these developments in the shape of protests from the excluded and the victims, with religion providing the language of ideological protest. He writes: 'It is against the background of a struggle between court and country rather than between capitalism and anticapitalism that I see the period of Reformation and Counter-Reformation.'[14]

In an article on 'Country House Radicals' published in *History Today* seven months later, in July 1953, he develops the court–country theme in its specifically English context.[15] But what is so striking about the Stubbs Society talk is the way in which, in a period of marked insularity in so much British historical writing, he is so alive to the continental dimensions of his subject. Continental connections and comparisons would lie at the heart of his approach.

In an attempt to capitalise on the great interest aroused by Hobsbawm's article, the editorial board of *Past and Present* organised a conference in London in the summer of 1957 on the theme of the 'contemporaneous revolutions of the seventeenth century' and asked Trevor-Roper to give the opening paper.[16] Unfortunately he pulled out of this because of a trip to Russia, but I think we can see in this invitation the genesis of the article that the journal would publish two years later. I do not know whether he was formally asked to submit an article or whether he offered it on his own initiative, but he must have seen in *Past and Present* – the country cousin of Braudel's *Annales* – an effective forum for placing before a growing national and international readership his ideas about court versus country as a general European, or at least West European, phenomenon.

A response to Hobsbawm in the pages of *Past and Present* had the additional advantage of providing another welcome chance to take a swipe at the Marxist interpretation of history. In his 1956 essay on 'Karl Marx and the Study of History', he had duly excoriated Christopher Hill and his fellow Marxists for depicting the English Revolution as the triumph of capitalism over feudalism – a depiction that, he pointed out, was not supported by the recent researches of French economic historians which indicated that production and commerce were in general decline in the seventeenth century. Then, with a mischievous glint in his eye, he interrupts the flow of his paragraph in characteristically dramatic fashion: 'But behold, a miracle! In 1954 another English Marxist, Mr. E.J. Hobsbawm, wrote a long article on "The General Crisis of the European Economy in the Seventeenth Century", in which he accepted the change of premises' and endorsed the arguments for the seventeenth century as a century of decline.

> It would seem then that such a complete reversal of Mr. Hill's premises would logically entail at least some adjustment of his conclusions. The English Revolution can hardly be painted as a victory for rising capitalism if capitalism is everywhere in decline.

Christopher Hill, then, would seem to have been well and truly skewered. But Hobsbawm too would not escape unscathed. 'Mr. Hobsbawm dogmatically tacks the old conclusion on to the new premises [...].' In Trevor-Roper's reading, Hobsbawm, 'using completely different evidence', still found 'a "logical" path to the same general "conclusion": in spite of the reversal of its basis, the English Revolution signified the triumph of the capitalist bourgeoisie. One is forced to assume that the "conclusion" was not really derived from the evidence at all, but preceded it.'[17]

Having polished off the Marxists, it was obviously incumbent on Trevor-Roper to advance his own alternative reading of seventeenth-century history; the general European character of Hobsbawm's article made it important for Trevor-Roper not to confine that alternative reading to British history, but to range widely, as he had done in his Stubbs Society talk, over the European continent. While there is no doubt that the court–country antithesis derived initially from his search for an explanation of the English Civil Wars, he had found enough indications, particularly in his reading of the correspondence of Spain's ambassador at the court of James I, the Count of Gondomar,[18] and the writings of seventeenth-century Spanish moralists and economic projectors, collectively known as *arbitristas*, to suggest that this was a formula that lent itself easily to transportation across the Channel.

I joined the editorial board of *Past and Present* in 1958, and in the summer of 1959 Trevor-Roper asked me to look at his essay, which he hoped the journal would be able to take, in spite of its length. I made one or two suggestions for minor changes, which he duly incorporated, and raised some more general points, one of them about the greater cost of warfare in the seventeenth than in the sixteenth century. Here he said he agreed with me and would put in a 'saving formula'. The article came out in the November issue of that year. It begins with a summary list of the revolts and revolutions of the middle of the seventeenth century, although, rather surprisingly, he makes no mention of Merriman's *Six Contemporaneous Revolutions* – a book which tended to be ignored in the subsequent debate, perhaps because Merriman was more interested in examining the revolutions for themselves and the interaction between them than in identifying possible shared characteristics. Instead, Trevor-Roper followed his list of contemporaneous revolts with a contemporary quotation from a House of Commons sermon delivered in 1643 by Jeremiah Whitaker: 'These days are days of shaking, and this shaking is universal.'

The question he posed and set out to answer was the following: 'What was the general condition of western European society which made it, in the mid-seventeenth century, so universally vulnerable – intellectually as well as physically – to the sudden new epidemic of revolution?'[19] He dismissed the Thirty Years War, and indeed the European wars of the sixteenth century, as an insufficient explanation, on the grounds that those wars had 'led to no such decisive breach in historical continuity'[20] – an assertion that might seem to be open to question, raising as it does the whole problem of what constitutes 'continuity'. Did not the Reformation disrupt continuity? Not for Trevor-Roper. The sixteenth century, as he saw it, absorbed its revolutions, whereas the seventeenth century did not. Instead the century was, he wrote, 'irreparably broken' during its middle decades, in ways that made its second half a 'new age', virtually unrecognisable to those who had lived through its first half.[21]

This reading was not, in fact, original. Roland Mousnier had published in 1953, the year before Hobsbawm's article, his massive survey of what we now know as the 'early modern' period in which he depicted the sixteenth century as the age of Renaissance and the seventeenth as the century of crisis and of the struggle against crisis – a struggle that led to the creative transformation of European society.[22] 'The Renaissance – how loose and vague is the term!', writes Trevor-Roper.[23] For him, as for Mousnier, it is loose enough to cover the entire sixteenth century, but the novelty of his interpretation – or at least partial novelty, for he acknowledges in a footnote the inspiration provided by half a dozen pages of Braudel's *Méditerranée*[24] – lies in the distinctive twist he gives to the century, by placing at its heart the defeat of the cities and of the urban civilisation of late medieval Europe by Renaissance princes, the Renaissance state and Renaissance courts.

The general argument of the article follows that of his Stubbs Society talk. The Renaissance state, he writes, was 'at bottom, a great and expanding bureaucracy, a huge system of administrative centralisation, staffed by an ever-growing multitude of "courtiers" or "officers"'.[25] In what is almost a glancing aside in the article of 1959 he adds that 'the Church, which was now everywhere a department of State, was similar.'[26] By the last years of the sixteenth century the growth of the increasingly top-heavy bureaucratic apparatus of state and Church was placing growing strains on society. Then, with the general return of peace in the early seventeenth century, the strains multiplied as princely courts embarked on an orgy of conspicuous consumption. The 1620s, when the years of peace came to an end, saw a widespread anti-court puritanical reaction in the 'country', and 'the "revolutionary situation" of the 1620s and 1630s developed.'[27] After a rapid and undeniably selective overview of the varying responses of different Western states to the crisis, with the response of the English state proving the most ineffective of all, the article concludes that this was 'a crisis not of the constitution nor of the system of production, but of the State, or rather, of the relation of the State to society'.[28]

In view of the interest generated by the article, the board of *Past and Present* invited six historians to respond from the standpoint of their own special areas of expertise, and their responses were published in the November 1960 issue of the journal, along with Trevor-Roper's reply.[29] Although recognising the ingenuity and the stimulating character of Trevor-Roper's essay, all six responses were to a greater or lesser degree critical. To many of the contributors he appeared to underplay the impact of war on seventeenth-century states and societies, and to draw an excessively rigid distinction between a vaguely defined 'court' and an allegedly puritanical 'country'. I remember him telling me some time later that we had let him off pretty lightly, but there is no doubt that he took the criticisms to heart and was determined to rebut them where he could.

Evidence for this comes from the revised version of the original article, as published in his anthology of essays, *Religion, the Reformation and Social Change*, published in 1967.[30] The revisions, which seem to have passed unnoticed, are revealing. There are a number of relatively minor changes and additions. For instance, after telling us that Queen Elizabeth's notorious parsimony became after her death one of her great retrospective virtues, he adds: 'how favourably it compared with the giddy extravagance of James I, the fiscal exactions of Charles I!'[31] He also adds a certain amount of detail about the complaints of the Cortes of Castile and the partial success of reform in France and its failure in Spain, although he omits to address the point that I made in the course of the debate, that it was Catalonia and Portugal, neither of which had a court, which revolted, while the heavily burdened Castile remained quiescent. One or two of the changes are more substantial. They are designed to shore up what some may see as a dangerously shaky edifice. Perhaps the most significant change is a long new paragraph devoted to matters ecclesiastical – a paragraph designed to flesh out his thesis of the top-heavy bureaucracy of the Renaissance state. 'The Reformation movement,' he writes, 'Catholic as well as Protestant, was in many respects a revolt against the papal "Court" – using the word "Court", as I always do, in the widest sense.' 'For although', he goes on to say, 'in one sense, the Counter-Reformation may have been a movement of moral and spiritual reform, structurally it was an aggravation of the bureaucracy.'[32] In a clear response to the criticism made by Mousnier and others about the gulf that separated court from country, he now strengthens his argument by telling us that 'men who think of themselves as "country" at one moment often discover that they are "Court" at another, and such discoveries may lead to unpredictable apostasy.' (Was he thinking here of Charles I's minister Thomas Wentworth, Earl of Strafford, a critic of the regime of Charles I who became its powerful leading minister?) 'For this reason, social tensions seldom if ever lead to a clean split.'[33]

In these changes we can see a skilled craftsman hard at work on repairs, and it is in this revised and repaired form that the article stands as his final judgement on the general crisis of the seventeenth century. How well has it stood the test of time? In terms of its argument my answer would be: not too well. As his critics pointed out at the time, what he had done was to transpose to continental Europe a court–country explanation of the origins of the English Civil Wars which may, or not, work reasonably well for England, but fails to explain adequately the continental upheavals of the mid-seventeenth century.[34] In doing this, he was essentially operating within the same frame of reference as Hobsbawm, although reversing the terms of the equation. A rising bourgeoisie is replaced by a declining gentry, but in both instances a social and economic explanation is being put forward for what Trevor-Roper himself recognised as a highly complex phenomenon, with many other forces at work, and not least those of local separatism. He defended himself by arguing that it is to the structural weaknesses of monarchies that we must look first, rather than to the forces that exploited them. Yet what state, after all, does not have structural weaknesses of one kind or another? What impresses, or at least impresses me, is the determination of monarchs and their ministers, whether in France, Spain or England, to impose – particularly in response to international rivalries and the demands of war – their own revolution from above by infringing traditional rights and liberties in their increasingly desperate attempts to raise more men and money. The effect of this revolution from above was to provoke revolution from below.

He was also taken to task, particularly by Mousnier, for neglecting the 'crisis of ideas' that led to the great intellectual transformation of the later seventeenth century. In response he admitted the neglect. 'To embark on this topic', he wrote, 'would be another task and any summary might prove grossly simplified.'[35] This is a fair point, and it could be argued that he spent a great part of his later career making good the deficiency.

What, then, are we left with? In the first instance, a brilliantly wide-ranging essay, brimming over with new insights and ideas. Here we have a British historian, at a time when so much of British history was insular and parochial, daring to look across the Channel in an attempt to find explanations and analogies for what was happening at home. We also have a historian who was thinking comparatively at a time when not much comparative history was being attempted. As an effort to explain the mid-seventeenth-century revolutions as a universal phenomenon the essay may have been flawed, but by identifying a range of issues – from the origins of mercantilism and the impact of office-holding to the character of courts and the nature of court culture – he either set up or helped renew lines of inquiry which have occupied the attention of historians from that day to this. But above all he presented his ideas and his insights with a style and a panache that are in a class of their own, and that should be a lesson to us all. We shall not, I fear, see his like again.

eighteenth century, which, as he wrote in the war, he liked for 'its elevated self-assurance, its complete and orderly world'.[5] The eighteenth century was the home of his intellectual heroes Gibbon and Hume. It was also the field of the historian who, among those he knew personally, had influenced him most, Sir Lewis Namier.[6] Trevor-Roper applied to the seventeenth century, on his own terms, Namier's principle that political events can be understood only once the social structure and social connections of which they are expressions have been reconstructed.[7] Yet Namier's name rarely figures in Trevor-Roper's historical studies. He saw that Namier's conclusions, which held political ideas to count for less than self-interest, were suited to a period of relatively static politics and of relative ideological consensus, and were of only limited value in explaining the convulsions of the previous century.[8] Trevor-Roper was drawn to convulsions: most of all to those of the seventeenth century and those of his own time. We saw in the Introduction some of the parallels in his mind between Nazi and seventeenth-century ideologies. We shall find others in this chapter.

Yet if such correspondences informed and inspired his interest in the political and religious conflicts of the seventeenth century, he came to the area for reasons remote from his eventual attitudes to it. As an undergraduate his historical priorities had lain in other fields. In his first year, while reading for a degree in Classics, he developed an extracurricular passion for medieval history and read Ferdinand Gregorovius's long work *Die Geschichte der Stadt Rom in Mittelalter*, partly to teach himself German, for he found languages easiest to learn by reading interesting books in them. After his change to a History degree he chose the nineteenth century for his period of foreign history and St Augustine for his special subject. He did not study seventeenth-century Europe, a gap perhaps evident in his early book *Archbishop Laud*; only from around the end of the war does there begin his excited engagement with both the history and the historiography of Renaissance and seventeenth-century Europe. As an undergraduate he was taught seventeenth-century English history by one of its leading authorities, his college tutor Keith Feiling, the historian of the origins of the Tory Party. But though Trevor-Roper expressed admiration for Feiling in retrospect,[9] there was little meeting of minds at the time. Feiling declined to supervise Trevor-Roper's doctoral thesis, stating that he knew too little of the subject.

The thesis, on which Trevor-Roper embarked late in 1936, was originally to have been on 'The Influence of the Puritan Revolution in Determining the Character and Organization of the Anglican Church'. Though the subject quickly yielded to a study of Laud, the architect of ecclesiastical policy under Charles I and the target and victim of Puritan hatred, the initial title demonstrates the early formation of Trevor-Roper's instinct to place historical subjects in long-term perspectives and to seek their enduring significance. In this case the significance had a personal dimension. All his life he was fascinated by religion, in both its historical and its psychological manifestations. By the time he wrote his book on Laud he had come to study religion from the outside. But his initial choice of subject was related to his own religious preoccupations. His public school, Charterhouse, was pledged to conventional Anglican piety. As an undergraduate at Christ Church he attended the High Church services in the cathedral that is part of the college, where even after his religious inclinations had been lost he would be stirred by the devotional singing.

Early in his graduate career he was courted by Oxford's Jesuits. It has often been supposed that he was susceptible to their persuasions and that he contemplated conversion to Rome. Support for that hypothesis might be sought, at the level of psychological speculation, in the aggression with which Trevor-Roper, who had a tendency to turn on convictions to which he had been attracted, came to assail Roman Catholicism in general, and converts to Roman Catholicism in particular. Yet there is no factual evidence for the assertion. His discernible inclinations lay within Anglicanism; they were Anglo-Catholic, perhaps, but not Roman Catholic.[10] They were not held without scepticism; they did not tie him to a group of worshippers or inhibit the jocular secularity of his social life; and they may not have amounted to faith. But they were intellectually earnest. In January 1937, in the early weeks of his thesis, he attended what his diary[11] called a 'very good' sermon by Alfred Blunt, the Bishop of Bradford, at Pusey House, the centre of Oxford's High-Church Anglicanism. The bishop addressed the 'position of the Church as interpreter, and function of the sacraments as the means of establishing connection with reality, etc.' He also, as the diary (briefly, alas) tells us, condemned 'vulgarity' as the opposite of 'faith'.

Yet Trevor-Roper was on the verge of an anti-religious reaction. The diary records that in late February, when he was 'fed up with Laud', he heard himself, on a Sunday, 'inadvertently referring to St Paul as a stupid old bugger', not a prudent assertion in so clerical a college as Christ Church or so clerical a university as Oxford. The break was not abrupt. By the start of May his religion had become 'more detached from my life', but he remained impressed by the social function of Anglicanism. He discussed with a friend 'the position of the Church as an educator and legislator to the layman, on which we agreed'. The title which, after his change to the subject of Laud, he registered for his thesis intimates the same respect for ecclesiastical authority: 'The Attempt of Archbishop Laud to Establish the Independent and Uniform Character of the English Church'.[12] Evidently he had some way to travel before reaching the opinion he voiced in 1965 that 'in a civilized society some lay control of the clergy [...] is the only thing which keeps the clergy within the bounds of sense.'[13] Nonetheless he told the friend that he had 'scrapped all my previous high-church views, together with the foundations on which such views must necessarily rest – original sin, divinity of Christ, and such-like mumbo-jumbo'. In the same month he described his ineffectual supervisor Claude Jenkins, the legendarily eccentric canon of Christ Church and Regius Professor of Ecclesiastical History, as a 'high-church old humbug'. Jenkins responded indignantly to the anticlerical direction the thesis quickly took, though Trevor-Roper was freed from his supervision later in the year, when the younger man was appointed to a research fellowship and was able to drop the thesis in favour of a book. It was probably also in May 1937 that there occurred Trevor-Roper's meditative solitary walk round Christ Church Meadow – or whatever experiences are concentrated into his account of it – when, as he remembered during the war, he

realized the undoubted truth that metaphysics are metaphysical, and having no premises to connect them to this world, need not detain us while we are denizens of it. And at once [...] I saw the whole metaphysical world rise and vanish out of sight in the upper air, where it rightly belongs; and I have neither seen it, nor felt its absence, since.[14]

Though Trevor-Roper preferred the substance of history to the abstractions of philosophy, his new attitude to religion was shaped and sustained by two young philosophy dons in his college: Gilbert Ryle; and Freddie Ayer, whose book *Language, Truth and Logic*, published early in 1936, had as Trevor-Roper would put it in 1950 'demolished the entire metaphysical world'.[15]

Trevor-Roper's work on Laud adapted to his new convictions. He studied not the spiritual content of seventeenth-century religion but its political and material base. He found guides ready to hand. The book owed debts of thought and language to Marxism, to Max Weber, and above all to R.H. Tawney, whose *Religion and the Rise of Capitalism* had appeared in 1926.

Tawney had depicted the erosion of medieval communal ideals and the rise of capitalist individualism in the sixteenth and seventeenth centuries; had associated that process with the Reformation and with Puritanism; and had included Laud among the defenders of the old social order. In Trevor-Roper's book Laud is the doomed champion of the same medieval values against 'the Puritan outlook of the businessman', and against 'progressive classes' and 'improving landlords' who 'consecrated their individualism by the profession of a strenuous Puritanism'.[16]

Tawney returned to the landlords (though not to their religion) in an essay of 1941 published in the *Economic History Review*, 'The Rise of the Gentry 1558–1640'. There he explained how the price revolution of the sixteenth century, and the volatile conditions of the land market, had counted against the great landowners of the aristocracy and enabled the rise of the gentry as their expense. Briefly Tawney made a further assertion, which in the same year he also adumbrated in a lecture, a less substantial contribution entitled 'Harrington's Interpretation of his Age', published both on its own and in the *Proceedings of the British Academy*. In it he drew on the arguments of the political thinker of the 1650s James Harrington to present the successful challenge to the Crown in the Civil Wars as a political consequence of the economic transformation Tawney had described. He made the same claim in 'The Rise of the Gentry', which presents the war as a challenge to a debtor class, the aristocracy, and to its fellow victim of economic change, the Crown, by the creditor class of rising gentry, who, as Tawney fleetingly asserted, found that 'as a method of foreclosure war was cheaper than liquidation.'[17]

Though Tawney made no attempt to demonstrate the connection between politics and economics which he asserted, the effect of his thesis on the study of the Civil Wars was revolutionary. In the later Victorian and Edwardian era interpretations of the Puritan Revolution, an event which since its occurrence had been the most divisive and controversial event in the nation's memory, had been set on a new footing by the scholarly labours and narrative accounts of S.R. Gardiner and his protégé C.H. Firth. But since 1914 investigation into the period had been becalmed. Gardiner's and Firth's nineteenth-century predecessors had seen a social dimension to the revolution. Projecting the social conflicts of their own age onto the seventeenth century, they had equated parliament's cause with the middle and industrious classes and the Crown's with an oppressive and effete aristocracy.[18] Gardiner and Firth likewise indicated, though more dispassionately, that the parliamentarians had looked to the future, both socially and politically. But their great narratives and editions had placed political rather than social conflict at their centre. Gardiner and Firth had more to say about political individuals and their intentions than about classes. It would not have occurred to them to present politics as the expression of economics. To readers drawn to Tawney's approach, mere political narratives now seemed naive and superficial. The impact of the article, and the primacy of economic explanation, were aided by the appearance in the previous year – the same year as *Archbishop Laud* – of the Marxist Christopher Hill's pamphlet *The English Revolution 1640*, which likewise equated the parliamentarian cause with economic advance.

Trevor-Roper was excited by the new perspective. The development of his own interest in the economic fortunes of the ruling class, as in Laud, was strongly influenced by Tawney. It also had an independent impulse and an independent focus of research. Sometime before the completion of *Archbishop Laud* he had chanced, at an antiquarian bookstall in Newcastle, on a seventeenth-century pamphlet which made mention of Thomas Sutton, the Elizabethan founder of Trevor-Roper's school,[19] who had been portrayed to the pupils as a benign philanthropist but whom Trevor-Roper, following the pamphlet's lead, found to have been a 'grasping and philistine' money-lender,[20] indeed the great lender of Elizabethan England and the creditor of large numbers of the English aristocracy and gentry. Trevor-Roper's inquiries were suspended by his wartime work, but by 1944 he was finding time to return to them. He wrote an article, 'The Bishopric of Durham and the Capitalist Reformation', which was published in the obscurity of the *Durham University Journal* in March 1946 (and which was, as in its original version it remains, hard to find). It placed Sutton's role in the financing of the coal trade around Newcastle within a national economic picture. Tawney had himself touched on the financing of the coal trade in the region.[21] Trevor-Roper's article owes a continuing debt to Tawney, though also to Weber, in its association of Protestantism with capitalism. Sutton is described as 'a perfect example of Max Weber's sociological type, the Spirit of Capitalism'.[22] The article is also indebted to Tawney's work on the gentry. Tawney seems, too, to have influenced Trevor-Roper's plan of 1944 to write a book called 'A History of the Ruling Classes', for in envisaging the volume Trevor-Roper took for granted a point that is a premise of 'The Rise of the Gentry': that the sixteenth century had created a new and lasting ruling class – even if he was less unsympathetic to it than Tawney and less convinced of its rapacity.[23]

Although Trevor-Roper's historiographical thinking around this time is mostly visible only in casually expressed statements, it is evident that Marx also remained in his mind.[24] At this stage indeed he paid more attention to Marx than to Weber, a priority that would be reversed in the years ahead. He also subscribed to a form of Whiggism, with which he contrasted the misguided 'neo-toryism' of Feiling, and to which, under Tawney's influence, he brought a modern sociological dimension. The process 'by which the essentially static, feudal society of the middle ages had been replaced, or was being replaced, by a modern, competitive, capitalist society' was, he held, 'an advance' not only 'economically' but 'constitutionally and intellectually', for 'the eighteenth-century conception of freedom, and the English parliamentary constitution, which has guaranteed and preserved that conception, spring from it.' What Trevor-Roper blamed the Whigs for missing was what Tawney had illustrated in *The Agrarian Problem in the Sixteenth Century* (1912), the cost of human suffering brought by the agricultural transformation on which Whig freedom had been built. Trevor-Roper decided that 'the Fabians', as he loosely called Tawney and his followers, were the 'best adjusters' of Whig history.[25]

The decade and a half or so that followed the war saw Trevor-Roper tussling with, and by stages emancipating himself from, the dominant nexus of Marxist, Weberian and Tawneyesque historical premises and mounting an often-solitary challenge to it. The repudiation went deeper than that, for over more than a century the notion that Puritanism and the parliamentarian cause had, however vaguely, represented forces of advance had become an almost instinctive premise, sometimes qualified but encountering little open opposition beyond either reactionary postures or nostalgia for medieval society or religion, positions for which, at least in their blinkered or sentimental forms, Trevor-Roper had no time. The protracted confidence of the postwar world in a better future, which would demolish the surviving oppressions and deprivations of the past, had wide if largely subconscious historiographical reverberations. His reaction against the progressive inter-pretative impulse extended beyond the spheres of economics and politics and religion to intellectual history, where Puritanism was likewise saluted as an agent of progress. His rejection of Marxist frameworks of interpretation, to which in any case his commitment had long been circumscribed, was the quickest and cleanest of his repudiations. He would conduct a mental struggle with the Weber thesis until the early 1960s, by which time he had concluded that the connection of Protestantism with capitalism was a mirage. The struggle with Tawney's thesis of the rising gentry came earlier.

It can be glimpsed in the drafts of his continuing work on Sutton, on whom he had written five chapters of a book when he abandoned it in 1951.[26] Papers in the Public Record Office, which had barely been explored, enabled him to reconstruct Sutton's relations with his aristocratic and gentle debtors and so to form his own picture, which the book was intended to convey, of the economic circumstances of the ruling class.

In 1948 Lawrence Stone, a former undergraduate pupil of Trevor-Roper, published in the *Economic History Review* an article, 'An Anatomy of the Elizabethan Aristocracy', which caused something of a sensation in the academic world, not so much for its thesis, which was an extension of Tawney's, as by the force of its expression and the dazzling parade of documentary authority and statistical techniques, features which announced Stone as the coming man of economic history. In 1951 Trevor-Roper would publish the reply to Stone that opened one of the most famous of academic civil wars. Tawney had portrayed the Elizabethan aristocracy as a class in difficulties. Stone, going further, alleged that the peerage had stood on the verge of bankruptcy. Trevor-Roper, who had accepted Tawney's thesis, had, on a first reading, no objection to Stone's. He knew about aristocratic indebtedness from his own studies, and with part of his mind viewed it as the deserved fate of a class made superfluous by economic change.

Trevor-Roper's biographer Adam Sisman states that his subsequent attack on Stone arose from pique, at the sight of a former pupil overtaking him in academic esteem: 'Stone's success was galling to him.'[27] The evidence adduced by Sisman is at odds with his claim. Trevor-Roper did have grounds for personal resentment. He had drawn Stone's attention to pertinent documents in the Public Record Office of which he had made a preliminary study, and had lent him his notes on them, only for Stone to cease communication and publish the article without acknowledgement. Even so, Trevor-Roper wrote to congratulate Stone on a 'really excellent' article, and told a friend that 'I think Lawrence's article is very good and drop all potential criticisms. I shouldn't have done it nearly so well, and the work is nearly all his own.' When Menna Prestwich, Trevor-Roper's spiky Oxford colleague, tried to persuade him that Stone had extensively plagiarised Trevor-Roper's article on Sutton, he privately derided the idea. He ignored her suggestion that he mount a counter-attack.[28] In the winter of 1949–50 he backed Stone's successful application for an Oxford Fellowship, for which Stone's article was his leading qualification and which made him an equal in the Faculty. It was when, in the summer of 1950, Trevor-Roper returned to the Public

Record Office that his attitude changed. As he worked on the documents which Stone had swiftly interpreted, he concluded that Stone had not merely misunderstood them but practised 'deliberate falsification on a shocking scale', with the result that there were 'gigantic statistical errors'.[29] As so often in Trevor-Roper's career, it was a betrayal of a historian's responsibility to honesty that incensed him.[30] Many people, Stone among them,[31] were to describe Trevor-Roper's reply to him as 'vituperative'. It was no such thing, but its exposure of Stone's errors was coldly and mercilessly annihilating.

As he thought about Stone's thesis Trevor-Roper began to have doubts about Tawney's. He had not yet rejected it *tout court*. In any case Tawney stood in Trevor-Roper's mind in the gallery of major historians who deserve 'great admiration' because, even though they may make errors, they 'have changed the historical climate'.[32] He told his Oxford lecture audience in 1950 that Tawney was 'one of the greatest of English historians'. In January 1951 he saluted in print 'the great work of Professor Tawney',[33] and demurred when the American historian Wallace Notestein suggested to Trevor-Roper that someone would one day do to Tawney what Trevor-Roper was doing to Stone. 'I am critical of Tawney', he replied, but 'I also greatly admire him [...] I don't believe that anyone will be able to do to him what I am doing to Stone, i.e. proving (as I submit) that he is neither honest nor a scholar.'[34]

Nonetheless his doubts about the rise of the gentry grew and hardened into rejection. In 1953 Trevor-Roper's long essay 'The Gentry 1540–1640', published as a supplement to the *Economic History Review*, took on Tawney's articles of 1941, which, as he put it elsewhere, had become 'with miraculous speed the orthodoxy – I would say the error – of a generation'.[35] Trevor-Roper was again charged with vituperation. In reality intellectual proposition is calmly met with intellectual proposition, firmly but not discourteously or disrespectfully; in that respect the article differs from his reply to Stone.[36] Its manner would now be unexceptionable. Yet it startled a generation wedded to professional decorum and not used to candid scholarly debate, at least with the revered Tawney. Trevor-Roper's statement in his inaugural lecture of 1957 that 'history that is not controversial is dead history' was itself more controversial than it would be now.

For five years the disagreement between Trevor-Roper and Tawney was mainly confined to the academic world, but in May 1958 a polemical essay by the American historian J.H. Hexter, which found more merit in Trevor-Roper's essay than in Tawney's but assailed the premises of both writers, appeared in *Encounter* and – an unimaginable prospect today – brought complex arguments about economic history into the public arena (to the distaste of Stone, who reproached Hexter for 'conducting very complicated academic discussions by bellowing through a megaphone in the market-place'[37]). If first Trevor-Roper and then Hexter had held their peace, no doubt Tawney's findings would gradually have succumbed to detailed and piecemeal objections and their interest would have quietly faded. Instead, the period attracted an intensity of study and debate that has never gone away. All of us who have worked on the Civil Wars have been the intellectual children or grandchildren or by now great-grandchildren of the gentry controversy. But the more thickly populated and intensively researched the study of the seventeenth century has become, the more primitive and sketchily supported the claims made during the gentry controversy have appeared. We need to remember the empty spaces into which the combatants ventured.

Trevor-Roper's work on Sutton, and his debate with Stone, had taken him from the seventeenth century to the sixteenth. Yet his seventeenth-century interests persisted. On his return to Oxford after the war he had plunged, not into the causes of the Puritan Revolution, but into its course. In the spring and summer of 1947 he gave 16 lectures on 'The Commonwealth and Protectorate'. By 1950 the series had swelled into 24 lectures.[38] The period was the main subject of his Oxford lectures over 15 years. Though they were addressed to the undergraduate body at large, they also had a base in a popular undergraduate option. In 1949 a long-running special subject in the Oxford History degree, 'Protectorate and Restoration 1654–1662', was altered to 'Commonwealth and Protectorate 1647–1658', the title it still retains. It is likely that Trevor-Roper joined forces with Christopher Hill, who had returned to Oxford from wartime work in 1945, to secure the change. Hill wanted to replace the study of the reactionary Restoration by attention to the Leveller movement of 1647–9, which figured largely in the new syllabus.[39]

The two historians knew that their perspectives on the period differed. Hill liked revolutions and Trevor-Roper didn't. But Trevor-Roper, like Hill, was at that time concerned with the Levellers. His studies of Nazism had roused his interest in the public appeal of revolutionary programmes. What happened in England in 1642–60 was, in his view, both 'a political revolution' and 'a social revolution',[40] and the Levellers were among the revolutionaries. He wanted to discover their social and economic background. Earlier he had been struck by the attraction of Nazism to the 'casualties' of economic change.[41]

Behind the Leveller movement, he now decided, there lay the grievances of craftsmen and smallholders, especially in East Anglia and the Midlands, who had fallen victim to agricultural change and economic depression. His interest in the Levellers was part of a wider approach to the Puritan Revolution, which would persist through his writings on it. He wanted to know how the moderate aims of the parliamentarian leaders during the approach to civil war had yielded to a revolutionary movement with the appeal and power to destroy the constitution. Following contemporary usage, he loosely called the coalition of MPs and soldiers, itself a loose alliance, which achieved the revolution 'the Independents'. In November 1947 he gave a lecture to the Cambridge Historical Society entitled 'Who Were the Independents?' (though as usual his mind was on many things, for at the dinner afterwards he enthralled the company by a long and animated monologue on Macaulay[42]). The identity of the Independents would exercise him many years. He saw them, too, as victims of social and economic change, whether as 'mere' gentry or as members of humbler ranks. Here was the origin of his challenge to Tawney. He found a parallel explanation for political grievances and conspiracies in the late Elizabethan and the Jacobean period. Characteristically he applied the same explanatory tool to other eras too, so that in 1950 he maintained that nineteenth-century English Catholicism had drawn its converts from 'the casualties of change'.[43]

The shadow of Nazism provides a second explanation of his interest in the Levellers: their involvement with the Cromwellian army, which oversaw the revolution of 1649 and dominated politics and government for the next 11 years. By the spring of 1948 Trevor-Roper was discussing with his publisher, Harold Macmillan, the future prime minister, an idea for a book on Oliver Cromwell and the New Model Army.[44] Down the ages perceptions of the Civil Wars have turned on Cromwell, whose reputation has been a barometer of changing social and political attitudes. In and after the inter-war years his career and character, and his use of his army as an instrument of devastation and of rule, had attracted frequent comparisons with the dictatorships of Hitler and Mussolini.[45] Trevor-Roper saw Cromwell in that light. In 1947 *The Last Days of Hitler* listed Cromwell among 'the great modern dictators', and, to illustrate a generalisation about politically unintelligent courts, compared the behaviour of Cromwell's 'satraps' to that of Hitler's entourage.[46] In 1948–9, while eschewing crude parallels between the characters of the recent tyrants and that of Cromwell, 'the most sympathetic of the great dictators', he was fascinated by the rise of the Cromwellian army, through the logic of revolutionary events, to 'naked power'.[47] Other modern parallels with the Cromwellian army intrigued him too.[48] The spirit of *The Last Days* persisted in his reflections on the murder of Charles I by a 'hated and despotic army' whose 'arbitrary power' was 'consecrated by the solemn barbarities of religion'.[49]

In July 1948 Berenson urged him to write a full-length biography of Cromwell, and was told in reply that 'I really do mean to write about the Cromwellian interlude.'[50] Trevor-Roper's first publication on the politics of the upheaval would be his essay of 1956, 'Oliver Cromwell and his Parliaments'.[51] After its appearance he committed himself to writing a book on Cromwell for the tercentenary of the Protector's death in 1958, only to withdraw from the obligation after deciding that 'this piddling anniversary' would supply too cramped a theme.[52] It was in its place that he embarked on his magnum opus on the Puritan Revolution, in which Cromwell would be only one of many prominent figures, though it was widely supposed that the work would be either a biography of Cromwell or something like one.

His view of Cromwell as a dictator had long yielded to a different perception of the Protector. Trevor-Roper's work on the revolution led him not only to question Tawney's thesis but to an alternative interpretation of the Civil Wars, one to which the conduct of Cromwell and other parliamentarian gentry pointed him. Not only did Trevor-Roper come to judge the thesis of a declining aristocracy and rising gentry mistaken; it seemed to him to obscure a different conflict which, he decided, was the real key to the political tensions of the era and which belonged to a European pattern. He was no less sure than Tawney that the war had social and economic origins. But they lay, he maintained, not in the agrarian changes described by Tawney but in the relationship between what contemporaries had called 'the court' and 'the country'.

The concentration of power in courts, and the irresponsible characteristics it promoted there, had long interested Trevor-Roper.[53] Now he placed it at the centre of his interpretation of the Civil Wars. The thesis took time to evolve. Many of the features of his later work on the revolution, and many of his points of departure from the progressive interpretation of the conflict, are already present, at least in embryo, by the time of his lectures of 1949: the attribution of revolution to economic discontent; the resistance to determinist explanation; the emphasis on the gap between the moderate aims of 1641 and the radicalism that followed; the refusal to think of the parliamentarians as forward looking. The parliamentarian cause, he maintained, reacted against rather than championed the dominant developments of society. The Independents, as he put it in a lecture of 1950, 'represented the victims, not the profiteers, of those great changes which can be summarized as the centralization of government, law and business in Westminster and the city of London'.[54] But at this stage the court is but one among other economic grievances of the depressed classes. Tawney had been alert to the economic power of the court, which he described, in a phrase which Trevor-Roper's book on Sutton approvingly quoted, as 'a lottery of unearned fortunes'.[55] But to Tawney, too, the court was only one strand of the story. Only from 1952 did Trevor-Roper give the court centre stage. Until then he had supposed, with Tawney, that the key to the rise and fall of landed families was the struggle among them for landed wealth, a conflict shaped by their success or failure in the management of landed income. Now he found the key not in land but in the competition for the remunerative offices controlled by the court interest. Around the monarchy there had grown an expensive, wasteful system of reward. It was supported by racketeering arrangements of indirect taxation that financed a parasitic and ostentatiously luxurious court at the expense of the regions and of the nation at large.

The thesis was able to evolve smoothly enough from his earlier argument about the reaction against centralisation of government, law and business. For in explaining the impact of 'the court' he used the term broadly, to cover not only the royal entourage but a network of associations that extended to the City of London and to the law courts. In an early formulation he compared the gulf between court and country to Disraeli's two nations, so divided that they knew nothing of each other. He would modify that picture and recognise divisions within the minds of individuals who in some ways benefited from courtly connections and in others were victims of them.[56] But he remained sure that it was 'the country' which broke Stuart rule in the 1640s. Its characteristic representatives belonged to a class not of rising gentry but of declining or 'mere gentry' who had watched richer and better-connected men prosper at their expense. The country's central demand was for decentralisation: of political power, of the Church, of the law, of education, of trade, all of which were controlled from the metropolis or by privileged interest groups. Trevor-Roper had long been sceptical of the Marxist perception of the protectorate of Oliver Cromwell as a 'bourgeois' regime.[57] Now he presented it as a government bent on implementing the country-party programme.

From the early 1950s Trevor-Roper used the thesis of court and country to explain not only the Civil Wars but the tensions of the half-century preceding them. The book on Sutton had explored the late Elizabethan conflict between the Queen's leading monster Robert Cecil and her favourite the Earl of Essex, in which Essex, though so great a courtier himself, had mobilised 'the excluded classes', especially the excluded gentry, in his support. Trevor-Roper wanted to expand that study into an account of the late Elizabethan succession crisis, on which he gave university lectures from 1952. Having found leading conspirators of the Gunpowder Plot among Sutton's debtors,[58] he examined the conspiracies early in James I's reign from a similar perspective. In replying to Tawney, and in widely read essays published in *History Today* in 1953 and 1955,[59] and then in a review in 1955 of C.V. Wedgwood's narrative of the prelude to civil war,[60] he placed those late Elizabethan and early Jacobean episodes in a line of protest leading from the northern rising of 1569 to the Civil Wars.

He also examined the relationship of political and economic discontent to religious dissidence. Having described Puritanism, in *Archbishop Laud*, as a creed of businessmen, he now saw it as the religion of excluded gentry. In both cases he insisted on the secular basis of religious profession, at least in its social and political manifestations. This was an enduring premise of his thought, from the book on Laud to his reflections on the Civil Wars late in his career. It may have been strengthened by his studies of Nazism and by reflection on the revival under it of forms of persecution that in previous centuries had enforced theological orthodoxy, a parallel which showed 'that social stereotypes are more lasting than religious systems – indeed, that religious systems may be only temporary manifestations of a more deep-seated attitude'.[61] On that front, at least, he could be found on the same side as the Marxists even after his revulsion from Marxism. For all his disagreements with Christopher Hill, he applauded (with polite qualifications) Hill's book of 1956, *Economic Problems of the Church*, which brought a materialist perspective to the conduct of pre-Civil-War Anglicanism.[62] Trevor-Roper himself maintained that seventeenth-century Puritanism had provided the religious voice of the mere gentry not because of the content of its faith but as an available ideological channel of moral repugnance against the corruption and ostentation of the court. There was another available channel, Catholic recusancy. Sociologically Puritanism and Catholicism, faiths so opposite in doctrine, were rival magnets to secular discontent, the difference being that whereas Puritan grievances could find an outlet in parliaments, Catholic ones, being proscribed by the state, could not. He never thought that the Puritanism of the landed opposition to Charles I ran deep, for 'the vast majority of the articulate English laity were indifferent to theological niceties.'[63] In the early eighteenth century, he observed, politically excluded Protestant gentry would turn with equal readiness to Tory Anglicanism.

Trevor-Roper's disagreement with Tawney went beyond their differences of economic analysis. He reacted against Tawney's failure to illustrate his connection between economic processes and the Civil Wars. Now, as so often in his career, Trevor-Roper protested against the separation of the study of politics from the study of society.[64] He believed that his own connection between economics and Civil War politics was demonstrable. He had, however, created a difficulty for himself. In accommodating political material within a reply to an article which had excluded it, he needed to speak not to Tawney's arguments but past them. Uncertain how to handle that challenge of presentation, he set out his case in a 'digression' too brief to establish it. By devoting the bulk of the reply to a refutation of the thesis of the rising gentry, he allowed the impression that he, like Tawney, regarded political history as subordinate to economic history. The impression was fostered by Hexter, who on reading Trevor-Roper's essay had written to congratulate him effusively on 'the classic piece of social history of the last two decades', but whose tone changed in his essay in *Encounter*, where he found it convenient to attack Tawney and Trevor-Roper alike as abettors of an economic determinism which for his part Trevor-Roper, as he had patiently explained to Hexter, could not have been further from embracing.[65] The misrepresentation to which Trevor-Roper had exposed himself had a lasting effect on perceptions of his article.

Trevor-Roper's emphasis on the court inescapably led him to analyse the political arena. He had already related economic struggles to court politics in his article on Sutton and in his unfinished book on him. Yet his departure from Tawney was deeper than that, for he believed Civil War politics to be inexplicable within the range of Tawney's conceptions. 'Economic interests', as Trevor-Roper put it in 1957, 'are abstractions which cannot mobilise themselves; [...] their force depends on personal manoeuvres, temporary alliances, procedural devices'; and 'the study of politics is [...] always also the study of politicians.'[66] The rebellion of the gentry, whether rising or falling, could never have been explained by statistics or impersonal categories. The challenge was to reconstruct the political contexts, moods, contingencies and decisions from which war had arisen.

That reconstruction could not be done in articles. It needed a book, which by 1957 Trevor-Roper had resolved to write. The politics of the Civil Wars, he had resolved, could only be understood, and explanations of the origins and course of the wars could only be tested or illustrated, through a narrative of events. Gardiner's narrative had focused on constitutional and religious conflicts. Now a new narrative was needed, to absorb the dimension of social explanation. It would have to be detailed, for in a period of events so crowded and fluctuating and confused the contexts in which politicians made their choices, and revealed their motives, were inevitably complicated. Only an 'ambitious', indeed 'vast', book could recreate them. It was not only the setting of political calculations and decisions that needed to be restored. It was the emotional framework of events, 'their cumulative pressure on the human mind', a force missed by 'historians who coldly and scientifically anaylze the structure of society' but 'easily overlook the power of human ideas, and even more easily of human moods, which are less definable'.[67] Somehow one had to do what social interpretation had not thought to attempt: to 'share the emotions of men long dead', and recreate, 'out of the dry litter of old facts, the white-hot mould of hope and fear and suspense in which their thoughts were fused'.[68] That was a recurrent preoccupation and endeavour of Trevor-Roper's writings. There was, it is true, one historian of the Civil Wars who was essaying the imaginative recreation which Trevor-Roper urged: C.V. Wedgwood, whose political narratives of the 1630s and 1640s, *The King's Peace* and *The King's War*, appeared in 1955 and 1958 respectively. But to Trevor-Roper's mind they fell short. Though Wedgwood 'writes excellent, readable narrative history', 'nothing is explained', for she keeps to 'the surface of society'. She shared, though from the opposite angle, the failing of Tawney, for she too divorced political from social history. Unable to grasp, from the study of politics alone, the passions and anger which motivated the parliamentarians, she 'sometimes seems to describe only unfortunate misunderstandings' in a 'polite society'.[69]

How were social and political history to be brought together? From the outset Trevor-Roper was conscious of a basic problem: 'The methods of social and political history are different. One is analytical, one narrative [...]. How can the two be combined in one book?' How was political movement to interact with social structure? Wedgwood's account 'moves', but without the social dimension that would give her account depth. 'The sociological historians', on the other hand, 'dive into the depths: but there is no movement at all. How can one *both* move *and* carry along with one the fermenting depths which are also, at every point, influenced by the pressure of events above them? And how can one possibly do this so that the result is readable?'[70]

That difficulty, which troubled, even obsessed him through the writing of the book, he thought of as 'the problem of form'. The perfection of 'form', and an aversion to formlessness, were lifelong preoccupations, driven by aesthetic and psychological impulses and also by a sense that deficiencies of form must reflect ones of argument. The characteristics of literary 'form' were a subject of his wartime ruminations.[71] It was during the war that he planned a book to be called 'A History of the English Ruling Classes', 'although how to impose form on so vast a subject is a problem which at present baffles, and may ultimately frustrate me.'[72] One reason he wearied of his early book on Laud was that 'the matter is not sufficiently adapted to the form.'[73] He repeatedly voiced his anxiety that the book on the Puritan Revolution might be 'formless'. Early in the writing it prompted a prophetic fear lest the book prove 'abortive'.[74]

From 1957, the year he became Regius Professor, he intensively wrote and rewrote. Initially he envisaged three volumes, to amount to about 300,000 words. The first volume was to trace the origins and outbreak of the Civil Wars. It would end either in 1642, the year war broke out, or in 1643, with the death of the parliamentary leader John Pym. Its title would be *The Crumbling of the Monarchy*, or else *The Crisis of English Government, 1640–2*, or else *Reform and Revolution? 1640–3*. The other two volumes were to take the story through the Civil Wars and their aftermath. They faded from his attention as he worked on the first volume, and were dropped. The first volume, which was divided into five long chapters, itself grew into around 300,000 words, three times the length he had originally envisaged for it. That was not the whole of it, for he proposed to add a sixth chapter.

After an opening passage on the meeting of the Long Parliament, the type-script takes us back to the 1590s, the era of acute factional strife when the divisions of court and country had assumed a dominant political role. He picks up the theme of court and country from his earlier studies. He describes the bloated and parasitic English court of 1590–1640 as an *ancien régime* – a term he had used for early Stuart rule since the late 1940s – in need of structural and administrative overhaul and curable only by the tackling of entrenched interests. A commanding if selective narrative shows us the unravelling of the Tudor system of government under the irresponsible and spendthrift rule of James I, when 'the whole Tudor system of government was allowed to dissolve'.[75] It was then, he believed, that 'the structure of society had been disastrously weakened'.[76] Then the book moves to the 1620s, where a theme develops which perhaps owed its initial inspiration to his friend Gerald Bre-nan[77] and which would reappear throughout Trevor-Roper's career. In England as in Europe, he argued, the economic depression and religious and political confrontations of the decade scarred the generation that lived through it, an experience parallel, he proposed, to equally defining ones of the 1920s and 1930s. The 1620s marked the end of the Renaissance, of its confidence and expansion, and brought a new mood of gloom, contraction, doubt. It also made England at least as vulnerable to revolution as it would be in the early 1640s, a fate it escaped, as in the 1640s it would succumb to it, through contingencies and human choices.[78] The memory of the 1620s had always to be borne in mind amid later events, for 'the iron of the past enters men's souls.'[79] From the 1620s we move to the conflict of 'the court' and 'the country' in the 1630s, the era of personal rule, of the policy of 'Thorough' pursued by Laud in the Church and Strafford in the state. But it is with the return to 1640 that the main part of the volume begins. It takes us, in close-up, through the course of events from the meeting of the Long Parliament to the outbreak of civil war in 1642. An 'epilogue' then takes us into 1643.

We misunderstand the book if we think of it as an attempt to answer critics who charged him with having failed to write a long work. He was indeed determined to write another book, but, whatever he might say about a huge one 'dispersing his critics', length for its own sake had no attraction for him. He was uneasy about the bulk of his draft, and especially about the quantity of detail which, he had decided, the argument required.[80] To readers today, bombarded as they have been by minutiae of the years 1640–2, the detail does not seem thick. At a number of points it seems thinner than the argument needs. Trevor-Roper was used to bringing detail to order and to subordinating it, confidently, to interpretation. But now the scale of his project posed a new challenge, aesthetic and organisational. He was uneasy about the result. His account even of the years before 1640, we are told, has been 'long and tedious'.[81] He apologises for the 'close' and 'great detail' of the narrative of 1640–2, which has been necessary because only under the inspection of events does the relationship of social to political developments emerge. Only under it, too, do determinist explanations of the Civil Wars fall away.[82]

In Trevor-Roper's argument the political preoccupations of the Long Parliament were not the constitutional ones emphasised by Gardiner. The constitutional demands of 1640–2, though fully exploited by the parliamentarians and though brought to the fore by the breakdown of trust between them and the Crown, were distractions from underlying objectives. The constitutional grievances did not go deep. The threat to legality by royal action was no greater, and the uses of the prerogative no more oppressive, under Charles I, whose government was 'mild enough',[83] than under the Tudors. Ship money was a just, indeed 'a model tax',[84] which the parliamentarians were to imitate once in power. He suspected that the opponents of the court attacked ship money because it was legally vulnerable, whereas the grievance of wardship, a burden which Trevor-Roper particularly emphasised and which he believed to matter much more to 'the country', was not.[85] He was not impressed by John Hampden, the hero of ship money, who owed an undeserved fame to the episode.[86] The essential parliamentarian goal was reform of the court and of the society which the court had drained and corrupted. Earlier, Trevor-Roper had wanted to write a full-length study of Robert Cecil, whom James I made Earl of Salisbury. In the book, as at that time, Trevor-Roper saw Salisbury as a statesman of towering ability and perception who understood the grievances of the country and, through the Great Contract which he offered to parliament in 1610 and through other proposals, set out to rectify them.[87] His death in 1612, by ending that hope, ended an age of responsible government and introduced a politically dissolute era. But in 1640–1 Salisbury's programme was revived. Its champion now was the parliamentarian leader the Earl of Bedford. The difference was that where Salisbury had planned reform from within the court, Bedford sought it by the exertion of parliamentary pressure on it. Bedford's efforts were thwarted by his death in his late thirties in May 1641.

Trevor-Roper's text glances only occasionally at other modern historians. Tawney and Weber are named only briefly.[88] He had put the gentry controversy behind him. There is nonetheless a rarely spoken target: the Marxist interpretation – particularly Christopher Hill's – of the Civil Wars, which had appropriated Tawney's arguments. Three claims interweave in Trevor-Roper's narrative: the Civil Wars were not desirable; they were not progressive; and they were not inevitable. At least since 1946 he had reacted against Marxist delight in revolutions, which to his mind were likelier to destroy than to create, to impair human advances than to achieve them.[89] He even finds a rare moment of agreement with A.L. Rowse, whose assessment of 'the odious, the superfluous civil war' he endorses.[90] To Trevor-Roper the wars were an 'unnecessary revolution',[91] brought about by contingencies and by bad politics on both sides. The subjection of the events of 1641 to narrative inspection disproved the modern view that the parliamentary reform programme of 1641 was doomed: that it merely tinkered with a revolutionary situation which inevitably overtook it.[92] If only Bedford, 'perhaps the ablest, deepest, most constructive statesman of the disastrous reign of Charles I', had lived, 'how different the history of England might have been'. For Bedford, 'who is, in a sense, the hero of this book',[93] possessed, like Salisbury before him but perhaps like no one else in 1641, the qualities of statesmanship needed to hold court and country together.

Viewed in the context of narrative, rather than from the distorting perspective of the unforeseen developments which followed, the reform programme of 1641 looked no mere prelude to revolution. In 1641 'no Englishman contemplated revolution, while almost all Englishmen wanted reform.'[94] Even as Bedford put pressure on the Crown he understood that reform depended on its cooperation and thus on its strength. The question was how a reform movement which should have been containable within constitutional processes escaped them, and how the events were set in motion that would bring the Independents to power. The answer lay in those pressures which narrative could reconstruct and to which sociological theory was deaf. The movement for reform, though it made its gains in 1641, was thwarted by mistrust and by events – the army plots, the trial of Strafford, the Irish rebellion – which created new lines of division. Soluble conflicts over the constitution and the Church produced entrenched and lasting positions, until the opposing parties had 'taken the government to pieces'.[95] A struggle over reform gave way to a struggle for sovereignty, which arose from, rather than caused, the crisis of 1641–2.

For parliament's leaders of those years were not prototypes of modern revolutionaries. Trevor-Roper saw the destruction of the ancient constitution as revolutionary, but not in the forward-looking sense in which Marxist and progressive historians used the term. In any case it was not the initial leaders who wrought the destruction but the Independents, whom they could not restrain. The men who commanded parliament in 1641–2 were 'fundamentally moderate and conservative'. They looked not towards the future but back to the reign of Elizabeth I, whose government and Church they idealised. The 'mental furniture' of the 'profoundly unrevolutionary' parliamentarian leader John Pym was a 'fossilized Elizabethanism'.[96] The Independents were if anything still less forward looking. Economically and politically the parliamentary party was reactionary. Examination of the conduct of the City of London and of the merchant classes showed that parliament did not represent the forces of capitalism. The parliamentarian cause was intellectually retrograde too. To Marxists, and to others who with them divided the thinkers of the past into friends or enemies of progress and portrayed ideas as ideological expressions of economic or political facts, the feudal monarchy stood for intellectual as well as political and social obstruction. In that view the Civil Wars were needed to 'liberalize the Church' and 'release the forces which led to the Enlightenment'. On the contrary, replied Trevor-Roper, 'Baconian science and rational theology' were held back by the war. Arminianism, the challenge, which prospered under Laud, to the Calvinist doctrine of predestination, was to Marxists a reactionary doctrine, the intellectual expression of the Caroline political programme. That claim, answered Trevor-Roper, confused the Arminian doctrine of free will with the political and ecclesiastical programme to which Laud had misguidedly annexed it. In reality 'intellectual liberalism' was

> on the side of the court. If only the heavy structure of the court could have been attenuated, if only Laud had not burdened his church with the oppressive weight of a new clericalism, if only the Stuarts had listened to the reformers while there was still time, the Enlightenment was at hand, without revolution.

So the Civil Wars were no more necessary to the advance of the intellect than they were 'to advance English capitalism'.[97]

To Trevor-Roper the revolution was a cause not for celebration but for lamentation. Once civil war had started, the parliamentarians needed to control and enlarge the resources of the state. It was then that the shallowness of the constitutional views they had proclaimed in 1641 was demonstrated. For to win the war the parliamentarians rode roughshod over constitutional liberties – only to be subjected in turn to the lawless rule of the army that had been their instrument of victory. 'How few revolutions', Trevor-Roper reflected as he was conceiving his book,

> have achieved their original aims! How few of the great changes which they have caused have been the direct consequence of their first mobilization. Men fight for liberty and achieve despotism, and liberty emerges from quite other battles: from the deadlock of the forces bent on tyranny.

'This paradox' was 'the great tragedy of English history'.[98]

Early in 1961 Trevor-Roper sent the text to two young colleagues: the men, though no one could have guessed it at the time, who would be his successors as Regius Professor at Oxford, Michael Howard and John Elliott. At some point, too, he read passages to the Regius Professor of Greek, Hugh Lloyd-Jones.[99] None of those colleagues was a specialist in English history, though Elliott, a historian of Renaissance and seventeenth-century Spain, knew enough about English developments to question some of Trevor-Roper's findings. Howard, a former undergraduate pupil of Trevor-Roper, had started a graduate thesis on the subject of seventeenth-century republicanism,[100] but had soon moved to modern military history. Trevor-Roper had a young friend with expert knowledge of the Civil Wars, Valerie Pearl, whose work on the City of London in the early stages of the revolution he drew on and influenced,[101] and who would have been delighted to read the typescript.[102] He evidently preferred to have readers who would judge its shape and its argument from outside the field. The shape worried him more than the argument. He looked to Elliott for judgement of both. In 1956 Elliott, commenting on Fernand Braudel's famous huge work on the history of the Mediterranean, had written to Trevor-Roper: 'I don't believe that Braudel has solved the supreme problem of uniting the social and economic analysis to the history of events, and I sometimes wonder if anyone ever will,'[103] though in 1963 Elliott himself would accomplish such a feat, admittedly with less massive and less overwhelmingly complicated material than Trevor-Roper's, in *The Revolt of the Catalans*, which, like Trevor-Roper's projected book, placed a mid-seventeenth-century revolution against a long-term background.

Elliott reassured Trevor-Roper about the structure of the book, which he found 'intensely readable, fast-moving, lucid and gripping'.[104] It was the argument that worried him. The strength of the book, he suggested, lay not in its thesis of court and country but in its refutation of determinism and its claim, which was 'absolutely right', that the revolution was 'unnecessary'. Elliott was not convinced by the court–country interpretation or by the subordination of constitutional to social motive. As he read, he found himself 'becoming increasingly Whiggish – simply by reaction'. Since the late seventeenth century Whig and then liberal historians had maintained that the Civil Wars had set the cause of liberty, espoused by parliament, against that of absolutism or tyranny, espoused by the Crown. Trevor-Roper's rejection of that thesis seemed to Elliott too sharp. 'Does the Petition of Right' of 1628, a key document in the Whig interpretation, 'deserve so little attention?' he asked. 'Do the legal struggles of the first decades of the century deserve such total neglect? Surely *liberty* and *property* are crucial themes in this society – just as crucial as the hatred of the court?' Elliott put his finger on a basic problem. Artistically the narrative was 'superb' and the 'construction' of the book was, within its author's 'own framework of reference', 'extremely successful'. But analytically the narrative was 'lop-sided'. It purported, or seemed to purport, to offer 'a *total* picture of the political behaviour of England's ruling class between 1640 and 1643', but gave only a partial one. Michael Howard, who had his own shrewd observations to contribute, described the narrative as 'deliberately unbalanced'.[105] Elliott proposed the addition of a chapter which would address the constitutional themes head-on.

Though at first he seemed inclined to take some such course, in the event Trevor-Roper did something different and much more extensive. Early in 1964 his wife, Lady Alexandra, wrote in despair to Randolph Churchill. Her husband, she remembered, had 'read most of the book to me and I thought it marvellous and was *horrified* when', after receiving Elliott's comments, 'he started to re-write the whole thing.'[106] He did not quite do that, but he did embark on a large and fundamental expansion of the project. At least to begin with he seems to have been more gratified by Elliott's approval of the structure of the book than troubled by his reservations about the argument. Though his subsequent steps are not easy to trace,[107] he evidently decided that the problem lay not in his thesis of court and country or in the subordination of constitutional to social issues, premises from which Elliott's letter did not shake him, but in his failure to do his thesis justice. It could not be demonstrated, he seems to have resolved, from the origins and early stages of the revolution alone. To illustrate it properly he would need to go back to the work that had given rise to it and that had informed his answer to Tawney: his studies, from the late 1940s, of the course of the revolution through the wars, the regicide, and the constitutional expedients of the Interregnum.

So his initial plan to move beyond 1642 or 1643 was revived. He returned from the origins and beginnings of the war to the field to which he had devoted so much energy in the years before his challenge to Tawney. He now wrote an account of around 125,000 words on 'The Fall of the *Ancien Regime* 1642–9', and a further 85,000 words on the period from the execution of the King in 1649 to the death of Oliver Cromwell in 1658.[108] His lectures on the Commonwealth and Protectorate lay ready for use and revision. He had already drawn on that earlier work in his essay of 1956, 'Oliver Cromwell and his Parliaments', which made a powerful impact for many years but which he perhaps overvalued. It was, he seems to have reasoned, only after the failure of the parliamentary leaders of 1640–2 that the extent of the country's hostility to the court had revealed itself: that the country-party radicals, the 'Independents', having swept their leaders aside, pressed home the grievances of the 'mere' or declining gentry. Though he did not now return to the debate about the economic condition of the gentry, he did repeat the claim that the Independents represented the backwoods. Being excluded from politics, they had no political skill – to Trevor-Roper always a fatal defect. The 'perfect representative of the unpolitical country party' was that member of a declining gentry family, Cromwell. The Protector could never understand constitutional objections to his rule because he regarded politics as 'secondary, even irrelevant'.[109] It was for supposing politics to be 'irrelevant' that Trevor-Roper had castigated Albert Speer.[110]

Trevor-Roper was hard at work on the book in September 1961, seven months after Elliott's letter. That is the last we hear of its composition. There is, however, a stray, undated document in his archive which could, though it need not, belong to 1965. It suggests that he was contemplating the contraction of the whole work into a single volume, in which the material from the abandoned first volume would be boiled down into the first of eight parts, the last of which would take the story to around the end of the Cromwellian protectorate.[111] At all events the Puritan Revolution stayed in his mind in 1962–5, when he gave lectures in Oxford, and in French at the Sorbonne, on the Civil Wars. But in 1965 he ceased to lecture on the subject.[112] The publication of *Religion, the Reformation and Social Change* in 1967, into which much of the argument of the book was reduced, was implicitly a declaration of abdication. New interests had usurped the subject of the book and perhaps had already threatened to do so as he wrote it. It was in the university term after his correspondence with Howard and Elliott that he first ran a class on 'Intellectual Movements of the Sixteenth and Seventeenth Centuries'. The publication in 1960 of his essay on the Hartlib circle, the only material, during the time he was working on the book, to be borrowed from it for publication elsewhere, suggests the tug of intellectual history, as do his reflections within the book on the intellectual liberalism of the court.

After his abandonment of the book his stepson James Howard-Johnston despairingly urged him to rescue it. James wanted him to publish the first volume, which was in a reasonably polished state, and to worry about the rest later. Certainly it was the first volume that was the most assured and coherent part of the text. Yet its problems were considerable. The thesis of court and country was one of startling brilliance and originality, which over-impressed its author. It left too much unexplained or unaddressed, not only in politics, the defect noted by Elliott, but in religion too. Trevor-

Roper's subordination of both spheres to social grievances concealed passions and fears of the very kind he was committed to recovering. The religious divide of 1640–2, he maintained, had been exaggerated, for the mainstream opinion represented in parliament 'supported the Church' and 'desired the same ends as Laud himself: creditable, preaching, resident ministers in their parishes.' Here was another 'tragedy', for Laud's failure to build bridges with the laity had created a needless polarisation.[113] Laud and his Puritan enemies had more in common than they understood, for both were reacting against failings and depravities of the Jacobean age. Laud's outlook is described as the 'Puritanism of the Right'.[114] Yet the book pays little attention to the ceremonialism of the Laudian Church, to its hostility to the Puritan emphasis on plainness of worship and on the centrality of the written and spoken word, or to the depths of anxiety and antipathy which those Laudian postures provoked. Trevor-Roper's argument that Puritanism, at least in its political forms, could be largely explained by moral repugnance at the court,[115] or by the hope of fortunes to be gained by piratical attacks on the New World territories of popish Spain, explains too little.

The character and composition of the 'country party' which he sets in opposition to the court are imperfectly delineated. The argument is undermined and confused by a characteristic ambivalence of feeling. He was torn between describing 'the best' and 'the worst' aspects of the gentry's mentality.[116] With one half of his mind he saw the country party as unthinkingly parochial and destructive, an image from which the disparaging account of the backwoods gentry in the third chapter of Macaulay's *History of England* does not seem far away.[117] With the other he saw it as a more positive force, crediting it with an admittedly inarticulate appetite for a sensible programme of decentralisation. It can be hard to tell whether the opposition to the court represented a bitterly excluded class or a reputable silent majority. In the second vein he intermittently presented the country party as the voice of the intelligent laity who spurned the factional divisions of the Civil Wars and favoured an undogmatic 'lay piety'[118] in religion, of the kind that had prospered outside the warring clerical ideologies since the Reformation. We can sense Trevor-Roper wanting to call the country-party laity – as elsewhere he did the devotional habits of 'simple gentry' in other times and places[119] – 'Erasmian'.

The problems are not ones of argument alone. Howard described the volume as 'wonderfully written', which in its way it inevitably is, but also as 'overwritten'. There is a sense of literary strain. The writing goes wrong partly because the thinking goes wrong, and partly because its spaciousness precludes the compression of thought that marks Trevor-Roper's most incisive prose. In other ways, too, his matter is not best suited to his gifts. His most compelling scholarly writing tends to have at least one of two features. The first is historical comparison. Perhaps to keep the work within manageable bounds, the book on the Puritan Revolution only rarely makes comparative points. The European crisis of the seventeenth century, a subject to which, as Sir John Elliott observes in Chapter 1, Trevor-Roper was at this time bringing an exciting comparative perspective, is only touched on,[120] and he makes little of the relationship, which keenly interested him and on which he wrote pioneering studies elsewhere,[121] between Civil War developments in England and those in Scotland and Ireland. Comparison being so important to the expression of his historical 'philosophy',[122] we miss, in its absence, the usual sense of a general reflective framework. In consequence the blows he aims at forces beyond his sympathy – at Puritan or provincial philistinism in particular[123] – lack the elevation of irony and look wanton or snobbish.

The second absent feature is textual detective work. His reply to Lawrence Stone had revealed a formidable mastery of documentary technicalities. Now his use of evidence was conventional and impressionistic. A joke he made against himself early in the writing of the book, that 'the whole Trevor-Roper interpretation of the whole history of England in the seventeenth century hangs upon one crucial sentence in the notebook of Sir John Oglander',[124] a country gentleman with the social attitudes which the book delineated, is wide of the mark, but not as wide as it should be. One source with which his argument required him to grapple, the papers of the Earl of Bedford, is cursorily examined (though we cannot tell whether he was given extended access to them; if he was, perhaps his weak eyes were defeated by the earl's complicated private notes). Compared to Gardiner's narrative, which was based on years of single-minded application to the reconstruction of seventeenth-century events, his is superficial. Trevor-Roper, who wrote the book among so many other commitments, was intellectually and temperamentally averse to single-mindedness. He had taken on an epic project, requiring a grasp of social structure, of administrative history and of complex events. So conscious of the challenge of form, he underestimated the challenge of substance.

For all its difficulties the first volume does hold together. In the added material, full as it is of striking individual insights, the book falls apart, as no other surviving manuscript of his does. The density and scale of the events of nearly two decades demanded, as he acknowledged, a highly selective treatment of events. Having apologised for the quantity of detail in the first volume, he now admitted to have gone 'briskly [...] perhaps too briskly' over the Civil Wars and the aftermath.[125] A problem that had pervaded the earlier portion becomes starker. In his interpretation the issues that occupied most of the time and energy of the parliamentarians arose not from their underlying goals but from the immediate demands of political success or survival. That became still truer after the outbreak of a war which, having needlessly and artificially divided the nation, had to be run and ended. Likewise the Church, having similarly been needlessly divided, had to be reconstituted. War brought new splits and new issues, which piled new problems onto politicians. The nation's divisions were entrenched by 'the mere fact of prolongation, the mere despair of settlement', which 'drove men on both sides to invest [...] both economically and emotionally' in the loyalties which war had created.[126] Trevor-Roper, wanting to concentrate on the issues of social reform, found his focus in the 'Independent' programme of the New Model Army and its civilian allies and then of the Cromwellian protectorate: a programme for reform of the law, of trade, of the Church, of education, of the electoral system. But 'throughout' the revolution 'immediate politics take precedence and long-term policy is submerged or pushed aside.'[127] His problem was to demonstrate among the parliamentarians an underlying commitment to the reform programme so deep-rooted as to vindicate his social interpretation of the wars.

There was a further difficulty. It was hard to disentangle the issues of reform from the 'blind ends and wearisome repetitions' of the political conflict, among which he feared to 'founder', and through which he dispiritedly picked his way.[128] He was used to writing about events and people he did not like, but not at such length. Though the added part of the book is vivacious enough, its authority is undercut, and its analytical spirit impaired, by his basic distaste for the destructive course and barren outcome of the revolution which he had eagerly made his subject in the postwar years, but of which he had wearied. The problem posed by his want of sympathy is already visible in the first volume, where we learn that with the coming of war the 'affable, civilized' grandees of the parliamentary leadership, who wanted only constructive reform, had yielded dominance to 'the grim, repellent face of middle-class English Puritanism'. 'The patrons of Inigo Jones and Van Dyck and Nicholas Stone would see their once obedient followers at work: Palladian mansions gutted, pictures slashed, statues hewed down, theatres closed, monumental tombs shattered and defiled.' 'How', he asked plaintively, 'could such limited and laudable intentions lead to such catastrophic consequences?'[129]

The challenge of representing the years after 1642 defeated him. Near or at the end of the writing he began a 'first draft' of his introduction.[130] If he made other attempts at it they do not survive. The draft is a melancholy document. What historian of such stature has thought of introducing so long a book in so apologetic a manner? Addressing 'the problem of form', he is 'well aware' that he has written 'an untidy, some may say a formless book. In self-defence I would reply, first, that the revolution itself was untidy and formless and cannot, without misrepresentation, be brought into neat symmetry.' The challenge posed by the disorderliness of the revolution to the requirements of literary form had long troubled him. He saw that the great contemporary historian of the wars, the Earl of Clarendon, had struggled with it.[131] But Trevor-Roper would not have accepted such an explanation as a book reviewer or from a graduate student. Secondly he would reply 'that in threading this tangled, smoky haze I have at least attempted to keep my eye on certain basic problems, even if this has involved, here, a selective treatment, there, an uneven pace'. Then he turns to the 'difficulties' he has faced: the problems of combining structural analysis with narrative, high politics with the movement of society. He has decided that a narrative form is indispensable, and yet acknowledges the perhaps insuperable problems of writing the story of such intricately chaotic events. For if, through narrative, we are to 'do justice' to 'events', 'how can we fail to become', like contemporaries, 'lost in the labyrinth? And if we are lost, then' – and there, in mid-sentence, the draft ends.[132]

If the book was a failure, it is questionable whether any ambitious account of the causes and course of the Civil Wars could have succeeded. A durable magnum opus is attainable only where conditions exist for its author to command a field. The growing population of Civil War studies, largely attracted by the gentry controversy, was creating the interpretative flux that has persisted ever since. Had Trevor-Roper's book, or its first volume, been published, it would quickly have become a dartboard for the PhD industry, which accelerated in the 1960s. Outside the academic world the first volume, at least, would have fared better. But how much better? Readers of a long narrative are likely to look for magisterial writing: not only magisterial in style, as the book mostly is, but conveying a sense of definitive authority. That is not Trevor-Roper's aim. In accordance with his own lights the book is controversial history, advancing and widening a subject but not aspiring to seal it. Not merely are analysis and long narrative hard to bring together: so are controversy and long narrative. And even readers without the professional knowledge to follow Trevor-Roper in his tracks might have sensed the problems with his thesis or spotted the 'lop-sidedness' of the story he told.

Much of the content of the book did reach the public, but in other contexts and mostly in abbreviated forms, in which the narrative framework was removed or much reduced. Essays in *Religion, the Reformation and Social Change* either condensed or incorporated themes of the book. In them the loss of the narrative was less damaging than, on the principles he had declared, he should have expected. Moments of deft chronological scene-setting do work which in the manuscript had taken many pages. His narrative had succeeded in separating events which determinist and neo-determinist writing had conflated and in showing their successive stages and changing contexts. Yet it had never overcome a basic problem of persuasion. Narratives, however long, are selective. Trevor-Roper's reader always wonders whether an alternative narrative might not support an alternative case. The impact of the essays which arose from the book is hard to measure or pinpoint, for as he himself remarked, in warning of the difficulty of identifying influences in intellectual history, 'so many ideas, at any time, are in the air,' and one needs to have breathed the air.[133] Influence cannot be gauged either by agreement with his claims or by the extent of citation of them, for thought can be provoked by arguments which we reject, or be subconsciously affected by them. It is in any case difficult to separate the effect of the essays from the aftershocks of the gentry controversy. Yet in fundamental respects his interventions on both fronts, which challenged the methods and the conclusions of current orthodoxy, have prevailed or anyway been vindicated. Neither the progressive nor the determinist view of the Civil Wars has survived. Few historians now think that the parliamentarians were forward looking. Everyone sees the difference between the reforming aspirations of 1641 and the revolutionary breakdown that followed. Everyone accepts – though the view came under attack in the late 1960s and early 1970s – that the aims and priorities of politicians are intelligible only through chronological reconstruction.

Like those of his opponents, Trevor-Roper's social explanation of the Civil Wars would fade. Even so, many of the interpretations that flourished in the aftermath of his work on the revolution bear his influence, whether direct or indirect. The thesis of court and country was developed.[134] The delineation, in an influential book on the Civil Wars by John Morrill in 1976, of 'the paradigm of the pure country squire', swayed more by moral revulsion against the court than by constitutional issues, might almost be a precis of one of Trevor-Roper's themes.[135] The term Trevor-Roper used to depict the Civil Wars as the protest of the regions against the centre, 'the revolt of the provinces', is the title of Morrill's book.[136] A number of historians have shared Trevor-Roper's view that the bureaucratic and fiscal burdens imposed on the regions mattered more than the legal or constitutional issues they raised.[137]

Interpretations later than Trevor-Roper's have also, though in these cases unknowingly, repeated and developed arguments made in his unpublished book but not in the essays that arose from it. There is his insistence that the nation did not, 'as is too often supposed', line up into 'royalists' and 'parliamentarians' in 1642: that the heart of the nation, unimpressed by the constitutional arguments on either side, tried to stay neutral[138] and, even when that had proved impossible, 'regarded the social substance of England as more important than its political form'.[139] It is now usual to emphasise, as he did, the malleability and what he called the 'obstinate political indifference' of the leaders of the shires as the successive governments of the Interregnum sought their support. Another unconventional claim made by Trevor-Roper only in unpublished form is now likewise broadly accepted. Against historians who tried to explain local Civil War allegiances by the economic forwardness or backwardness of the regions – the forward counties being parliamentarian, the backward ones royalist – he maintained that in individual shires 'it was generally the chances of war, rather than the economic character of the county, that decided which party should have control of it.'[140] He anticipated later interpretation too by his protest against the tendency of a post-aristocratic age to treat the House of Lords as secondary to the House of Commons, which, in that 'fundamentally aristocratic society', was 'in general [...] subordinate to it'.[141] For the great peers held the great offices and 'by the numerous bonds of patronage [...] exercised effective social dominance over the gentry'.[142]

The collapse of the book was a heavy blow to him. Yet it was followed by a period of extraordinary fecundity in other fields.[143] When he returned to the mid-seventeenth century in the 1980s, most fully in the mature long essays that he brought together as *Catholics, Anglicans and Puritans* in 1984, it was the intellectual history of the period, and its relationship to political history, that most interested him. His long-standing arguments about the reactionary qualities of Calvinism, and the enlightened ones of Arminianism and its sister tendency Socinianism, were given enlarged scope.[144] But if his interest in seventeenth-century religion survived, so did his conviction that the forms it took had secular explanations. He took issue with new claims, from a succeeding generation of historians, for a position he had long mistrusted: that the Civil Wars were 'wars of religion',[145] in which, at least in leading minds and at decisive moments, religious issues mattered more than political ones. In reply he returned to the subject of Laud and reiterated, within a revised framework, his belief that the religious conflicts had been of political importance only when, and because, they were used for political purposes.[146] He took on a second claim to emerge from a younger generation too: that the seventeenth-century politics which mattered were 'high politics', to which social movements were irrelevant. Tawney had subordinated politics to society. Now society, and indeed all long-term developments, were being presented as irrelevant to politics, so that the revolutions of the seventeenth century were being divided from their 'long context in time – i.e. from the accumulated [...] experience of those who' made them.[147]

What he called that 'jejune' approach was being applied more fully to the Revolution of 1688 than to that of 1640–60. Provoked by it, he gave a lecture in 1990 on the continuity of purpose between the two events, which historical specialisation had characteristically separated. There he returned to earlier preoccupations: to the reform programmes of Salisbury and Bedford, and to the messianic aspirations – which are treated in the next chapter – for the transformation of society that the parliamentarian leaders of the 1640s had taken up, even if he now presented demands for social reform, implicitly at least, as the partner of a constitutional programme rather than its superior.[148] Unfortunately his claims, made in a lecture written in a tired state at the age of 76, were uncharacteristically lacking in flair and coherence. The pressure of thought which, for all the problems of the abandoned book, had animated its arguments about the relationship of social to political history had dispersed. The mountain of the Puritan Revolution remained unclimbed. Yet, since he attempted the book, nothing published on the period by the increasingly fragmented specialist world has begun to rival the breadth of inquiry and of vision that characterises the abandoned manuscript. Nothing, too, has approached its author's capacity, displayed in the essays on the Civil Wars and their origins that preceded the writing of the book, to excite public interest in a complex historical subject. In that respect no less than in perceptions of the issues of debate, the era of the storm over the gentry seems far away.

3

Three Foreigners: The Philosophers of the Puritan Revolution

Mark Greengrass

'Three Foreigners and the Philosophy of the English Revolution' was the title Trevor-Roper gave to the bravura essay that, in the first of its two forms, he published in *Encounter* in February 1960.[1] It heralded a shift in his interests, away from the economic preoccupations of the 'storm over the gentry' towards the relationship, which would dominate his work on early modern Europe for the rest of his life, between the history of ideas and political engagement. In the gentry controversy Trevor-Roper had characterised the parliamentarian cause as a destructive movement, bent on the removal of social and political oppressions and abuses. But by now he also detected, in the angry, mainly negative agenda and in the inarticulate, confused pronouncements of 'dim squires', a 'positive' programme, which in the 'Three Foreigners' essay was his 'only' concern. It was a programme of practical reform, even if the practicalities were sometimes clouded by messianic speculations and language. The reform would be achieved by processes of decentralisation, which would liberate the Church, education, the law and the economy from top-heavy monopolistic systems and revive social energy and humanity.

To articulate that agenda, what he called the 'country party' needed stand-ins, surrogate *philosophes* from another shore. Enter an unlikely trio. John Dury was a Scottish Calvinist pastor who had spent most of the decade of the 1630s abroad on a personal mission to overcome the confessional divisions between Calvinists and Lutherans that were blighting the Protestant common front in the Thirty Years War. Their reconciliation would be the first step towards the termination of Europe's religious divisions. Samuel Hartlib was the son of a merchant from Elbing who moved to England in the late 1620s to escape the Thirty Years War. Jan Amos Komenský (John Amos Comenius) was a minister of the Moravian Brethren, living in exile in Poland after the disastrous failure of the Bohemian Revolt at the beginning of the Thirty Years War. He had outlined a 'pansophic' vision, for the reunification of knowledge with experience, in a work which Hartlib had published (without his consent) in 1637. The three surrogates were hardly the Abbé Sièyes, still less the Diderot or the Rousseau, of the English Revolution. They were not household names in 1960 and had not been in 1640. Only Comenius had a reputation – and in 1640 it was on the basis of his innovative and successful textbook for teaching Latin, *The Gate of Languages Unlocked* (*Janua linguarum reserata*, 1631), an enterprise distant from the concerns of Trevor-Roper's essay. In 1640 most of the published works and achievements of all three men (such as they would be) lay ahead, in a future whose turbulent political changes shaped them more than they did it. In 1960 the historical reassessment of their contribution, individually and collectively, had a long way to go.[2] The critical reader of the essay might have reckoned that the degree to which the three were either 'foreigners' or 'philosophers' was open to debate, and the nature of their *common* purpose still more so. The evidence for the latter rested on Samuel Hartlib's archive, which was not in the public domain. To the degree that a shared goal existed, it was emblematised by a 'covenant', drafted in Comenius's hand and signed on 3 March 1642 in London.[3] It bound each of them to commit the rest of his life to undo the confessional divisions of the world around them; to educate young people in the unfashionable acquisition of useful knowledge; to remain in discreet communication one with another; not to divulge their pact to outsiders without their mutual consent; and only to do so with those who shared their objectives. The three were outsiders, uncomfortable in the world as it was, misfits even. It was a tall order to believe that the 'philosophy of the Puritan Revolution' lay in their hands, but that was Trevor Roper's proposition.

How had Trevor-Roper arrived at that proposition? He had encountered Hartlib's archive, albeit briefly, some time in 1959 whilst working on his essay. He had gone to Prestatyn, where George Turnbull, the former Professor of Education in Sheffield and the custodian of the papers, lived following his retirement in 1954. Turnbull and Trevor-Roper were entirely different personalities. It is impossible to imagine Trevor-Roper writing the archival-retentive book that Turnbull published in 1947 as *Hartlib, Dury and Comenius: Gleanings from Hartlib's Papers*. But they shared a first in Classics, a wartime past and a love of fishing. Trevor-Roper was shown 'six crates' of papers and

Turnbull's transcription of Hartlib's diary, or *Ephemerides*.[4] There must have been a reorganisation of the archive whilst it was in Turnbull's hands, for when Turnbull took trusteeship of them he had received them in a 'large box, tied in 68 bundles'. Trevor-Roper was told something – though by no means all – of the curious history of how Turnbull had come by them.[5] He sent a draft of the *Encounter* article to Turnbull, who replied on 22 January 1960 thanking him for 'this synthesis of so much material'. He restricted his critical comments to points of detail.[6] Through the text, and through the somewhat enlarged version republished (as 'Three Foreigners: The Philosophers of the Puritan Revolution') in *Religion, the Reformation and Social Change* in 1967, one can deduce what Trevor-Roper went looking for in Prestatyn.[7] He was in search of the political links between Hartlib, Dury and Comenius and members of the country party in and around parliament. He found them in Nicholas Stoughton, William Waller, Sir Cheney Culpeper and (above all) John Pym.[8] By 1967 the papers were in the public domain. Turnbull himself had wanted to deposit them with the British Museum (where the manuscripts now in the British Library were then housed), whilst being aware that the right to dispose of them might properly rest in the hands of Lord Delamere.[9] After Turnbull's death in 1961 they were returned to Sheffield by his successor, W.H.G. (Harry) Armytage. They spent a couple of years in Armytage's own office until his appointment as Pro-Vice-Chancellor prevented him from carrying out further significant work on them. He deposited them in the university library, whose new building (opened in 1959) was equipped with a strong-room. The highlighting of Hartlib's significance by Trevor-Roper's essay of 1960 was an important contribution to the seriousness with which their conservation was eventually taken.

The content of those papers was bound up with Hartlib's life and its contexts. Born in around 1600 in Elbing (Eblag in Polish), in Polish Prussia, to a refugee merchant from Poland and his English-born wife, who was the daughter of a rich Baltic merchant there, Hartlib studied at Brieg (Brzeg) in Silesia and at the famous Calvinist Academy at Herborn. That was where the Czech encyclopedist and educationalist Comenius had matriculated in 1611, although Hartlib probably knew him through his younger brother Georg, who studied with Hartlib at the University of Heidelberg in 1613.[10] Hartlib then spent time in Cambridge, certainly in 1625–6 and perhaps earlier too, under the aegis of the Puritan divine John Preston, which is where he first met the Scottish divine and irenicist John Dury. The Cambridge interlude preceded his permanent relocation to England after the Baltic coast had been ravaged by the conflicts of the Thirty Years War. Hartlib first tried to establish a school in Chichester in 1630, where he sought, through his gradually emerging pedagogical notions, to advance his 'universalist' ideal to bring about a 'reformation, both of Religion, Learning, and propagation of the Gospel'.[11] When that failed he moved to London. By then Comenius's innovative 'look and say' method of learning Latin, set out in *The Gate of Languages Unlocked*, was beginning to make the headlines. In (or perhaps even before) 1634 Hartlib, recognising in Comenius's pansophic manifesto a kindred programme, wrote directly to offer his support. Comenius would be somewhat taken aback, however, to find that in 1636 his reply – a brief outline of his plan for educational reform as the basis for a more profound human reformation – had been published without his knowledge by the indefatigably enterprising Hartlib, who was committed to the open sharing of knowledge. In collaboration with Comenius (whose visit to England in 1641–2 he facilitated and hosted) and Dury (whose irenicism he promoted), Hartlib became, in the years of the English Civil Wars and the Commonwealth, the promoter of a multiplicity of projects. His interests and publications ranged from medicine to agriculture, from natural science to colonial development, from politics to education, and to much more besides. He was a London 'intelligencer' from whom one could learn all sorts of knowledge – from the best ways to cultivate bees to the latest developments in Cartesian philosophy. Writing (probably in 1643) a form-letter to be circulated to divines at the Westminster Assembly in order to secure its support for Dury's irenicist endeavours, he alluded to the range of contacts which he and Dury had

> with the great many distressed Princes and other Men of Eminencie of several ranks in Moscovia, Lithvania Prusia Polonia Silesia Moravia Bohemia Hungaria Transylvania Vpper and Lower Germanie Sweden Denmark Fraunce yea in Turkie New England and other remoter Parts of the World.[12]

It was the surviving part of the correspondence from such commitments, together with the attachments, scribal drafts, memoranda and miscellaneous papers that accompanied the letters, that confronted Trevor-Roper in 1959: over 5,500 items of manuscript, a 'rich and daunting resource for the historian', as Richard Yeo describes it in his recent analysis of seventeenth-century scientific notebooks.[13]

How had the papers come into Turnbull's hands? A significant figure in his own lifetime, Hartlib had succumbed to the agonies of kidney-stones and a humiliating reversal of his fortunes at the Restoration. As his vision of universal reformation fell from fashion, his reputation faded. The collection of his papers, the heart of which resided for a while at Brereton Hall in Cheshire before being acquired by the Cholmondeley family and integrated into their library at Vale Royal at some date after 1669, was subjected to pillaging by various individuals, some of them Royal Society virtuosi, who used what they found to sustain their designs and preoccupations, others men who were concerned to obliterate evidence of their own pre-Restoration activities.[14] It was only in the nineteenth century that Hartlib's significance gradually emerged. Even then he was scarcely known outside the few scholars who came across his papers in visits to Vale Royal, though Milton's dedication of his treatise *Of Education* did win him attention elsewhere. He was called 'Milton's familiar friend' in 1865 by the English impresario Henry Dircks.[15] But the existence of the papers eluded the Slovak scholar-sleuth, Ján Kvačala, who made it his business to search through English archives in the 1890s to discover the traces of Comenius.[16] His publications, along with those of a fellow Czech philologist, Adolf Patera, were what led Turnbull, who had undertaken a Liverpool University MA on the little-known German late-humanist pedagogue Wolfgang Ratke, to turn his attentions to Hartlib.[17] Turnbull's work was interrupted by the war, but in 1919 he completed a PhD thesis in the Philosophical Faculty of the Friedrich-Wilhelms-Universität in Bonn on the subject of Hartlib's relationship to Comenius. It was published as a short book the following year.[18] So it was Hartlib's contacts with Comenius and associated German encyclopedist pedagogues that heralded his rehabilitation. The phrase 'the Hartlib circle' (now in common currency) was first coined, as Leigh Penman has discovered, by Timothy Corcoran as early as 1907 to delineate those contacts.

Meanwhile the papers remained quietly out of view. Trevor-Roper remembered being told that the documents 'having been lost for many years [...] were re-discovered in a solicitor's office in (I think) Chester during the war, [...]. It was decided, by the solicitor I think, that they had been deposited there by the Delamere family – i.e. the Booths of Booth's Rising – in the last century.'[19] The papers were, indeed, in the possession of Birch, Cullimore & Co., Chester, the solicitors for the Delamere family from the middle of the nineteenth century. Their removal from Vale Royal, the family seat, explains why they were not auctioned off in 1923 by Hugh Cholmondeley when he disposed of other valuable manuscripts and heirlooms to fund his estate and lifestyle in Kenya. They came to light when the Delamere muniments were reorganised after the death of the third baron Delamere in November 1931. Instead of auctioning them the solicitor in question contacted Turnbull, whose monograph on the subject had come to his attention, and they were 'allowed to be inspected' by him and placed at his disposal. Turnbull published the results in 1947. He did not, however, let on that he had been in possession of the archive since 1933, an omission that explains Trevor-Roper's confident statement that the papers had been rediscovered 'in 1945'.[20]

One might imagine that the initial stimulus for Trevor-Roper's essay came from his reading of Turnbull's work. Certainly he showed himself interested in Comenius the year after its publication.[21] But the real prompt may have been his reading of William Vincent's study of grammar schools and of projects for state education in the 1640s and 1650s, which he reviewed in the *New Statesman* in February 1951. Its first chapter is entitled 'Hartlib, Comenius and Dury' – Trevor-Roper's three foreigners.[22] Vincent was headmaster of the Cathedral School of Christ Church, Trevor-Roper's Oxford college, and so may have been known to him. The review reads like a prospectus for the essay published a decade later:

> In 1640, these [three cosmopolitan specialists – i.e. Hartlib, Dury and Comenius] (patronised by Opposition peers and bishops) seemed to have the world before them; the eager reformers of the Long Parliament listened to their ideas and allocated funds and privileges to education. The outbreak of the civil war temporarily extinguished such hopes; but with peace the Republic, in a more pedestrian way, resumed the interest. Schools and universities revived; the position and stipends of schoolmasters were improved [...]. [But] after 1660 the force was spent, the policy reversed.[23]

However, the notion that the three foreigners voiced the aspirations and enthusiasms of a 'country party' in an 'English Revolution', whose 'dim squires' were mostly inarticulate, only took full shape when Trevor-Roper wrote his projected opus on the Great Rebellion, which had been sketched out by the end of 1957.[24] Around the same time his article on the 'General Crisis of the Seventeenth Century', published in *Past and Present* in 1959, sketched a European ideological context for the three foreigners and gave a European dimension to the court–country paradigm. It too would reappear in *Religion, the Reformation and Social Change* in 1967.[25]

The brilliance of Trevor-Roper's essay lay in its absorption of the three marginal figures into the historiographical mainstream. Hartlib in particular had been dismissed by historians of science and medicine in the 1950s as beyond the accepted and acceptable canon of the Scientific Revolution. His exclusion was based on what now seem artificially narrow definitions of 'ideas' and 'thought' as well as on a prejudice against the naiveté of Hartlib's utilitarian, millenarian and utopian ideals. Trevor-Roper's essay shared that prejudice, but transcended it by explaining that the ideas of Hartlib and his circle, whatever their limitations, had found a historical moment that gave them power. The argument placed the essay in the broadening of the scope of the 'history of ideas'.

Running through the 'Three Foreigners' essay is the theme of the difficulties encountered by one generation in speaking to another. It is not difficult to detect in the piece Trevor-Roper's sense of the historian's obligation to bridge inter-generational gaps. He wrote:

> If we are to understand changes in human history, human philosophy, we must always remember the importance of single generations. One generation of men may be bound together by common experiences from which its fathers and sons are exempt; and if those experiences have been signal, terrible, inspiring, they will give to that generation a character distinctive to itself, incommunicable to other men. How can we who lived through the 1930s, whose minds and attitudes were formed by the terrible events of those days, understand or be understood by men to whom those events are mere history, reduced to the anodyne prose of textbooks? [26]

In that passage he was discussing specifically men whose outlooks had been shaped by the 1620s and the (from a Protestant perspective) climacteric disasters of the first decade of the Thirty Years War. But the whole essay is grounded in the theme of inter-generational incomprehension. He uses it in depicting the bicephalous legacy of the thought of Francis Bacon, which he saw as divided between the 'vulgar Baconianism' generated in the distinctive atmosphere of the 1620s by Hartlib's empirics and enthusiasts, and an intellectualised 'Baconianism' which would occupy the high ground in the new generation after the Restoration. Seeking, at the end of the essay, to explain the evaporation after 1660 of all that the three foreigners had contended for, and their consequent absence from what he took to be the background of the Royal Society, he wrote: 'There is continuity in history, but there is also discontinuity: each generation profits by the acquisitions of its predecessors, but sheds its mood, the mere deposit of incommunicable experience.'[27]

What, then, of our chances of recovering the mental outlook of readers of *Encounter* more than half a century ago? Trevor-Roper was already known to them. He had published an essay on Erasmus there in May 1955, and an attack on the historical philosophy of Arnold Toynbee in June 1957. It was in *Encounter* than the 'storm over the gentry' broke in June 1958. The English Revolution (as it was known to that generation) seemed a pivotal way of understanding the ideological struggle between East and West which dominated the mental outlook of a postwar generation, and which is vanished now. Other concerns addressed by the issue in which his article appeared seem equally remote. C.P. Snow gives his 'Afterthoughts' on the 'Two-Cultures Controversy', which remind us how science, within whose history Hartlib's ideas were conventionally (and unflatteringly) assessed, was at that time placed in a special box, separate from other area of intellectual inquiry.[28] An article by Noël Annan attacks the moralising tones of Snow's adversary in the controversy, the then-eminent literary critic F.R. Leavis. A review of two books on the Hungarian Revolution of 1956 asks why the 'revolution' had turned out not to happen. Katherine Anne Porter's contribution is on the collapse of the *Lady Chatterley's Lover* trial in the United States. Pamela Hansford Johnson (C.P. Snow's wife) seeks to recover the year in which Proust notionally situated his famous novel. Asa Briggs's book *The Age of Improvement* gets a small review under the heading 'Victoriana'.

Foreign as much of that material may seem to us, the mental world it summons is essential to any estimate of the impact of Trevor-Roper's piece. The essay offered a double challenge to Marxist history. Its paradigm of 'court and country' attempted to replace the interpretative framework of class conflict and it insisted that ideas have a life of their own, which cannot be reduced to social or economic explanation. Those premises, though they voiced a historical philosophy that it would be reductive to regard merely as a Cold War position, spoke to the preoccupations of that war. Yet to confine speculation about the concerns of Trevor-Roper's readership to the ideological struggle of East and West would be another kind of simplification. The kaleidoscope of topical concerns addressed in that issue of *Encounter* – the first issue in what Bernard Levin would later christen the 'Pendulum Years' of the 1960s, on account of the tug-of-war between the past and the future –

should remind us that the recreation of the mental landscapes in which ideas or interpretations make their mark is a complex matter.[29]

Seven of the Pendulum Years separate the publication of 'Three Foreigners' in *Encounter* and its enlarged version in *Religion, Reformation and Social Change*. The alterations that Trevor-Roper made to the text were substantial but not fundamental. Footnotes were added. New paragraphs were inserted – probably as a consequence of the reading which he did in order to substantiate the footnotes. Much more, however, had changed, and was in the course of changing, in the intellectual terrain to which the essay belonged. The shift had begun six months after the *Encounter* publication with the celebrations to mark the tercentenary of the Royal Society in July 1960. The event attracted a confetti of commemorative publications. The Oxford physicist and Fellow of the Royal Society Sir Harold Hartley edited the substantial volume *The Royal Society, its Origins and Founders*, published later in 1960 in plush red covers under the imprimatur of the Society itself.[30] Hartley's pupil, Sir Cyril Hinshelwood, president of the Society that year, gave the Tercentenary Address, which garlanded a special tercentenary volume of the *Notes and Records* of the Society.[31] Accompanying media presentations readily accepted the conventional view that the Society's origins lay in an 'Invisible College' which met in London in the 1640s and which preserved Bacon's influence.[32]

A flock of Fellows of the Royal Society was also despatched in July to complementary celebrations in Oxford and Cambridge. The delegates to Oxford were each treated to a complimentary copy of a 15-page pamphlet, specially printed by the Clarendon Press, entitled *The Beginning of the Royal Society*. Its authors were E.J. (Ted) Bowen, an Oxford physicist who, like Hinshelwood (who had asked him to write the little piece in question), was a student of Harold Hartley, and Margery Purver, whom Bowen insisted upon as a collaborator, since her Oxford doctoral thesis, completed a year previously in 1959, had been on precisely the subject of the origins of the Royal Society.[33] The pamphlet dismissed the evidence for the London origins of the Society, and roundly declared that, in the words of Thomas Sprat in his early history of the institution, it was Oxford that had furnished 'the foundation for all this that followed'.[34] 'Not only were the Oxford men innovative,' wrote Bowen and Purver, 'they were conscious of their role' of innovation.[35] The pamphlet was not well received. When Trevor-Roper, who was not present, enquired of Cyril Hinshelwood in May 1962 whether it was true that the publication had occasioned an incident, Hinshelwood denied that the reaction had gone that far but recorded the (understandable) reaction among the delegates that the pamphlet was 'a little *pro domo*' – i.e. that it had come across as special pleading for Oxford.[36] The reasons for Trevor-Roper's enquiry are not hard to fathom. Earlier that spring he had read Margery Purver's doctoral thesis and thought well of it.[37] Her forensic and combative style would have appealed to him, and the work provided just the supporting evidence he needed of a rupture between, on the one hand, the 'vulgar Baconians' and the erudite ancestors of the Royal Society. He urged publication of the thesis in the Historical Monographs series at Oxford University Press.

It was also in the early spring of 1962 that Christopher Hill had given the Ford Lectures at Oxford on 'The Intellectual Origins of the English Revolution', which were subsequently published in 1965. Hill argued – over a breathtaking compass, but confessedly selecting evidence that supported his case – that unnoticed intellectual connections linked the opponents. Hill did not, on this occasion, claim that the drive for intellectual advance lay in Puritanism, though he did draw on Robert K. Merton's thesis, published initially in 1936, that there was an inherent link between Protestantism and the advance of science.[38] Instead Hill sought to show that controversies in the fields of science, history and law, which to immediate appearance were separate from each other, had common roots in the social and political conflicts of the society that gave them birth.[39] Hill concentrated not on a 'country party' but on Londoners. The 'three foreigners' were consigned to a modest ten-page section which begins, 'we must pause for a moment over the Comenian group' and ends, 'If we see the Comenians […] as active agents in bringing together the group which later formed the Royal Society, as I think we must, then we should also see [the parliamentarian leader] John Pym as one of the founding foster-fathers of the Royal Society.'[40] In those ten pages, implicitly and explicitly, Hill rejected the proposed Oxford genesis of the Royal Society.

Purver, a faun caught between the big beasts of the Oxford forest, was frightened. She developed what Trevor-Roper later thought might have been symptoms of paranoia. She thought that one of her examiners was blocking the publication of her work. She believed that Christopher Hill was spying on what she was reading in the Bodleian Library, and that her thesis was circulating among unauthorised persons. She placed it on closed access, where it remains even after her death in 2013.[41] Trevor-Roper twice tried to persuade her to represent more fairly the views of those her work sought to contradict, to no avail.[42] The delegates at the Clarendon Press declined to publish the work. Probably through Trevor-Roper's influence it was published instead by Routledge in 1967, with an Introduction by him which referred pointedly to forces which 'have resisted, and resisted strongly' its appearance in print.[43] Trevor-Roper himself published a long review of Christopher Hill's book in *History and Theory* in 1966.[44] Hill had made no secret of the fact that he had assembled his evidence selectively. The trouble, as Trevor-Roper showed with panache, was that an alternative selection could produce different conclusions. The review focused on Hill's material concerning the historians William Camden and Sir Walter Raleigh and on what Hill called 'puritan historiography'. Privately Trevor-Roper was appalled by Hill's way with the evidence.[45] In 1967 the revised version of 'Three Foreigners' conspicuously made no reference to Hill's book.

That omission, however, left the 'Three Foreigners' essay exposed. If Hill had been selective with the evidence in one part of the work, then his method of working brought into question the rest of his scholarship. But Trevor-Roper had himself postulated unsuspected intellectual connections among the parliamentarians. To demonstrate that his were right and Hill's wrong, he would have needed the time to work through the mass of Hill's material. He would also have had to confront directly Merton's thesis about Protestantism and science, on which Hill had drawn for support. Trevor-Roper, who had long wrestled with Max Weber's thesis about the connections between Protestantism and another kind of advance, in economics, published his conclusions on that subject in *Religion, the Reformation and Social Change*. But he had not paid the same attention to Merton. Instead he expressed his enthusiasm for a historian with a very different approach to early-modern science, Frances Yates, in whose work he found confirmation of the shortcomings of Hill's claims.

As the 1960s drew to a close the approach that characterised Yates's work was also adopted by other historians. Among them, Trevor-Roper developed a high regard for Pyranali ('Piyo') Rattansi, whom he met first in 1961, and whose appointment to the history of science unit within the Department of Philosophy at Leeds he supported. In 1966 Trevor-Roper gave a lecture in Leeds, where he met another young historian of science, Charles Webster.[46] Webster had trained as a teacher in the University of Sheffield's Department of Education in 1958 and had there met Harry Armytage. He went on to teach Chemistry at the Sheffield City Grammar School, where he developed an interest in the seventeenth-century physician from Halifax, Henry Power. That was when he became aware of the Hartlib Papers, though it was only once he had established himself in Rattansi's department in Leeds that he was free to devote himself to studying them. By the time he moved to Oxford in 1969, most of the work and writing for what became *The Great Instauration, Science, Medicine and Reform 1626–1660* had been completed. Webster's immersion in Hartlib's papers enabled him to reconstruct the connections Hill had drawn into a different and more convincing picture. His book relegated the 'Three Foreigners' essay to the footnotes.[47] On Webster's broad canvas Protestant religious affinities and anxieties were related to aspirations for the advancement of learning, medical change and the dominion over nature. He showed those preoccupations appealing across social frontiers to all who saw a role for themselves in the shaping of society and in the Coming of the Kingdom. He took his subject outside parliament, on which Trevor-Roper's account of the foreigners' influence had centred, into a larger, more dynamic and more varied world, even if the movement Webster depicted could be as unpolitical and inarticulate as Trevor-Roper's country party. Webster also showed that clear distinctions between vulgar and erudite Baconians would not work. Trevor-Roper's premises were being undermined or refined on other fronts too. In an article of 1974 Webster had recontextualised and reinterpreted the evidence for the existence of the 'Invisible College' in such a way that the debate about the origins of the Royal Society became a classic *'question mal-posée'*.[48] Michael Hunter, one of Trevor-Roper's doctoral students, based a major reassessment of the early Royal Society on the first prosopographical study of its Fellows.[49] In the field of political history the publications of John Morrill, David Underdown, Blair Worden, Anthony Fletcher and others gradually exposed the thesis of a 'country party' for what it was: a brilliant first stab at trying to get at the characteristic mind-set behind the parliamentarians, but not an enduring term of art, and not the last word.

On 19 January 1989 Trevor-Roper kindly took up my invitation to revisit the 'Three Foreigners' essay in a public evening lecture in Sheffield. The local agenda was to raise the profile of the Hartlib Papers Project, one of three flagship research initiatives launched in the late 1980s by the British Academy in conjunction with the Leverhulme Trust. The project was then in its second year of transcribing and digitising the archive. When I picked him up at the station he declared that he wanted time to himself before the lecture. As became clear, he had not finished it. The habits of a lifetime had not deserted him: 'Congenitally incapable of preparing lectures, articles, anything, ahead of time', he wrote to Robert Blake in 1977, 'I go through agonies of tumultuous industry at the last minute.'[50] There was agony of a different sort at a dinner before the lecture, presided over by the Vice-Chancellor, Geoffrey Sims, whose own lack of small-talk, coupled with the lack of any talk at all from Trevor-Roper (who hated eating before lecturing), made for an excruciating two hours.

The one thing that Trevor-Roper had asked for beforehand was a map of Central Europe in the seventeenth century. I dug one out from a slumbering collection of old Westermann roll wall-maps, which had been rendered redundant by overhead transparencies. As we entered the lecture room, where the great and good of Sheffield were assembled in number, he turned to me and said: 'Can you tell me where Herborn is?' I was baffled. Did he not know? Only later did I realise that of course he knew but that he could not rely on his short-sighted eyes to locate it quickly enough as he spoke. When the only moment in the lecture when the map had a purpose arrived, he gestured with a grand sweep encompassing roughly the Holy Roman Empire ('that powerhouse of the Calvinist international at Herborn', 'here'), and we moved briskly on.

After the lecture he invited Mike Leslie, who was the genus and managing genius of the Hartlib Project, and me back to his hotel. Taciturnity banished, he wanted to drink northern bitter and to talk. His principal interest was not in the three foreigners of the seventeenth century, but in an intelligence agent in the twentieth. The penny had dropped that my brother was the writer Paul Greengrass. It was Paul who had had persuaded the former MI6 agent Peter Wright to go on record with his experiences in British intelligence, in a *World in Action* documentary in July 1984. Paul subsequently drafted the book *Spycatcher* on the basis of Peter Wright's testimonies, a book which appeared in Wright's name and which became notorious as a result of the British government's humiliating failure to secure an injunction against it in an Australian court on 31 March 1987. Around this period Paul had lunch with Trevor-Roper three or four times a year at a restaurant in Piccadilly frequented by intelligence operatives. Now, over the beer, he asked us nothing about the Hartlib Project (whose commitment to the transcription of endless documents, and to their electronic publication, he might have disparaged) or about the archive.

My memory of that January 1989 lecture is now fragmentary and impressionistic. I recollect a first half that was dull – a reworking of the 'Three Foreigners' essay without the punch. Looking back on it I sympathise with him. He must have felt that the essay had not stood the test of time as long as he would have liked, and that he was struggling, as he addressed the audience, with his own experience of inter-generational incomprehension. The international ideological tensions of the contemporary world, which had given the essay resonance in 1960, had receded. The essay must have seemed to belong to his past. The lecture came to life in the second half, where he adumbrated the 'European international' of early seventeenth-century Calvinism and the 'antiquated metaphysical notions' of the scholars at Herborn, whose encyclopedic aspirations and circles of influence Howard Hotson has now taught us to see so differently.[51] He ended the lecture with a *tour de force* plea for the integration of English history into a broader European perspective, the goal which had inspired his essay on the 'General Crisis', and which is one of the lasting legacies of his work on the early modern period.

Which of us, anyway, would expect an essay that had been written on any subject to have a shelf-life of as long as a quarter-century? Trevor-Roper's distinctive prose style doubtless contributed to the longevity of the 'Three Foreigners' essay. It is a style that cries out to be read aloud. That, indeed, is how I first encountered his essays, at Epsom Grammar School in the later 1960s. The small sixth-form group studying History heard them from a portable Grundig tape-recorder into which they had been dictated by our teacher, who stopped the machine after each paragraph for us to discuss the argument and analyse the style.[52] The result had predictably bizarre effects upon our own essay-writing. But it was an enduring lesson in the power of words to convey ideas. In that sense, Trevor-Roper's essays have entered my bloodstream and, I suppose, the bloodstream of others of my generation.

PART TWO

Ideas and their Contexts, *c.*1500–1800

4

Ecumenism and Erasmianism: The Wiles Lectures, 1975

Noel Malcolm

Among the various substantial typescripts in the archive of Hugh Trevor-Roper is one entitled 'The Ecumenical Movement and the English Church, 1560–1640'.[1] It is the text of the Wiles Lectures, delivered by him in Belfast in May 1975. To call it an unpublished book would be something of an exaggeration; although the prose is, as always, beautifully polished and cadenced, much further work would have been needed in order to convert this sequence of four one-hour lectures into a publishable volume. But it was certainly expected and intended, both by the lecturer himself and by his hosts, that a volume would eventually appear. And while the subject matter may seem, at first sight, obscure, these lectures brought together a number of strands of research and argument that came to have a special importance in Trevor-Roper's view of the religious history of early modern Europe. So it may also seem that the failure to publish these lectures is something deeply to be regretted.

The Wiles Lectures, which have taken place almost annually since 1954, are administered by the Wiles Trust at Queen's University, Belfast. The trust was set up and named in honour of the industrialist Thomas S. Wiles of Albany, New York, by his daughter, Mrs Austen Boyd (née Janet Wiles), who had settled in Northern Ireland. Under the terms of the trust, the purpose of the lectures is to 'promote the study of the history of civilisation and to encourage the extension of historical thinking into the realm of general ideas'; as with some other famous historical lecture-series, the speaker is asked to perform the delicate tightrope-walking task of addressing simultaneously both a scholarly audience and any interested members of the general public who may wish to attend. The Wiles Lecturer is also required to turn his or her lectures into a book, and the general rule, to which there have been only a handful of exceptions since 2002 (and none before then), is that the book is published by Cambridge University Press. The roll call of important works that have emerged from the Wiles Lectures is an impressive one, of which the Boyd family (which is still represented on the board of the Trust) can feel very proud. These are books that have captured wide audiences, while also speaking to scholars: they include Herbert Butterfield's *Man on his Past: The Study of the History of Historical Scholarship* (1955), Jon Nef's *Cultural Foundations of Industrial Civilisation* (1958), Denys Hay's *The Italian Renaissance in its Historical Background* (1961), John Elliott's *The Old World and the New, 1492–1650* (1970), Moses Finley's *Politics in the Ancient World* (1983), Eric Hobsbawm's *Nations and Nationalism since 1780* (1990), Linda Colley's *Captives: Britain, Empire and the World, 1600–1850* (2002) and Robert Bartlett's *The Natural and the Supernatural in the Middle Ages* (2008).[2]

The special format of the Wiles Lectures was and is as follows. The lectures take place on four successive afternoons and are followed by drinks and dinner; after that meal the discussion continues among an inner core which consists of historians from Queen's University and a number of scholars from elsewhere (mostly nominated by the lecturer) who are flown in, accommodated and wined and dined at the Trust's expense. While one might have expected the atmosphere thus created to be a very convivial one, in most other ways Belfast in the early years of 'the Troubles' would not have seemed an attractive destination. The tally of violent deaths in Northern Ireland would pass the 1,000-mark by April 1974, and the Wiles Lectures that were due to be given (by Professor Jack Gallagher) in the following month had to be postponed to November because the province was paralysed by a strike organised by the Ulster Workers' Council. (The 1975 lectures, however, took place during a lull in the conflict.) It is conceivable that Trevor-Roper, far from being put off, might at first have envisaged a visit there as a positive opportunity to investigate the political situation; but there is no particular evidence of such plans, and in the event he was too busy working on his lectures to take part even in the daytime excursions to places of historical interest that were organised for the visiting scholars. Among other reasons for agreeing to give the lectures, the fee of £400 – which, as the Trust's rules specified, was 'payable on delivery of the typescript ready for publication' – should not go unmentioned: at the time when he accepted the invitation, this was the equivalent of £4,605 in 2013.[3] But in any case, like many a canny lecture-organiser keen to capture a star, Queen's University issued its invitation so far in advance that it would have been hard to find a plausible reason to say no. The invitation to give the Wiles Lectures in May 1975 was sent in November 1971, and accepted by Hugh Trevor-Roper in February 1972.[4]

The list of the so-called 'external guests' who came to Belfast for the lectures is a very distinguished one. There were three younger scholars, all of them pupils of Trevor-Roper: Blair Worden, Toby Barnard and Kevin Sharpe. And there were four more senior figures: Anne Whiteman, Geoffrey Nuttall, John Kenyon (who was invited by the University at rather a late stage, as a replacement for Owen Chadwick) and Margaret Aston (who was external but also local, having moved to Ulster when her husband began work at the Northern Ireland Office in 1974).[5] One other eminent historian from outside Queen's University also attended: Geoffrey Elton, who had given the Wiles Lectures in 1972 and was now a trustee of the Wiles Trust. The expertise of these eight historians covered a wide range of topics in political and religious history, from the late Middle Ages to the early eighteenth century – albeit mostly British and Irish.[6] The History Faculty at Queen's University was, understandably enough, less well supplied with early modernists. Michael Roberts, the authority on Sweden, had retired as Professor of Modern History in 1973, but the Faculty did include John Bossy, an expert on relations between English and continental Catholicism in the sixteenth and seventeenth centuries, and Ian Green, who had recently completed his doctoral dissertation on the Restoration Church under Trevor-Roper in Oxford.[7] With the exception of Green, who was still an Oxford research student when the invitation to give these lectures was issued and accepted, there does not seem to have been any special acquaintance or friend of Trevor-Roper's in the History Faculty at this time. In retrospect, one of the participants has suggested that the choice of topic for the lectures – the history of ecumenism – may perhaps have been made with the ulterior purpose of riling the Belfast (Protestant) academic establishment.[8] Such behaviour would not have been entirely out of character, and some dignitaries from the Union Theological College might well have been expected both to attend and to dislike certain aspects of what they heard. But if Trevor-Roper formed any such intentions with the History Faculty in mind, he was under a misapprehension; in the words of Alistair Cooke (now Lord Lexden), who was one of their number, 'they did not have a bigot among them. Condemnation of religious extremism would have pleased, not shocked them.'[9]

From the recollections of some of the participants one gets a rather mixed impression of how the lectures went, and how they – and the giver

of them – were received. Blair Worden recalls that 'Hugh had been ill
beforehand and his lectures weren't in an orderly state (at one point he had
to stop to find the next page), but they were wonderfully entertaining.'
(The text of the lectures, typed by a secretary, does bear many small
changes and additions in Trevor-Roper's hand, testifying to his last-minute
perfectionism, and in some places there are larger hand-written additions
or sequences of additions on one or more pinned-on pieces of paper.) Of the
inner core of discussants, Toby Barnard writes: 'Other than the Oxonians,
the only one whom I recall was Kenyon, who showed very little interest
in the lectures or the discussions. The Oxonians, knowing Hugh (indeed
nominated by him), were (I think) talkative and generally supportive.'
According to Blair Worden, Trevor-Roper 'coped genially enough' with
the questions until 'one persistent and slightly truculent questioner asked
him, "for the 58th time", to explain the difference between ecumenism and
irenicism. "I think", replied Hugh frostily, "I shall rest content with my
previous 57 answers."'[10] Geniality and frostiness were sensed in different
quantities by different observers. Alistair Lexden recalls: 'Mrs Boyd [the
founder of the Trust] looked on this occasion, as on all others, for charm in
the distinguished visitor; she was largely disappointed. Was he disdainful?
I rather think so.'[11] An alternative interpretation might be that for much
of the time he was so preoccupied with putting the final touches to his
lectures that he failed to supply the social sparkle that was expected of him,
and that during the discussions he sometimes felt the burden of having to
justify his arguments to an audience that was almost entirely lacking in
relevant specialist knowledge.[12]

  For the topic he had chosen was genuinely innovative, opening up a field
of study that had never received any general treatment of this kind. And it
involved, in classic Trevor-Roperian fashion, both the sketching of some very
broad-brush arguments about nearly a century of European religious history,
and the exploration of some quite recondite matters, such as the curious life
story of the Dalmatian bishop Marcantonio de Dominis and the rollercoaster
career of Patriarch Cyril Lukaris of Constantinople. The broadest of all his
themes was stated at the start of his first lecture:

> For the beginning of wisdom, in approaching the whole subject of the
> Reformation, is to admit that, as so often in the history of great strug-
> gles, spiritual or secular, nobody wanted what in fact they were ultimately
> to get. The Reformers did not seek to create a separate Protestant

Church in Northern Europe in opposition to the Catholic Church of the Mediterranean lands any more than the Catholics sought to create a Counter-Reformation Church in opposition to them. Both parties, indeed one can say all parties, envisaged a continuation of the universal Church.[13]

The person who aimed most consistently at developing a reformed but continuing universal Church was Erasmus, 'the first ecumenical reformer who seemed, at one time, to speak for the whole Church'.[14] His project failed, the victim of the extreme polarisation of religious attitudes that was brought about by Luther on the one hand and the Counter-Reformation assault on Protestantism on the other; but elements of his thinking lingered on. Trevor-Roper finds a strong element of Erasmianism in Calvin (again he urges us not to look at history backwards by reading 'the fierce, narrow, intolerant religion' of 'the embattled dominies of Scotland' back into Calvin himself, that Renaissance intellectual), and comments: 'The Erasmian content of early Calvinism [...] is what led so many of the élite of Europe to become Calvinists after the failure of Erasmianism. It took half a century, perhaps more, before that Erasmian content was driven out of Calvinism.'[15]

After the Roman Catholic reaction was codified at the Council of Trent (1545–63), in a way that ruled out any kind of ecclesiastically approved ecumenism from the Catholic side, Erasmianism could survive in Catholic countries only in a minimal or hidden way, 'as private intellectual heresy or (as in Spain) suspect mysticism'.[16] Individual Erasmians with active reformist ideas moved from those territories either to places where some toleration was practised (Poland, Transylvania) or to Protestant countries, where the name of Erasmus was still honoured. But it was one thing to celebrate Erasmus as a proto-Protestant, another to accept and promote his universalist agenda, which must now involve resolving or otherwise superseding the differences between the Protestant and Catholic camps. For a while, in the final decades of the sixteenth century, tentative steps were taken in that direction by a small network of intellectuals in the Netherlands and France – men such as the Flemish classical scholar and moral philosopher Justus Lipsius (who was first Catholic, then Protestant, then Catholic again), the French Catholic historian Jacques-Auguste de Thou and the Huguenot scholar Isaac Casaubon. In the first decade of the seventeenth, a movement along these lines gained strength on both sides of the confessional divide in France, and a potentially reunionist 'national synod' was planned, but the assassination of Henri IV in 1610 put paid to all such hopes. In 1611 Casaubon left

France for England, 'and with him, it can be said, the movement which he represented moved to England also'.[17]

Hence the central focus of these lectures on the Church of England. As Trevor-Roper explains in the second of them, the ground there was already 'well prepared' for Erasmianism: after the failure of the Spanish Armada radical Puritanism had been on the retreat, subjected to 'the great Anglican counter-attack', of which the intellectual high point had been the publication of Richard Hooker's *Laws of Ecclesiastical Polity* in 1593 (Books I–IV) and 1597 (Book V). As Trevor-Roper admits, this was 'not, in any explicit sense, an Erasmian work [...]. Nor was it explicitly ecumenical'; but in its recognition of 'the relativity, the legitimate variety, the necessary comprehensiveness of any Church which claims universal validity', it expressed an 'Erasmian philosophy' nonetheless and can be viewed as 'potentially' ecumenical.[18] The implications in favour of ecumenism were grasped by Hooker's friend and disciple Edwin Sandys, who went on a tour of continental Europe, studying the religious and political conditions he found there, and shortly before his return in 1599 wrote an account, *A Relation of the State of Religion*, sketching 'the possibility of a re-union of the Churches'. He did not publish it then; but four years later Elizabeth was succeeded by a bookish king with grand intellectual horizons, a mixed confessional background and a newfound devotion to the Church of England. So conditions now seemed ripe for a campaign of Erasmian consciousness-raising. Sandys's book appeared in 1605 and enjoyed a rapid publishing success, before being no less rapidly suppressed (for reasons that are quite obscure). James I's interest in Erasmian and/or ecumenical ideas seemed to come and go; nevertheless Isaac Casaubon, who moved to England and became his court scholar, was convinced that the King's interests in such projects were deep and genuine. Casaubon urged his Dutch friend Hugo Grotius to come to London and lobby for James's patronage of a reunionist project which would involve, in the first place, calling a General Council of all those Christian Churches (Western and Eastern) that rejected the decrees of the Council of Trent. Grotius was already one of the leaders of the Arminian movement – Arminianism being, 'after all, only Erasmianism re-emerging from its coercive Calvinist carapace'.[19] There were senior Arminians in the Anglican hierarchy too, men such as Lancelot Andrewes and John Overall. Fatefully, however, the new archbishop of Canterbury appointed by James in 1610 was not one of those, but a Puritan academic, George Abbot, for whom ecumenist projects of this kind held little appeal.

On his visit to England Grotius was rebuffed by the Archbishop. And much worse was to follow: at the Synod of Dordt, the representatives of Abbot's Church would give their support to the most intransigent Dutch Calvinists, who would then persecute Grotius and his allies. For there was another model of inter-Church cooperation: establishing a united front, not to resolve disagreements with opponents but to anathematise and crush them.

In his third lecture Trevor-Roper turns to the one place in Roman Catholic Europe that, after the collapse of ecumenism in France, still offered some hope of a Catholic–Protestant reconciliation: Venice. The Venetian government viewed the Counter-Reformation papacy with caution, coldness and, during the jurisdictional clash between them that led to a papal interdict against Venice in 1606–7, real hostility. Venice's leading ideologue and political counsellor, the friar Paolo Sarpi, was fiercely opposed to the papacy; he corresponded widely with Protestants and anti-papal French Catholics, and over many years he gathered the materials for a very damaging account of the Council of Trent, presented as a case study in power politics and the manipulation of all-too-human interests. The English saw Venice, with Sarpi as its guide and spokesman, as a suitable place in which to extend their own influence – not just in politics, but in religion too. After the interdict the ambassador there, Sir Henry Wotton, organised the distribution of the Anglican liturgy in Italian, and Sarpi was soon making a close study of an Italian translation of Sandys's *Relation of the State of Religion*. Trevor-Roper rejects the idea that this was just a one-way attempt to convert Venice to Protestantism; rather, it was

> another chapter in the search for an ecumenical Church – always remembering that, after the Council of Trent [...] ecumenism was essentially anti-papal: it consisted in an alliance of non-papist Catholics and moderate Protestants made possible by an agreement to differ, to suspend judgement, in inessentials.[20]

In 1616, while Sarpi was completing his history of the Council of Trent, a colourful new recruit to this cause suddenly appeared. Marcantonio de Dominis, who was a Venetian subject (from the Dalmatian island of Rab) and Catholic archbishop of the Venetian-ruled see of Split, travelled to London and publicly declared his wish to join the Church of England – which, he said, represented the true catholic and universal Church, purged of Rome's corruptions. He was welcomed and honoured by James I, who appointed him dean of Windsor, and while in England he published not only Sarpi's history of the Council of Trent (with a dedication to King James by de Dominis, so polemical that it caused serious embarrassment to the author) but also his own lengthy treatise on the true Church. Archbishop Abbot favoured these developments and had taken active steps to arrange the smuggling of Sarpi's text to England. Abbot's main concern, Trevor-Roper suggests, was to get the book published in time for the Synod of Dordt. (It is not clear from the account he gives whether this was with a view to hardening the Synod's anti-Catholic resolve, or reminding it that anti-papal Catholics were still worth cultivating.) The eventual publication of Sarpi's work came too late to influence that gathering, and the Synod's decisions moved the Reformed Churches of Northern Europe, and the Church of England, further away from any ecumenist path. De Dominis, Trevor-Roper argues, was a true ecumenist, and during the next few years he underwent a process of bitter disillusionment with the English Church. It was thus not only out of vanity and false hopes (though those do seem to have been present) but also for principled reasons that in 1622 he decided to leave England and reconcile himself again with the Church of Rome. The story – and the third lecture – ends on a sad note: once installed in Rome, he was put to work writing retractions, willy-nilly, of all his previous writings. Having shown some reluctance shortly before he fell ill and died in 1624, he was formally condemned as a relapsed heretic, and his corpse, portrait and books were ceremonially burned.[21] For the post-Tridentine papacy, reunion was something to be achieved in only one way: reducing the Protestants to total submission. And with the Thirty Years War already raging, a Catholic *reconquista* was an imminent or actual reality in several of the territories of Protestant Europe.

Direct reconciliation between the two great religious blocs in Western Europe was not possible – nor had it ever been a realistic scenario in the years since the conclusion of the Council of Trent. Nevertheless, ecumenist impulses of a kind could still be directed along a different track, in a kind of grand out-flanking manoeuvre. The aim here was reunion not with Western Christians but with those of the East; and this forms the subject of the fourth and final lecture. For Protestants the Eastern Orthodox Church, with its history of direct descent from some of the first Christian communities, represented a repository of early traditions that could be used to show that important doctrines had been distorted and corrupted by Rome. For Roman Catholics, the Orthodox – who had formally separated from them in 1054

— were 'schismatics', erring sheep who should be brought back into the fold. While the Counter-Reformation papacy engaged, from the 1570s onwards, in a series of initiatives to win over to Rome the Orthodox Christians of Greece, the South Slav lands, Ruthenia (i.e. the western Ukraine) and Moldavia, Protestant intellectuals began making contacts of their own with the Orthodox world. Some senior Orthodox clerics welcomed their advances, to counteract what could already seem undue pressure from the Catholic side. In this they were responding also to the changing balance of diplomatic power in Istanbul, where, in the early seventeenth century, thanks to the growing presence of English and Dutch traders in the Levant, the ambassadors of England and the United Provinces began to exert significant influence.

The key figure here was Cyril Lukaris, a Cretan who had studied in Venice (adding good Latin to his fluent Italian) before being raised, in 1601, to one of the highest positions in the Greek Orthodox Church, as Patriarch of Alexandria. Trying to establish the true nature of Lukaris's thinking about Protestantism and Roman Catholicism is a task which, as Trevor-Roper notes with some wryness, has deeply perplexed every one of the handful of modern scholars who have attempted it:

> Three biographers, a Greek Methodist, a Greek Orthodox Archbishop, and a German Jesuit, have contrived to reach firm conclusions doctrinally comforting to themselves but entirely incompatible with each other. Unfortunately, to reach them, each has had to ignore, or to discount as forgeries, important documents used by the others.[22]

The puzzle is further compounded by references in the scholarly literature to letters in private hands, of which the whereabouts are now quite unknown. It is clear that, having pledged his agreement with, and allegiance to, the papacy in 1608, Lukaris then turned to the Protestant side, which he cultivated over quite a long period. In 1612, for example, he contacted Archbishop Abbot, proposing the education of Greek priests in England; one was duly sent to Balliol, Abbot's own college. While it is hard to tell what distinctions, if any, Lukaris made between different varieties of Protestantism, Trevor-Roper believes that Abbot began to suspect him of improperly favouring the Arminians and others who veered away from the strict Calvinist path. When the Greek student at Balliol reached the end of his studies in 1623 and set off for Constantinople, Abbot was irritated to learn that he planned to travel overland via various other Protestant

2

The Puritan Revolution

Blair Worden

'The twentieth century, I find,' wrote Trevor-Roper to Bernard Berenson in January 1948, 'is a fascinating century to live in and to study.' For, 'when, since the fifth century, was Europe so interesting and mutable to observe?' He had recently returned from Czechoslovakia, whose precarious present condition, as the Communist takeover approached, he had been eager to study. Yet modern politics had been 'only one' reason for his journey. 'Really I am, or pretend to be, a seventeenth-century historian, and Bohemia to me is the Bohemia of Wallenstein and Comenius, of Wenzel Hollar and the White Mountain, of aristocratic palaces and baroque Jesuit churches. Only the chance of war' – the chance that had led him to investigate the circumstances of Hitler's death – had 'projected my studies' into contemporary history.[1] He wrote more on the seventeenth century than on any other, though more on its first half than on its second, and though much that he wrote on its first half stepped back into the sixteenth century. In 1976, when he was working on the Huguenot physician Theodore de Mayerne, he casually referred to the time of Mayerne's career, from the late sixteenth century to the mid-seventeenth, as 'my natural area of study'.[2]

Why, amid so many periods that he wrote about, did he choose that one? It was not a taste for the flavour of the era. Admittedly he rejoiced in the 'wonderful, rich vocabulary' of the age of Donne and Browne and Milton and Aubrey.[3] His wartime friend Logan Pearsall Smith, who was something close to a literary mentor, was the editor of Browne and Jeremy Taylor and the biographer of Sir Henry Wotton. In 1970 Trevor-Roper's *Letters of Mercurius*, a book which may have a suggestion by Smith distantly behind it,[4] was modelled on Aubrey's prose and carried loving echoes of his phraseology. Yet literature is the subject of only a small proportion of Trevor-Roper's writings on the seventeenth century. If his selection of period had been determined by a sense of personal affinity we might sooner expect him to have opted for the

territories, including centres of moderate Lutheranism such as Helmstedt.
'What I am suggesting', Trevor-Roper explains, 'is that by 1623 the official
English attitude towards Reunion had hardened. The concept was too tied to
Arminian ideas. Circumstances had changed, and it is circumstances, rather
than intellectual development or argument, which alter ideas.'[23]

In the final part of this lecture, Trevor-Roper tells the story of the last
years of Lukaris's career. Having become the Patriarch of the Greek Church
in Constantinople in 1620, he was much cultivated by both the English
ambassador there, Sir Thomas Roe, and the Dutch, Cornelis Haga. In 1629,
under the influence of a Swiss Calvinist chaplain supplied to him by Haga,
he issued a 'Confession of Faith' directly based on the *Confessio belgica* of
the Dutch Churches. This was a hugely imprudent act, as such doctrinal
innovation alienated all those bishops of the Greek Church (a waning
number, in any case) who had hitherto remained his supporters. Trevor-
Roper suggests that Lukaris tried to align his Church with international
Calvinism because he thought this was the only way to protect it from
the growing pressure that came from the Roman Church – which, having
already absorbed one Orthodox Church, in Ruthenia, now had its eye on the
main prize, in Constantinople.[24] Over the next nine years Lukaris became the
shuttlecock of Western diplomacy in the Ottoman capital, being dismissed
and then reappointed by the sultan several times; and in 1638 he was both
dismissed and executed. During those years, however, his support had come
only from Holland, not from England. For even though Abbot had been
succeeded at Canterbury by a churchman of a very different kind, William
Laud, the spark of Anglican ecumenism had finally been extinguished. As
Trevor-Roper writes, in conclusion, about the Church of England:

> In the flourishing peace of King James, it could offer itself as a model for
> a reunited Christendom; but when the iron age returned, it must give up
> this comfortable but perhaps unreal position. The alternatives before it, in
> the real world, were now two. Either it must move to the Left, accept the
> domination of militant Calvinism, and thus retain its leadership in the world
> that would not yield to the Counter-Reformation; or it must contract out
> of the struggle and aim at preserving its own inheritance, the inheritance
> formulated for it by Hooker and Andrewes, on a more static, private base.
> The Puritan archbishop Abbot had turned away from the fair-weather
> Arminianism of the early peace-time years and preserved the international
> rôle of his Church by allying himself with Paolo Sarpi and Cyril Lucaris and

supporting the Predestinarians at the Synod of Dordt. But in the next reign, when the English contracted out of the Thirty Years War, the English Church retreated from that exposed position. Sir Thomas Roe might continue to advocate a forward policy, in Europe, but Archbishop Laud would not have it. He believed in Anglicanism in one country.[25]

The shift of focus back to England, and indeed to a figure on whom Trevor-Roper was the leading authority, provided a neat and satisfying ending. But the subject matter of the whole lecture-series had ranged very widely, raising many important questions and opening many possible avenues of research. This set of four lectures had very much the character of a sketch of a larger work; it was not something that could be published as it stood. A few Wiles Lecturers had been able to issue their lectures almost verbatim, merely supplying them with the necessary references to sources; Sir Steven Runciman's *The Last Byzantine Renaissance* (delivered as lectures in 1968 and published as a slim volume in 1970) is one example. But a great deal of work would be needed to flesh out the rather schematic account which Trevor-Roper had given here.

A few days after the final lecture, Lewis Warren, the head of the History Department at Queen's University, wrote to Trevor-Roper thanking him enthusiastically, and reminding him of the Trust's rules about publication. Whilst no particular timescale was mentioned, he also said that 'I shall be writing to the Press shortly to make preliminary arrangements.'[26] Responding to this, Trevor-Roper asked whether he might publish not with Cambridge University Press but with one of the London publishers that he knew; this notion was politely but firmly quashed. As Warren explained in his reply, there was a point of principle behind the idea of having every set of lectures published at Cambridge: 'some of the volumes of Wiles Lectures cannot be expected to have wide sales, and [...] indeed some may be published at a loss (and are subsidised by the Trust); it is therefore important to have a permanent arrangement with a publisher who will give as much care and consideration to the unprofitable as to the profitable.' Trevor-Roper's annotation at the foot of this letter reads: 'Would it pay me to forfeit £400 & publish with ?Collins in order not to subsidise the grubs?'[27] He hinted at such a possibility in his reply; and there the matter rested until Warren returned to it in February of the following year, repeating his earlier point and enclosing a copy of the original letter of invitation to Trevor-Roper, which had clearly stated that all Wiles Lectures were published by Cambridge University Press.[28] Five weeks later came a letter from a Cambridge University Press editor, Patricia Williams, and at this point Trevor-Roper capitulated: he promised that he would duly submit a 'revised, perhaps extended' version of the lectures.[29] But there was still no sign of a finished typescript by October 1978, when the Vice-Chancellor of Queen's University wrote on behalf of the Wiles trustees to ask when it might be expected to appear. On 8 November Trevor-Roper replied:

> I do intend to put these in publishable form, and I will of course offer them to the Cambridge University Press. On the other hand I also want to expand them a little – I felt that the limit of four lectures was cramping to the subject which I would like to present a little more fully. The trouble is, I have so little time in which to do this at present. So will you bear with me a little longer? I promise that it will be done.[30]

There is no reason to think that that promise was insincere. Among Trevor-Roper's papers there is a notebook, the first page of which is inscribed 'Wiles Lectures etc. 1976', in which he entered materials that would be used in the expanded version. One page bears an additional note dated 1977. Towards the end of the entries there is a page entitled (in Greek) 'schema', which sets out the plan of a book with ten chapters: it begins with 'Erasmus & More', reaches Hooker in Chapter 4, then discusses Hooker's disciples; Grotius; Sarpi and de Dominis; and Lukaris (Chapter 8), concluding with a ninth chapter called '1618 & re-polarisation', and a tenth entitled simply 'derniers reflets'.[31] But at some point, at the end of the 1970s or in the early 1980s, the impetus to proceed further with this project was lost.

That he had made slow progress since his return from Belfast is entirely understandable. During the rest of 1975 he was putting the finishing touches to two books, both published in London in the following year: *Princes and Artists: Patronage and Ideology at Four Habsburg Courts, 1517–1633* (itself based on a set of just four lectures, but with the advantage that its subject matter called for lavish illustration, which added to the page count), and *A Hidden Life: The Enigma of Sir Edmund Backhouse*. In 1976 and 1977 much of his energy was devoted to combating proposals for Scottish devolution. In 1978 he was hard at work on the draft of his biography of Theodore de Mayerne. And in 1979 his career took two unexpected turns, both of which would lead to new demands on his time: appointment as a life peer, and election to the Mastership of Peterhouse.[32] Precisely when (and why) the project of the Wiles Lectures book was abandoned remains, however, mysterious.

As often happens to academics with embryonic works in their filing-cabinets, from time to time Trevor-Roper received requests for lectures or conference papers which could conveniently be satisfied by working up one small part of the projected book. Sometimes these texts would then appear in print. In this way, several pieces that derived from the Wiles Lectures did appear before the public. Thus some elements of his account of Richard Hooker (and Edwin Sandys) were presented in 1977, first in a lecture in Washington and then in a review article in the *New York Review of Books*.[33] Also in that year Trevor-Roper gave a lecture to the Ecclesiastical History Society which was published (in 1978) in their conference proceedings under the title 'The Church of England and the Greek Church in the Time of Charles I'.[34] The essay on Hooker was reprinted in Trevor-Roper's *Renaissance Essays*, and a subsequent collection, *Catholics, Anglicans and Puritans: Seventeenth Century Essays*, would include a long essay on 'Laudianism and Political Power', containing material on Grotius's doomed attempt to enlist the English in an Arminian ecumenist project. A more detailed account of that affair, first given as a lecture to an Anglo-Dutch historical conference in 1991, was printed in Trevor-Roper's next collection, *From Counter-Reformation to Glorious Revolution*. And, although it was not completed in Trevor-Roper's lifetime, the biography of Theodore de Mayerne also offered a taste of one of the topics discussed in the Wiles Lectures, with its comments on the politico-religious predicament of Isaac Casaubon and Jacques-Auguste de Thou at the beginning of the seventeenth century.[35]

Of course, Trevor-Roper was not the only person working on some of these subjects. A short biography of de Dominis – the first to appear in English since the mid-nineteenth century – was published in 1984; this at least can have caused Trevor-Roper few qualms, as it tended to confirm, on the central issue of de Dominis's commitment to ecumenism, the line developed in the Wiles Lectures.[36] On the other hand, a long-awaited biography of Sir Edwin Sandys by the American historian Theodore Rabb, which remained awaited until 1998, would present a convincing analysis of Sandys's *Relation of the State of Religion* that arrived at a conclusion precisely opposite to the one Trevor-Roper had favoured. In Rabb's words,

> Sandys did the research [on religion in Europe] to expose the futility of the hopes to which believers in Christian unity still clung [...]. Christians had to face up to a rather different situation: implicit in the abandonment of a single faith was the acceptance of a more or less permanent split.[37]

But of all the later works that encroached on Trevor-Roper's chosen field, by far the most important was W.B. Patterson's *King James VI and I and the Reunion of Christendom* (1997). This wide-ranging, deeply researched and carefully argued work was itself the product of several decades of study. It covered all the topics of the Wiles Lectures that belonged to the period of James's reign – Casaubon, Grotius, de Dominis, Sarpi, the Synod of Dordt, relations with the Greek Church – plus some others, such as James's involvement, via the leading Huguenot pastor Pierre du Moulin, in the planning of the French Protestant Synod of Tonneins (1614), where a project of Protestant union was seriously discussed.[38] Patterson gave a much fuller account of James's own interest in Church reunion and the idea of a General Council; he distinguished carefully between positions that Trevor-Roper had tended to run together, such as the attitudes of Grotius and Casaubon; and in the one substantial passage where he discussed Trevor-Roper's own various publications on these matters, he gently suggested that the emphasis on Erasmianism as a driving force in the English case had been overdone:

> Trevor-Roper's interpretation needs to be modified to do justice to the important role played by King James. It was the king's conception of the mission of the Church of England that largely defined its place in Europe in the early seventeenth century. James, a political theorist and a theologian as well as a statesman, does not really fit the Erasmian pattern.[39]

But what, in any case, was the Erasmian pattern? Had Trevor-Roper persisted in his plan to develop a full-length book out of his Wiles Lectures, this is the question that would have stood most urgently in need of an answer. The characterisations of Erasmianism that are given here and there in the lecture typescript are very general. For example:

> human reason was to limit the area of necessary belief; scepticism, suspension of judgement, was to prevent frontal collisions in genuinely contested areas. In this way a hard core of recognised truth, a wide agreement to differ, and mutual toleration, would preserve the unity of the Church.[40]

Or again: 'an agreement to differ, to suspend judgment, in inessentials [...] scepticism round a hard core of reason'.[41] What notion of 'reason' was to be applied, and on what basis were inessentials to be distinguished from essentials? Such issues are not addressed. During the course of the lectures, the 'Erasmian' label is applied to a bewildering range of people, including the conservative natural law theorist Richard Hooker, the members of the Family of Love (whose foundational texts expressed an exalted spiritualism), the pragmatic *politiques* of the French Wars of Religion, and a fiercely anti-Roman thinker, Paolo Sarpi, who, although nominally a Catholic, seems to have held a more or less Lutheran conception of the Church and yearned not for the integration of Protestantism with Catholicism but rather for the utter destruction of Roman authority in all its forms. Trevor-Roper tends to merge Erasmianism with both ecumenism and irenicism (which are not the same things – that persistent questioner in Belfast may have had a point) and, for good measure, with almost any attitude that favoured religious toleration.[42] To take just the last of these: there were many different kinds of argument that could be used in early modern Europe to promote toleration – theological, ecclesiological, political, epistemological. Distinctions need to be made; and any term, such as 'Erasmianism', that not only blurs those distinctions but also implies that there was a single continuous tradition from which all tolerationists drew and to which they all contributed is unlikely to illuminate the intellectual and religious choices that people actually made. At the heart of Trevor-Roper's account of this crucial period of post-Reformation history, one cannot help sensing the presence of that 'Whig' approach which goes through the past identifying friends and allies. To the question 'what do these people really have in common?', the most truthful answer may be that they are all admired, for their actual or imputed opposition to religious bigotry, by Hugh Trevor-Roper. However sound his likes (and dislikes) may have been, that is hardly a sufficient basis for identifying an objective historical tradition.

So although these Wiles Lectures were undoubtedly enlivening and enlightening at the time when they were given, we need not mourn for too long over the failure to publish them in book form. The central thesis, if placed under the spotlight in that way, might not have stood up to all the close scrutiny that it would surely have attracted. As things turned out, all was for the best in the best of all possible worlds. Those who attended the lectures enjoyed four days of intellectual stimulation; in later years, readers were able to benefit from some of the fruits of Trevor-Roper's researches as they were published, piecemeal, in other venues; the 'grubs' who might have burrowed destructively into a full-scale statement of the argument were never given such a target; and in the end the Wiles Trust, which has done so much to promote serious historical thinking and publication, kept its £400.

5

Intellectual History: 'The Religious Origins of the Enlightenment'[1]

John Robertson

In 1967 Hugh Trevor-Roper published an essay entitled 'The Religious Origins of the Enlightenment' in his collection *Religion, the Reformation and Social Change*.[2] Personally and historiographically, the essay appeared to go against the grain. Personally, Trevor-Roper had an established reputation as an anticlerical, for whom religious doctrine had no meaning. He had recently reinforced that reputation by reissuing his first book, *Archbishop Laud*, in which he discounted Laud's beliefs in favour of a rigorously secular interpretation of his career and contribution to the downfall of the Stuart monarchy.[3] Yet here, in this new essay, he explicitly ascribed 'religious' origins to the Enlightenment. Such a thesis was also at odds with the prevailing assumptions of scholarship in the field. In 1967 it was still widely assumed that the Enlightenment had an irreligious inspiration. This had been the accusation of the Enlightenment's critics from the 1790s onwards: in their eyes the *philosophes* were subversive atheists, dedicated to undermining the Church and Christian morality alike. Even in the twentieth century, the thesis of irreligious origins continued to prevail.[4] In 1966, the year before Trevor-Roper's essay was published, Peter Gay confidently entitled the first volume of his major, synthetic study, *The Enlightenment: An Interpretation*, 'The Rise of Modern Paganism'.[5]

What led Trevor-Roper to go against the grain both of his own past, and of a tradition of scholarship with which he might have been expected to sympathise? The purpose of this chapter is to investigate this apparently unexpected intervention, and to offer an explanation for it. To do so, I shall explore the broader development of Trevor-Roper's historical interests from the mid-1950s into the 1960s and beyond. What this reveals, I shall argue, is a conscious redirection, or rebalancing, of his historical interests in the early 1960s, as a result of which he gave much more weight in his work to intellectual history. Against the view that his thinking remained set in the mould established by *Archbishop Laud*,[6] I shall argue that there was a significant change in the 1960s, and a continuous development thereafter.

In what follows, I shall work from the inside out: from the essay on the religious origins of the Enlightenment to other essays to which it was immediately related, and from these essays to their identifiable sources. For this purpose I shall set the essays in the context of Trevor-Roper's evolving interests in the later 1950s and 1960s, making extensive use of correspondence and papers from his archive. From there, I shall explore the significance of the redirection of his interests, and of the 'religious origins' essay in particular, for the subsequent development of his work. Finally, I shall attempt to characterise Trevor-Roper's conception of the history of ideas, or intellectual history, and to locate within it the main themes of the 'religious origins' essay.

It is important to emphasise the limits to my inquiry. This is not a comprehensive study of Trevor-Roper the historian.[7] Trevor-Roper was not only extraordinarily intelligent; he had a quite unusual breadth of interests, and ability to maintain them alongside each other. My argument that there was a shift in the balance of his interests in the early 1960s does not imply that all his work thereafter should be thought of as intellectual history. Nor do I presuppose that the course of Trevor-Roper's development was representative of trends throughout historical scholarship in Britain at the time. In that wider setting, Trevor-Roper's was one case among many, and more individual than most. As we shall see, the process of intellectual adjustment took place on Trevor-Roper's terms: he did not align himself with any existing approach to the history of ideas, nor did he set out to establish a new methodology for others to follow. If there was broader significance to the change to which I point, it will not be clear until there are comparable studies of other leading historians of the period.

'The Religious Origins of the Enlightenment' took as its point of departure the still-fashionable association of Protestantism with the cause of progress.[8] A Whig theory in the nineteenth century, it had passed to the Marxists by its end. What Trevor-Roper called this 'neat theoretical lampadophory' had been reinforced by the work of Max Weber, who had given the association of Protantism and progress a new social content. Now apparently as strong as ever, the theory had recently been extended to the intellectual sphere, in

Christopher Hill's *Intellectual Origins of the English Revolution* (1965). Trevor-Roper, having previously criticised this book in a review,[9] set out to test Hill's thesis more generally. He acknowledged that the thesis seemed to have objective facts on its side. The evidence that intellectual life was freer, heresy safer, in Protestant countries was undeniable. It was also true that in the eighteenth century leading *philosophes* looked to Calvinist Holland, Puritan England, Calvinist Switzerland and Calvinist Scotland for inspiration from the past and refuge in the present. But it was not clear that these facts established a causal connection. To know which tradition had led to the Enlightenment, Trevor-Roper suggested, we should look more closely at those whom the men of the Enlightenment had themselves identified as their precursors.

These precursors, we would see, derived from three distinct phases of Europe's recent history: from the late Renaissance, from the brief period between the Wars of Religion and the Thirty Years War, and from the last years of the seventeenth century – all periods of ideological peace, of theological reconciliation and of cosmopolitan exchange within the 'Republic of Letters'. Moreover, if we looked at these precursors in their separate countries, we would see that they had in fact been opponents of Calvinist orthodoxy. They were the Arminians and their clients the Socinians in early seventeenth-century Holland, groups named respectively after Jacob Arminius and Fausto Sozzini (Socinus), divines who had renounced Calvin's doctrine of predestination and insisted that salvation involves the exercise of free will. These were followed by the Independents in mid-seventeenth century England and, at the end of the century, by the Huguenot exiles who after their expulsion from France by Louis XIV in 1685 had done so much to promote the cause of Enlightenment in Holland and in Switzerland. These last – Jean Leclerc and Philip van Limborch, Jean-Pierre de Crousaz and Jean Barbeyrac – had been the self-conscious heirs of the earlier Arminians and Socinians. As for Scotland, Enlightenment had only come after the Kirk had been 'de-Calvinized' by the Revolution and the Union, and had come under the sway of 'the Arminian historian, William Robertson'. 'Arminianism or Socinianism', therefore, 'not Calvinism, was the religion of the pre-Enlightenment'.[10]

It might be objected that Arminianism and Socinianism had been Calvinist heresies, and that insistence on their importance only modified, and did not disprove, the thesis that Calvinism was the religious origin of the Enlightenment. The refutation of this objection was crucial to Trevor-Roper's argument. In both Holland and England, he pointed out, Arminianism had been a heresy of the right. Its exponents had been accused of crypto-popery. They had also been accused of Socinianism. But Socinianism too was not, initially, a radical heresy. In Holland the Arminians had protected the Socinians. In England the first to engage with Socinianism had been the moderate Anglicans Lucius Cary, Viscount Falkland, John Hales and William Chillingworth; both Arminianism and Socinianism were movements within the Anglican establishment before they were adopted by radicals such as John Bidle during the Civil Wars.

Nor was this surprising, for in historical fact Arminianism and Socinianism had a distinct origin, which preceded Calvinism. That origin was Erasmus, whose philosophy of free will and of the application of reason to religious texts made him, in effect, the first Arminian and the first Socinian. Even the 'peculiar tenet' of the early Socinians, their rejection of the origin of the Trinity, derived from Erasmus's biblical scholarship. (In other words, it was a matter of philology and applied reason, not theology.) Erasmus's paternity was recognised by the early Italian heretics, Sebastiano Castellio, Jacobus Acontius, and Lelio and Fausto Sozzini; it was recognised by the Dutch Arminian jurist and theologian Hugo Grotius, and by his English disciples Falkland and Chillingworth. Arminianism and Socinianism, Trevor-Roper suggested, were simply the new names taken by developments of a philosophy received from Erasmus.[11]

Even within the Catholic Church, Trevor-Roper believed, 'the Erasmian tradition – to use a convenient phrase' had survived throughout the seventeenth century, and by the century's end was challenging established orthodoxy there too. It was to be found where Catholic humanism still found shelter, between 1590 and 1625, in the Venice of Paolo Sarpi and in the France of Montaigne and of the historian Jacques-Auguste de Thou, before even they were condemned for heresy. But then it resurfaced among the Oratorians in the second half of the century, flowering in the 'Socinian' biblical scholarship of Richard Simon. In Naples the historian Pietro Giannone had turned from Descartes back to de Thou and Montaigne, as well as to Locke and Newton – 'both Socinians in religion'. Giving this argument a final twist, Trevor-Roper claimed that it was Catholic, or at least Jacobite Erasmianism which had inspired the Scottish Enlightenment in the eighteenth century, through the mystics of the Episcopalian north-east, the Chevalier Ramsay, and David Hume, 'a Jacobite till 1745'.[12]

But it was the relation of Calvinism to Erasmianism which was the primary focus of the essay. And Calvinism, Trevor-Roper ended by acknowledging, had done the Erasmians one service. At certain periods it had provided them with a suit of armour with which to defend themselves against the Counter-Reformation Catholic Church. Erasmianism was a philosophy for peaceful times, Calvinism for belligerent ones. But this was a political service, and entailed nothing about the religious origins of the Enlightenment as an intellectual movement. In answer to that question, he had made his case that the eighteenth-century Enlightenment was not an outcome of Calvinism, but 'a reunion of all the heretics', a recomposition of the original Erasmian message of free will, reason and tolerance.[13]

'The Religious Origins of the Enlightenment', which had not been published previously, was withdrawn from a *Festschrift* for Theodore Besterman in order to be included in *Religion, the Reformation and Social Change*. Justifying its inclusion, Trevor-Roper emphasised its natural connection with the other essays in the volume.[14] It is most obviously related to the title essay itself.[15] For that was also concerned with the supposed relation between Protestantism and progress, and specifically with Max Weber's thesis of a causal connection between Calvinism and capitalism. Accepting that 'much of Weber's thesis is still firm', Trevor-Roper set out to test the historical facts to which it was supposed to apply. Where Weber had concentrated on describing a theoretical connection, Trevor-Roper would identify actual capitalists and test their commitment to Calvinist 'worldly asceticism'. The capitalists he chose to examine were the great entrepreneurs of the Thirty Years War, the men who had financed, armed and supplied the armies of both the Protestant and the Catholic combatants, Calvinists such as Louis de Geer and Hans de Witte. These were no ascetics, nor were they (de Geer apart) particularly good Calvinists. Their religious attitude was, for want of a better name, basically Erasmian. They had an idea of a 'calling', a purpose in life, but it was Erasmus's idea, an idea of a layman's calling which was commonplace before Protestantism. Moreover, though these capitalists might reside in Protestant countries, they or their forebears had come there as refugees from the once-great commercial and manufacturing cities of southern, Catholic Europe. If there was a critical connection between religion and capitalism, therefore, it was a negative one: the hostility of Counter-Reformation Catholicism, and of the courtly, bureaucratic monarchies which supported it, to the Erasmian religious culture and commercial freedom of Europe's urban, bourgeois elites. The argument sets up that of the essay which immediately follows, the great essay on 'The General Crisis of the Seventeenth Century'. For this was precisely a crisis of the great monarchies, their lavish courts and bloated bureaucracies – a crisis, in Weberian terms, of state and society.[16] Equally, the argument of 'Religion, the Reformation and Social Change' provides social foundations for the essay on the religious origins of Enlightenment, explaining both why the Erasmian Arminians should have enjoyed the support of the Dutch mercantile elites, and why they reverted to Calvinism when they needed a suit of armour to defend themselves against the Catholic Church and its princely allies.

Between the essays on 'The General Crisis' and 'The Religious Origins', lay another, the long essay on 'The European Witch-Craze of the Sixteenth and Seventeenth Centuries'. While ostensibly on a very different, antipathetic subject, this too was not unrelated to the religious origins of the Enlightenment. 'The European Witch-Craze' was an essay in intellectual history, more concerned with the genesis and spread of systematic demonology than with popular witch beliefs and their persecution. The witch-craze, Trevor-Roper began by pointing out, gave the lie to any simple assumption that Renaissance and Scientific Revolution marked stages in a linear history of intellectual progress. The demonology which inspired witch-hunting had engaged not only the lurid imaginations of Dominican inquisitors, but many of the best minds of the age, from Jean Bodin, the political thinker of the French Wars of Religion, to the Cambridge Platonists of the later seventeenth century. Overt sceptics had been very few. The most prominent was Johann Weyer, court doctor to the Duke of Cleves in the 1560s, who had an Erasmian, Platonist pedigree. Trevor-Roper did not posit a Manichaean opposition of demonological evil and Erasmian reason: both Erasmus and Grotius, he acknowledged, had remained silent in the face of witch persecution, as had Bacon, Selden and Descartes. The process which led to the decline of the early modern witch-craze was slow to get under way and drew on more than Erasmianism. Nevertheless, he was able to discern the religious origins of the Enlightenment at work by the end. The final victory came when nature was liberated from biblical fundamentalism by the English deists and the German Pietists, 'the heirs of the Protestant heretics of the seventeenth century, the parents of that eighteenth-century Enlightenment'.[17]

A complex web of threads thus joined these essays which Trevor-Roper published together in *Religion, the Reformation and Social Change* in 1967. By his subsequent admission, another, earlier essay might have joined them. For the Italian translation of the main essays in *Religion, the Reformation and Social Change*, whose title was the more direct *Protestantesimo e trasformazione sociale* (1969), Trevor-Roper accepted the suggestion of the reviewer of the English original in the *Times Literary Supplement* and added an essay on Erasmus which had first appeared in *Encounter* in 1955, before being republished in the *Historical Essays* of 1957.[18] Here Erasmus was presented as 'a giant figure in the history of ideas', 'the intellectual hero of the sixteenth century'. It had been his personal tragedy, but also his legacy, that he had stood out against the division of Europe into two great ideological camps; he had thus set an example to intellectuals now, in the 1950s, to reject the efforts of Western and Soviet politicians to gather them into rival intellectual 'congresses'. In this early essay Trevor-Roper described Erasmus's philosophy at greater length than he would do in 'The Religious Origins'. He underlined the extent to which it was a synthesis of anti-scholastic thinking, combining evangelical piety with the scholarship of Valla and the Platonisms of both Pico's Florence and Colet's Oxford. He also described how it was reconstructed after it had been assaulted by Luther and condemned by Rome. The first to attempt it had been the exiled Italian heretics, Castellio, Acontius and the Sozzini; they had been followed by the Dutch Arminians. Then there was the revival of religious liberalism in Oxford in the 1630s, as 'Socinian' books poured into England and Falkland made his house at Great Tew in north Oxfordshire a centre of Socinian studies. Within the Catholic Church Erasmian piety (though not Erasmian tolerance) had been adopted by the Jesuits, and later, in the seventeenth century, by the mystics. By the early eighteenth century, an age of 'rational, tolerant piety' had begun.[19] This is not yet the argument of 'The Religious Origins of the Enlightenment', but many of the component pieces are in place, and the earlier essay, as Trevor-Roper acknowledged, provides a helpful way into the later one.

Having set the 'Religious Origins' essay alongside those with which it was published, we can attempt to reconstruct the reading and the intellectual preoccupations from which these essays derived. Most immediately obvious is the preoccupation with Max Weber's *The Protestant Ethic and the Spirit of Capitalism*. Trevor-Roper is likely to have encountered the book in the 1930s, while he was writing *Archbishop Laud* (1940); and at first, as he later admitted, he was inclined to accept Weber's identification of Calvinism with capitalism.[20] Soon after the war, he began to have doubts. He rejected R.H. Tawney's account of the rise of the gentry, and his scepticism came to extend to Tawney's endorsement of the Weber thesis in the 'Foreword' to the English translation of *The Protestant Ethic* and in *Religion and the Rise of Capitalism* (1926). By the summer of 1956 Trevor-Roper had embarked on a book of his own on the problem. In August that year he told Bernard Berenson that he was working 'on the subject of the Reformation and Social Change – two processes which, I now think, are quite distinct', but which had been confounded by 'those German sociologists – Marx, Weber, Troeltsch, Sombart, etc.'. He depicted himself as trapped in a 'morass'.[21] If so, he had entered it willingly enough, being at that point deeply engaged in economic history.

Surviving notes from this period indicate an intensive programme of reading in early modern economic history, British but also continental. Of particular interest to Trevor-Roper were works on the metal and cloth industries of the Low Countries; 'the Entrepreneur Controversy', as it evolved in the pages of *Explorations in Entrepreneurial History*; and the literature devoted to economic diasporas. A constant stream of requests to the Bodleian for the purchase of foreign books accompanied and fuelled this reading. The book on Weber which he set out to write in 1956 addressed the question of whether the Protestant Reformation was the origin of modern capitalist Europe, and was to have 12 chapters. He wrote, in whole or part, seven of these.[22] He then seems to have abandoned the book and in 1957, the year of his appointment to the Regius Chair, he began instead to write another on the Puritan Revolution.[23] But the interest in economic history remained strong. At the instigation of the young Cambridge historians Peter Matthias and John Elliott, he met the German economic historian, Herman Kellenbenz, for whom he prepared a list of questions.[24] In 1958 he turned to Eric Kerridge and E.H. Phelps-Brown to provide him with information on prices, particularly during the 'crisis' period of 1590–1660.[25] Although by now engaged on a full-scale study of the Civil Wars, he nevertheless took time to write a powerful riposte to Eric Hobsbawm's 1954 *Past and Present* article on 'The Crisis of the Seventeenth Century'; this, the first version of the 'General Crisis' essay, was submitted to *Past and Present* in 1959, Lawrence Stone welcoming it as reinforcing the journal's recent rupture with its Marxist past.[26] Nor was the problem of the Reformation and social change forgotten. In March 1960 he gave a lecture in Paris on 'Religion et réalités économiques aux XVIe et XVIIe siècles', followed two days later by one in Rome on 'The Crisis of the Seventeenth Century in England and Europe'.[27] The essay published as 'Religion, the Reformation and Social Change' took final form as a lecture delivered to the Fifth Irish Conference of Historians in Galway in 1961, where it received, he recalled, an unsympathetic reception from an audience 'powerfully reinforced by local monks and nuns'.[28]

When viewed in the light of its extended genesis, what is striking about the argument in 'Religion, the Reformation and Social Change' is the depth of Trevor-Roper's perspective. He knew that the question of Protestantism's contribution to the economic and social transformation of Europe had been asked long before Weber, and that it had quickly become a subject of confessional controversy.[29] He likewise knew the German debate in detail, discussing the contributions of all the 'academic German sociologists', Marx, Weber, Sombart and Troeltsch.[30] Trevor-Roper's decision to correct Weber and re-state the connection between religion and economic and social change was based on two conclusions of his research. First, Weber had mistakenly distinguished between commercial and industrial capitalism. Trevor-Roper's reading had shown him that the great entrepreneurs of the Thirty Years War and their forebears in late medieval Italian and Flemish cities had been both commercial and industrial capitalists.[31] Second, as the existence of such capitalists before the Reformation testified, capitalism had been perfectly compatible with a form of Catholicism. If the two had subsequently ceased to be compatible, this was not because of the superior appeal of Calvinism as an ideology of capitalism; it was because the Counter-Reformation had reconstructed the Catholic Church in a form which obstructed capitalist enterprise. The apparent incompatibility of Catholicism and capitalism was the outcome of contingent social, political and institutional developments. These were the same developments as had produced the expansion and bureaucratisation of the Renaissance courts, subjects of the 'General Crisis' essay. Together Catholic Church and Catholic monarchs had siphoned off the resources which could have been used by Catholic industry.

But Trevor-Roper's argument combined intellectual with economic history. Those who were actively engaged in economic life in 1500 had possessed a distinctive religious attitude, 'Erasmianism'. There was even, he suggested, an Erasmian version of the 'calling'. But it was quite different from the one which Weber attributed to Calvinists. Weber deduced his concept of 'worldly asceticism' from the Calvinist's anxiety over his salvation, his utter dependence on a decision which had already been taken by an all-powerful, transcendental God.[32] By contrast, the Erasmian idea of a calling had no comparable theological content; it was simply 'the real, inner piety of the active layman in his calling above the complacency of the indolent monk'.[33] Whence, then, had Trevor-Roper derived his understanding of Erasmianism, the idea which would, a few years later, play such an important part in the essay on the 'Religious Origins of the Enlightenment'?

An account of the beginnings of his interest in Erasmus and Erasmianism was obtained by the American historian Peter Miller in 1999. Then working on the early seventeenth-century scholar and republican of letters Fabri de Peiresc, Miller wrote to Trevor-Roper to ask whether his interest in Erasmianism had derived from his work on Laud, and whether he had been led towards the 'Libertins Erudits', and Peiresc in particular, by reading Pintard.[34] In reply, Trevor-Roper discounted both suggestions. His interest in Erasmianism had not been the direct result of his work on Laud,[35] and he read Pintard's work very late, long after he had discovered the *libertins* through de Thou. Instead, he identified two other works as his sources of inspiration. The first of these had been Marjorie Hope Nicolson's edition of the *Conway Letters* (1930), to which he was introduced, during the war, by Logan Pearsall Smith. Reading these letters of Anne Conway, her doctors and the Cambridge Platonist Henry More had shown him that study of the interaction of politics, war and ideas was far more interesting than their separate specialisation.[36] The second inspiration, read in 1951, was Marcel Bataillon's *Érasme et l'Espagne, recherches sur l'histoire spirituelle du XVIe siècle*, originally published in 1937.[37] Through Bataillon, Trevor-Roper recalled, he saw that Erasmus was not merely an exact scholar and a humanist philosopher, but also 'an intellectual radical and a spiritual thinker'. Reading beyond Bataillon, he realised that the ideas of Erasmus persisted in both Catholic and Protestant Europe, resurfacing in a brief age of Enlightenment before the renewal of ideological war in the seventeenth century. 'So I discovered, through Erasmus and Grotius, something of the character and pedigree of Arminianism which I had not realised when I wrote about Laud, and had accepted the conventional view of it.'

Evidently the interest in Erasmus, and in the history of ideas more generally, had been aroused early, even if it played second fiddle for much of the 1950s to research into economic and political history. Its first fruit had been the 1955 essay on Erasmus. In that essay, Trevor-Roper identified two more sources which had helped him to appreciate the afterlife of Erasmianism and its subsequent mutation into Arminianism and Socinianism. The first of these was Delio Cantimori's *Eretici italiani del cinquecento* (1939), a classic, detailed study of all the Italian heretics and exiles: Castellio, Acontius, Lelio and Fausto Sozzini, Giorgio Biandrata and many others.[38] It seems unlikely, however, that Cantimori's work was a source of more than information. Cantimori emphasised the links and common ground between the early Socinians and the Anabaptists and interpreted Lelio Sozzini and later Biandrata as making much of Christ's poverty. For his part, Fausto Sozzini was portrayed as increasingly isolated in his insistence on non-resistance, which Cantimori seemed to equate with the old Italian tradition of Nicodemism. There was no suggestion that these remote, intrepid radicals owed much to Erasmus, or supplied the religious origins of the Enlightenment.

Another book, it is clear, was much more important. This was H.J. McLachlan's *Socinianism in Seventeenth-Century England* (1951). Trevor-Roper acquired his copy in the year it was published – the same year that he read Bataillon – and evidently read it closely.[39] He cited it in the essay on Erasmus as an 'important work', and cited it again in 'The Religious Origins', incorporating additional references which illustrated Laud's vulnerability to the charge of befriending Socinians.[40] Given the extent of Trevor-Roper's debt to the book, its argument merits extended exposition.

McLachlan was a tutor and librarian of Manchester College, Oxford, a Unitarian foundation, and might have been expected to write the book as an account of the genesis of Unitarianism. But this was not what he did. Rather, he presented Socinianism as it reached England in the seventeenth century as the theological legacy of the Italian humanist sceptics, Acontius above all, and of the Dutch Arminians, as much as of the Sozzini. Behind the Italians, McLachlan also remarked, was the textual editing of Erasmus. The opening chapter contains a brief account of early Socinian theology, in which the critique of the doctrine of the atonement is put before the rejection of the Trinity. But thereafter Socinian theology is mentioned only in the most general terms. Socinianism is characterised as the application of reason to religious problems and to the Bible in particular; it is closely identified with religious tolerance.[41]

When Socinian ideas and books began to enter England in significant quantity in the 1630s, moreover, the first to be interested were Anglicans. The key figures in McLachlan's story were Lord Falkland, John Hales and William Chillingworth, the last being a particular intimate of Falkland's and a regular at Great Tew, with access to Falkland's library. None of these, McLachlan emphasised, was a Socinian in doctrine. But they collected and read Socinian books, discussed Socinian ideas with each other and approached religion by the application of reason to the scriptures, and by accepting diversity of opinion in all but a few essentials. On this last point, a key text was Acontius's *Stratagematum Satanae* (1565), whose republication in 1631 was probably the work of Dr Christopher Potter, provost of Queen's College, Oxford, and a lesser Laudian. Laud himself, McLachlan observed, had tolerated and even encouraged these 'Socinian' Anglicans. (Here McLachlan picked up a hint in the first edition of *Archbishop Laud* that Laud's theology had been liberal even if his ecclesiastical policy had been reactionary.) McLachlan also documented the accusations of Socinianism made against Hales, Chillingworth and Laud himself, most aggressively by the Presbyterian Francis Cheynell, and he noted that John Owen, dean of Christ Church and Oliver Cromwell's chaplain, had later singled out Grotius as a dangerous Socinianising influence on English theologians. All of the accused had vigorously defended themselves, but if their denials were justified in strict point of doctrine, their interest in Socinian ideas was evident in their libraries and in their broad approach to religious argument.[42]

A few years later, indeed, the radicals Paul Best and John Bidle emerged from the maelstrom of the Civil Wars openly professing and publishing Socinian beliefs, in defiance of the wrath and harsh sanctions of successive Presbyterian and Independent authorities. But in the context of McLachlan's story, they were properly seen as offshoots of Anglican Socinianism, not as a separate or novel development. By the end of the century, moreover, Socinianism was safely back within the Church of England. Its most public proponent, the clergyman Stephen Nye, had kept his Hertfordshire living through the 40 turbulent years from 1679, while its most distinguished intellectual sympathisers, Locke and Newton, took care never to admit their heterodoxy in public.[43]

McLachlan's argument that seventeenth-century English Socinianism was an Anglican phenomenon, whose intellectual commitments derived as much from the Italian followers of Erasmus and from the Dutch Arminians as from the theology of Sozzini, was not, perhaps, the most surprising of historical insights. To a considerable extent it followed and accepted (in substance if not in spirit) the main lines of Cheynell's bitter, partisan case against the Laudians and Chillingworth in particular. But read alongside Bataillon, McLachlan seems to have provided Trevor-Roper with a historical connection he had hitherto been missing. When, in 1940, he had recognised that Laud was more liberal intellectually than ecclesiastically, he had been unable to develop the thought, or explain what liberal Anglicanism was. Now he adopted the McLachlan thesis, and adopted it almost wholesale. Ignoring McLachlan's few more precise remarks about Socinus's theology, he took over and generalised the suggestion that the ultimate father of Socinianism was Erasmus, and that the line of descent lay through the mid- and later sixteenth-century Italian humanists, then through the Dutch Arminians and particularly Grotius, until it reached the liberal, moderate Anglicans of the Great Tew Circle. Only incidentally a theology, this Socinianism was an attitude of mind, liberal and tolerant, and an intellectual commitment to the application of reason to the Bible and all religious issues. Along with its slightly less heterodox relative, Arminianism, Socinianism was Erasmianism by another name.

On this basis, Trevor-Roper's concept of Erasmianism did not lack substance. As an attitude of mind, it might not match Weber's standard of theological conviction, but it enabled Trevor-Roper to mount a critique of the Weber thesis both as economic and as religious history. More than that, it was clear that the understanding of Erasmianism he had acquired from Bataillon and McLachlan had critical implications not only for the Weber thesis in its original form, but also for those who wanted to identify Calvinism with intellectual progress. Trevor-Roper had made this point in a lengthy footnote to 'Religion, the Reformation and Social Change', [44] and it was quickly picked up by readers. Thanking Trevor-Roper for an offprint of the essay, his Oxford colleague John Cooper expressed regret that he had not had occasion to deal more fully with Hill's theses, though he had enjoyed the note on Hill's 'Ptolemaic attempts to save the phenomena'.[45] Helmut Koenigsberger was another to recognise the intellectual implications of the argument, comparing it with his own attempt to assess 'Decadence or Shift' in European intellectual, artistic and musical culture after 1600.[46]

By 1963, therefore, the road towards the argument of 'The Religious Origins of the Enlightenment' had been clearly signposted. It was, to a considerable extent, a logical extension of his long and close engagement with the Weber thesis, and his almost equally long-standing interest in Erasmus. But then, in 1963, this logical progression was interrupted and enriched by something akin to a crisis in Trevor-Roper's intellectual life. At the very least, he paused to reflect. Since the late 1950s, his major preoccupation had been the big book on the English Civil Wars. He had continued to work on it, rewriting it and changing its scope and title, until at least the summer of 1961. But by then he knew that he faced serious structural problems in combining narrative with long-term social analysis. Gradually, it seems, he realised that he could not finish it, or would not publish it.[47] Yet his family, his colleagues and the wider scholarly and literary world still expected it. He had reached a turning-point. During the Christmas and New Year vacation of 1962–3, which he spent at Chiefswood, in the Borders, he took stock. He made a series of resolutions, which he recorded in a notebook. The first was 'to be better-tempered, more tolerant, etc.'; the second was to resume the notebook in which the resolutions were recorded; the third was to re-read the Greek tragedians, 'even if I fall behind in the latest historical periodicals'. He did maintain the notebook, the only one of its kind he kept after the war, until September 1963. Although there is a late entry dated 30 August 1964, it is clear that the notebook is primarily a record of the first nine months of 1963. The substantial entries are those devoted to books which made a particular impression, and to the historical problems which were exercising him at the time. Every so often, he would also round up the rest of his reading in a list, with briefer comments. Written in a clear hand, with only occasional corrections and insertions, the notebook documents a period of reading and reflection which was to shape his subsequent development as a historian.[48]

He records that he spent the first term of 1963 in Paris, at the Ecole Pratique des Hautes Etudes at the invitation of Fernand Braudel. He was there to lecture (in French) on the English Civil Wars. But he received little guidance as to the lectures, found French scholars elusive, and even had difficulty obtaining access to libraries. So he read: Wesley's *Diary*, Voltaire's *Essai sur les Moeurs*, and some of Giannone's *Storia civile del regno di Napoli* and *Triregno*. This reading was directed towards a paper which he had promised to give to the inaugural International Enlightenment Congress the following summer, on the historical philosophy of the Enlightenment.[49] Then he turned to 'that other topic which interests me, international calvinism', and read works on Geneva, Béarn, Sedan and La Rochelle in the late sixteenth and seventeenth centuries.[50] Two figures stood out from this reading and were the subjects of what are virtually free-standing essays.

One was John Wesley, who repelled yet fascinated Trevor-Roper by his philistinism and intellectual conservatism. Wesley, he noted, had condemned all the great Enlightenment historians; he was certain that Captain Cook's anthropological discoveries were mere fiction; and 'in spite of Erasmus, Bentley, Gibbon, Porson, he goes on regularly preaching on the Three Heavenly Witnesses.'[51] Wesley was, in effect, the antithesis of Enlightenment as Trevor-Roper was coming to understand it, and a reminder of what he valued in its intellectual achievement.

The other figure to receive close attention was the historian Pietro Giannone, who had been kidnapped at the behest of the pope for writing the *Storia civile del regno di Napoli* (1723), the 'civil history' of the Kingdom of Naples. Trevor-Roper had been drawn to Giannone through his interest in the historiography of the Enlightenment. Having read parts of his two main historical works in Paris, he got hold of Giannone's autobiography on his return. 'Of all the books which I have read recently,' he wrote in the notebook, 'none has so seized my mind as Giannone's Autobiography.' He found himself drawn to Giannone personally by his love of rural solitude, and of the sea. He compared the 'incredible persecution' suffered by Giannone, and the conditions of imprisonment in which he wrote his autobiography, with the good fortune of Gibbon, free to write in Protestant Lausanne, just across the lake from Savoy, where Giannone had been kidnapped. He sought to explain the cowardliness of the Italian princes whose rights Giannone had attempted to vindicate: they were too keen on securing patronage at the papal court, but also afraid that the religious orders might turn their peoples against them unless they deferred to Rome. More particularly, Trevor-Roper was intrigued by the English translation of the *Storia civile*, which had so delighted Giannone when he received a copy and read the distinguished list of subscribers, archbishops and bishops among them, who had made the publication possible. What Trevor-Roper noticed, however, was the large number of Scots among the subscribers.

> Surely, I said to myself, this is relevant to that great problem, the Scottish Enlightenment. Generally, scholars agree with Dugald Stewart that it was 'soon after the rebellion of 1745' that the Enlightenment dawned in Scotland; but here, in 1729–30, are Scotsmen of all literate classes subscribing to the first great work of enlightened history.

Moreover the translator, Captain James Ogilvie, seemed to be a Tory, perhaps even a Jacobite, as were most of the great figures of the Scottish Enlightenment, including David Hume and Lord Kames. Trevor-Roper believed he now had a key to unlock the puzzle of the sudden flowering of Scottish intellectual life in the eighteenth century, a problem of which he had been aware at least since the winter of 1957–8, when he read the *History* and letters of David Hume. That eminent Scottish historians were still denying even the existence of a Scottish Enlightenment only added relish to the challenge.[52] The result would be the enduringly provocative essay, also published in 1967, 'The Scottish Enlightenment'.[53]

The growth of Trevor-Roper's interest in the Scottish Enlightenment is traced by Colin Kidd in the chapter following this one.[54] What is important here is the coincidence of interests in Enlightenment historiography, the Scottish Enlightenment and the religious origins of the Enlightenment: all came into focus in the early 1960s, and specifically, it seems, in 1963.

The figure of Giannone – his intellectual formation, his 'civil history' and his persecution at the hands of the late Counter-Reformation state – runs through and links all these interests. Giannone's recognition that history and law were inseparable, and that the legal codes of Theodosius and Justinian were the key to understanding the fall of the Roman Empire and the subsequent kingdoms and republics of Europe, was the 'very doctrine' of Montesquieu, Voltaire and Gibbon.[55] The English translation of his *Civil History* helped to explain the origins of the Scottish Enlightenment, since it suggested that it was Jacobites who infiltrated the new historical thinking into Scotland behind the fortified lines of Presbyterian hostility.[56] Finally, Giannone's professed debt to de Thou demonstrated that the Catholic Erasmian tradition had survived to nourish Enlightenment even in such a stronghold of Counter-Reformation as Naples.[57]

The interplay of these interests is also evident within the essay on the Enlightenment's religious origins. It was the Enlightenment historians, Voltaire and Gibbon, whom Trevor-Roper called upon early in the essay to identify their precursors as the Arminian heretics of the seventeenth century. The Scottish Enlightenment is likewise summoned in evidence to demonstrate that even where Calvinism had hitherto succeeded in suppressing Arminianism, the Erasmian seed was brought in and scattered by dissident Catholics and Jacobites, who thus made possible the subsequent de-Calvinising of the Kirk by 'the Arminian historian' William Robertson. These claims were exaggerated: there is no evidence that the young Hume was a Jacobite, and Robertson never admitted to Arminianism in doctrine. But they confirm the extent to which the essay on the Enlightenment's religious origins was fertilised by a confluence of interests in intellectual history.

Between 1963 and the essay's publication in 1967, further stimuli can be identified. Trevor-Roper's first resolution in the New Year of 1963 had been to be 'better-tempered, more tolerant, etc.', but the temptation to smite an erring colleague was not to be resisted. The publication of Christopher Hill's *Intellectual Origins of the English Revolution* in 1965 was too great a provocation. Trevor-Roper's irritation with the book was not with the Marxism of its author. In his 'Preface to the Second Edition' of *Archbishop Laud*, he had paid tribute to Hill's 'profound and illuminating book', *Economic Problems of the Church*, a book with a Marxist thesis.[58] But in the *Intellectual Origins*, Hill had committed the cardinal sin of arraying thinkers in opposed ideological and political camps, the very sin against intellectual freedom and historical perspective which Trevor-Roper had decried in his essay on Erasmus ten years before. The review of *Intellectual Origins*, published in *History and Theory* in 1965, concentrated on Hill's treatment of historiography and his claims for the significance of Raleigh as a Puritan historian; but its criticism in detail was devastating in its implications for Hill's thesis as a whole. Having noted Hill's debt to R.K. Merton's sub-Weberian argument for a connection between Puritanism and scientific progress, he reinforced his earlier remarks, in the note in 'Religion, the Reformation and Social Change', on the flimsiness of Hill's evidence in support of such a connection. Confident that he had disposed of this thesis, he simply set it aside, after an initial mention, when he came to write 'The Religious Origins of the Enlightenment'. For he was now in a position to respond to John Cooper's request to deal with Hill's theses with a positive argument of his own.[59]

Another intellectual encounter in the years immediately after 1963 was to prove far more stimulating. Frances Yates was an independent scholar attached to the Warburg Institute in London, author of a series of innovative studies of Renaissance philosophy and iconography. Although they did not meet until after the publication of *Religion, the Reformation and Social Change* in 1967, Trevor-Roper's admiration for her work was already evident by 1964. He wrote to her in June of that year, telling her that he read everything she wrote with the greatest interest, and asking for any offprints she might have to spare. She replied expressing interest in his recent *Encounter* article 'Three Foreigners and the Philosopher of the Puritan Revolution'.[60] When he wrote again, two years later, he was able to inform her that he had built up an almost complete collection of her works. He congratulated her on her article in the *New York Review of Books* on the Globe Theatre, and at the same time congratulated the editor, Robert Silvers, on securing it. 'I think she is the most interesting historical writer in England', he told Silvers, 'and she never takes up any subject without illuminating it.'[61] What he admired in her work, as he wrote a few years later in an article in the *Listener*, was:

> the power not merely to answer old problems but to discover new, not merely to fill in details, but to reveal a new dimension which alters the whole context in which the details must be seen. She does this by a technique which is very simple to state but very difficult to acquire: by re-creating the mind of the past.

She had done so by reconstructing the unconscious contexts of thought, using the iconographical method pioneered at the Warburg Institute by

Fritz Saxl, Rudolf Wittkower and Ernst Gombrich, to interpret 'the whole mental structure of the Renaissance'. Refusing to treat history as only what happened, her books had recovered a whole series of 'lost moments', when alternatives had been possible. Even when those alternatives had failed – as had the 'Erasmian' dream of William of Orange to preserve the unity of the Netherlands under the tolerant patronage of the Duke of Anjou – they had left a legacy – in this case the Valois tapestries which Yates had made the subject of a book. Her historical imagination 'recreates not only the facts but the mental world, the possibilities, the frustrated hopes of the past'.[62]

In themselves Yates's studies of Renaissance neo-Platonism and the hermetic, cabbalistic philosophy of Giordano Bruno overlapped to only a limited extent with the religious origins of the Enlightenment as Trevor-Roper presented them. Although she would tell Bataillon in 1967 that she regarded herself as a 'humble disciple of Erasmus' in her sixteenth-century studies, it was Bruno, not Erasmus, who caught her historical imagination.[63] But she had alerted Trevor-Roper to the 'Erasmian' potential of Renaissance Platonism, an insight which he put to use in the essay on the witch-craze, where he observed that Platonism had inspired the critics rather than the adherents of demonology.[64] Moreover, as the correspondence between the two intensified following the publication of his essays in 1967, it became clear to Trevor-Roper that the congruence of 'The Religious Origins of the Enlightenment' with Yates's interests was greater than he had initially realised. He would have liked, he told her in December 1969, to use her findings to develop that essay, which he now called 'Calvinism and the Enlightenment'. Specifically, he wished he had extended its scope to include the liberal Calvinism of the Palatinate, which he recognised as having an importance matching that of the Dutch and the Swiss. In all three cases it was important to distinguish the urbane Calvinism of the cities (Heidelberg, Amsterdam) from the sterner, rural Calvinism which surrounded them.[65] A month later he told her that he had been doing work on Falkland's circle at Great Tew, which was certainly 'Socinian', and whose models were plainly Erasmus, Acontius, Hooker and Grotius. But he also admitted that he had not, in 'The Religious Origins', sufficiently documented the internal change which Calvinism underwent in the later sixteenth century. If one distinguished the Calvinism of Calvin from the Calvinism of Beza (his successor in Geneva) and of 'the siege-minded Huguenots, Scots etc.', Calvin himself emerged as much nearer to Erasmus. Perhaps, he speculated, German Calvinism seemed so much more liberal because it did not have a Beza, or an Andrew Melville.[66]

Trevor-Roper did not confine himself to such speculation for long. By 1971, if not earlier, he had begun research into the career of Theodore de Mayerne, the Paracelsian physician who served in turn Henri IV, James I and Charles I. The first (and for long the only substantial) fruits of this research were the essays on 'The Paracelsian Movement' and 'Medicine at the Early Stuart Court'.[67] The full-length book on Mayerne which was in large part written during the 1970s would not be published until 2006, three years after his death.[68] The interest which culminated in *Europe's Physician* was in fact older than this, having first been aroused when Trevor-Roper encountered Mayerne in the pages of the *Conway Letters*. But it was Yates who had prompted him to recognise that Mayerne was, in his different way, as much the product of liberal Calvinism as Grotius and the Great Tew Circle, and it was to Yates that he continued to report the progress of his research on Mayerne in the early 1970s.[69]

As he told Yates in 1970, he was also doing fresh work on the Arminian or Socinian variant of Erasmianism which had provided the central thread of 'The Religious Origins of the Enlightenment'. In the 1980s this would bear fruit in two new, longer essays, on 'The Great Tew Circle' and on 'Hugo Grotius and England', published respectively in 1987 and 1992.[70] The first of these contains the fullest statement of Trevor-Roper's understanding of the English, Anglican version of Erasmian Socinianism, which, he suggested, had been nurtured and then kept alive by the members of the Great Tew Circle, before and during the Civil Wars. They had not been Socinians in the 'strict', unitarian sense of the term; theirs was not, in other words, a narrowly theological position. Rather, they had been Socinians in the 'wide' sense, committed to 'the use of human reason generally in matters of faith'. Once again he identified the intellectual forebears of this position:

> first of all, Erasmus; then the 'libertine' continuators of Erasmus – Castellio, Acontius, Ochino, Cassander, Socinus himself; then, the liberal Protestant thinkers of the turn of the century, and, in particular, the French Huguenot and Platonist Philippe du Plessis Mornay, the Anglican Richard Hooker, and the Dutch Arminian Hugo Grotius.

What these and the members of the Great Tew Circle had in common was best described as a philosophy, whose key elements were an abhorrence of violence in the cause of religion, a commitment to toleration, intellectual scepticism, political conformity and an enduring hope that Christendom might yet be reunited. Focusing now on the leading individual members of the circle, Trevor-Roper sought to show the different ways in which they had put this philosophy to use. As the most troubled by doubt, Chillingworth had applied it both to defend Anglicanism against the lure of Rome and to save the Church of England from Laudianism. As the group's leading statesman, Clarendon had expressed the Socinian philosophy by writing 'civil' history: like de Thou and the Italian vernacular historians, he refused to appeal to the workings of divine providence and sought empirical, human explanations for the disaster of the Civil Wars. The third leader was Hammond, the circle's most durable controversialist, who defended Great Tew's ideal of Anglicanism against a formidable trinity of opponents: the Independent John Owen, the Presbyterian Richard Baxter and the Erastian Thomas Hobbes. It was no surprise to Trevor-Roper that a defence of Grotius against improper charges of 'Socinianism' was central to Hammond's exchanges with Owen and Baxter.[71]

In many ways, the Restoration in 1660 seemed to vindicate the stance taken by the Great Tew Circle. Headed by Sheldon at Canterbury and Hammond at Worcester (though he died before he could be consecrated), several surviving members of the group were appointed to bishoprics, while Clarendon held sway at court. But it was not an enduring victory. The solvent of sceptical reason, which had inspired the 'wide' Socinianism of the circle, would continue to be put to work by others: by the Catholic biblical scholar Richard Simon, and by the Protestant Deists. Trevor-Roper ended the essay on the Great Tew Circle without mentioning the Enlightenment, but the essay's portrayal of Anglican Socinianism was entirely consistent with the account he had offered 20 years earlier of the Enlightenment's 'religious origins'.

Along with its sequel on Grotius in England, the essay on Great Tew thus stands in an even more direct line of succession to 'The Religious Origins of the Enlightenment' than the book on Mayerne. Concerned with the early and mid-seventeenth century, these works explore subjects which had become central to Trevor-Roper's interests in the 1960s, when he turned to write on intellectual history. They did not, of course, exhaust those interests. Throughout the 1970s and 1980s he continued to lecture and publish essays on the Enlightenment historians and their nineteenth-century heirs, including Gibbon, Dimitrie Cantemir, Macaulay, Carlyle and Burckhardt. Fittingly, his last published essays were on Giannone and Gibbon. He also wrote, but did not bring to publication, a long essay on the then-neglected Conyers Middleton, 'From Deism to History'. The essay filled a gap in his account of the genesis of Gibbon's *Decline and Fall*, but he did not present Middleton as an Erasmian.[72] Trevor-Roper also, of course, continued to write on a wide variety of other subjects, from Renaissance and early modern political and religious history to the Second World War and the impostor-adventurer Edmund Backhouse. However important it became and however broadly he conceived it, intellectual history never crowded out those other interests.

Even so, a conscious reordering of Trevor-Roper's historical interests took place in 1963, with the result that he began to write on a range of subjects in intellectual history. An interest in the history of ideas was itself long-standing, reaching back to his reading of the *Conway Letters* and Gibbon's *Decline and Fall* during the war, and to his discovery of the larger significance of Erasmus early in the 1950s. But during the 1950s this interest had not amounted to more than a diversion from his primary engagements, which were with economic history, the Weber thesis, and the social and political causes of the English Civil Wars. These last were the subjects he researched most intensively, and on which he tried to write. With the failure to complete the major study of the Civil Wars, however, he needed to redirect his energies, and intellectual history provided the outlet. His development as a historian had changed course, decisively.

The change of direction did not go unremarked at the time. The anonymous *Times Literary Supplement* reviewer of *Religion, the Reformation and Social Change*, who suggested that the volume might well have included the earlier essay on Erasmus, also observed that Trevor-Roper's recent work showed a greater ability than before to discriminate between ideas, and to allow for the independent importance of beliefs. He now related ideas to social structure in a manner different 'from all but the most heterodox of Marxists'. The reviewer noticed that Bacon and Baconianism had joined Erasmus and Erasmianism as a focus of Trevor-Roper's attention. Even so, it was clear that Trevor-Roper's warmest sympathy was reserved for the 'neo-Erasmians' who were the subject of the most recent essay to be included, that on 'The Religious Origins of the Enlightenment'.[73]

In this essay, more fully, perhaps, than in any other, Trevor-Roper set out the arguments which lay at the heart of his 'turn' to intellectual history. For there he brought centre stage a philosophy to which he was already sympathetic – Erasmianism – and showed how it was connected to another intellectual movement to whose historical vision he was also drawn, the Enlightenment. In the course of the essay he was able to settle his final accounts with Weber, whose interpretation of the relation between Protestantism, capitalism and intellectual progress had preoccupied him for so long. More positively, he could respond to the pleasure he had received from reading Giannone, whose determination to resist the attempts of the papacy to silence him had been such an inspiring antidote to the chilly intellectual climate of Braudel's Paris. After the essay's publication in 1967, it was clear that intellectual history had become a major, if not a predominant, interest for Trevor-Roper. In the long run, the collection *Catholics, Anglicans and Puritans*, which contained the Great Tew essay, together with the posthumously published study of Mayerne, *Europe's Physician*, and his essays on historians, collected in *History and the Enlightenment*, may be regarded as the fullest, most developed products of this reorientation of his interests. But 'The Religious Origins of the Enlightenment' was among the first and most important signposts of the new direction. For its own arguments, and for their subsequent elaboration under the influence of Frances Yates, it stands out as a seminal essay.

So far, this study has been concerned to place 'The Religious Origins of the Enlightenment' in the context of Trevor-Roper's development as a historian. In conclusion, I shall attempt to add historiographical perspective to the story, with a brief assessment of Trevor-Roper's conception of intellectual history. As Irene Gaddo has observed, it is not easy to pin down.[74] While Trevor-Roper passionately believed that good historical writing required a philosophy of history as well as a commitment to scholarship, this did not entail adherence to a formal methodology. In writing about ideas and their role in history, he occasionally acknowledged predecessors whose approach had given him inspiration. But these were as likely to be remote as recent; he did not identify himself with any of the approaches current when his interest in the subject was first aroused, and after his own interests had taken a developed form, he never sought to place himself at the head of a school. In the context of this study, therefore, insight into Trevor-Roper's conception of intellectual history may best be achieved simply by retracing the steps by which his interest emerged, and asking what each reveals.

A first and fundamental point is revealed by his early enthusiasm for the *Conway Letters*. Ideas interested Trevor-Roper when connected with wider social and political developments: he was never attracted by Isaiah Berlin's concept of *Ideengeschichte*, in which ideas are treated as if they were self-generating, separate from their social context.[75] Perhaps significantly, the thinker who fired his own engagement with the subject, Erasmus, was one in whom Berlin showed scant interest.

Erasmus excited Trevor-Roper for three reasons, each formative of his conception of intellectual history. The first was his philosophy. By this Trevor-Roper understood his fundamental principles, above all his commitments to reason, free will and moral engagement with this world (as opposed to withdrawal to prepare for the next one). To grasp this philosophy did not require intensive study of how Erasmus developed his arguments in specific texts; it was enough to identify his central propositions. But these still required extensive reading among his works, and an interpretative perspective capable of identifying and connecting their major themes. A second reason for Trevor-Roper's enthusiasm for Erasmus was the communicability of his ideas. Having read Bataillon's great work, he realised that Erasmus's ideas had been able to spread even further than Bataillon had established. One reason for this was Erasmus's correspondence and the example it set to the Republic of Letters – correspondence was a form of evidence to which Trevor-Roper always attached great importance. Another was the adaptability of Erasmian ideas, and their ready appeal to other men of letters, philosophers and scholars. The commitment to free will was one aspect of this. But the most important was Erasmus's defence of an ideal of the intellectual life as transcending political and religious partisanship, disdaining the bitter divisions which such partisanship fomented.

This, the political implication of Erasmus's ideas, was the third and perhaps the most compelling reason for Trevor-Roper's excitement. As the *Encounter* essay of 1955 made clear, Erasmus offered Trevor-Roper a model of intellectual independence amidst the polarised ideologies of the Cold War. It was not that Erasmus had been unable to make choices, any more than Trevor-Roper was indifferent between capitalism and communism. But Trevor-Roper had rebelled as soon as attempts were made to recruit him to the platform of the anti-Communist, State Department-funded 'Congress of Cultural Freedom', and spoke out of turn at its first meeting in Berlin in 1950.[76] Erasmus, he knew, had taken the same stand in the not dissimilar circumstances of the 1520s. The political dimension of Trevor-Roper's enthusiasm for Erasmus remained a constant. It was noticed by his 1967 *Times Literary Supplement* reviewer, who remarked in closing that Trevor-Roper's writing betrayed the voice of the pulpit: as Erasmus had preached unsuccessfully to the elite of his day, so, the reviewer feared, would the Regius

Professor now.[77] In fact, as Cold War gave way to détente, Trevor-Roper grew confident that others shared his stance: 'we are all Erasmians now,' he wrote in a *Sunday Times* review in 1976.[78] With the ending of the Cold War in the 1990s, the 'period' character of Trevor-Roper's commitment to Erasmus has become more obvious, although others of that generation have continued to defend its validity.[79]

The discovery of Erasmus took Trevor-Roper so far as a historian of ideas. The protracted investigation of the Weber thesis took him further, by obliging him to consider how ideas could become intellectual movements, capable of shaping social forces and political events. For Weber's mistake, he came to argue, was not simply one of economic history. It was not even the sociologist's unwillingness to take account of historical contingency – his overlooking of the political imperatives which led the Counter-Reformation Church, like the Renaissance courts, to invest in the proliferation of offices at the expense of economic enterprise. It was his failure, in his fascination with the Calvinist doctrines of predestination and the Calling, to recognise that an alternative intellectual outlook, equally if not more favourable to economic enterprise, already existed in the form of Erasmianism. The philosophy of free will and insistence on the morality of worldly engagement, Trevor-Roper wanted to argue, had given Erasmus an appeal beyond philosophers and scholars: his ideas had reached and been adopted by the cultivated, enterprising elites of the great cities of the Netherlands and northern Italy. It was a claim as bold as any made by a 'total' historian, Weberian, Marxist, or *Annaliste*; the problem was to document it. That the Arminians were supported in the early seventeenth century by the leading merchants of Amsterdam was not evidence that the commercial–industrial elites of early sixteenth-century Europe were already 'Erasmian'. A 'social' historian of ideas, as the term came to be understood in the 1970s, would have looked for evidence of the diffusion and reception of humanist ideas in urban contexts. In this vein Erasmus's gift for self-publicity, his dealings with printers and, more generally, the links between humanists, printers and magistrates responsible for social policy have all proved fruitful lines of investigation.[80] But such scholarship was in its infancy when Trevor-Roper engaged with Weber in the late 1950s and early 1960s, and his notes indicate far less reading in the subject than he was able to undertake in social and economic history. The conviction that ideas shape social and political change would remain fundamental to Trevor-Roper's philosophy of history, but it would not dominate his own later work in intellectual history.

By contrast with 'Religion, the Reformation and Social Change', 'The Religious Origins of the Enlightenment' was wholly an essay on the history of ideas. Underpinning it was the same conviction that 'Erasmian' philosophy had exerted an appeal far greater than Bataillon's study of its immediate influence could reveal. But Trevor-Roper now made the most of McLachlan's insight into the Erasmian character of Anglican Socinianism, treating Erasmianism as a tradition able to mutate into forms which, while superficially confessional, nevertheless continued to express the same general philosophy. For this Trevor-Roper had evidence far stronger than he had been able to call upon for the imputed Erasmianism of the great entrepreneurs. He could trace the passage of the Erasmian philosophy through books, correspondence and personal contact – connections epitomised in Grotius's reception in England, and the conversations of the Great Tew Circle. The story was weighted towards England; Trevor-Roper's dependence on McLachlan is underlined by the absence of a comparably extended treatment of the Dutch Remonstrant tradition after Grotius. Even so, Trevor-Roper was confident that the intellectual phenomenon of Erasmianism was Europe-wide in its reach. He would have none of the reservations subsequently expressed by Bataillon himself, or by Dutch scholars tired of hero-worship of Erasmus, who thought that the term 'Erasmianism' was being over-used.[81]

'The Religious Origins of the Enlightenment' may have been written before Trevor-Roper had become fully aware of similarities between his own approach and that of Frances Yates. Only after its publication did he appreciate her point that there had also been a German strain of liberal Calvinism. But his enthusiasm for Yates does suggest that here, at last, was an approach to the history of ideas with which he could identify – and with which, therefore, his own approach may fruitfully be compared. In some respects this was surprising. Frances Yates was a devotee of the Warburg Institute in London, where the preferred methods – textual philology in the study of ideas, iconography in the history of art – were specialised and precisian. Nevertheless, Trevor-Roper found the Yatesian approach congenial for two reasons. First, she conceived of intellectual history as the discovery and reassembly of associated ideas – not as the reconstruction of specific patterns of argument and conceptual usage, in the manner of historians of political thought. Like Yates, Trevor-Roper preferred to use the idea of intellectual tradition flexibly, permitting a tradition to change its identity over time, while preserving its core principles. The second, still more attractive feature of Yates's approach was her openness to alternative possibilities, to the ideas which did not 'succeed'. In the history of ideas, at least, Trevor-Roper had a strongly anti-Whiggish streak: those who chose wrongly, especially when they still strove to uphold the principles of free will and reason, deserved study at least as much as those whose ideas enjoyed the endorsement of posterity.[82]

Even so, a fundamental difference between Yates and Trevor-Roper seems to remain, in the matter of religion. Yates was a devout Anglo-Catholic, for whom the presence of religious ideas in Renaissance and early modern thought posed no problem of understanding. How did Trevor-Roper, who apparently lacked any such conviction, find a place for religion in the history of ideas? Few aspects of Trevor-Roper's intellectual personality are as difficult to capture as his perception of religion. His wartime journals have revealed a man with a strong sense of the numinous in the natural world, able to appreciate pagan beliefs in natural spirits, and puzzled by his indifference to the more human and more intellectually developed religion of Christianity.[83] But he was always curious about the person of Christ and the early history of the Church. He was sufficiently intrigued by the successive attempts of G.A. Wells, Professor of German at Birkbeck, to demonstrate the inadequacy of the Gospels' evidence for the existence of Jesus, and to explore the likelihood that Jesus was the imaginary creation of the early Christians, to give encouragement to the author and shelf-space to his books.[84] He was even more keenly interested in the doctrine of the Trinity. Why did Christians believe this doctrine, and why did Churchmen periodically become so agitated in its defence? But he did not think that the question was capable of an intelligible answer. The doctrine was 'palpable nonsense', to which no rational person could subscribe with intellectual conviction.[85] As such, it epitomised the intellectual incredibility of all theology: none of it could be taken seriously. What was left, accordingly, was an idea of religion as expressed in piety and in respect for established forms and ceremonies – but which could fertilise intellectual life only by setting aside theology and by adopting a rational philosophy. Such had been, he thought, the achievement of the Erasmians and of their Arminian and Socinian heirs, who had not so much denied as discounted the doctrine of the Trinity.

In the light of more recent developments in scholarship, this is likely to seem an inadequate view of religion's potential contribution to intellectual history. Trevor-Roper's positive lack of interest in theology may have been characteristic of many historians working on religious phenomena (including witchcraft) during the 1960s and 1970s. But it contrasts markedly with current work on subjects overlapping with Trevor-Roper's interests, on Anglican Socinianism and Great Tew,[86] on Henry More and the Conway circle,[87] and on the 'Socinianism' of Locke.[88] Even if Trevor-Roper discounted theology, however, this does not mean that religion had no place in his conception of intellectual history. He did not argue that Erasmians, Arminians and Socinians were committed to a version of Christianity so attenuated that it should not count: on the contrary, he emphasised their belief in the example of Christ, and in the centrality of the Bible, rationally understood. When Trevor-Roper argued that they were the religious ancestors of Enlightenment, we have no reason to suppose that he meant other than what he said. However the Enlightenment was to be understood, it should not be divorced from earlier manifestations of rational philosophy within Christianity.

As it was, Trevor-Roper's understanding of the Enlightenment was very much of its time, the 1960s. The agenda of Enlightenment studies was then being set by the Italian historians of ideas, Giuseppe Giarrizzo and Franco Venturi. Giarrizzo had published substantial studies of Gibbon, Conyers Middleton and Hume; Venturi was already laying out his vision, not only of Enlightenment in Italy, but of the 'rhythms' of the movement as a whole.[89] Trevor-Roper's essays on Enlightenment historians and the Scottish Enlightenment reveal how much he shared their understanding of the subject. He wrote confidently of 'the Enlightenment': awareness of the diversity of Enlightenment's manifestations, which by the 1990s had led many – though not all – scholars to drop the definite article and think in terms of plural Enlightenments, was still in the future. He was confident too that the Enlightenment should be studied for its intellectual originality. Its adherents' most distinctive contributions had lain in their conception of 'the progress of society' and in the philosophies of history which accompanied it.[90] Here his enthusiasm for Giannone and Gibbon inclined him more to Giarrizzo's Enlightenment than to Venturi's; though always alert to the practical implications of ideas, Trevor-Roper did not adopt Venturi's concept of a 'political history of ideas'. Nor did he pursue the 'social history' of the Enlightenment, as Daniel Roche, Robert Darnton and Nicholas Phillipson propounded it in the 1970s.[91] When Trevor-Roper reached the Enlightenment, the ideas themselves mattered more to him than the mechanisms by which they were diffused through society.

In one important respect, Trevor-Roper appears to have gone directly against the approach to the Enlightenment advocated by Franco Venturi. The very suggestion that the Enlightenment might be approached through its 'origins' was anathema to Venturi. Two years after the publication of 'The Religious Origins', Venturi was lecturing in Cambridge on 'Utopia and Reform in the Enlightenment'. In the opening lecture he explicitly denounced the search for the Enlightenment's origins as nostalgic and misconceived: it detracted from the historian's proper task, which was to identify the function of Enlightenment ideas in the history of the eighteenth century.[92] On closer inspection, however, it is clear that Trevor-Roper's use of the term 'origins' was not quite the one Venturi rejected. For Trevor-Roper was not arguing that the major figures of the Enlightenment were themselves Erasmians. Giannone may have drawn inspiration from the Erasmian de Thou, but that did not make him an 'Erasmian'. Voltaire and Montesquieu were Deists, not Erasmians. Hume might be claimed as a Jacobite, but he was certainly no Erasmian. Trevor-Roper did suggest, repeatedly, that William Robertson was an Arminian, but the claim was never supported by evidence. On the face of it, Gibbon's claims were stronger. He had been the first historian to identify Erasmus as the father of a distinct tradition of rational theology, which had later been revived by the Dutch Arminians, Grotius, Limborch and Leclerc, and in England by Chillingworth and the Latitudinarians of Cambridge. An important moment in his own education in Lausanne had been reading the philosophy of Jean-Pierre de Crousaz, whose divinity was that of the Arminians Limborch and Leclerc.[93] But this is the closest Trevor-Roper came to suggesting an Erasmian lineage for Gibbon: his Swiss re-education may have saved him from Catholicism, but it only exposed him anew to the Deist scepticism of Middleton, who was not, for Trevor-Roper, an Erasmian.[94]

Instead of tracing a continuous line of intellectual inspiration, what Trevor-Roper meant to convey by 'origins' seems rather to have been the existence of comparable periods of intellectual liberalisation in the two centuries before the Enlightenment: in the age of Erasmus himself, during the precious years of peace between 1600 and 1620, prolonged in England until 1640, and in the closing decades of the seventeenth century. The adherents of the eighteenth-century Enlightenment, he suggested, had looked back to those periods as anticipations of their own – as earlier moments of 'enlightenment' – and had drawn inspiration from the example of their leading thinkers. Argued in this way, Trevor-Roper's thesis of 'origins' was not as regressive in its implications as Venturi's critique would suggest. He was not positing the existence of a continuous line of intellectual inspiration of which the Enlightenment was the culmination. What interested him was the intellectual struggle which had been fought to deflect the contending claims of Reformation and

Counter-Reformation and to preserve intellectual freedom, and to which, he thought, the Enlightenment had been heir. The Enlightenment was another phase in that struggle – not the final phase, given the recovery which the Churches would stage in the nineteenth century, but one marked by major new intellectual achievements.

Comparing 'The Religious Origins of the Enlightenment' with more recent scholarship on similar subject matter has the inevitable consequence of highlighting the 'period' character of the essay's arguments and approach to the history of ideas – its distance from the present. But without distance, historiography cannot be written. It is what makes it possible to clarify what was distinctive in Trevor-Roper's approach and argument. At this distance, what stands out is the originality of the essay's subversion of the cliché that Enlightenment and religion were intrinsically opposed, and the suggestiveness of its central thesis of an Erasmian tradition in European religious, historical and moral thought from the sixteenth to the eighteenth centuries.

6

The Politics of the Scottish Enlightenment

Colin Kidd

Throughout Hugh Trevor-Roper's career an elegant scepticism – self-consciously fashioned after Hume's and Gibbon's – and a refined pugnacity (which was all his own) marked his distinctive contributions to a series of lively debates on matters of historical and public interest. We see the combination in his contributions to the 'storm over the gentry', in his investigation into the private world of the Führer, and in his analysis of the findings of the Warren Commission. Though sometimes depicted as a man of the Establishment – accurately enough, though his preferences were, more precisely, for a patrician Whiggery unconstrained by mandarin caution – Trevor-Roper appeared to take a dissident's delight in stepping on toes. To the joy of his readers, he had no respect for the frontiers which demarcate the fiercely defended bailiwicks and modest cabbage patches of less versatile academics. Yet academic freebooting has its costs as well as rewards. The anonymous *Times* obituary – whose curious matter and baroque mode of expression bore the imprint of Maurice Cowling, Trevor-Roper's foremost adversary during his years as Master of Peterhouse – pointedly noted, from close personal acquaintance, that Trevor-Roper 'was able to make himself liked as well as disliked in any community in which he settled'.[1]

There were, perhaps, few communities of historians in which Trevor-Roper made himself quite so disliked as that which covered the field of early modern Scottish history running from the Reformation through to the onset of romanticism in the early nineteenth century. Trevor-Roper's iconoclastic views on a range of historical topics, which ranged from the scholarly improprieties of the sixteenth-century political philosopher George Buchanan to the shallow and commercial provenance of the nineteenth-century cult of tartanry,[2] won him many enemies in the Scottish universities. Understandably,

Scottish intellectuals responded peevishly to the activities of an Oxbridge muckraker apparently bent on exposing fraudulence in the darker corners of their nation's past.[3] However, there was no pleasing the Scots. By a curious irony, Trevor-Roper's patent admiration for the achievements of Scotland's eighteenth-century Enlightenment elicited still louder expostulations of outrage from his fellow historians north of the border.[4]

This affair merits investigation, not least because it brings into focus the problematic reception afforded the Scottish Enlightenment in modern Scottish politics, culture and historiography. In particular, the Scottish Enlightenment has occupied, in the words of Tom Nairn, 'a curious limbo of non-recognition'[5] in the nationalist worldview. Such quirks did not escape Trevor-Roper, who pointedly described the Scottish Enlightenment as 'very unpopular in departments of Scottish history in the universities of Scotland'.[6] Indeed, it is necessary to make clear that the controversy surrounding the Enlightenment within Scottish historiography has differed dramatically from the wider international debate on the politics of the Scottish Enlightenment. The Scottish Enlightenment has become the subject of intense political debate in think-tanks and universities across the world. How far were David Hume and Adam Smith the intellectual progenitors of modern conservatism? Did Smithian political economy provide an unambiguous warrant for reduced state sectors and untrammelled markets? Or did the eighteenth-century Scottish science of society lead in a leftward direction, with its distinctive stadial strain of sociological analysis anticipating the Marxist theory of base and superstructure?[7] Within Scotland, debates over the ideological significance of the Scottish Enlightenment do not run along a left–right axis, but have been framed in terms of unionist and nationalist explanations of the origins of Enlightenment. To what extent was the Union of 1707 the driving force behind the achievements of eighteenth-century Scotland's culture and economy? Twenty years ago Nairn, the Marxist theorist of neo-nationalism, noticed that the Scottish Enlightenment, 'the country's one moment of genuine historical importance, its sole claim to imperishable fame', did not, as one might assume, play a leading role in the nationalist interpretation of Scottish history. Rather, nationalists found the theoretical detachment of Enlightenment social science to be a matter of reproach and condemned the Scottish Enlightenment for its rootless, cosmopolitan betrayal of Scottish cultural distinctiveness. Nairn pondered the dismal irony that, 'if Scottish nationalists have ever been really united on one thing, it is their constant execration and denunciation of Enlightenment culture.'[8] The ideological status of the Scottish Enlightenment is no longer quite so contentious today. Although a nativist suspicion still lingers that the Scottish Enlightenment was an anglicising movement, intent on the eradication of scotticisms, more recently some nationalists have begun to reclaim the Enlightenment as a part of Scottish heritage, insisting upon its deep indigenous roots in pre-1707 – even pre-1603 – Scottish culture.[9]

Yet this shift owed much – though no Scot has conceded as much – to Trevor-Roper's bitterly resented remarks on the origins of the Scottish Enlightenment, which, by popularising the topic and by suggesting certain fruitful lines of research, did much to map out the possibility of this nationalist rehabilitation. Indeed, Trevor-Roper's insights on several topics in Scottish history converged (unconsciously) in content and analysis, if not in rhetoric, with the findings of nationalist historians and intellectuals. Nor, it transpires, did Trevor-Roper's historical politics lend themselves to easy parsing, his reputation as a leading Conservative notwithstanding. As a historian, Trevor-Roper was decidedly Whiggish and an acknowledged thorn in the side of Tory historians such as Cowling. Scottish historians have missed not only the nuances in Trevor-Roper's work, but also the bigger picture. The stridently Scotophobic mood music which accompanied Trevor-Roper's excursions into Scottish history has contributed to a serious misunderstanding of his intellectual project. Trevor-Roper's current standing in Scottish historiography is that of the caricaturist caricatured. It is time to fix his contribution with greater accuracy and to establish the *multiple* contexts which help to explain his curious fascination with early modern Scotland.

Trevor-Roper's literary talents – not least his feline taste for satire – had a tendency to distort certain aspects of the past, if sometimes for the best of motives: to enhance his readers' comprehension of what was at stake in remote squabbles over apparent trifles which now seemed decidedly esoteric. At a pointed remove from the academic pedantry he despised, Trevor-Roper worked hard to foreshorten the distance between his readership and the alien obscurities of the past, to make vivid sense of context and to resurrect long-dead personalities. But there were other, less worthy motives too. A native Northumbrian whose peerage alluded to these origins, Trevor-Roper does appear to have felt an inherited ancestral obligation to engage in cross-border warfare. In addition, the historian was all too quick to recognise – or possibly sought out with malice aforethought – the historical antecedents of his own contemporary bêtes noires – fanatical religious enthusiasms of a

Calvinistic stamp, the rampant clericalism of seventeenth-century Peterhouse, anticipations of totalitarianism, manifestations of Scotch nationalism.[10] More ambiguously, Trevor-Roper found himself drawn to twisted characters whom he affected to disdain, but whose perverted ingenuity tantalised and inspired him, such as literary hoaxers and sophisticated conmen.[11] Trevor-Roper imported these obsessions into his study of the Scottish Enlightenment, drawn as he was to the mystery of its unaccountable origins in the totalitarian Scotch Calvinism of the mid-seventeenth century and to the influential fraud perpetrated by James Macpherson on behalf of Ossian, the purported 'Scotch Homer'.[12]

This much is understood. Yet a national self-regard barbarises the Scottish historiographical response to Trevor-Roper. A solipsistic assumption prevails that Scotophobia – fuelled by a superficial knowledge of Scottish history – provides a satisfactory explanation of Trevor-Roper's interventions in the field. Angus Calder has described Trevor-Roper's initial piece on the Scottish Enlightenment as a 'farrago of prejudices'.[13] In their attempt to unmask the 'inferiorist' assumptions which have distorted Scottish historiography, the neo-nationalist intellectuals Craig Beveridge and Ronald Turnbull devote considerable attention to the pernicious influence of Trevor-Roper. His denigration of seventeenth-century Scottish backwardness bore a strong affinity, they have argued, with the rhetorical strategies of Third World colonialism as deconstructed by Frantz Fanon.[14] The late Don Withrington – with all the zeal of a Scot by adoption – denounced Trevor-Roper for insinuating a school of anti-nationalist fifth columnists, including Nicholas Phillipson and John Robertson, into the study of the Scottish Enlightenment with the objective of explaining it in terms of the domestication of *external* influences.[15] Scottish historians seem oblivious of the intellectual substance behind the Scotophobic satire, and of the wider European themes which drew Trevor-Roper – again and again – to case studies in Scottish history. Trevor-Roper was not monomaniacally obsessed with the Scotch: he had other fish to fry.

Critics of Trevor-Roper's interpretation of the Scottish Enlightenment have directed their dudgeon at one piece in particular – his address to the Second International Congress on the Enlightenment held at St Andrews in 1967,[16] published as part of its transactions as an essay in *Studies on Voltaire and the Eighteenth Century* (*SVEC*) – and have tended to ignore amplifications and reformulations of his position on the Scottish Enlightenment found in essays, variously, on topics including David Hume, the religious origins of the

Enlightenment, the Jacobite reception of Giannone, the Scottish dimension of European romanticism and the reading habits of an early modern Scottish *politique*, as well as a significant reworking in 1977 of his earlier treatment of the Scottish Enlightenment.[17] When read in its entirety, Trevor-Roper's remarkable series of essays which address – or which touch upon – the Scottish Enlightenment, a clearer sense emerges of the wider European context which informed Trevor-Roper's opinions. Beyond the immediate battlefield of Anglo-Scottish chauvinism lay a less-visible hinterland of cosmopolitan erudition which provided reinforcement for Trevor-Roper's position.

More oddly, the controversy which followed the publication in 1967 of Trevor-Roper's notorious essay on the Scottish Enlightenment was predicated upon a partial reading and obtuse misinterpretation of that piece; though, to be fair, there was obtuseness on both sides. The rhetorical excesses deployed by Trevor-Roper in his negative portrayal of late seventeenth-century Scottish political, religious and economic life served to detract attention from other elements of his case. At its core was a mystery: 'By what social, political or intellectual alchemy did a country which had recently seemed so barbarous suddenly – in the fashionable jargon of the sociologists – "take off"?'[18] Trevor-Roper found the sharp and sudden contrast between the dark theocracy of the Covenanters and the free speculation of the Scottish Enlightenment 'very perplexing'.[19] Despite his staunch unionism, Trevor-Roper did not resort to a straightforwardly unionist interpretation of the rise of the Scottish Enlightenment. Although Trevor-Roper claimed that the 'liberating effects' of the Union of 1707 were 'unquestionable', he explicitly denied that the Union provided a secure or persuasive explanation for the remarkable transformation of Scottish culture during the eighteenth century; nor did he present the Scottish Enlightenment as an anglicising affair.[20] He pointed instead to other cultural contacts across the North Sea, especially from the United Provinces of the Netherlands during the 1690s, and the resumption by way of Jacobitism of intellectual links with France. Furthermore, Trevor-Roper did not disdain to search for the pre-1707 origins of the Scottish Enlightenment, although he detected the emergence of a new liberal spirit in Scottish culture no earlier than 1680. While Trevor-Roper could find no redeeming features in the fanatical religion of the Presbyterian Covenanters, he noticed that the Episcopalian culture of north-east Scotland had constituted a 'leaven in the Presbyterian lump'.[21] Its estrangement from hardline Presbyterian orthodoxy liberated the imagination and the intellect, notwithstanding the awkward fact that this same culture of Episcopalianism would provide the ideological underpinnings of eighteenth-century Scottish Jacobitism, and as such was tarred by association, politically, with the forces of royalist reaction and, historically, with a dead end.

Three lines of a priori reasoning drew Trevor-Roper towards research on that supposed absurdity, the Jacobite origins of the Enlightenment in Scotland. First, as a historian of seventeenth-century England and early modern Europe, Trevor-Roper was unimpressed by the Weberian-inspired[22] assumption that Calvinism – or Puritanism in its English form – was the radical, liberating intellectual force behind the Scientific Revolution. In his essay entitled 'The Religious Origins of the Enlightenment' Trevor-Roper suggested an alternative genealogy for liberal thought running along Erasmian and Arminian channels.[23] G.D. Henderson's work on the irenic quietism of Aberdonian theology during the seventeenth century[24] persuaded Trevor-Roper that Scotland provided a fascinating and revealing case study in Arminian liberality, one which threw into relief the narrow-minded fanaticism of the supposed Calvinistic progressives – at least according to Weberian theory – of the Covenanting movement. The quietist mysticism of north-east Scotland bore none of the marks of the ascetic Puritan rationalism which the Weberian tradition associated with the rise of science, but was a local manifestation of a more conservative, but equally, more latitudinarian, Arminian pre-Enlightenment. The principal targets here of Trevor-Roper's revisionism were far removed from the claustrophobic world of Scottish history: the Erasmian–Arminian tradition was counterposed as a corrective to the influential versions of Puritan progressivism variously associated with R.H. Tawney's *Religion and the Rise of Capitalism* (1926), Robert K. Merton's *Science, Technology and Society in Seventeenth-century England* (1938) and the works of Trevor-Roper's Oxford colleague Christopher Hill.[25] Nor, it seems, did his own Scotophobia account for Trevor-Roper's bleak portrayal of the arid fanaticism of seventeenth-century Scottish Presbyterian culture, a verdict which merely confirmed a distinguished tradition of precedents among historians – including H.T. Buckle, W.E.H. Lecky and J.M. Robertson[26] – who shared Trevor-Roper's dislike of clericalism in all its forms.

In the second place, Trevor-Roper, who was a keen student of English Whig historiography, identified David Hume as a Tory historian, critical of the Puritans and sensitive to the historical predicament of the early Stuarts.[27] Hume's Toryism suggested a possible non-Whig provenance for Scotland's Enlightenment. However, it is worth noting that Hume's purported Toryism might well constitute a red herring. For one of Trevor-Roper's many antagonists, the Cambridge historian Duncan Forbes, parsed Hume's historical politics, more persuasively, as those of a 'sceptical Whig'.[28]

Thirdly, Trevor-Roper held decided ideas about the Enlightenment as a movement directed against religious authority. His interest in Hume's historical writing helped Trevor-Roper to formulate his position. Hume had brought something distinctively Scottish to the English historiographical tradition. In England and Scotland, as elsewhere on the continent, argued Trevor-Roper,

> the Enlightenment was largely the triumph of lay reason over clerical bigotry. But the bigots in the two countries were different. In England they were Tory parsons; therefore the English Enlightenment wore Whig colours. In Scotland they were the ministers of the whiggamore Kirk; therefore the Scottish Enlightenment was a Tory movement.[29]

It was because of Hume's Tory distance from the Whig-Presbyterian Kirk that, according to Trevor-Roper, he was able to see through the English Whig mythology that those who 'opposed the Stuarts, or were oppressed by them, were thereby necessarily friends of liberty or truth'.[30] In a later essay, Trevor-Roper would reject more decisively the received assumption that Jacobites were 'mental fossils buried permanently beneath the detritus of the Glorious Revolution'.[31]

Hunches of this sort, underpinned by careful chains of reasoning held together by logic, experience and comparisons, led Trevor-Roper in certain promising directions, hitherto obscurely signposted within Scottish historiography. However, they also drew him into unwarranted assumptions, most notably the ascription of an Arminian position to the liberal Moderate Party of the eighteenth-century Kirk, which allowed him to substantiate his otherwise tenuous claim that the Scottish Enlightenment was an anti-Whig affair.[32] By contrast, what seems most striking is the un-Arminian nature of the Scottish Enlightenment. At the very least, the Moderates were notional Calvinists, who – happily or not – subscribed to the tenets of the Westminster Confession of Faith.[33] Nevertheless, Trevor-Roper's intervention does acknowledge the problem of continuity in reconciling a Presbyterian Enlightenment and its Episcopalian origins. Arminianism, moreover, was only part of the story. Trevor-Roper also recognised that alongside the Arminian tradition another kind of pre-Enlightened thinking had developed among the temporal elites of early modern Europe's sectarian trouble spots: the anticlerical gentry Erastianism of the *politiques*. In a charming pamphlet on the library of Thomas Hamilton, the first Earl of Haddington, Trevor-Roper showed how this strain of hard-headed pragmatism in religious matters found its way – albeit tenuously and exceptionally – into late sixteenth- and early seventeenth-century Scotland by way of its French connections.[34] More recently, historians have begun to recover the part played by a *politique* dislike of religious extremism in the emergent latitudinarianism of Restoration Scotland.[35]

Trevor-Roper's essay of 1967 on the Scottish Enlightenment concluded with a tantalising suggestion that the process of social change in eighteenth-century Scotland which had stimulated 'analysis of human progress' had also thrown up the 'raw material of the new romanticism'.[36] In 1969 he took the opportunity offered by the Coffin Memorial Lecture at the University of London to explore more fully the connections between Enlightenment and romanticism in Scotland. Why had romantics across Europe honoured Scotland as the seat of primitivist and historic authenticity? Why had the poems of Ossian and the novels of Scott exercised an unparalleled fascination upon the continental imagination? Unlike scholars content to plough narrower furrows, Trevor-Roper tried to explain why a small and hitherto impoverished and insignificant country such as Scotland could generate within the space of a century *both* a distinctive Enlightenment of international repute and, in addition, a strain of romanticism which, through the works of Macpherson and Scott, exercised tremendous appeal across Europe. Trevor-Roper perceived that historians ought to address the cultural achievements of Enlightenment and romanticism as connected manifestations of the same underlying social phenomenon. Whereas the 'direction' of Scotland's cultural energies had changed, 'the power behind them was the same.'[37] Trevor-Roper claimed that the 'same social chemistry which released, in one generation, the genius of Hume and Adam Smith, formed, in the next, as its secondary product, the genius of Scott.'[38] Eighteenth-century Scotland's remarkable and speedy social transformation, Trevor-Roper argued, had led in the first instance to a new configuration of social thought as a generation of Scots intellectuals – abetted by the insights of Montesquieu, the midwife of the Scottish Enlightenment – theorised the remarkable changes of the age of improvement they had lived through; while the generation which followed had responded wistfully to the redundancy of Scotland's old order. The charm of romantic archaism lay on the obverse side of rapid social progress:

The Scottish Enlightenment, like every era of enlightenment, had its social foundations. Its great writers – Hume, Robertson, Ferguson, Adam Smith – directed their minds to the progress of society not merely because they had read Montesquieu, but because their own society presented them (as English society did not provide Englishmen) with a case-history for the application of Montesquieu's social laws. They saw before them, simultaneously, the old, static introverted society of pre-Union Scotland and the new transforming energies released by the renewed post-Union contact with the world. The dynamics of progress were visible before them, and they delighted in that progress. A generation later Scott looked more nostalgically at the same process. For him, the old society, whose relics had seemed barbarous to his predecessors, had acquired, in retrospect, a new charm.[39]

Thus Scott came to mythologise the relics of the old Border society of castles and peel-towers, just as Macpherson had imparted a proto-romantic gloss to the passing of clan society in the Highlands. Scotland's unique exposure to the processes by which the functional shaded visibly into the archaic had stimulated the emergence of two quite divergent modes of historical expression with broad appeal to intelligentsias across Europe which recognised the same social changes but had experienced them without the same intensity or vividness.

A critic might cavil here, and elsewhere in his oeuvre, at Trevor-Roper's reductive treatment of Enlightenment and romanticism as epiphenomena of deeper social changes. However, that objection never appeared to play any part in the Scottish critique of Trevor-Roper. His notoriety in Scotland owed something to the natural tendency to pigeonhole Trevor-Roper as an English Conservative. Such a classification is correct, but somewhat crude, and a peculiarly inappropriate way of describing Trevor-Roper's interpretation of the Scottish Enlightenment, which verges on the Marxisant. Although in politics a Conservative, Trevor-Roper distanced himself from the wilder excesses of anti-Communism. In *The Philby Affair*, he recounts how during his wartime service in intelligence he stood at a considerable remove from the 'lunatic'[40] anti-Communist prejudices of his superiors. Trevor-Roper maintained this dispassionate outlook during the early phase of the Cold War. At the Congress for Cultural Freedom held in West Berlin in 1950 he had stood out for his reluctance to endorse, and openly subversive attitude towards, the prevailing anti-Communist hysteria, a stance which profoundly irritated the event's – secret? – sponsors in the CIA.[41] Over time, however, he came to view Philby and his fellow moles as fanatical modern-day successors of the confessional extremists of the Reformation and the Counter-Reformation, and to see through the superficially secular ideology for which they sacrificed so much as a new kind of religiosity.[42] Nevertheless, although as a historian Trevor-Roper rejected the central tenets of the Marxist theory of history, he accepted in a non-doctrinaire way the common-sense proposition lurking within Marxist history – though, in fact, with a longer pre-Marxist pedigree stretching back to James Harrington by way of Adam Smith – that political and cultural developments were inexplicable without reference to their economic underpinnings.[43] He gave historical sociology a similarly guarded welcome, at least in so far as it reformulated for a new age the insights of Montesquieu, another of Trevor-Roper's intellectual heroes. In an oration given at the London School of Economics in 1968 he pronounced: 'Today, I cannot conceive of good history without a sociological dimension.'[44] This did not mean that history was a science, or that historians should place much, if any, reliance on static sociological models, but it still marks a significant gulf between the latitudinarian eclecticism of Trevor-Roper's historical philosophy and the rigidly anti-materialist interpretation of history espoused by some of his fellow conservatives on the revisionist right. The dogmatic certainties of the right were no more congenial than those of the left,[45] and had no place in historical scholarship. Indeed, Trevor-Roper made a signal contribution to the emergence of the new social history, by way of his work on the declining gentry, the general crisis of the seventeenth century and the witch-craze.[46]

By the time Trevor-Roper returned to the subject of the Scottish Enlightenment in his address to the Fifteenth International Congress of the History of Science, held at Edinburgh in 1977, his agenda may well have become more narrowly Scotophobic. For Trevor-Roper's contributions to Scottish history during the late 1970s were coloured in good part by his personal experiences in Scottish affairs. From 1976 Trevor-Roper, who had a home in Scotland which he used during vacations from the Regius Professorship of Modern History at Oxford, campaigned vigorously against the Callaghan government's devolution proposals. In a robust piece of anti-nationalist journalism published in 1976, entitled 'Scotching the Myths of Devolution', Trevor-Roper reminded readers of *The Times* that devolution was not a step in the dark. Twentieth-century Britons knew all too well what Scottish home rule might be like in practice, for they had observed 50 years of it from 1922 to 1972 in the 'Scotch province of Ulster'.[47] In further contributions to *The Times*, whether on the opinion pages or the letters column, he elaborated upon the folly of devolution.[48] The cause of the Union was of such constitutional importance that it transcended immediate party loyalties. Trevor-Roper contributed a foreword to the anti-devolutionist polemic *Devolution: The End of Britain?* (1977) written by Tam Dalyell, then the Labour MP for West Lothian.[49] Personal complications compounded disillusionment with contemporary Scotland. In 1977 Trevor-Roper also found himself involved in political – and Pooterish – controversy at a local level when he tried to fight off proposals to site the 402-bed Borders General Hospital adjacent to his house, Chiefswood, near Melrose, which had been built for Sir Walter Scott. The location and the angry response it provoked in the staunchly unionist Trevor-Roper did not fail to delight the local Scottish National Party (SNP). Trevor-Roper feared not only that the new hospital would reduce the value of his property – which was then estimated at £75,000 – but that the philistinism of the local planners would irrevocably damage a piece of Scotland's heritage. Trevor-Roper went as far as to promote an alternative solution: that the new hospital be more appropriately situated at a new town development outside Galashiels.[50] It was built as planned near Melrose.

Under the inspiration of his contemporary campaigns on the Scottish scene, the historian turned again to Scottish history, in part to find some welcome relief from his travails in the comforting hobby of historical mischief-making. Trevor-Roper's anti-nationalist sentiments did nothing to discourage his deconstruction of the Scottish Highland tradition, the subject of a substantial essay published in 1983.[51] By a further irony, Trevor-Roper was at work on this problem when a new generation of intellectuals – some nationalist, others on the New Left but with nationalist leanings – was engaged on the same mission of demolishing the Great Tartan Monster – which the neo-nationalists believed had stifled the creative energies of the Scottish people.[52] Not that the neo-nationalists wanted to hear this sort of thing from Lord Dacre, newly ennobled in part for his robust defence of the Union during the later 1970s.

The Scottish Enlightenment retained its capacity to irritate Scottish nationalists. Trevor-Roper's address of 1977 on the Scottish Enlightenment, subsequently published in *Blackwood's Magazine*, renewed some of the controversial lines of interpretation advanced in the essay of 1967, and added several more. Trevor-Roper confronted an influential nationalist strategy for accommodating the Scottish Enlightenment: the notion, which would find its fullest expression in the works of G.E. Davie, that the Enlightenment had emerged out of a thriving indigenous culture of democratic intellectualism which, as Davie noted, was later threatened by anglicising reforms in the educational sphere during the nineteenth century.[53] Trevor-Roper argued that the social basis of the Enlightenment in Scotland was decidedly anti-democratic. The Patronage Act of 1712 had removed the selection of ministers from the bigotry of the common people and placed the appointment of clerics in the hands of an Erastian gentry. Indeed, in so far as Trevor-Roper was able to identify a democratic intelligentsia in eighteenth-century Scotland, he alighted upon the scholastic Calvinists of the Secession who, frustrated by the Patronage Act's confounding of the spiritual and temporal realms, left a corrupt – because more enlightened – Kirk in 1733.[54]

As an outsider, Trevor-Roper decided to reiterate his sense of why the Scottish Enlightenment still exerted such a fascination over scholars throughout the world. It did not, he explained, derive from any fascination with Scottish history per se, nor with those aspects of the Scottish Enlightenment which followed the broad contours of the Enlightenment elsewhere in Europe. Trevor-Roper warned historians not to conflate the 'Scottish Enlightenment' with the 'Enlightenment in Scotland', a quite different phenomenon.[55] Between 1650 and 1750 the general phenomenon of Enlightenment, disseminated from its main centres in France, the Netherlands and England, had transformed the cultures of several peripheral nations and provinces, such as Hanover, Denmark and even Livonia. In this regard, Scotland was no exception. Trevor-Roper notes that 'what foreigners admired in late eighteenth-century Scotland, what they found, in a peculiar form, there and nowhere else, was not art or literature or medicine or natural science or even philosophy.'[56] These were matters for Scottish historians; the flowering of political economy or science of society in eighteenth-century Scotland was a matter of international interest.

Moreover, Trevor-Roper insisted that the Scottish Enlightenment was not simply a label for a period in Scottish cultural history. By Trevor-Roper's lights, the Scottish Enlightenment was a distinctive strain of social inquiry, an intellectual movement comprising the likes of Hume, Smith, Robertson, Ferguson and Millar, but from which he explicitly excluded James Beattie, Thomas Reid and Lord Monboddo: 'A movement which includes Thomas Reid and James Beattie as well as David Hume and Adam Smith is not a movement at all: it is merely a set of dates.'[57] Indeed, Trevor-Roper went further, assigning the antiquarian learning of Monboddo, the pious philosophy of Beattie and the common-sense philosophy of Reid to the highest rung of an anti-Enlightenment which operated on several levels, from a sophisticated intellectual counter-movement of anti-Humean philosophy and erudition down to the popular bigotry of the anti-Catholic mob of 1779. Trevor-Roper surely went too far in aligning the Common-Sense school with the rebarbative bigotry of Auld Licht diehards.[58] Common-Sense philosophers strove rather to effect a plausible – if makeshift – concordance between the potentially destructive insights of eighteenth-century philosophy and the old core truths of Christianity.[59] Presbyterian backwoodsmen, on the other hand, had tended throughout the eighteenth century to reject the perceived equivocations involved in any serious engagement with the Enlightened challenge to Christianity. Nevertheless, Trevor-Roper did ask a pertinent question: whether a philosophical movement so self-consciously devoted to a rebuttal of Hume's irreligious scepticism, notwithstanding the sophistication of its analysis or the cordiality of its champions' personal relations with Hume,[60] belongs more properly to the category of anti- or counter-Enlightenment. Such is the current drift of scholarship on the Scottish Enlightenment that this sort of question tends no longer to be posed, and the issue is quietly fudged as an intra-Enlightenment conversation.

Indeed, Trevor-Roper's legacy in this area is Janus-faced. On the one hand, he advanced a narrow definition of the Scottish Enlightenment which excluded much of what scholars of eighteenth-century Scottish philosophy now find most fascinating and worthy of study: the culture of science which ushered in significant developments in chemistry and the new uniformitarian geology as well as Reid's anticipation of Kant's solution to the riddle of the Pyrrhonian cul-de-sac mapped by Hume. On the other hand, however, Trevor-Roper's explorations in the Episcopalian culture of the north-east and its cosmopolitan connections with the erudition of the Jacobite diaspora suggested – even insisted upon – a more variegated Enlightenment which was far from an exclusively Presbyterian phenomenon. In particular, we have become sensitive to the Roman Catholic dimensions of Enlightenment in the Scottish world, by way of the late Jim McMillan's explorations of the cisalpine Jansenist culture of the Scots College in Paris and Mark Goldie's rehabilitation of a late eighteenth-century Scottish Catholic Enlightenment.[61] Trevor-Roper's autumnal piece on the British reception of Giannone[62] further illuminates a lost eighteenth-century realm of enlightened Catholicism too easily overlooked, for their own different reasons, by both modern champions of Enlightenment and Catholicism.

Trevor-Roper's critics in the field of Scottish history have been quick, of course, to recognise his failings, and understandably slow to acknowledge his worthwhile contributions to the field, if they are conscious of them. Demonised as a Scotophobe, the nuances of his work consigned to an oubliette, Trevor-Roper has proved a convenient butt of nationalist historiography, allowing its practitioners to evade the contradictions in their treatment of the Scottish Enlightenment. But the whirligig of time brings its revenges. When historians of a later era revisit the debates of an earlier generation, often it is the similarities rather than the differences of rival protagonists which leap out at the visitor.

In the field of Scottish history Trevor-Roper's leading public critic has been Dr William Ferguson (b. 1924) of the University of Edinburgh. Within the internal politics of Edinburgh University during the 1960s and 1970s Ferguson won renown as a feisty defender of local particularity against creeping anglicisation. This troubled environment would shape his response to Trevor-Roper. Ferguson, moreover, was deeply immersed in the political controversies and learned literature of a bygone Scotland, and where questions of cultural preference arose he instinctively – and endearingly – took the side of ancients rather than moderns. On the topic of the Scottish Enlightenment Ferguson stands representative of an archaic nationalist position which now seems less representative of current orthodoxy in several important respects than the thesis advanced by Trevor-Roper. Ferguson appeared to take the line that the Scottish Enlightenment was a retrospective historical reification, a unionist Trojan horse smuggled into Scottish history. Consider Ferguson's pointed remarks in his book *Scotland's Relations with England* (1977) about the 'so-called, and perhaps mis-called, "Enlightenment" of the eighteenth century'.[63] What did Ferguson mean by this? In a later volume, *The Identity of the Scottish Nation* (1998), Ferguson directly reproached the achievement of the Scottish Enlightenment in the sphere of history:

> Whatever did not square with their philosophy was not knowledge, and they loftily dismissed anything they could not understand. In no other area of human knowledge were the serious intellectual shortcomings of the Enlightenment so obviously exposed as in the study of history. As far as their attitude to the past was concerned they were regressive, and they seriously impeded the triumph of record scholarship on which historical science depended.[64]

Ferguson has a serious point to make here about the divergence of Enlightenment conjectural history from a culture of scrupulous antiquarianism, but he exaggerates the issue out of a manifest distaste for the Enlightenment.

Ferguson's brand of nationalism now seems as outdated as Trevor-Roper's unionism. Both belong to a world we have lost. It should be clear by now that Trevor-Roper's Scotophobia was focused and took a particular form: he admired Hume keenly, and he issued a positive reappraisal of the north-eastern intellectual tradition from the Aberdeen Doctors onwards. Trevor-Roper trained his fire on what he considered a perverted Scotch nationality grounded in an enthusiastic and theocratic brand of Calvinist bigotry.

It was this highly targeted Scotophobia which irked Ferguson, a son of Muirkirk in the Covenanting heartland and the sympathetic interpreter of a tradition of Scottish national consciousness inaugurated by George Buchanan which – perhaps surprisingly – fused Presbyterian political theory and an identification with Gaelic antiquity.[65] Ironically, Trevor-Roper had an unreliable ally of sorts within Ferguson's own department. Trevor-Roper's detection of the Enlightenment's origins in the episcopalian culture of Restoration Scotland found a striking echo in the work of Ferguson's immediate superior, Professor Gordon Donaldson (1913–93),[66] who championed, with the zeal of a convert from the United Free Church tradition, by way of the Kirk, an episcopalian interpretation of Scottish history.[67] Nevertheless, Donaldson, whose dislike of nationalists and the cause of the Highlands did nothing to dim his intense patriotism, stressed the indigenous provenance of Scottish episcopalianism and had little truck with Trevor-Roper's description of late seventeenth-century episcopalians as 'anglophil',[68] though recent research does emphasise their awareness of the theological and political strategies of their co-religionists within the Church of England. Indeed, Donaldson had ambivalent relations with Trevor-Roper, who sponsored Donaldson's nomination to the British Academy,[69] and with his supposed views of the Enlightenment. In 1988 Donaldson published an article in the *Scotsman* which denounced the Conservative secretary of state Malcolm Rifkind for his suggestion that the Scottish Enlightenment was a direct product of the Union of 1707.[70] Donaldson's views occasioned little surprise in the University of Edinburgh. While head of the Department of Scottish History there, he had prevented his students from attending classes on the Scottish Enlightenment given by Nicholas Phillipson,[71] an alien of English stock who lectured in the suspiciously rootless Department of History. Trevor-Roper, a friend of Phillipson, gazed on this scene with fascination. It confirmed his impression that Scottish History Departments were akin to sects, thirled to a nationalist theology and staffed with yet another fanatical Scotch clerisy. Here were scholars of prodigious erudition, but prone to a suffocating insularity which, while it saved Scottish historians from the pitfalls of modish pretension, left them happily remote from wider trends in historical scholarship and most especially from the insights to be gleaned from comparative history.

Trevor-Roper's metropolitan perspective on the exotic fauna found in Scottish History Departments did not preclude his sharing some of their assumptions. By a further irony, Trevor-Roper and Ferguson held a not-dissimilar outlook on the politics of the pre-Union period. Ferguson came to prominence for his telling analysis of the role of bribery in obtaining Scottish parliamentary ratification for the Articles of Union.[72] Although they disagreed about the meaning of the Union, Trevor-Roper and Ferguson endorsed a Namierite reading of the seamier side of pre-1707 Scots factionalism and corruption.[73] What now strike the reader are the shared professional assumptions of a generation of historians who recognised the contribution made by Lewis Namier at the cutting edge of their discipline.[74] Of course, Trevor-Roper made his point with an extravagant Scotophobic flourish which served to distance him from the nationalist school of history.

Ferguson's older strain of nationalism seems now decidedly antiquarian and ecclesiastical, and his position on the Enlightenment now diverges considerably from the scholarly – and nationalist – consensus. Today's nationalism is self-consciously civic in orientation and aligned with the liberal inheritance of the Enlightenment. Where Ferguson took refuge in denial when confronted with the Enlightenment of Hume, a newer breed of nationalist appropriates the Scottish Enlightenment by emphasising its indigenous pre-1707 roots in the Scottish past.[75] Yet, directly and indirectly, Trevor-Roper encouraged much of the scholarship on which this thesis depends. His notorious essay suggested how the intellectual history of late seventeenth-century Scotland might be tackled, while his Oxford research students Hugh Ouston and John Robertson traced, respectively, the cultural developments initiated in the Scotland of *c.*1680 by James, Duke of York, the future James VII,[76] and the underappreciated intellectual lineages which led from the patriot laird Andrew Fletcher of Saltoun into the militia issue which so engaged the Scottish Enlightenment.[77] Robertson's further work on the theoretical sophistication of the Union debates also points to the vitality of Scottish political discourse prior to the supposed cultural watershed of 1707.[78]

The controversy surrounding Trevor-Roper's contributions to the study of the Scottish Enlightenment throws into relief the broader ideological dilemma faced by Scottish intellectuals who wish to forge a compelling identity out of the materials of the Scottish past. For the core values of democracy, liberalism and nationalism seem to have taken their rise, respectively, from different sources, each in its own way contaminated. While the Covenanting tradition inspired democracy, it was democracy of an illiberal and intolerant sort. On the other hand, the liberal ideas which sprang up during the Enlightenment emerged in a milieu which witnessed enthusiastic anglicisation and an undemocratic cultural elitism exemplified by the reluctance of most of its political and moral philosophers to criticise an unreformed electoral system. By the same token, the nationalist legacy bequeathed by Jacobitism was irredeemably associated with authoritarian monarchy, its later appropriation by romantics such as Scott inspiring only the further deformations of the Great Tartan Monster. Liberalism, democracy and nationalism belong to three incompatible traditions whose bequest to the modern Scottish intelligentsia is a mingled puzzlement, irritation and embarrassment. Trevor-Roper had the audacity – as well as the insight and integrity – to explore the treacherous ambiguities of these traditions, and it seems apparent that he revelled in the opportunity to point out to Scots aspects of their history which were awkward and unsightly. Nevertheless, he also held historical attitudes in common with an older generation of nationalists and functioned as an unlikely and unintentional John the Baptist for the revisionist historiography which accompanied a newer – and less reverential – strain of civic nationalism. It is hard to avoid the conclusion that Trevor-Roper has been criticised for some statements which, coming from another source and couched in a less offensive idiom, might have been easily aligned with the nationalist interpretation of Scottish history.

PART THREE

Hitler and his World

7

Special Service in Germany and *The Last Days of Hitler*[1]

E.D.R. Harrison

Hugh Trevor-Roper's study of Hitler's death[2] was published to remarkable acclaim. Lewis Namier, at that time the most distinguished historian in Britain, wrote to Trevor-Roper:

> I read your book, if I may say so, with the greatest interest and admiration. You have made a truly excellent job of it and combined very thorough scholarship with a lightness of touch and a style which I am glad to see is not yet extinct at Oxford.[3]

A.J.P. Taylor reviewed *The Last Days* as 'an incomparable book, by far the best book written on any aspect of the second German war: a book sound in its scholarship, brilliant in presentation, a delight for historian and layman alike. No words of praise are too strong for it.' And *The Last Days* has remained a standard work. In the best recent study of Hitler's death, *Inside Hitler's Bunker*, Joachim Fest praised 'Hugh Trevor-Roper's superb overview, his sound judgement, and his splendid style'.[4] How did Trevor-Roper produce this modern classic? What were contemporary reactions to the book and to what extent has Trevor-Roper's analysis of Hitler's regime indeed stood the test of time? These questions can now be answered by drawing both on public sources and on Trevor-Roper's own remarkably extensive and carefully maintained personal archive.

Trevor-Roper achieved fame as a historian, but he began his Oxford career with the study of Classics. As he wanted to read the classical scholar Wilamowitz in German, during March 1935 he went to Freiburg to improve his grasp of the language. He would recall that his landlady's son was devoted to Hitler: 'I was made to witness processions and marches, fluttering swastika flags, harangues by party bigwigs. I was disgusted by this inflammatory oratory; disgusted also by the abject conformity of the German people.'[5] When he returned to Oxford, Trevor-Roper drew up a balance sheet for his visit to Germany and decided it was in deficit. Although Trevor-Roper had mastered German, now that he could read Wilamowitz he concluded that the great scholar was actually a silly fellow, so that all the effort had been for nothing.

Only the Munich Agreement of September 1938 redirected Trevor-Roper's attention to Germany. He was particularly impressed by the insight of the British historian Robert Ensor, who had predicted in 1935 that Hitler would annex Austria in spring 1938 and in the autumn of the same year would either provoke a European war or force the capitulation of Europe to avoid war over Czechoslovakia. So Trevor-Roper studied Ensor's pamphlets about Hitler and Nazism. Because Ensor stressed that reading Hitler's *Mein Kampf* was the precondition for understanding international affairs, Trevor-Roper read the book in German and concluded that Hitler was a man with ideas and goals. Later Trevor-Roper's knowledge of German was to provide the basis of a remarkable career in British Intelligence. After the outbreak of the Second World War he joined the Radio Security Service and in early 1940 broke a hand-cipher used by the German secret service. This success pointed the way for British professional code-breakers who then decoded substantial quantities of Abwehr (German Military Intelligence) messages.[6]

In 1941 Trevor-Roper became a member of the British Secret Intelligence Service (SIS, also known as MI6) and developed into its leading expert on German secret wireless. Inside SIS he became fascinated by Hitler's court. He studied the transcripts of conversations recorded without their knowledge between two German generals captured in North Africa, Ludwig Cruewell and Ritter von Thoma. Trevor-Roper noted privately:

> Even the politicians aren't safe from von Thoma's merciless tongue. – Hess [...] will only eat vegetables planted at full-moon; Hitler [...] can't sleep any more at night, and has ever wilder attacks of rage, – in Munich they call him Teppich-beisser, carpet biter [...] Thoma goes on, it's quite true, he lies on the floor, and snaps around like a mad dog [...]. But best of all is Thoma's description of Goering [...]. He was dressed completely in white silk – a white silk shirt such as the Doges used to wear, with big puffed sleeves [...]. On his head he wore St. Hubert's stag, with a swastika of gleaming pearls set between the antlers.[7]

From 1943 Trevor-Roper headed a section in SIS which produced research papers on the Abwehr and the Security Service of the SS and highlighted the competition between the two organisations. As Trevor-Roper studied the politics of intelligence within Nazi Germany he became familiar with Admiral Canaris, the head of the Abwehr, and Heinrich Himmler, the Reichsführer SS.

Trevor-Roper, who always brought a historical perspective to the war, was surely bound to write a historical work of some kind about it. But how did he come to find his subject in the death throes of Hitler's regime? His interest in Nazi Germany was channelled this way by Cold War politics. The chaos and destruction which attended the fall of Berlin made the circumstances of Hitler's death mysterious. Uncertainty could only distract the German population from reconstruction. It was politically necessary to solve the mystery of Hitler's fate. Brigadier Dick White, head of the Counter-Intelligence Bureau in the British zone of occupation, would remember that

> this seemed to me important at the time for the general security and stability of the occupied zones [...]. The idea of an enquiry into Hitler's fate was wholly mine. I explained it to [Field Marshal] Montgomery [Commander-in-Chief of British Forces of Occupation in Germany] who suggested that I should begin by seeing the Russians and he immediately signalled [Marshal] Zhukov proposing this. I visited Berlin [...] and [was] [...] entertained to lunch by a Russian General – a cheery, knock about and rather boozy occasion. He assured me Hitler and Goebbels had committed suicide in the Chancellery and their bodies burned. He produced Hitler's identified false teeth in evidence.[8]

But while his General was reassuring Dick White, Stalin decided to muddy the waters. On 1 May he had been informed of Hitler's death, and on 5 May officers from Soviet Military Counter-Espionage (Smersh) had dug up Hitler's corpse. On 11 May the technician who had made Hitler's dentures confirmed that the body was indeed the Führer's. Hitler's false teeth were then passed to Dick White's Russian general. On 31 May Laventi Beria, the head of the Soviet secret police, was told about this important dental evidence and ordered the information to be given to Stalin.[9] Yet the Soviet dictator defied this positive evidence because an undead Hitler concealed by the West could prove a valuable propaganda asset.

On 6 June 1945 Stalin told President Truman's envoy Harry Hopkins that 'he was sure Hitler was still alive.' On 9 June Marshal Zhukov, Soviet commander in Germany, was asked at a press conference what had happened to Hitler. Zhukov replied that 'we have not discovered any corpse which could be identified as that of Hitler. He could have left Berlin by air at the last moment.' The Soviet commandant of Berlin added that in his opinion Hitler had gone into hiding, possibly with Franco. Next the Soviet news agency TASS announced that Hitler had been seen in Dublin, where he had cleverly disguised himself in women's clothes. It was also rumoured that Hitler had become President de Valera's butler. More pointedly, the Russians accused the British of concealing Eva Braun and Hitler in their zone. This allegation made it all the more necessary for British Intelligence to collect the available evidence about Hitler's fate and establish the truth.[10]

But to whom should Dick White entrust the inquiry? He regarded Trevor-Roper as the foremost German expert in British Intelligence. Although other officers had spent more time in Germany, none could match him for sharpness, determination or expertise. In March 1943 White had minuted, 'I can think of no single officer, either in MI5 [the British Security Service] or MI6, who possesses a more comprehensive knowledge of the Abwehr organization, particularly on its communication side, than Capt. Trevor-Roper.' Trevor-Roper later recalled the occasion in September 1945 when Dick White sounded him out: 'it was when I was drinking hock with Dick White [...] in Bad Oeynhausen [headquarters of the British 21st Army Group] that my researches were first instituted [...] over the third bottle of hock [...] Dick [...] asked me if I would accept the job, and of course I said yes.'[11]

Before Trevor-Roper could start, White had to prise him out of his current work in the War Room of Allied Counter-Intelligence in London. This was a temporary but important piece of the Allied war effort. The initiative to set up a War Room came from Major-General K.W.D. Strong, intelligence chief at the Supreme Headquarters Allied Expeditionary Force (SHAEF). On 10 November 1944 Strong wrote to Sir David Petrie, head of MI5, that 'an adequate sized and comprehensive German War Room is necessary [...]. It should contain all the best personnel which the Special Agencies can make available for the task.' An accompanying note stressed that 'CI [Counter Intelligence] Staffs in the field require [...] one comprehensive organisation, constituted as their expert advising staff on all questions of German clandestine activity.' As MI5 realised, the great advantage of the arrangement was 'that information from all sources would for the first time be effectively brought together'.[12]

The War Room was an intelligence centre for collating incoming material on the German secret service and initiating further action. It was active from 1 March 1945 under the direction of MI5's Colonel T.A. 'Tar' Robertson. It provided Allied armies in the field with advice and information on the organisation, operations and personalities of German Intelligence. It included a publications section, which was a misnomer as its reports on German Intelligence were classified secret and circulated only to relevant officers within Allied Intelligence, whose attention was drawn to particular gaps in Allied knowledge and the methods by which they might be filled. The publications section consisted of three officers brought in from SIS, namely Trevor-Roper, Stuart Hampshire and Charles Stuart. While in SIS the three officers had studied the radio traffic and other material of German Intelligence and issued regular reports on these. So much of their basic work stayed the same. But now they had considerably more information. Their section had access to all the evidence which flowed through the War Room, such as decrypts of the German enigma machine, captured documents and records of prisoner-of-war interrogations.[13]

War Room staff advised Allied officers who were questioning captured intelligence functionaries and also took part in interrogations themselves. So Trevor-Roper's work in the War Room developed his interrogation skills and knowledge of the German opponent. His section was particularly concerned with gaps in existing knowledge and these did not come any bigger than the mystery of Hitler's death. Yet Trevor-Roper was still busy with paperwork from earlier tasks.[14]

He was rescued from this bureaucratic treadmill by White, who on 10 September 1945 wrote to Trevor-Roper's boss, T.A. Robertson, pointing to

> a considerable amount of comment in the Press on the subject of whether or not HITLER is still living [...] the chap who has kept the closest tabs on the matter appears to be Trevor-Roper. I am, therefore, anxious that he should prepare a brief [...] subject to your agreement [...] a job like this, unless it is done now, will never get done and unless it is done by a first-rate chap, won't be worth having [...] it should I think be a work of some considerable historic interest.[15]

This last comment was remarkably prescient. Robertson replied,

I agree with you entirely that the idea of clearing up this business about Hitler is essential and that it should be done now. The only thing that worries me slightly is that you should have picked upon Trevor-Roper to undertake this task, as, although he may not think so, he has a fairly formidable job in front of him writing two papers: one on Economic Espionage and the other on Successes and Failures of the German Intelligence Service, before he can really be turned on to any other work.[16]

Although on 10 September it was decided to close the War Room from 1 November, the planned reports still had to be finished. Fortunately Trevor-Roper succeeded in convincing the reluctant Robertson of the importance of White's task and that the other jobs should be done later.[17]

How did Trevor-Roper carry out his inquiry? His position as a British intelligence officer gave him considerable advantages. He could call on the assistance of British Army intelligence staff, the Field Security Police and the administration of prisoner-of-war camps. He had access to much captured documentation, such as the papers of the Dönitz government which briefly followed that of Hitler, and the diaries of the Luftwaffe Chief of Staff Karl Koller and Hitler's finance minister, Lutz Graf Schwerin von Krosigk. The American occupation authorities at Frankfurt also put their material at his disposal and he was helped by the American Counter-Intelligence Corps. Much relevant evidence from British and American interrogations or bugging of prisoners was circulated to the War Room in London or the Counter-Intelligence Bureau in Germany and routinely passed on to Trevor-Roper. He could request British and American agencies to carry out inquiries or interrogations on his behalf like a team of research assistants armed with powers of arrest. Usually the witnesses did not want to be found. But if they drew British or American attention Trevor-Roper could get access to them. Even so, he suffered from a major handicap. Although the Russians promised White their cooperation, this was not forthcoming. They excluded various key witnesses, some of whom Trevor-Roper finally tracked down with the help of Hans Rothfels, the first director of the Munich Institute of Contemporary History, when they were released from Soviet captivity in 1955.[18]

The search for Trevor-Roper's witnesses in the British Zone was orchestrated by Major Peter Ramsbotham, who worked on the intelligence staff at British Army of the Rhine Headquarters. On 18 September 1945 Ramsbotham wrote to the intelligence staff at the three British Army

Corps in Germany and at Berlin Army Headquarters. He told them that 'an exhaustive enquiry is being undertaken by this Headquarters into the circumstances surrounding Hitler's death, in order that it can be established definitely whether or not he actually died, and under what circumstances his death occurred.' Ramsbotham requested any information held about witnesses on a list of 33 names which he enclosed.[19]

Trevor-Roper concentrated on finding witnesses for what he called the 'dark period' between 22 April, when much of the Nazi elite left Berlin, and 2 May, when the Russians reached Hitler's bunker: 'seven witnesses of the dark period, from different and independent groups, had been located and interrogated [...] by 1st November 1945, when the report of my conclusions was due.'[20] The seven witnesses included a guard detective, Bormann's secretary and Hitler's chauffeur. The questions Trevor-Roper put to witnesses were brief and specific, usually focusing on events and whom the witness saw on a particular occasion. He treated the evidence with scepticism, as he explained later in a letter of 6 February 1946:

> It is quite impossible to arrive at a complete estimate of events if one begins by accepting any individual statement as accurate throughout. All witnesses in the present case are fallible, as is only to be expected at this distance of time. They are particularly fallible in the matter of dates: they could not possibly be otherwise, living as they did, perpetually underground, not distinguishing night from day, in circumstances of siege and bombardment, and only asked to remember the details at least five months later [...]. All the dates which I have given are based on external evidence.[21]

In his eventual report Trevor-Roper admitted that 'the only conclusive evidence that Hitler is dead would be in the discovery, and certain identification, of the body.' Nevertheless he felt that the evidence for Hitler's death was

> positive, circumstantial, consistent and independent. There is no evidence whatever to support any of the theories [...] which presuppose that Hitler is still alive [...]. It is considered quite impossible that the versions of the various eyewitnesses can represent a concerted cover-story; they were all too busy planning their own saftey [...] to learn an elaborate charade which they could still maintain after five months of isolation from each other and under detailed and persistent cross-examination.[22]

On 10 November 1945 Trevor-Roper presented his report in person to the Quadripartitite Intelligence Committee of the four Allied Powers in Berlin. An appendix to the report asked whether any of the powers held eight further witnesses from the bunker and asked the Russians to make a statement on the body recognised as Hitler's by the teeth. But 'very interesting' was the only comment the Russians would make.[23]

Trevor-Roper's report only proved inaccurate in one significant respect. He stated that Hitler married Eva Braun on 30 April. In fact the wedding took place a day earlier. This detail emerged from the discovery of Hitler's marriage certificate and wills. Trevor-Roper would recall that 'at the end of November 1945 a document purporting to be Hitler's will was discovered in the coat-lining of a suspect [Heinz Lorenz] detained by the British authorities at Hannover and I was asked to return to Germany and investigate this matter too.' Lorenz was being held in a prison camp for using false papers when a sergeant of the guard told him to move on. Not satisfied with Lorenz's reaction, the sergeant grabbed the prisoner by the shoulder, and pushed him in the right direction. In doing so he felt paper in Lorenz's shoulder pad. When the jacket was searched, Hitler's will came to light.[24]

Lorenz had in his possession Hitler's personal and political testaments with an appendix to the latter by Goebbels. Lorenz had been a senior editor at the German News Service. He was responsible for collecting typescripts of broadcast news and bringing them to the bunker. On 29 April 1945 Bormann gave him the wills, which he was to take to Munich. According to Lorenz, Wilhelm Zander, an official of the Nazi Party Chancellery, was also given copies of the personal and political testaments, which he was to take to Hitler's appointed successor, Grand Admiral Dönitz. Major Wilhelm Johannmeier, assistant to Hitler's chief Wehrmacht adjutant, was given the political testament to take to Field Marshal Schörner, Commander of Army Group Centre in Bohemia. In his will Hitler appointed Schörner Commander-in-Chief of the Army. Although the three messengers succeeded in escaping from Berlin, they quickly realised their missions were hopeless and abandoned them.[25]

On 14 December 1945 Trevor-Roper left for Germany on his new mission, and stayed for three weeks.[26] Lorenz and his documents were in British hands. Trevor-Roper set out to locate Zander and Johannmeier and find their documents. Johannmeier was living in the British Zone, but claimed he was merely escorting the other two messengers. Trevor-Roper was not wholly convinced, as Johannmeier was a veteran of the Eastern Front. He reasoned that,

If Johannmeier was considered a more experienced and determined man than the others, and one who could be relied on to get them through the Russian lines [...] it would seem natural and obvious to use him not solely as an escort, but also as a bearer. Equally it seems eccentric that Johannmeier, if he were merely escorting the bearers of vital documents, should have no instructions as to what he should do if [...] the bearers met with an accident or were killed on the way.[27]

As Johannmeier was obdurate, on 18 December 1945 Trevor-Roper interrogated Lorenz, who protested that he had seen Hitler's political testament in Johannmeier's hand.[28] However, before returning to Johannmeier, Trevor-Roper began the search for Zander. When questioned by the British Field Security Police in Hanover, Frau Zander claimed that

she had last heard from her husband on April 12th 1945. She said she was herself anxious for news, and gave many details which seemed evidence of her sincerity, including photographs and the names and addresses of Zander's mothers and brothers in Saarbruecken. In fact [...] these details were intended as smoke in our eyes.[29]

Zander's wife had spun such a convincing tale that even his mother believed he was dead. The story unravelled after an American intelligence officer learned that Zander had been treated under an assumed name in a hospital near Munich for injuries sustained walking from Hanover to Bavaria.[30]

With the help of the American Counter-Intelligence Corps, on 26 December 1945 Trevor-Roper interrogated contacts of Zander near Munich, one of whom revealed Zander's false identity. This enabled Trevor-Roper to track Zander down to an address near Passau, as he later recalled:

having motored all day and all night in a jeep, through mud and sleet and snow, I stood, at 3.0 in the morning, in the village of Aidenbach, near the Austrian frontier, and posting a man with a revolver at each corner of the crucial house, since no one answered on knocking, I sent a German policeman to climb through a window and open the door. Then I went in and broke into a bedroom; and from the bed saw emerging [...] a giant nose, the unmistakeable nose of Bormann's assistant, SS Standartenfuehrer Wilhelm Zander.[31]

On interrogation Zander confirmed much of what Trevor-Roper already knew about Hitler's last days and admitted that he had been given copies of both Hitler's wills and two other documents, namely the Hitlers' marriage certificate and a note from Bormann to Dönitz. These documents now came into the possession of American Intelligence.[32]

Zander confirmed that Johannmeier had also been given a copy of Hitler's political testament. On 1 January 1946 Trevor-Roper re-interrogated Johannmeier, yet in the face of all the evidence the Wehrmacht veteran stuck fast to his story. As he did not have any documents he could not produce them. So Trevor-Roper appealed to Johannmeier's reason, saying that the others had already given the game away and all the relevant information was against his story. The British had no interest in holding him captive but had to do so as long as there was this discrepancy. For two hours Johannmeier firmly resisted. Then Trevor-Roper took a break from his interrogation, and during this interval Johannmeier caught up with the argument and realised the futility of his silence. As the two Nazi officials had already spilled the beans, it was absurd for a simple soldier to suffer further in the cause they had abandoned. When the interrogation resumed, there was some precautionary fencing, during which Johannmeier sought assurance that he would not be punished. Then he finally admitted: 'Ich habe die Papiere [I have the papers].' He led Trevor-Roper to a corner of his garden in Iserlohn and dug up a bottle containing, as his interrogator expected, Hitler's political testament and a covering note from the Chief Wehrmacht Adjutant to Schörner.[33]

The tracking-down of Hitler's wills was Trevor-Roper's finest hour as a British intelligence officer. Afterwards Peter Ramsbotham wrote that 'everyone [...] is full of admiration for the speed and efficiency with which your investigations were concluded.' As with his original report, Trevor-Roper's triumph in locating the wills was only made possible by Stalin's silence. As early as 17 May 1945, Hitler's personal adjutant, Otto Günsche, had stated to Red Army Intelligence that Johannmeier, Lorenz and Zander had received copies of Hitler's will, but this information was kept secret. In any event, Trevor-Roper's success quickly turned sour. As he was leaving Munich, he asked his American counterpart to keep the discoveries quiet until there could be an agreed Anglo-American statement. He was assured that the documents were locked up in the safe of General Truscott, Commander of the United States Sixth Army, where they would stay pending an agreed statement. But next day, when Trevor-Roper had reached Frankfurt, he was shown a copy of *Stars and Stripes*, an American armed forces paper, which had banner headlines about the great coup of the Sixth Army, personally communicated by General Truscott. There was no reference at all to any British participation. To redress the imbalance in the media coverage, Trevor-Roper drove to British Headquarters and held a press conference giving details of Hitler's personal and political testaments.[34]

Shortly after his press conference Trevor-Roper received a telephone call from Colonel Sands of American Intelligence in Frankfurt, who asked: 'Did you, on your recent visit to the U.S. Zone, discover any documents other than those handed to Sixth Army HQ?' The implication was that the Lorenz documents had in fact come from the US Zone. Trevor-Roper denied any further discoveries and gave Sands a guarantee that he had not taken any documents out of the US Zone. Despite his protestation, from January 1946 Trevor-Roper was for a time *persona non grata* in the US Zone. So Sands promised that he would arrange any future interrogations Trevor-Roper required according to his brief. Trevor-Roper recalled that this 'was not very satisfactory, as the interrogators did not have the necessary background to pursue such topics as might emerge during interrogation, or to detect possible errors or lies at the time.' Trevor-Roper's forced absence was a handicap in respect of various prisoners, in particular Artur Axmann, head of the Hitler Youth, captured by the Americans in December 1945. In retrospect, Trevor-Roper felt that General Truscott had double-crossed him twice: first by prematurely publishing the story and taking all the credit, and second, by twisting Trevor-Roper's press conference over the Lorenz papers to blacken his name falsely as a document thief and so justify having rushed into print. Truscott's bad case of Hitler fever marred Trevor-Roper's remarkable triumph in finding the wills.[35]

The historical possibilities of the inquiry had struck the History graduate Dick White from the beginning. While he was carrying out the inquiry Trevor-Roper had no plans to write about it for the public, as he thought this would not be allowed. In January 1946 Trevor-Roper took up a teaching appointment at Christ Church, Oxford. Then White proposed that Trevor-Roper should write up his research as a book which would need to be authorised by the British Joint Intelligence Committee (JIC), the body which coordinated British security and espionage.[36] White advised Trevor-Roper not to submit a proposal to the JIC:

No government agency will ever sanction a proposal of which they cannot foresee the effect [...]. But if you were to write it first, and take the risk of their decision, and submit the text to them, then they would at least see the limits of what they were allowing.[37]

Reassured by White, Trevor-Roper found the idea of a book very appealing: 'above all, I was attracted by the unique opportunity to write a book of contemporary history which I believed, if done carefully, would stand the test of time.' Normally works of contemporary history quickly become obsolete due to the release of new documents,

> but in this case the circumstances were unusual, even unique. Hitler spent his last days enclosed under siege in a subterranean bunker. The number of witnesses was limited, and there were very few primary sources. Everything suggested that the facts could be reconstructed without any fear of later contradiction [...]. I was vain and young enough to believe that I could write a book which combined immediacy and historical value. So even though the events were so close and dramatic I decided to consider them from a distant historical perspective.[38]

Trevor-Roper would remember that he wrote *The Last Days* during 'the spring and summer of 1946, in the evenings, during the term'. Dates on the manuscript itself suggest he may have written most of the text even more quickly than he remembered. Dates are rubber stamped in red on some of the pages and suggest an astonishing tempo. It seems he wrote more than two-thirds of the book in less than a month between 18 February and 15 March 1946, for example about 12,000 words during four days in late February. This impetus would certainly help to explain the fluency and consistency of style in *The Last Days*. Once he had fixed the topic in his mind he wrote it out very quickly. The main text was finished by 22 May and entitled *Hitler's End*.[39]

Trevor-Roper had written to White on 12 March asking him to read the book. On 18 March White replied enthusiastically that 'I think the whole world ought to be told your story and I don't doubt that your elegant pen has done justice to it. Incidentally I read your writing easily so please send me the MS as soon as possible. I am all eagerness.' White also pressed on with obtaining official approval for publication. On 16 May he discussed the book with Harold Caccia, a senior British diplomat and chairman of the JIC. Caccia told White that the Foreign Office was responsible for the policy aspect, namely any international implications, and the JIC should give a ruling on the security aspect.[40]

Next White submitted a minute about the book to the JIC, which discussed the matter at its meeting on 14 June 1946. Colonel I.I. 'Tim' Milne of SIS pointed out that 'whereas Mr Roper was in SIS at the time, the material for his book had not been obtained as a result of his SIS work [...]. [So] 'C' [General Sir Stewart Menzies, Chief of SIS] [...] had no objection to one of his officers publishing such a book after demobilisation.' Other committee members mentioned the

positive advantage in publishing this book, to which view the Foreign Office gave their full support. The book had as its object the preventing of the creation of a Hitler 'myth', and in its detailed and readable form was likely to appeal to a wide public. Further, the Foreign Office might be invited to consider the translation of the book into Foreign Languages, including German, for dissemination as propaganda.

However, the committee considered that 'there might be objections to publication before the War Crimes Trials at Nuremburg had ended.' The point was also made that,

in view of the propaganda value of the book, added weight might be given if a foreword to the book was written by a responsible Commander in authority at the time of the incidents described. The foreword [...] would thereby gain the support of a famous man to the publication. Mr. Roper might like to approach, for example, Lord Montgomery or Lord Tedder [Deputy Commander, Allied Expeditionary Force, 1944–5].

Lastly, the JIC invited the Foreign Office to undertake the final clearance of the book for publication. This was more of a formality than anything else, as White told Trevor-Roper in a letter which enclosed the relevant section of the JIC minutes.[41]

Trevor-Roper was content for the Foreign Office to consider the issue of translation into German. As he told White on 19 June,

I should certainly be glad if some such authority would take the decision (at least as regards translation into German), as at present I find it difficult to decide myself. The book is intended as history rather than propaganda: I think the facts are true as given; and I have been more concerned to understand the events and their causes and relations, than to push a point of view.[42]

Trevor-Roper also promised to wait until the conclusion of the Nuremburg Trials before publication. The delay was necessary because, as Caccia pointed out at a later JIC meeting, 'to publish the book before might embarrass the Court and the British President, who would deliver the principal judgement. This was in no way acceptable.' Trevor-Roper further set about recruiting a great man to write the foreword, telling his friend Solly Zuckerman that, 'of the two names mentioned, I would greatly prefer Tedder. Do you think he would consider writing such a foreword if asked? (that means, if asked by you?) [...]. I do not think that I want a foreword by anyone else.' On 4 July Zuckerman reported that 'I have seen Tedder and shown him your draft introduction and synopsis of contents. He is definitely interested.' In due course Tedder completed the foreword on 21 October 1946.[43]

While Zuckerman was recruiting Tedder to write the foreword, Dick White had passed the manuscript to Harold Caccia. On 4 July he wrote to Trevor-Roper that 'Harold Caccia is still reading your book but hopes to let me have it back at the end of the week. Incidentally he describes it as "enthralling" and is most complimentary about it.' However, Caccia felt that any intelligent reader was bound to ask himself how this collection of monkeys had been able to control Germany and thought Trevor-Roper might like to put in an extra page on this aspect. Trevor-Roper replied to White on 6 July, 'I agree entirely with Harold Caccia's point about the necessity for some explanation, and am in fact finishing the book with an epilogue which will try to answer the question.' When he eventually saw the epilogue, Cacccia felt that it 'certainly gives me an adequate answer to the points which I raised, and, like the rest of his writing, is lucid and coherent. But who am I to set myself up as a critic of so excellent a work?' All the same, the JIC had asked the Foreign Office to undertake the final clearance of the book, so on 27 September Trevor-Roper called on Caccia to enquire whether any further formality was required before publication. Caccia said not. By leaving the matter there he missed an opportunity to raise the question of the German translation for propaganda purposes which the JIC had explicitly invited Caccia to consider, and disregarded a remarkable propaganda opportunity for influencing the German public.[44]

While the book was going through its Foreign Office vetting, Trevor-Roper's publisher was waiting eagerly. Initially Trevor-Roper had flirted with the publisher Hamish Hamilton, feeling that Macmillan, who had published his first book on Archbishop Laud, were 'mugwumpish'. Nevertheless, in the event he stayed with Macmillan, whose representative

Lovat Dickson wrote to him on 14 June 1946 asking, 'Have you any news yet? We are anxious to have the MS as soon as possible.' On 8 July Dickson wrote to acknowledge receipt of the manuscript and the signed contract. Dickson also acted as a channel for communication between Trevor-Roper and Macmillan's American company. In a letter of 8 August Trevor-Roper queried why the title had been changed for the American contract.[45] On 17 September Dickson wrote:

> The American Company are very anxious to call the book *The Last Days of Hitler*. This seems to us a much better title than *Hitler's End*, and as I think you said at one stage you did not mind [...] we should now settle on that.[46]

So the idea for the particularly apt title came from an anonymous American editor.

Trevor-Roper agreed to the new title but the change made him suspicious of his publisher. When Macmillan offered to correct the proofs to save time, Trevor-Roper declined. Dickson then complained that 'there has been further delay at the blockmakers owing to the fact that you made corrections on the drawings in red ink, instead of making them on the margins. These corrections have had to be carefully erased.' But in December Dickson wrote with the news that the Book Society was going to make *The Last Days of Hitler* its March choice and would take at least 15,000 copies. Macmillan now ordered an initial printing of 30,000 copies, twice as many as their next largest for a new book in December 1946. Although the book's subject and topicality meant it was bound to do well, Macmillan's shrewd alteration of the title vindicated Trevor-Roper's decision to stay with them.[47]

The Last Days of Hitler was published in March 1947. It attracted great public interest. Much of the attention was very favourable, though sometimes praise was tempered by criticism. The Cambridge reviewer David Thomson, while admitting that Trevor-Roper had done an admirable job in piecing together the evidence, observed that with his 'sweeping generalizations about the character of the Nazi regime and some of its leaders [...]. Mr Trevor-Roper treads on thinner ice [...] in a way all too common among Oxford historians.'[48]

Sweeping the conclusions may have been, but Trevor-Roper's general comments on the Nazi regime were also compelling:

we must recognise that Hitler was not a pawn; that the Nazi state was not (in any significant use of the word) totalitarian; and that its leading politicians were not a government but a court [...]. In Nazi Germany neither war production, nor man-power, nor administration, nor intelligence, was rationally centralised [...]. The structure of German politics and administration, instead of being, as the Nazis claimed, 'pyramidal' and 'monolithic', was in fact a confusion of private empires, private armies, and private intelligence services.

Hitler's clear mastery over the National Socialists was not matched by clarity in the exercise of power within the Nazi regime, which disintegrated into manageable empires in the hands of the dictator's subordinates, as 'the rule of a court conceals a political anarchy [...] [of] jealous feudatories, with their private armies and reservations of public resources.'[49]

Trevor-Roper was not the first to deny that Nazi Germany was totalitarian. Franz Neumann's *Behemoth*, published in 1942, had emphasised that the Nazi ruling class was a fragmented assortment of powerful groups. Neumann argued that the Nazi state was far from homogenous and that no one organ had monopolised political power. But Trevor-Roper's argument was based on more extensive evidence and was enforced by his characteristic power and clarity of statement. His perceptive account of institutions competing for power in a way which was partly independent of Hitler was confirmed by later historians such as Martin Broszat.[50]

Trevor-Roper drew controversial material for *The Last Days* from Hermann Rauschning, a former Nazi president of the Danzig senate who had fled abroad in 1935. Once in exile, Rauschning became a critic of Nazism and in 1938 he published *Die Revolution des Nihilismus*. The following year this thoughtful book came out in English as *Germany's Revolution of Destruction*. In 1939 Rauschning published another book, *Hitler Speaks*, which purported to be a collection of conversations with Hitler from the period 1932 to 1934, when Rauschning was supposedly one of Hitler's intimate circle. In early 1940 Goebbels noted in his diary that Rauschning was 'the most cutting propagandist on the other side. His book *Hitler Speaks* is exceptionally skilfully written and a huge danger for us.' Rauschning was difficult to refute due to his great skill in blending fact and fiction.[51]

Trevor-Roper's use of Rauschning prompted some criticism. Namier, who thought so highly of *The Last Days*, told Trevor-Roper:

one thing about which I cannot quite agree with you is the valuation you put on Rauschning [...]. Like a real German he rides every point to death, and the general style of his 'Hitler Speaks' with its imaginary ending does not give me sufficient confidence in the man ever to quote any passage from that book as authoritative.[52]

In a Historical Association pamphlet published in 1943, Norman Baynes had observed that the conversations recorded by Rauschning

> took place in the years 1932 to 1934; the book was published in 1939. The form in which these conversations are here presented, it must be confessed, awakes suspicion. We are told that 'the writer jotted [these conversations] down under the immediate influence of what he had heard. Much may be regarded as practically a verbatim record.' The question of course is 'How much?' The student would have welcomed a reproduction of the contemporary 'jottings.'[53]

In *The Last Days* Trevor-Roper took issue with Baynes and wrote that 'the vast mass of intimate matter since available has shown Rauschning to be completely reliable.' Trevor-Roper repeatedly quoted from *Hitler Speaks* in *The Last Days*. He championed the book in his introduction to *Hitler's Table-Talk*. Trevor-Roper felt that Rauschning's predictions had been vindicated, and as he told Namier, 'it seems to me more reasonable to suppose that Rauschning was reporting the truth than that he accidentally invented what turned out afterwards to be true.' Rauschning's book was also drawn on by Alan Bullock in his classic biography of Hitler, and applauded by A.J.P. Taylor. But in 1971 Rauschning admitted that *Hitler Speaks* was not a publication of his original notes: 'instead I wove together an overall picture of Hitler from notes, memory and indeed information from others about Hitler.'[54]

Ten years later Rauschning's press agent Emery Reeves explained to the Swiss historian Wolfgang Haenel how Rauschning came to write *Hitler Speaks*. In 1939 Rauschning had found himself in Paris with high medical bills, an expensive flat and five children to support. Reeves told Rauschning to write up his experiences and conversations with Hitler in the form of quotations so as to interest the public, and gave him the largest advance payment ever made in France. In fact, Rauschning had only met Hitler four times. Even with Hitler's propensity to monologue, these meetings scarcely sufficed for a book of more than 300 pages. So *Hitler Speaks* is not the verbatim record of conversations with Hitler which it appears to be, though fragments of the book may indeed be authentic scraps from the four meetings. But, for the most part, Rauschning simply recycled material from his *Revolution of Destruction* and various contemporary publications, including Hitler's speeches and *Mein Kampf*. Trevor-Roper's personal copy of Haenel's booklet shows that the Oxford historian carefully worked through the pages, marking particularly telling passages. By 1990 he had concluded that he had given Rauschning too much credit: 'Wolfgang Haenel has convinced me I should have been more careful in this respect.' But the error should not be exaggerated, as *Hitler Speaks* is consistent with more authentic records of Hitler's opinions.[55]

Hitler Speaks offered a beguiling trap, not least because Rauschning's earlier book, *Revolution of Destruction*, was so thoughtful and fluent. For *The Last Days* Trevor-Roper also drew on *Revolution of Destruction*, which provided a wide-ranging analysis of the motivation and goals of Nazism. Rauschning's analysis was not without flaws. The main weakness was his refusal to credit Nazism with ideas. Rauschning argued that Nazism had left behind its racialist origins and by 1938 was merely using them 'as a necessary element in propaganda. Racialism is its make-believe.' For 'intensive settlement in the east of Europe in territory won for Germany is no longer the central aim of National Socialist foreign policy [...]. It is no longer of any importance.' Rauschning considered Hitler an opportunist, not a man with goals: 'There was and is no aim that National Socialism has not been ready for the sake of the movement to abandon or to proclaim at any time.' As its title suggests, the main themes of Rauschning's book were revolution and destruction:[56]

> the revolutionary elite can maintain itself in power in its permanently critical situation only by continually pushing on with the revolutionary process [...]. When the political structure of the country has been razed to the ground, the elite will march over the frontier, to upset the existing international order.[57]

Trevor-Roper chose wisely in his use of *Revolution of Destruction*. He kept its perceptive emphasis on nihilism but departed from Rauschning in also giving weight to Hitler's other ideas. Trevor-Roper identified the purpose of the Nazi system as 'World power or Ruin'. 'World power' meant 'the conquest of Russia, the extermination of the Slavs, and the colonisation of the East'. If the quest for world power failed, the alternative was ruin or nihilism. Rauschning's influence is discernible in Trevor-Roper's statement that 'nihilism [...] had inspired the Nazi Movement in its early days [...] in the last days [...] it was to this nihilism that it returned as its ultimate philosophy and valediction.' Nearly 60 years later Joachim Fest supported Trevor-Roper's emphasis on the essentially destructive nature of Nazism when he wrote: 'the intent to demolish had always been Hitler's first and preferred course of action, an expression of his true voice, which now could be heard once more.'[58]

Trevor-Roper believed that the isolation of Hitler's bunker and the limited evidence about its circumstances guaranteed that his account would remain valid and protected from subsequent revision. Yet, as well as Hitler's last days, the book also discussed the general development of Nazi Germany. This wider vision gave *The Last Days* much of its depth and explanatory power but also allowed scope for errors to creep in. The position of Albert Speer, Hitler's minister of armaments and war production, illustrates Trevor-Roper's reluctance to restrict his analysis to the bunker. Speer particularly caught Trevor-Roper's attention, but Speer was not a bunker inmate; he only paid occasional visits, and otherwise travelled widely around Germany. In *The Last Days* Trevor-Roper wrote:

> Speer was not an artist, nor a politician. He had no common interests or ambitions with the rest of the court. He observed their antics, but did not compete in their field [...]. Speer was a technocrat and nourished a technocrat's philosophy. To the technocrat, as to the Marxist, politics are irrelevant.[59]

Trevor-Roper's account of Speer stressed his attempts to frustrate Hitler's scorched-earth policy inside Germany at the end of the war and his plan to assassinate Hitler in his bunker. Nevertheless, in his epilogue Trevor-Roper characterised Speer as 'the real criminal of Nazi Germany' because Speer supposed politics to be irrelevant.[60]

Trevor-Roper's treatment of Speer, like his use of Rauschning, raised questions among his readership. J.K. Galbraith, the American economist, wrote to Trevor-Roper in July 1947 complimenting him on 'an exceedingly fine and wonderfully restrained exercise in history'. Yet Galbraith saw Speer differently. As a director of the American Strategic Bombing Survey he had questioned Speer, and after the first few days of interrogation I found myself concluding that, among his other notable qualities, he was a really superb actor [...]. He was aware, in those early days, that his colleagues were putting on a rather bad show. To be, as later Goering became, the unregenerate Nazi was unwise as well as unbecoming [...]. [Speer] chose, instead, the mantle of the aloof observer and made this convincing by holding forth on his personal loyalty to Hitler. Then, since he is both a man of personal courage and also aware that no one respects a coward, he assumed an attitude of complete indifference as to his personal fate. The whole, I conceive, to have been an admirably devised and executed scheme for survival [...] here is a truly first-class rascal, [...] who played with the gang, cherished his success, and in the end had a somewhat better alibi and a much better story than his companions [...]. Not one man in a million could have handled himself so well in a crisis.[61]

Later research has supported Galbraith by showing that Speer was a super-lative politician who took to the power struggles of the Third Reich with consummate ease. Speer's qualms came after the war. In 1939 he contentedly kept in line with Nazi racialism as his office redistributed stolen Jewish prop-erty in Berlin.[62] In 1945 Speer sought to keep Germany fighting by putting the interests of the armed forces and war manufacture before those of civilian survival. On 15 March he circulated a Hitler decree which on Speer's sug-gestion ordered that priority for transport was to be determined 'only by its immediate value for the conduct of the war'. The operational needs of the Wehrmacht were given priority over refugees trying to escape. In consequence there were virtually no more refugee trains and millions of civilians in eastern Germany were overtaken by the Red Army. Speer never asked Hitler to sur-render. Indeed, in a memorandum of 18 March he urged drastic measures to defend the Reich at the rivers Oder and Rhine. He had no scruples about the deploying of Hitler Youth and old men as cannon fodder. Instead he wanted 'to win the enemy's respect' in a final battle and so achieve a favourable con-clusion, very much the illusion from which Hitler was also suffering.[63]

Looking back on *The Last Days* more than 40 years later, Trevor-Roper honestly conceded that he had been misled by Speer. He had despised most of the Nazis he questioned. They had lost all dignity in defeat. By contrast, Speer neither cringed nor tried to deny his past:

Speer attracted me through his apparent ability to look honestly at events and himself and to judge his own responsibility and admit it – or at least a great part of it. Later, as the evidence grew, and I got to know Speer better, I was compelled to modify my view of him. Now I regard him as a highly intelligent man in whom the sense of right and wrong was undermined by the experience of power [...]. Conversations with him after his release from Spandau confirmed this. How, I asked myself, had this cultivated man been able to share the podium at the Berlin Sports Palace on 28 February 1943 with Goebbels and applaud his dreadful tirade of hate against the Jews? [...] After I had spent a day with him in Munich, I went to the Institute for Contemporary History and read [the speech] [...] I felt sick.[64]

If Trevor-Roper overestimated Speer, he gave a vivid and accurate portrayal of less subtle members of the Nazi elite. He delighted in Goering's grotesque luxuries, first discovered when he listened to the surreptitious recordings of General von Thoma. Material from Thoma is reproduced in *The Last Days*. Trevor-Roper also showed a good understanding of the power struggle between Himmler and Bormann. In *The Last Days* Trevor-Roper emphasised the superstitious and credulous weaknesses of Himmler, but also brought out his efficiency as an administrator and in particular his gift for choosing able subordinates. He traced the growing power of the SS during the war, its successful encroachments on the powers of the armed forces, and Himmler's appointment as Reich minister of the interior in 1943. Himmler's SS came increasingly into conflicts of jurisdiction with the Gauleiter or regional leaders of the party who were backed by Martin Bormann, the head of the Party Chancellery. Bormann successfully asserted the role of the Gauleiter in the face of the SS, and in early 1945 crowned his victory by securing the appointment of Himmler, a former sergeant-major, to the hopeless task of commanding Army Group Vistula in the fight against the Red Army. Recent scholarship bears out Trevor-Roper's theme of the increasing power of the Nazi Party in the final year of the war.[65]

The most controversial aspect of *The Last Days* was provided by Trevor-Roper's observations on Christianity. He wrote that Hitler 'had no trouble from the Churches'. Dr Johann Neuhäusler, suffragan bishop of Munich, took issue with this statement, writing to Trevor-Roper that 'in my opinion you could only have reached this judgement in ignorance of the facts.' Neuhäusler drew Trevor-Roper's attention to his own book on the topic and the English book *The Nazi Persecution of the Churches* based on Neuhäusler's evidence.[66] The Bishop failed to persuade Trevor-Roper, who replied:

186 • *Hugh Trevor-Roper*

after careful consideration I am convinced that although individuals –
priests, pastors and devout Christians – fought actively against Nazism
[…] the Churches themselves as organised institutions did not plan
actions against the regime or carry them out, neither the Protestant nor
the Catholic Church. On the whole I share your opinion that the Church
was indeed persecuted, and also that you tried to defend your areas of
jurisdiction. But I can find no evidence of other opposition.[67]

Trevor-Roper retained the offending sentence in later editions.

Trevor-Roper's references to the Catholic Church produced even more
annoyance than his general dismissal of Church opposition to Hitler. These
comments were not intrinsic to the argument or evidence in *The Last Days*
but were rather comparisons drawn in order to explain the conduct of
Goebbels and Himmler. To illustrate the character of Goebbels's propaganda
he chose the Jesuits and to clarify Himmler's mentality he selected a Catholic
saint. These were not, perhaps, the most tactful of comparisons. Trevor-
Roper wrote:

> Joseph Goebbels was […] the prize-pupil of a Jesuit seminary, [and] he
> retained to the end the distinctive character of his education: he could always
> prove what he wanted […]. As the Jesuit persuades his penitent that all is
> well, that he had not really sinned at all, and that the obstacles to belief are
> really much less formidable than they appear, so Goebbels persuaded the
> Germans that their defeats were really victories […]. As the Jesuits created
> a system of education aimed at preventing knowledge, so Goebbels created
> a system of propaganda, ironically styled 'public enlightenment', which
> successfully persuaded a people to believe that black was white.[68]

Father Brodrick, a Jesuit reviewer in the *Tablet*, the English Catholic weekly
magazine, was incensed by this passage:

> Could Joseph Goebbels himself, with all his Latin and Jesuitical snakiness
> […] have hinted more evil of people whom he disliked in as brief a space
> […]. There is no proof whatever that Goebbels received his early education
> from the Jesuits. They had been driven from Germany by Bismarck and
> did not return until 1919 […]. To pass to another point, how on earth does
> he know what Jesuit confessors say to their penitents in the confessional? Is
> he God's spy or has his brief connection with the Secret Service given him

delusions of omniscience? [...] As for the Jesuits having created a system of education 'aimed at preventing knowledge,' I defy anybody, including Mr Trevor-Roper himself, to explain what that means.

Brodrick referred to the many Jesuits murdered by the Nazis and expressed his resentment at 'any furtive and despicable attempt, worthy of Goebbels at his worst, to plant swastikas on their graves'.[69]

Brodrick also resented Trevor-Roper's explanation of Himmler's combination of private virtue with mass murder by comparing him with a Grand Inquisitor. Trevor-Roper had written that

> The Grand Inquisitors of history were not cruel or self-indulgent men. They were often painfully conscientious and austere in their personal lives. They were often scrupulously kind to animals, like the blessed Robert Bellarmine, who refused to disturb the fleas in his clothes. Since they could not hope for theological bliss (he said), it would be uncharitable to deny them that carnal refreshment to which alone they could aspire. But for men who, having opportunities of worshipping aright, chose wrong, no remedy was too drastic.[70]

Brodrick objected that Bellarmine was never an Inquisitor, and that he was attended not by fleas but by flies which landed on the saint's large nose.[71]

In addition to the protest of outraged clergy, Trevor-Roper received a considerable correspondence from Catholic laity, including an open letter from the novelist Evelyn Waugh, who alleged:

> you give the unwary reader the impression that Bellarmine was Grand Inquisitor – a purely Spanish function. He was 'consultor' to the Holy Office in Rome. I do not know of any instance of his being zealous in securing death penalties. Do you? Can it be that you are one of those who believe Galileo was burned? The whole passage rather reminded me of the Englishman who, being told that the Americans have never forgiven the burning of Washington in 1812, said 'I never knew we caught the fellow' [...]. I wish you would direct me to the Jesuit confessor who would try and persuade me I am sinless. I find they take quite a different line.[72]

Trevor-Roper fended off the torrent of criticism from Catholic clergy and laity with a mixture of resistance and retreat. He was not convinced by the advocates of Bellarmine. In the second edition of *The Last Days*, published in 1950, he retained the offending passage and defended it against Brodrick in a footnote, drawing on a contemporary biography by Jacopus Fuligatus to insist that the insects in question were fleas not flies. On a more substantial point, he cited Bellarmine's opinion that it was an act of charity to liquidate heretics, 'since if they live longer they will only conceive more heresies, and deceive others, and thereby intensify their damnation'. Although Trevor-Roper defended his comparison of Himmler with Bellarmine, he abandoned his parallel between Goebbels and the Jesuits. It had produced more protests than any other aspect of *The Last Days*, and Trevor-Roper discovered that he was mistaken. Father Bernard Bassett, SJ, who knew Trevor-Roper from Oxford, assured him that Goebbels was never at a Jesuit school. Trevor-Roper had already turned to the biographer of Goebbels, F.W. Pick, from whose book he had drawn the information, but Pick would discover from further inquiries that he had been mistaken. Goebbels's old teacher informed Pick that there had been no Jesuit teachers at either of the schools Goebbels attended in Rheydt. So Trevor-Roper conceded his error in the introduction to the English second edition and removed four references to the Jesuits in the paragraph introducing Goebbels, though the offending material enjoyed a renaissance in the German edition of 1965.[73]

Whatever the shortcomings of individual passages, Trevor-Roper's book tore apart the pretensions of the Nazi regime as seldom before. So the volume quickly assumed political importance. On 13 July 1947 the prime minister's private secretary informed the private secretary of the chancellor of the Duchy of Lancaster that

> the Prime Minister [Clement Attlee] has recently been reading H.R. Trevor-Roper's 'The Last Days of Hitler' and feels that this damning exposure of the character and intrigues of the Nazi Leaders ought to be distributed in Germany as widely as possible. He has, therefore, asked me to enquire whether it has yet been translated with a view to publication in Germany, or whether any steps are contemplated to that end.[74]

At the time of Attlee's enquiry, the British element in the Allied Control Commission for Germany based in Berlin had already realised that plans for publishing the book in Germany had gone badly astray. In November 1946 Trevor-Roper's publisher, Macmillan, had offered the newspaper serialisation rights in the German language to the Control Commission. On 10 December came the reply that the leading papers in Vienna and in the British Zone of Germany did not think the time suitable: 'The policy at present is not to devote too much attention to the past, but to concentrate on the positive tasks of reconstruction.' Next Macmillan offered the German-language book rights to the Control Commission, but once again received a rebuff. The official concerned failed to grasp the political value of the book and missed an excellent opportunity. Macmillan also separately approached the American Military Government, to no avail. Trevor-Roper suggested his publisher try Switzerland, and Macmillan sold the book rights in German to the Swiss publisher Amstutz and Herdeg on 26 February 1947.[75] During March extracts from the book amounting to 10,000 words appeared in *Die Welt*, a German newspaper published with British sponsorship.[76]

The British edition of *The Last Days of Hitler* was published on 18 March 1947. Yet there was still no German book version in prospect for the British and American zones, although Michael Balfour and Robert Birley of the Control Commission felt that 'this is the kind of book which the Germans ought to read.' David Whyte of the Foreign Office wrote to the Control Commission that 'it is certainly a very unfortunate chain of events which have led to our not being able to secure the German rights of this book [...]. Macmillan are doing everything they can to help us and to bring pressure to bear on the Swiss publisher.' Meanwhile, in July 1947 Spiegel Press did bring out a German translation of *The Last Days*. This edition appeared in a rudimentary binding with a cyclostyled text, and there were only 800 copies.[77]

Trevor-Roper's book needed a mass edition for the German market, but the Foreign Office was stymied by the Swiss publisher. Whyte wrote to Amstutz on 6 September offering him the paltry sum of £100 for a licence to produce a German edition of 20,000 copies. Amstutz replied that '£100 is so inadequate that it would hardly be worthwhile for any publisher to consider it.' On 3 December Amstutz came to the Foreign Office and Whyte 'exercised all powers of persuasion possible, emphasising that we wanted to get a German edition of "L.D. of H." out quickly and the interest that was being taken in this case by the P.M.'s office', but to no avail. He concluded that Amstutz was 'a very self-willed man and extremely obstinate [...] in principle opposed to accepting any sterling offer we can make him. He is interested only in operating a branch of his publishing house in Germany.' In February 1948 Amstutz wrote again, informing Whyte, in case he wanted to buy copies, that the Swiss edition was due to appear in March. After Amstutz belatedly gained access to the German market, he complained to Macmillan that his edition of *The Last Days* had not gone well there, selling only 73 copies in the whole of 1951.[78]

In the late 1940s most Germans who wanted to read Trevor-Roper in full had to work through the English edition of his book. On 23 February 1948 the British Information Control Branch asked its Information Centres throughout the British Zone for German reactions to *The Last Days*. The centres were almost unanimous in recording a great demand. For instance, the Neumuenster Information Centre reported that 'everyone who can read English asks for this book.' German readers felt Trevor-Roper was objective in his judgements. According to the Information Centre in Schleswig, 'Readers say, that the book is written in a fair way. The author has tried to see things in a dispassionate way.' The Gelsenkirchen Centre reported that *The Last Days* was 'one of the most widely read books in our library', though it added that 'people are very cautious in making comments in the presence of the staff.' Another reporter stated that 'this book is generally returned without comment. If a reader does make a remark, it is to the effect that "Hitler deserved this fate."'[79]

Although Whyte ordered 90 copies of the Swiss edition for the Information Centres, the initial absence of a substantial German edition limited the readership. How much greater would have been the book's impact in Germany if the British government had required the German translation rights as a quid pro quo for approving a book which, after all, had been researched at their expense? The JIC had sanctioned the book not least with a view to a German translation, but the Foreign Office failed to ensure this was done in a way which would best serve British (and indeed German) interests. So the full intended value was not gained from Trevor-Roper's inquiry and the subsequent publication of his book.[80]

In conclusion, we should return to the questions posed at the beginning. Trevor-Roper came to write *The Last Days* because he was ideally qualified to do so. He had visited Nazi Germany in the 1930s, gained a mastery of the German language and used this to good effect while working for British Intelligence during the war, all the while further enhancing his knowledge of the Nazi regime. It was his obvious interest in Hitler's fate which led to his being chosen to carry out the official inquiry which was the basis of his book. And, as a professional historian with a uniquely appealing style of presentation, no one was better suited to turning the original inquiry into contemporary history. His penetrating explanation of Hitler and Nazism was largely confirmed by later historians, as was his emphasis on the late resurrection of the Nazi Party under Martin Bormann. Certainly Trevor-Roper was taken in by Hitler's persuasive armaments minister Albert Speer. Nevertheless, his book remains a compelling and invaluable study of Hitler's fall. He planned a book which would stand the test of time, and he succeeded. Anton Joachimsthaler's modern study of Hitler's death identifies few errors of detail in Trevor-Roper's account. The virtues of his book continue to outweigh its defects. Although Trevor-Roper had engaged in furious controversy with A.J.P. Taylor over Hitler, no one praised *The Last Days* more than Taylor, who wrote in 1968 that Trevor-Roper's 'brilliant book demonstrated how a great historian can arrive at the truth even when much of the evidence is lacking or, as in this case, deliberately kept from him [...]. This was all the doing of one incomparable scholar.'[81]

8

'The Chap with the Closest Tabs': Trevor-Roper and the Hunt for Hitler

Richard Overy

In September 1945 Brigadier 'Dick' White, one of the senior British intelligence officers who ran the Anglo-American Counter-Intelligence War Room, wrote to Lieutenant Colonel 'Tar' Robertson, overall director of the War Room, suggesting that continued speculation about the death of Hitler should be resolved by producing a report to be presented to the Quadripartite Intelligence Committee, set up to coordinate intelligence gathered by the four Allied occupation authorities in Germany. 'The chap who has the closest tabs on the matter', wrote White, 'appears to be Trevor-Roper.'[1] The report should be done as soon as possible, he continued, and 'unless it is done by a first-rate chap, won't be worth having'. So it was that the Secret Intelligence Service (SIS/MI6) officer, Major Hugh Trevor-Roper, found his imminent demobilisation back to Oxford interrupted by official instructions to assemble a small team under his direction to produce as definitive an account of Hitler's end as was then possible. The eventual outcome, it is well known, was Trevor-Roper's publication two years later of *The Last Days of Hitler*, a book that has remained a classic exploration of the grand finale of the dictator and his circle ever since.

The explanation for the origins of the decision to get Trevor-Roper to write a report on Hitler's death relies heavily on his own account. The well-known story of a conversation with Dick White and Herbert Hart at some time in September 1945 over 'three bottles of hock', during which he regaled his colleagues with stories of the last days in the Hitler bunker so enthusiastically that White, 'his eyes popping', realised that such an important story should be written down, seems to have been unduly influenced by the hock.[2] Concern over establishing the fate of Hitler in the final dark days in his Berlin bunker had been expressed for months, and a good deal of intelligence effort, by the

British and the Americans, had already gone into establishing a plausible account – a situation of which White must have been well aware. Indeed it is surprising that the decision to produce a report was not made much sooner. It is also possible that Trevor-Roper might never have been allowed to undertake the project if his seniors in the War Room had insisted that he was too busy with other things. Robertson doubted whether Trevor-Roper would have time to do it given his commitment to writing a lengthy report on the German Intelligence Services and German industrial espionage. SIS had already decided to dispense with Trevor-Roper's services on 12 October so that he could return to Oxford. Robertson discussed the issue directly with Trevor-Roper, who told him that he was anxious to get back to Oxford by late November or December but that he was confident he could do all the tasks he had been set, including a report on the death of Hitler, in time for the meeting of the Quadripartite Committee in mid-November. On 18 September Trevor-Roper's demobilisation was deferred at his own request until the report was ready.[3]

There were many advantages in tasking an officer from the Counter-Intelligence War Room with the responsibility. The organisation grew out of the joint counter-intelligence unit set up at General Eisenhower's Supreme Headquarters Allied Expeditionary Force (SHAEF) in 1944 between MI6 and the recently founded American Office of Strategic Services (OSS), which supplied detailed reports not only on the German intelligence services, but also on the police and SS, and the National Socialist Party, drawn from material supplied by the British Political Warfare Executive.[4] The unit was renamed the SHAEF Counter-Intelligence War Room on 1 March 1945 and given greater responsibility for collecting, evaluating and disseminating intelligence information, but particularly human intelligence gathered from the interrogation of captured Germans. The War Room was renamed again on 13 July when SHAEF was wound up. Based at the small German town of Bad Oeynhausen, the Counter-Intelligence War Room became the central clearing-house for all kinds of intelligence, with a staff of 70 officers from MI5/MI6 and 25 from OSS. The War Room had an Assessment Section, whose 22 officers, including Trevor-Roper, were responsible for drawing up more general reports on the beaten enemy using the wealth of interrogation material available.[5] The organisation was finally wound up on 1 November 1945 on the ground that its expertise was dispersing back to civilian jobs, as indeed would Trevor-Roper, and was less well-suited to the task of producing the more narrowly political and economic reports now required by the occupation authorities.

The Allies' concern over establishing the truth surrounding the death of Hitler did not begin with Robertson's inquiry about Trevor-Roper, and indeed a number of reports had already been drawn up before September on the intelligence available on the last days in the bunker and Hitler's suicide. The wider context for the decision to elicit yet another intelligence survey on the question from officers in the War Room puts Trevor-Roper's contribution into a perspective that he largely avoided in his own account of the genesis of his report.[6] The initial news of Hitler's death came from his appointed successor as president, Grand Admiral Karl Dönitz, who had left Berlin to establish the new government in the port town of Flensburg near the Danish border. Dönitz announced that Hitler had died a hero's death defending the German capital against the oncoming Soviet Army. The Allied response was mixed. The Soviet view was to doubt the sincerity of the claim and to assume that Hitler was probably on the run, even to imply that his Western partners might be sheltering him for their own political purpose. On 2 May, the day following Dönitz's announcement, *Pravda* concluded that this was simply a 'fascist trick' to cover Hitler's flight.[7] The speculation was not helped by the failure of the British and American military authorities to terminate the government in Flensburg and to arrest Dönitz and his colleagues. A campaign began in the Soviet press against Western cooperation with the new German government which, according to the official government journal *Izvestia*, 'has stunned the conscience of all sensible people'. The British Foreign Office recognised that the ambiguity surrounding Hitler's death, coupled with continued de facto recognition of the Flensburg regime, encouraged 'the morbid Russian fear that we may yet do a deal with the Germans to fight Bolshevism'.[8] What neither the British nor the Americans knew was that Red Army intelligence officers had found the charred remains of Hitler and Eva Braun and identified them from their teeth with the help of dental personnel they had tracked down within days.[9]

British concerns focused much more on fear that a 'heroic' Hitler death might pave the way for a Hitler legend to grow and a revival of radical German nationalism following the German defeat.[10] News arrived at the Foreign Office on 2 May from Washington that on 24 April Heinrich Himmler had told the Swedish Count Bernadotte that Hitler was physically finished and close to death, if not already dead. The German SS intelligence officer, Walter Schellenberg, claimed that Hitler had had a probably fatal brain haemorrhage. A report from Flensburg a few weeks later also suggested that Hitler, 'out of his mind and half paralysed', had probably been finished off by an injection from his doctor, Theodor Morell.[11] All these reports and rumours served the British hope that a sordid end in the bunker would make it difficult for a Hitler cult to revive around the idea of an embattled leader fighting to the last against a barbarous enemy. But there appeared no certainty yet that the German people might not be seduced by the myth of a heroic climax to the Third Reich. A report on the prisoner holding-centre at ASHCAN (Mondorf-les-Bains in Luxembourg) submitted to the British Control Commission in Berlin by a Foreign Office official explained how easily Hitler's death could be turned into legend:

> He would have wished to die in battle at the barricades but could trust none but his own hand to kill him; and assuming the drama to have been played out as then planned, his own hand will have done so; but first he was to murder a Miss Braun, a virgin by all accounts, to take with him. It is the ritual of the dying god, complete with preparation of a fire to burn their bodies: in orthodox folk-lore the date for these bonfires is May-eve [April 30]. In the telling and re-telling of the legend there will be German girls aplenty to envy Miss Braun, and the fight against Hitlerism may hardly have started.

The report concluded that the dead leader, if he was indeed dead, 'could no more be laughed off than can Satan himself'.[12]

It was nevertheless necessary in the first instance to demonstrate unequivocally that Hitler was dead, not only to ensure that he would not suddenly reappear and revive German resistance, but also to still the suspicions of the Soviet government and to quash the sudden upsurge in bizarre claims that Hitler was, as Moscow maintained, still alive and somewhere in the Western sphere. All the scraps of evidence and the claims, even the most ludicrous, had to be examined. In late May 1945 an Austrian who had worked on the construction of Hitler's Bavarian retreat at Obersalzberg claimed that there was a crypt under the building in which Hitler's body had been laid after he had been shot by a general in May 1944. Arrangements were made to take the builder there but were finally cancelled in June.[13] That same month the TASS news agency in Moscow published claims that Hitler, disguised as a woman, had landed secretly in Dublin and was in hiding somewhere in Ireland.[14] At last, on 6 June, a Soviet spokesman in Berlin announced to eager journalists that the Red Army had indeed found the bodies of Hitler and Eva Braun, identified by dental records and both dead by poison, only for the constantly suspicious Stalin to get Marshal Georgii Zhukov three days later to deny entirely the previous announcement. Stalin was given the autopsy reports on 16 June confirming the dental findings but he refused to allow the information to be shared with his Allies.[15] The climate of claim and counter-claim prompted parliamentary questions in London to which the government could only give assurances that investigation was continuing.[16]

Behind the concern to establish the whereabouts of Hitler, whether alive or dead, was the preparation for the international military tribunal agreed upon at the founding meeting of the United Nations in San Francisco in May. For the British government, which had favoured a quick execution of German leaders rather than a trial, the news of Hitler's death in Berlin was welcomed as an opportunity to abandon plans for a trial altogether, but the Soviet and American regimes insisted on it.[17] For the American prosecution team trying to decide whether a living Hitler would be a liability at a trial, exact intelligence about his fate was critical. The chief American prosecutor, Justice Robert Jackson, spent time in May and June trying to persuade the new president, Harry Truman, that the traditional immunity of a head of state would not apply in the case of this trial. These efforts have to be understood in a context in which there was nothing but sketchy evidence and the word of Grand Admiral Dönitz that Hitler really had died in Berlin. No trace of either Hitler or his secretary and head of the Party Chancellery, Martin Bormann, had been reported, and the American prosecution case, which rested heavily on the idea of a general conspiracy to wage aggressive war, needed to include both men in any possible indictment to make the concept of conspiracy work in legal terms.[18] The prosecution had to proceed on the assumption that there was something in the Soviet case that Hitler was still at large, and, sceptical though the Western powers were, they had to imagine what a Hitler trial might look like. There had been fears expressed in preparing a trial that Hitler might simply defy the jurisdiction of the court, or use the courtroom to present himself as a martyr, or seize the opportunity to reiterate the obnoxious content of *Mein Kampf*.[19] A definitely dead Hitler would make it simpler to construct the indictment and plan the case, without the risk of a sudden dramatic reappearance.

In June a sudden breakthrough occurred when a former guard at the bunker, Hermann Karnau, turned up at Field Marshal Montgomery's headquarters in the British zone of occupation with testimony that he had watched the bodies of Hitler and Eva Braun burning in the Reich

Chancellery garden on 30 April. This was the first eyewitness report of what had happened. In July the SHAEF intelligence unit produced a report on 'Hitler's Last Days' which, though wrong in some important details – above all the assertion that both had taken poison – anticipated Trevor-Roper's later report in its main conclusions:

> One prisoner, a security guard at the Reichs Chancellery, said that on 1st May [in fact Karnau stated correctly 30 April] he saw Eva Braun in the Reichs Chancellery crying that she would rather die there as she did not want to escape. Later that evening when he opened the door of the emergency exit he saw the bodies of Hitler and Eva Braun burning on the floor. Hitler's head was split and his legs were already consumed. Hitler was said to have poisoned himself and Eva Braun in his office, and his personal servant, Linge, had carried out his orders to cremate their bodies. His body is said to be buried 2 yards away from the emergency exit in a bomb crater.[20]

The information from Karnau was later corroborated by another guard, Hilco Poppen, who was interrogated in hospital in late September 1945 by intelligence officers from the British 30 Corps. Poppen remembered Karnau's comments that Hitler and Eva Braun were dead: 'Sie liegen im Garten und brennen [They are lying in the garden, burning].' Poppen added that both of them had taken poison, and that their bodies were then placed in a bomb crater, soaked in petrol and set alight.[21]

This was still not incontrovertible evidence (though it closely resembled the final report produced by Trevor-Roper four months later) and as the time drew nearer for the Allied prosecution teams to draw up the final Indictment of those now defined as major war criminals, the proper procedure to adopt in the cases of Hitler and Bormann remained far from settled. American interrogators even asked prisoners if there was any truth in the rumour that the Soviet side had spirited Hitler away to secret captivity, the mirror-image of Soviet suspicions of the West.[22] In the case of Bormann there was as yet no evidence at all of his fate or current whereabouts. The British and American prosecution teams, now as distrustful of the Russians as the Russians were of them, worked on the assumption that Bormann was probably in Soviet captivity, but for some reason had not yet been revealed for the purposes of the trial. The lists of major war criminals subject to the Indictment drawn up by the British and Americans included Bormann, whose name was followed by the comment 'in Russian hands (unconfirmed)'.[23] Gradually interrogation material emerged to suggest that Bormann had died trying to flee the bunker, on a bridge over the River Spree. British Intelligence came to the conclusion that Bormann was probably dead, but information continued to appear over the year that he had been sighted, and sometimes Bormann and Hitler together.[24]

The situation with Hitler was more complicated, since the common assumption was that he was dead, even if the evidence was lacking. In late June the Russians were still insisting on including Hitler, Himmler and Bormann as 'persons dead or not present', a deliberately ambiguous formulation.[25] The first draft of a possible indictment document, drawn up by Jackson's team at some point in August, opened with the words 'The United Nations *ex rel.* The Kingdom of Belgium, the Republic of France, The United States of America (etc. etc.) *versus* Adolf Hitler, *alias* Adolf Schickelgruber'.[26] Jackson had certainly intended to include Hitler, and even Heinrich Himmler (who committed suicide in British custody in May), because the conspiracy charge centred on Hitler as the gang leader. But by mid-September Jackson was expressing doubts about the wisdom of including Hitler and trying him *in absentia*, though he was still worried that if Hitler really were alive and were found during the trial, it would be embarrassing to have to begin a fresh indictment of the senior villain of the piece. The British chief prosecutor, Sir David Maxwell-Fyfe, had no objection to including Hitler's name on the list of defendants, but not Himmler's, whose death was beyond argument.[27] Nevertheless, the British War Crimes Executive, meeting in late September 1945, opposed the inclusion of Hitler as one of the indicted criminals because to include it 'would merely stir up public curiosity about his survival'. The British prosecution assumed that Hitler's responsibility was sufficiently explicit in the discussion of a general conspiracy and in the end this view prevailed.[28] In early October 1945, before the Indictment was served on the defendants, a minute on '30.4.1945' in the papers of the general secretary of the Tribunal, Harold Willey, concluded (correctly) that Hitler was 'burned and buried on that day', but because the fate of Bormann was still an open question, his indictment could go ahead.[29]

These arguments were played out against further rumours of Hitler's survival fuelled by the Soviet press. The Foreign Office collected British newspaper reports ('Hitler Still Alive Says Moscow', *Daily Herald*; 'Body Russians Found Was Not Hitler's', *Daily Telegraph*) and monitored *Pravda*. On 9 and 10 September the Soviet journal, almost certainly with Stalin's approval, published two fresh claims – one a report from Rome Radio that Hitler was living in Hamburg under an assumed name, the second a report that the deputy mayor of Berlin, Karl Maron, was convinced that Hitler was still alive. The British *Evening Standard* reported that even Scotland Yard now believed that Hitler was alive, so regular were the assertions emanating from Moscow.[30] Stalin's motives are difficult to explain, since there existed strong medical evidence from Soviet doctors that the remains of Hitler and Eva Braun had been clearly identified. But the effect in London was to launch what became Trevor-Roper's project on Hitler. The Political Department of the Foreign Office wrote the following minute on the news from Moscow on 12 September: 'we are not investigating at all. Should we be?' A week later Trevor-Roper had been confirmed as the man to lead the investigation, a decision framed by the months-long tension between the different prosecution teams over the status of an allegedly dead Hitler and the mischievous efforts from Moscow to leave their Western partners in a state of awkward uncertainty. It was not a decision derived out of the blue from an impromptu conversation one evening in mid-September, though that is the version which Trevor-Roper perhaps preferred, since the story, as he told it in the wartime journals, highlighted his own prior interest in the subject, on which, 'from a variety of casual sources', he had 'picked up a good deal of unsystematic information'.[31]

The subsequent story of the six-week investigation that resulted in the report 'The Death of Hitler', presented to the Quadripartite Intelligence Committee on 10 November (and in an abbreviated form released to the press on 1 November), has relied heavily on Trevor-Roper's own account in the Introduction to *The Last Days of Hitler*, published two years later. Two recent assessments of the Trevor-Roper version have appeared, one in German by E.D.R. Harrison, which appears in an English version in the previous chapter of this book, and a detailed reconstruction of Trevor-Roper's movements and activities during the investigation by the American historian Sara Douglas. Both have shown that Trevor-Roper relied not solely on his own efforts, but on the accumulated intelligence of the previous six months and the assistance of colleagues from the War Room, particularly Peter Ramsbotham, who appears to have played Watson to Trevor-Roper's Holmes.[32] Trevor-Roper was, nevertheless, ultimately responsible for testing the plausibility of the material and formulating a judgement about Hitler's fate. There is no doubt that once presented with the challenge, Trevor-Roper did indeed deploy his considerable forensic skills as a historian to the task of sifting and evaluating the, admittedly small, body of evidence available on the last days in the bunker and Hitler's suicide. The summary that he eventually produced has proved remarkably close to what is now generally regarded as the reality and has been corroborated almost completely since the opening of the archives of the former Soviet Union. His method he described in his wartime journals: to hold every version up to the light of reason and to dismiss all those that failed the test. The distilled account in his report was enough, he concluded, 'to convince any rational being'.[33]

There were, nevertheless, significant problems in producing an entirely convincing narrative, not least, as Trevor-Roper recognised, the difficulty of getting anything out of the Soviet side, 'those incompetent and obstructive barbarians of the East'. In late October he confessed to Peter Ramsbotham that he needed the testimony of Hitler's secretary, Gerda Christian, a member of the SS Begleitskommando (responsible for guarding the bunker), and someone from the Sicherheitsdienst (Security Service) who had personally witnessed the burning of the bodies.[34] The final version of the account listed those present in the bunker with some measure of completeness, but only five people had been found who could provide direct evidence about life in the bunker at the time of the suicide, including Karnau and Poppen. The other three were Bormann's secretary, Else Krüger, Hitler's chauffeur, Erich Kempka, and a security officer, Erich Mansfeld.[35]

With such a short timescale, Trevor-Roper had to rely on information supplied to the Counter-Intelligence War Room from field interrogations in the British and American zones, whose distribution had been centralised in August following a directive from the Intelligence Group Office of the Control Commission for Germany.[36] The material on Poppen arrived serendipitously ten days after Trevor-Roper began his work. A week later, on 8 October, the US Army Air Forces Interrogation Division in Austria was able to supply a very lengthy report, 'The Last Days in Hitler's Air Raid Shelter', based on interrogation of the pilot Hanna Reitsch, who made almost the last flight from Berlin on an improvised runway, shortly before Hitler's suicide.[37] Peter Ramsbotham circulated a list of 33 names to all Corps Intelligence staffs of those wanted in connection with the investigation. Trevor-Roper also had access to detailed reports produced by the OSS on Hitler's health, dental work and personality, and fragmentary evidence from the interrogations conducted by the Americans at Nuremberg. One important account, reproduced by the Berlin Advanced Headquarters of the British Intelligence Bureau three days before Trevor-Roper began his investigation, seems to have escaped his net. '"Nazidämmerung" or the Last Days of Berlin', written evidence from Thilo von Reibnitz, first given to the Russians, provided a very detailed account of the final military defence of the capital and of Hitler's slow realisation that it was all over. Reibnitz confirmed that Hitler and Eva Braun had killed themselves, and that Hitler had named Dönitz as his successor.[38] In the labyrinth of the Allied intelligence organisation, it was possible for nuggets to remain unmined.

The central body of evidence available for Trevor-Roper remained frustratingly small. The key witnesses were in Soviet hands and had already been subjected to strenuous interrogation, but the presence of Heinz Linge (Hitler's head of household), Otto Günsche (his adjutant) and Hans Bauer (Hitler's pilot) was kept concealed from the Soviet Union's allies throughout the period of Trevor-Roper's investigation and beyond. After four weeks of work, however, he was reasonably confident of his ground. He wrote to Ramsbotham that 'the first-hand evidence at our disposal is now so full and consistent that apart from *direct eye-witness* accounts of the events in the bunker *after midday on April 30th*, no further material is likely to add anything significant.'[39] Six copies of his final report were sent to the Quadripartite Committee, which Trevor-Roper also attended. The British headquarters of the Control Commission in Berlin was told by the Commission Public Relations Department that they had to make it clear that the report was the fruit of British labours and 'will go out to the world as a British story'.[40] A short press release (though not the full report) was given out on 1 November to assembled newsmen, though no questions were allowed. The announcement was made a week earlier than initially planned, in an effort to stifle the continued press speculation about Hitler's end. Just 19 days before the start of the trial in Nuremberg, the Allies were able publicly to state that Hitler was dead and would no longer threaten to menace proceedings once they were under way.

In his final report for the Quadripartite Committee Trevor-Roper insisted that all the numerous versions broadcast about Hitler's fate had 'no valid evidence whatever'. His conclusion was heavily derived from the interrogation of Karnau in June, which had also formed the basis of SHAEF's 'Hitler's Last Days', and the American interrogation of Kempka, Hitler's chauffeur. Hitler and Eva Braun had retired to his personal quarters in the afternoon of 30 April, where Hitler shot himself and Eva Braun (probably) took poison; the bodies were then taken outside, doused with petrol, set on fire with a blazing rag tossed by Otto Günsche and then, once incinerated, buried in a shallow grave a few yards from the bunker exit.[41] Trevor-Roper wrote in his wartime journal that he was convinced that in his report 'the main lines are certain'. He also hoped that his conclusions would at last silence the journalists – 'those indefatigable mythologists' – who preyed on the uncertainty for their own purposes.[42] But he also understood that more evidence was needed to make the account watertight. His version was at best provisional, and had served British political and legal interests. The caveats he gave in his report (the absence of the body, the failure to locate key eyewitnesses) were enough to prompt continued scepticism and did nothing in the end to quell the persistent stories about Hitler's survival; indeed, on its own the report had remarkably little impact beyond soothing anxieties at Nuremberg. In December a Paris police commissar, returned from Berlin, published in *Paris-Matin* a refutation of the report under the headline 'No Witness Saw the Body of Hitler'. Eyewitness testimony in the case of criminal matters, he continued, was worth 'practically zero'; the witnesses had rehearsed a common script and trumped the intelligence services. 'I am certain', he concluded, 'that the incineration did not take place.'[43]

Speculation continued unabated in the months that followed, during which the drama of the Nuremberg Trials finally got under way, with Hitler now no more than a ghostly presence. The British censors intercepted and transcribed letters between ordinary Germans on the possible fate of the Führer. One woman told her father that the popular view endorsed the Soviet doubts about Hitler's death: 'some say he will come back as a social-democrat [...]. The husband of an acquaintance of mother's, who worked on an airfield, says that he saw Hitler and Bormann get away in an aeroplane. Who knows?'[44] Two years later a letter was intercepted by the censors that showed how speculation had persisted long after the events of 1945. An old Sturmabteilung (SA) man writing to a comrade told him that there were thousands of opinions current about the fate of Hitler. 'I myself', he continued,

> spoke to a U boat sailor, who says that 2 boats of his flotilla were set aside which took him to SP [Spain?]. One of the two, either 88 [Adolf Hitler] or M.B. [Martin Bormann] is said to have lost a leg. Even English people are of the opinion that both are alive.[45]

The British authorities, perhaps sensitive to the fact that they had undertaken the principal investigation, continued to take the small nuggets of misinformation seriously, though all the political intelligence reports showed that Hitler, whether dead or alive, was not going to spark a nationalist backlash in Germany.[46] In the spring of 1946 the same authorities set in motion an intelligence operation codenamed Conan Doyle. It was prompted by an implausible claim. MI14 had interrogated a man and his wife who claimed that her dead spiritualist father had told them from beyond the grave to check on a Private Stanley Knight, who had written to his wife from Hanover, before shooting himself, that he had identified Eva Braun and Adolf Hitler in a house in the city. Eva was posing as her sister and Hitler as 'Heinrich', shielded from identification by a false birthmark, a blond wig and a facial operation. Intelligence officers found the house occupied by a clerk and his daughter, Eva, working as a prostitute but no trace of the famous couple. An officer scribbled at the foot of the Conan Doyle report, not altogether facetiously: 'we might ask these people to find out and let us know the whereabouts of Martin Bormann.'[47]

By this time Trevor-Roper had returned to Britain and to the prospect of picking up his life again in Oxford, 'looking forward to books, drink and intellectual society once more'. He did not leave the story of Hitler behind him. Copious notes and files accompanied him to Oxford, but it soon proved too great a temptation not to abandon the search where he had left it. He returned to Germany in December to pursue the eventually successful hunt for actual copies of Hitler's will, and again in March to follow up further interrogation leads. The work of filling out the story of Hitler's last days was now the responsibility of two intelligence officers, Captain Humphrey Searle and Brigadier E. Gask. Indeed, the initial report in November 1945 was the start as much as the end of the hunt for evidence. Trevor-Roper was fortunate that the intelligence community in Germany kept him supplied with a wealth of new and secret information that came in as one eyewitness after another was uncovered. Trevor-Roper's interest in the remaining investigation was the result of an idea, formed it is not quite clear when, of writing a book on the basis of his original intelligence work.[48] If he had not written *The Last Days of Hitler*, his investigation would have been little more than one piece in the jigsaw being put together by the Allied intelligence and security agencies during 1945 and 1946. The book transformed the story and Trevor-Roper's role in uncovering it. He began writing in February and much of the draft was finished by March. He was helped greatly by Searle, who drafted a 'Time Table of Events in Hitler's Bunker', based now on the testimony of 27 people who were in or had been to the bunker during the last days of the war. Searle summed up the stage of the investigation in early March. There were two outstanding issues to confirm: the first was the burning and disposal of the bodies; the second was the fate of Bormann.[49] Trevor-Roper had drafted a second report early in 1946 on Bormann, based on the new evidence collected since the Quadripartite meeting in November. Once again he got very close to the truth that Bormann had died on foot on a bridge in Berlin near the Invalidenstrasse.[50] But the American intelligence authorities did not want this account published in case Bormann was caught and put on trial. This prospect had sustained the decision to keep Bormann's name on the list of those indicted and if reports of his death proved premature, the stature of the Allied intelligence effort might, it was feared, be diminished.[51] Bormann's fate could not be corroborated with any certainty in 1946, and indeed the final evidence, based on DNA samples taken from bones found in Berlin, only surfaced more than 60 years later.

Trevor-Roper certainly felt he had enough material to draft what became *The Last Days of Hitler*, published in March 1947 after final approval (and the excising of some information) by the Joint Intelligence Committee. In historical terms it was a small story but, like the later fascination with Hess's flight or Kennedy's assassination, it has continued to excite the public imagination and to invite endless speculation. The research had not been all his own work by any means, though he gave scant acknowledgement to the large number of intelligence officers and interrogators who helped to piece the story together, bit by bit, and continued to do so well after publication of Trevor-Roper's account on the basis that following up any lead might provide 'useful historical information'.[52] The book was based on the best intelligence yet available, but it was not the last word. Though Trevor-Roper continued to tinker with each new edition as more evidence became available, the best recent accounts have taken a more critical view of the reliability and consistency of the testimony, which from the very nature of the story was certain to be conflicting and, as time passed, likely to be embroidered or altered.[53] The one thing that distinguished Trevor-Roper's initial report and subsequent history from earlier suggestions was the assertion that Hitler had shot himself. Though Trevor-Roper and the British intelligence community could not know it, this information caused some consternation for the Soviet secret services when it was presented to them in November 1945, for they had reported earlier in the year to Stalin that Hitler had died a coward's death by taking poison. It had generally been felt that this description of the dictator's end would be more in keeping with Stalin's own intuitive judgement of his enemy; changing the story of Hitler's death now had risks for those involved. There also remained the nagging fear, fuelled by months of Soviet insinuation, that Hitler might still be alive.

In January 1946 Lavrenti Beria, head of the People's Commissariat for Internal Affairs (NKVD), ordered a thorough investigation, codenamed Operation Myth, of the circumstances surrounding Hitler's death, and in particular the manner of his suicide. The key witnesses denied to Trevor-Roper, Otto Günsche, Heinz Linge and Hans Bauer, were subjected to such severe levels of interrogation and torture that it is surprising they did not immediately provide the details Beria wanted, since two of them had accompanied the bodies to the garden and set them alight. Eventually Linge and Günsche confirmed that Trevor-Roper had been right, that Hitler had shot himself while Eva Braun took poison. Further forensic investigation in the bunker in 1946 confirmed the intelligence that Hitler had shot himself, though it could neither confirm nor deny whether Hitler had also taken cyanide, a possibility still regarded by some historians, not unreasonably, as an open question.[54] In 1948 the Soviet security ministry decided to turn the interrogation material into a book, to be submitted to Stalin. The subsequent dossier, given the title 'The Hitler Book', was presented to the Soviet dictator on 29 December 1949 and was placed in his personal papers, only to surface to historical scrutiny in the 1990s.[55] The one significant difference from Trevor-Roper's account was the information that Linge, not Günsche, had set the bodies alight with a piece of paper after the two had struggled with matches in a high wind. *The Hitler Book* also reconciled the difference between Linge and Günsche over the exact position of the bullet wound by opting for the right temple, though later examination by Russian forensic scientists of the skull fragments found in the crater where Hitler had been buried suggested a shot from below, through the mouth or chin.[56] These are small differences in historical terms. The two sides reached roughly the same conclusion and, given the absence of any physical evidence and the key witnesses secretly held in Russian hands, this says much for the earlier British investigation.

There is a bizarre conclusion to the efforts of Trevor-Roper and the Counter-Intelligence War Room to demonstrate conclusively that the German leader had died on 30 April 1945. In 1953 the authorities in the German Federal Republic wanted to register Hitler's death, which until then had remained unofficial. The German Foreign Office wrote to the secretary general of the Allied High Commission asking the Allies to forward the materials of their earlier investigation so that the registration could be confirmed. The British Intelligence Organization in Germany replied a few weeks later that the work had been conducted chiefly by Trevor-Roper and recommended that the German Foreign Office obtain a copy of *The Last Days of Hitler* from the Research Department of the British Foreign Office.[57] Arguments between Bavaria and Berlin over who had the right to register the death postponed a formal declaration until the end of 1956, by which time eyewitnesses in Soviet captivity had begun to return to Germany.[58] Nevertheless, Trevor-Roper could claim some credit in the end for unwittingly laying Adolf Hitler to rest.

9

Himmler's Masseur

Gina Thomas

It may seem strange, given the many questions arising from *The Last Days of Hitler*, to focus here on a figure who, in the grand scheme of things, was little more than a bit-part player in the Third Reich. Indeed, Felix Kersten barely features in the gallery of grotesques who populate Trevor-Roper's account of the final convulsions of the Nazi dictatorship. Yet this ambiguous figure, who has been variously described as Himmler's masseur or personal physician, occupied an inordinate amount of Trevor-Roper's time. His involvement in Kersten's cause became a *cause célèbre* in Sweden. There were debates in the Swedish parliament, official communiqués and a government White Book,[1] a publication of which Trevor-Roper was, as one newspaper put it, 'both the cause and the villain'.[2] There are more files on Felix Kersten in the Dacre Archive than on almost any person except Hitler. They document the labyrinthine complexities of a controversy in which Trevor-Roper became entangled shortly after the publication of *The Last Days of Hitler* and which continued to dog him almost to the last. 'The subject seems never to die,' he sighed in 1997.

> I have never been able to escape entirely from Felix Kersten. After he had been granted Swedish citizenship [in October 1953], I supposed that I could forget him; but I was wrong. Since his death – he died in 1960, in Hamm, where he was on his regular European round, massaging rich Germans – he became an object of research. Scarcely a year passes without some reminiscent echo of his name; and behind the name I see once again that gross peasant figure with his huge hands kneading the stomach of the most sinister destroyer in modern history and incidentally, in the regular interludes of the exercise, saving a few random lives from the grim machinery of extermination. American doctoral students, biographers of one or other of the parties in his story, reviewers of their biographies,

historians, film and television producers, a seemingly endless series. At this moment, as I write, I am fending off a Finnish television company which is planning a film of this Finnish hero. They do not realise the depth of the water in which they are wading.[3]

At the heart of the affair lies an undignified contest between Felix Kersten and Count Folke Bernadotte, the vice-president of the Swedish Red Cross and nephew of the Swedish king, over a 'small but crucial' affair at the close of the Second World War. Himmler's masseur and Bernadotte each claimed the credit for the Swedish rescue operation which, as the Allies closed in on Hitler's crumbling empire, secured from Heinrich Himmler – who as head of the SS had overall command of the concentration camps – the release of many thousands of Scandinavian, Jewish and other prisoners. The documents accumulated by Trevor-Roper over several decades do more than just tell the extraordinary story of the masseur who with his nimble hands relieved Himmler's crippling stomach cramps and who used his intimacy with the Grand Inquisitor of the Third Reich, as Trevor-Roper liked to call Himmler, to gain humanitarian concessions. But in order to show how much the story reveals about Himmler's entourage, about the fall-out from the Swedish rescue mission and, not least, about Trevor-Roper himself, it is necessary to chart his involvement in the controversy.

He first heard about Felix Kersten and his role at Himmler's court from Walter Schellenberg, the suave head of counter-intelligence who had been one of Himmler's closest associates. Having lost confidence in Hitler's ability to win the war, Schellenberg had placed his misguided aspirations on a new postwar order under Himmler's control. By 1943 he had already begun to extend diplomatic feelers in the hope of persuading his vacillating superior to reach a separate peace with the Western Allies. Schellenberg, who was also treated by Kersten at Himmler's request,[4] used the masseur's foreign contacts to further this policy and ingratiated himself with Count Bernadotte. When Schellenberg arrived in Stockholm on 5 May 1945, with diplomatic credentials from Hitler's successor Admiral Dönitz to negotiate the surrender of German troops in Norway, Bernadotte gave him sanctuary in his house and promised to prevent Schellenberg's extradition. In return Schellenberg agreed to back up his protector's vainglorious version of the Swedish rescue mission. Large parts of Bernadotte's hasty memoir of the Swedish rescue mission, which was published a mere six weeks after the event, were ghost-written by Schellenberg. However, his Swedish sojourn proved shorter than he had hoped, for in June Bernadotte was forced to surrender his friend to the Allies to stand trial as a war criminal. It is a measure of the significance Bernadotte attached to this relationship that on 17 June he personally accompanied his protégé to Frankfurt, the administrative capital of the American zone of occupation, where Schellenberg was interrogated by British and American intelligence.[5]

He had used his time in Stockholm to write an account of his career, two copies of which he carried with him when he went to meet his captors. It was from this document and from transcripts of Schellenberg's interrogation by British intelligence that Trevor-Roper, who had been closely involved in his case, learned about 'Felix Kersten, his extraordinary influence over Himmler, and the way it was used – by Schellenberg himself among others – to bring prisoners out of the concentration camps'. Trevor-Roper recorded that 'Schellenberg's account of the personalities at Himmler's court made a deep impression on my mind: no one previously had revealed the sheer dottiness of Hitler's Lord High Executioner.'

Trevor-Roper became ever more aware of the contradictions and inconsistencies with which Kersten's life was riddled, and which gave rise to five diverging versions of his published memoirs, to one of which Trevor-Roper wrote a preface.[6] In one of many jottings he made at various stages of his involvement he noted:

Kersten's biography comes necessarily, to a large extent, from his own account and is likely to be indulgent towards himself. To have been the personal physician, the confidant, almost the confessor of the great ogre of Europe requires some extenuation and we are entitled to approach his own account with some scepticism.

As we shall see, that is a mild understatement. Years later, when his faith had been dented by Kersten's fantastic claims and dubious documentary evidence, Trevor-Roper wrote on a piece of paper headed 'Kersten': 'The beginning of wisdom in the matter of Kersten is to recognise: he cannot be accepted as a reliable authority for anything unless corroborated by external evidence.'[7] But then, as Trevor-Roper explained in a letter to the journalist Barbara Amiel: 'Yes, Kersten was a dubious character about whom I expressed my reservations. But the question at issue is not his character but the historical facts in the affair of Bernadotte.'[8]

The facts as presented by Kersten were, it now seems, even more dodgy than Trevor-Roper came to suspect. Indeed, few facts about Kersten's life remain uncontested. He claimed to have been born in 1898 as a Baltic German in the Estonian city of Dorpat, then under Russian control. Yet a recent German biography[9] asserts that Kersten was in fact born in Halle, Handel's birthplace, as Felix Huberti, and that he had fled to Finland in 1919 after being involved in the murder of a communist activist by an irregular militia group. There, it is alleged, he assumed the identity of Felix Kersten, fought with Finnish mercenaries against the Bolsheviks in the Finnish War of Liberation, joined the Finnish Army and became a Finnish citizen.

On these last points, at least, the discordant accounts converge. Kersten's Finnish military service and citizenship seem to be the only established details from his early life. What remained concealed until many years later was that Kersten was apparently dismissed from the Finnish Army for forging documents to further his promotion and for using coroneted business cards. Trevor-Roper was amused when a documentary filmmaker who came to interview him about Kersten in the late 1990s sent him a photocopy of the card. 'If I had seen it earlier', he replied,

> I might have given a more positive answer to your question, whether he was a multiple, or a split personality. The particular coronet he chose was that allotted, in Britain, to an Earl, so I suppose that, for a German Balt, it would indicate a Count of the Holy Roman Empire. At least this was an innocent, and (since it was before 1922) a juvenile foible. We all have our foibles.[10]

Later in his career Kersten, in an assertion worthy of Münchhausen's syndrome, claimed that – among other epic achievements – he had single-handedly saved the entire Dutch nation from deportation to the Ukraine, a claim which in 1972 the Dutch historian Louis de Jong exposed as a complete fabrication.[11] The same fantastical tendency had been evident much earlier. The SS discovered how difficult it was to establish the truth about Kersten. When Himmler asked the chief of his personal staff to research Kersten's background, the SS Race and Settlement Office, one of whose duties in the cause of 'racial purity' was to assess marriage applications of SS members, could find no record of his marriage in the place he had given. In the end the office encountered so many problems that it gave up. By then Kersten had made himself indispensable to his master.

Whether Kersten went to Berlin in 1922 to further his studies as a manual therapist, or whether he had to leave Finland in a hurry after his fraud had been uncovered, is of little consequence here. What has never been in doubt is Kersten's magic touch, which was to make the most feared man in Germany seem like putty in his hands. According to Kersten, it was the Tibetan healer Dr Ko who discovered his natural gift and taught him a special technique. When Ko returned to Tibet in 1925 Kersten took on his patients and became much sought after by captains of industry, for whom he worked wonders. One recommendation led to another, until Kersten was passed on by the Duke of Mecklenburg to his brother Hendrik, Prince Consort to Queen Wilhelmina of the Netherlands, who in 1928 appointed him as his personal physician.

Kersten accordingly moved his practice to The Hague. But he continued to treat his illustrious European clientele in Germany. In 1939 one of his patients, Dr August Diehn,[12] president of the German Potash Syndicate, orchestrated an introduction to Himmler with a view to furthering their interests. Diehn and his industrialist friends pressed Kersten to dissuade the Reichsführer from nationalising their businesses. It was the first of many such missions which the masseur, ever eager for recognition, readily took on.

When Hitler's troops occupied Holland Kersten found himself trapped in Germany. Himmler refused to let him go, and although he was allowed to treat patients in Berlin, Kersten spent long periods tending to the needs of his tyrannical master. He used his influence, from whatever motives, to mitigate the evil wrought by the regime. Himmler, who referred to him affectionately as 'my good Mr Kersten', introduced him to Mussolini's foreign minister, Count Ciano, as 'the magic Buddha who cures everything by massage'. Walter Schellenberg, who formed an allegiance of mutual benefit with Kersten, spoke of the masseur as Himmler's shadow.

As word spread that he had his master's ear, Kersten found himself increasingly in demand from supplicants who hoped that he could intercede for them. His many entreaties led the pliant Himmler to observe that, with every rub, his masseur squeezed a life out of him. When in the summer of 1942 seven Swedish businessmen were arrested in Warsaw by the Gestapo on charges of espionage, Kersten was approached by the Swedish ambassador in Berlin to help secure their release. This was the moment that gave him a bridge to neutral Sweden. Seeing that a German victory was becoming ever more elusive, Kersten was anxious for a safe haven. In return for his successful intercession on behalf of the Swedish businessmen he requested an apartment in Stockholm. There, in September 1943, he moved with his family. From then until the fall of the Third Reich he commuted between Himmler's court and Sweden. When the defeat of Germany became imminent, the Swedish government sought to negotiate the rescue of thousands of Scandinavian, Jewish and other prisoners from German concentration camps. Both the Swedish Foreign Minister Christian Günther and Hillel Storch, the Swedish representative of the World Jewish Congress, used Kersten as an intermediary. He undoubtedly helped pave the way for the astonishing concessions Himmler made in the hope that he could secure the goodwill of the Western Allies. Besides releasing thousands of prisoners who were brought to safety in Sweden by the fleet of white Red Cross buses marshalled by Bernadotte, Himmler agreed not to implement Hitler's order to blow up the concentration camps and shoot the remaining prisoners rather than allow them to fall into the hands of the Allies. In the early hours of 21 April 1945, ten days before the arrival of the Russian troops, it was at Kersten's estate of Hartzwalde, near the Ravensbrück concentration camp about 80 kilometres north of Berlin, that – to quote a personal memorandum written by Trevor-Roper – 'the man who had undertaken to exterminate the entire Jewish people greeted the representative of the World Jewish Organisation, the Swedish Jew Norbert Masur, with the wonderfully insensitive words, "it is time that we Germans and you Jews buried the hatchet."'[13] Kersten was adamant that Himmler's concessions were *his* achievement, and later told Trevor-Roper that it was the achievement of which he was most proud.

After the war the World Jewish Congress credited Kersten with saving tens of thousands of Jewish lives. But when in June 1945 Bernadotte rushed into print with his account of the rescue operation, he failed to mention Kersten's name.[14] Instead he presented himself as the hero of the hour and intimidated Kersten so that he would keep quiet. Denied recognition and citizenship in Sweden, Kersten appealed to his Dutch friends for help, foremost among them the economic historian Professor Nicolaas Posthumus, founding director of the Netherlands State Institute for War Documentation, who became the masseur's most energetic champion. Posthumus arranged for an official inquiry to be set up which confirmed Kersten's heroic deeds,[15] and in 1950 Kersten was rewarded with a distinguished royal decoration. But his desperate battle for Swedish citizenship continued.

It was through Kersten's Dutch connections that Trevor-Roper discovered in the late 1940s the lengths to which Bernadotte had gone to silence Kersten and polish his own image as the 'Prince of Peace'. A conversation with the Dutch historian Louis de Jong, Posthumus's successor as director of the Netherlands State Institute for War Documentation, drew Trevor-Roper's attention to the connection between Kersten, Bernadotte and the bitter

Swedish postwar debate between those who had opposed neutrality and those who defended it on the grounds that it had served humanity more effectively than military intervention.[16] By then Bernadotte had already succeeded in antagonising Trevor-Roper. For in April 1947 the Count had written a long letter criticising the characterisation of Himmler and Schellenberg in *The Last Days of Hitler*. Bernadotte suggested that the book had not done full justice to his own role both in rescuing prisoners from the concentration camps and in negotiating the surrender of German troops in Denmark and Norway. He also defended his own book, *The Fall of the Curtain*: 'You think the value in general of my book is very slight and that I only was a superficial observer of what happened in Germany during the last months of the German Reich. You must understand if I don't share your opinion 100%.'[17] Bernadotte was referring to a footnote in the first edition of *The Last Days* which misquotes the title of *The Fall of the Curtain* and states that Bernadotte's book 'contains some information; but he was a superficial observer and in general its value is very slight'.[18] It is hardly surprising that the Count could not agree 100 per cent. Trevor-Roper amended the footnote in the second edition to read: '*The Fall of the Curtain* contains some useful information about the personal part played by the author in the last days.' Privately Trevor-Roper was less magnanimous. In his lengthy reply to Bernadotte he had asked whether his correspondent had any other alterations or reservations to make which might be included in the forthcoming Swedish edition of the book. He even proposed a 'prefatory note, in which you could express disagreement where we disagree'. This offer seems to have slipped Trevor-Roper's mind, for he later declared himself puzzled by a request to include the correspondence with Bernadotte as an appendix in the Swedish translation of *The Last Days of Hitler* and questioned Bernadotte's motives for seeking this inclusion.[19]

It was after the meeting with de Jong in February 1949 that the pieces of the jigsaw began to fall into place in Trevor-Roper's mind. As he later recorded in a 'Note for my own memory',[20] the Dutch historian had told him:

the whole question of humanitarian work during the war was deeply involved with Swedish political interests; that in particular there was a strong party which had advocated participation in the war against Germany, and that its opponents, who had advocated neutrality, defended themselves on the ground that Sweden was able to save humanity better by such acts of humanitarianism as were only possible for a government which remained neutral in the struggle.

Bernadotte, Trevor-Roper surmised, had sought to bolster the cause of Swedish neutrality, of which he was the chief propagandist, and to justify his negotiations with Himmler and Schellenberg, by exaggerating his own role in the Red Cross mission. That would also explain why Bernadotte had been so keen to publish his book 'while the iron was still hot', and why the Swedish Foreign Office continued to support Bernadotte's claims even after his assassination in Jerusalem in September 1948. Trevor-Roper concluded that Bernadotte was the mascot of the neutralist party, which was anxious to justify its stance in the war. 'My crime appeared to be my omission, in my book *The Last Days of Hitler*, to give the credit for ending the war to Bernadotte, and my alleged failure to appreciate that neutrals too contributed to the defeat of Hitler.'[21] From a combination of personal vanity and political expediency Bernadotte had airbrushed Kersten out of the story. Furthermore, Trevor-Roper was convinced that, by requesting the inclusion of his letter, Bernadotte had used *The Last Days of Hitler* 'as a vehicle for his own self-advertisement'.

Trevor-Roper published his explosive attacks on Kersten's denigrators in the American journal *Atlantic Monthly* and in his preface to Kersten's memoirs. He even officially proposed Kersten for the Nobel Peace Prize – only to find that the rules disqualified him from doing so.[22] In his championship of Kersten the desire to redress a wrong mingled in his mind with the mischievous prospect of pricking the Bernadotte bubble and infuriating the Swedish establishment. His determination was strengthened by the publication in 1950 of a hagiography of Bernadotte. It was written, Trevor-Roper jeered, by Ralph Hewins, who was 'an amateur historian – he obtained a third in the subject at Christ Church'.[23] Trevor-Roper told Bernard Berenson he was convinced that Bernadotte's widow, the daughter of an American asbestos king, had hired the 'English hack' to write 'a savage attack on me, and it has caused governments and royal families in Sweden and Holland to take sides in the great struggle over the reputation of Himmler's Estonian masseur'.[24] This was before Trevor-Roper had published anything on the matter.

In seeking to unravel the story Trevor-Roper recognised that

all the persons had undeclared interests and motives for their action and none can be taken at his word: The Swedish government, Bernadotte, Schellenberg, Himmler, Himmler's courtiers who gave evidence for Kersten. There was vanity here, complicity there, fear of punishment for war crimes.

For all his readiness to support him, he had no illusions about Kersten. After several years of correspondence they eventually met for lunch at the *pension* 'Sunny Home' at Scheveningen, where Kersten was staying.

> I found him a huge, thickset man with coarse peasant features and powerful hands able to expel the most tenacious trauma from the richest stomach. He tucked his napkin behind his necktie and ate greedily. He was certainly not a sensitive character but would a sensitive man ever have willingly massaged Himmler?[25]

Trevor-Roper became convinced that Kersten was colluding with Himmler's former courtiers, who were furnishing their old mate with affidavits to support his claims. He viewed with suspicion a crude letter allegedly written by Bernadotte to Himmler on 10 April 1945, which stated that the Jews were as unwelcome in Sweden as they were in Germany and volunteered information on British military targets to improve the accuracy of German V2 attacks. The historian Gerald Fleming, who subjected the document to forensic analysis, subsequently proved it to have been a forgery by Kersten.[26] Equally, Trevor-Roper was not satisfied by assurances given on Kersten's behalf by Professor Posthumus, whom he kept pressing with questions. Trevor-Roper also called, as so often, on his old intelligence connections. Was it conceivable, he asked Dick White, that the British had ever planted deception material on Bernadotte, which might explain the letter to Himmler.[27] Though Trevor-Roper doubted the authenticity of the document, the suggestion implied therein that Bernadotte might have been motivated by anti-Semitism was never quite erased, as the pro-Zionist Labour politician Richard Crossmann confirmed. 'I never saw Bernadotte in Palestine,' Crossman told Trevor-Roper in 1956,

> but he left behind him the following clear impression: i) of an almost insane vanity and self-importance, and ii) of a readiness to jump to conclusions [...]. I did also hear rumours that he was anti-Jewish, but had not taken them seriously until I read your introduction.[28]

Even so, in his irritation with the 'great campaign to build up the late Count Bernadotte' at the expense of Himmler's masseur, Trevor-Roper may have held too lenient a view of Kersten and been too ready to take him at his word. When he looked back on the whole affair many years later, Trevor-Roper admitted that time has softened my views of that remote period, and if I were to write about it afresh now, I would be a little more favourable to Bernadotte and a little less favourable to Kersten [...]. Kersten was a somewhat unappealing character, and one could not love a man who had been so close to Himmler.

On the other hand,

Schellenberg had been equally close to Himmler, and had been involved in war crimes, whereas Kersten had actually saved lives, as Bernadotte must have known [...]. Even allowing that Kersten was more of a rogue than I supposed, I still think that Bernadotte improperly used his social position to silence him and to alter the historical record.[29]

*

Trevor-Roper's engagement with the Kersten affair illustrates recurrent characteristics of his life and writing. There is his zest for polemical combat; his fondness for *la comédie humaine* – he called the Kersten affair 'black comedy with a tragedy'; the fascination with questions of forgery; and his sympathy with the underdog against an establishment closing ranks. Above all we see Trevor-Roper's abiding preoccupation with the Nazi period: the drama of his era, from which, as he wrote to Nicholas Henderson at the end of his life, their generation of the 1930s would never escape.[30]

There were times when Trevor-Roper wearied of the countless demands made on him as a result of *The Last Days of Hitler*. He was sick of Hitler's teeth, he once exclaimed, as the argument over the odontological identification of the tyrant's purported remains dragged on and on. Hitler's skull had become, to him, like King Charles's head: 'It keeps popping up in the most troublesome way.'[31] And a correspondent who wrote to him – twice – about her search for biographical details of Hitler's vegetarian cook, Constanze Manzialy, was given short shrift: 'I cannot give you any facts beyond those to be found in my book,' he replied in 1980.

Also I am afraid I do not think that your project was so important as to deserve all this research. No doubt Miss Marzialy was very competent with the Brussel sprouts, but in seeking to reconstruct her life are you not scraping the bottom of the saucepan?[32]

Trevor-Roper also had little patience for a subplot of the Kersten affair: the battle of vanities between the Jewish negotiators Hillel Storch and Norbert Masur. As head of the Swedish branch of the World Jewish Congress, Storch had been closely involved in the negotiations for the release of concentration camp prisoners. Originally he was due to accompany Kersten to the crucial meeting with Himmler on 21 April 1945. But Storch, a refugee from Riga, was stateless and at the last minute it was decided that the risk of sending him into the lion's den without the protection of a passport was too great. His place was taken by Norbert Masur, a German-Jewish exile who had Swedish citizenship. On his return Masur published an account of his mission,[33] which incensed Storch, who felt that his preparatory work was being marginalised. The ensuing squabble mirrored the dispute between Kersten and Bernadotte. Both parties were relentless in seeking validation for their efforts from Trevor-Roper, who tried to keep them at bay.[34]

But even when he tired of such distracting intrusions, his boundless curiosity prevailed. Although he repeatedly declared a wish to extricate himself from the Kersten controversy, he still encouraged the aggrieved parties who bombarded him with self-justificatory letters to keep him up to date. At each new prompting he set off like an eager truffle dog on the trail of clues which might shed light on the murky affair. 'Please continue to keep me informed of events: I always enjoy hearing from you,' Trevor-Roper wrote to Kersten in 1959.

Over and above Trevor-Roper's engagement with the 'pernicious ideology' of Nazism and the 'stupefying insolence of absolute power' which never ceased to astonish him, the Kersten affair also chimed with his keen sense of the bizarre. He viewed the Nazi elite as 'a set of monkeys'[35] and 'flatulent clowns'.[36] The canny masseur appealed to the taste for 'phoneys, *fantaisistes*, mystery men, Backhouses' to which Trevor-Roper confessed in a notebook in the early 1980s, as he asked himself why, when he could have been at ease at Chiefswood, his home in the Scottish borders, happily reading and writing, he found himself 'a prisoner in an uncomfortable farm-house in Italy, in the heat of summer, being talked to death by a bore',[37] another *fantaisiste*, the self-styled Duc de Grantmesnil. When Trevor-Roper pieced together the melodramatic finale in the bunker he only knew the outlines of the strange case of Felix Kersten. But the more he learned about Himmler's court through the Kersten story, the more it confirmed his picture of Hitler's rule 'as a jungle of satrapies' and of Himmler himself as 'an indecisive crackpot mystic, ruled by astrologers and masseurs'.[38]

PART FOUR

The Mind and the Style

10

Trevor-Roper and Thomas Carlyle: History and Sensibility[1]

B.W. Young

More than any other historian of his generation, Hugh Trevor-Roper read and meditated on the literary and scholarly achievements of his great predecessors. And his was a constantly evolving pantheon. From *Historical Essays*, his first collection of studies, published in 1957, to the collection edited by John Robertson as *History and the Enlightenment*, which appeared in 2010, Trevor-Roper wrote imaginatively and often passionately about historians, from the ancient world to the eighteenth-century Enlightenment. For Trevor-Roper, History had a history, and it was one from which History, professional and lay, had much to learn. Most of those lessons were positive, but some were negative. In this essay attention will be paid to a historian whose example Trevor-Roper considered worse than unfortunate. In common with his fellow historian-prophets Karl Marx and Arnold Toynbee, and the once all-too-influential E.H. Carr, it was Thomas Carlyle (1795–1881) who represented to Trevor-Roper the antithesis of all that was required of, and all that was admirable about, the vocation of the historian. But even in Carlyle Trevor-Roper could discern one redeeming virtue: imagination.

Why was this, and what does it reveal about Trevor-Roper's own historical temperament? His antagonism to Carlyle was rather more about sensibility and personal experience than it was about the mere techniques of historical inquiry; other historians were at least as inaccurate as Carlyle, and yet they were admired by Trevor-Roper, and others were at least as idiosyncratic stylistically, yet it is Carlyle who suffers most in his literary appraisals. At root, Carlyle's thought and writings – excepting the need for the exercise of the historical imagination – ran directly counter to all that Trevor-Roper understood positively by 'philosophy' and how that philosophy was expressed in the writing of History.

There is a context to this sensibility, and to this 'philosophy', and it is to be found in Trevor-Roper's politically maturing experience of the 1930s, that uniquely troubled decade during which he reached his maturity. The 1930s, particularly at Oxford and Cambridge, was a decade of conversion, in which true believers and fellow travellers emerged with a new sense of religious conviction and/or political certainty; and in this anxious age, despite the temptations of certitude, Trevor-Roper never converted. Temperamentally, he was not *convertisable*; he ably resisted the machinations of that most fascinating *convertisseur*, Monsignor D'Arcy, SJ. Nor yet, for all its initial appeal as a means of historical understanding, was Trevor-Roper attracted to Marxism politically. The world of Oxford Catholicism was known to him socially, but he remained distant from it intellectually; the apostolic brotherhood of the 'Cambridge Spies' was naturally one from which he was excluded, and he was never committed to its much less politically destructive Oxford fraternity. Graham Greene, a friend of Kim Philby, eventually combined the two philosophies long before it became fashionable to do so. Greene – an Oxford contemporary of Evelyn Waugh, the noisiest of Catholic converts, and in common with Greene a decade older than Trevor-Roper – seems to have anticipated the trends that created the 'liberation theology' of the 1960s and 1970s as the solution to his own quandary in reconciling Catholicism with radical politics. Where Greene was in his element, however, the radicalisation of the Society of Jesus and the emergence of 'liberation theology' had effectively beached an intellectually exhausted Father D'Arcy, just as Vatican II similarly bemused the prematurely aged Waugh. To Trevor-Roper, the assuredly secular sceptic, such developments only reinforced his conviction that Catholicism and communism were both dubious total philosophies, terrible simplifications of the totality of human experience, and, therefore, of History.

And History, for Trevor-Roper, reflected the truth of human experience in a way that neither religion nor politics alone could. History was not to be confused with prophecy; although when a secular historian did prove prophetic, as Trevor-Roper thought was genuinely and tragically the case with Jacob Burckhardt's premonition in the 1870s and 1880s of the advent of fascism, he was ignored, and ignored most troublingly by the Marxist historians who despised what was, to them, his merely old-fashioned liberal conservatism. In his championship, especially in his reflective mood during the 1980s, of Burckhardt, Trevor-Roper was surely thinking about his own experience of the 1930s.[2] Burckhardt had founded no school and was a champion of the Italian Renaissance discovery of the individual; to Trevor-Roper, Burckhardt, a true historical innovator, incarnated the best qualities of the German Renaissance of the nineteenth century. But, above all, Burckhardt resisted the more troubling aspects of that later Renaissance, freeing himself from the dubious politics that gradually began to emerge among nineteenth-century German historians. Trevor-Roper appreciated that most of the great historians, if not exactly created *ex nihilo*, are certainly best understood as being *sui generis*. This is a humanist contention that will be explored in this essay in an attempt to understand how Trevor-Roper, a supreme humanist, thought and wrote about History.

Why, then, was Trevor-Roper's the very individual voice that it was? Why did he not adopt the British-accented varieties of Marxism that so many prominent historians of his generation found so attractive?[3] Influenced though he was by elements of Marx's thinking about history, he remained suspicious of programmatic approaches to the past of the kind provided for many historians of his generation by Marxism. His preferred models were the great historians of the past, and from them he learned how important the individual can be in shaping his or her own part in history. Just as political actors amounted to being more than a simple creation of the forces and contexts in which they lived, so likewise for Trevor-Roper the great historians were something over and above the circumstances in which they wrote and thought about history. Individuals are constituted by more than mere circumstance in time and place; the choices they make, and the nature of their individuality, cannot be reduced to, and in many ways transcend, those circumstances. One can seek to capture the contexts in which a mind and an intelligence, indeed a sensibility, developed – but can one easily chart the fluidity in which it moved? One can seek to capture, for example, the contexts in which Gibbon wrote the *Decline and Fall of the Roman Empire*, but it remains true that the best commentator on those contexts, in the various drafts of his autobiography, is Gibbon himself.[4] The great historians were the masters of the contexts which they explored; their writings were never completely determined by the historical situation in which they wrote. One cannot fully measure what Isaiah Berlin called 'The Originality of Machiavelli' by locating him purely and securely in the context of sixteenth-century Florence; Machiavelli thought for, but also beyond, Florence.[5] If his immediate context were sufficient to explain his political and historical thought, there would not have been the tumultuous afterlife of Machiavelli's daring thinking which J.G.A. Pocock charted in *The Machiavellian Moment* in 1975. Machiavelli, in common with many great historians, is at once a predecessor and a contemporary. So it was for Trevor-Roper that one should read the great historians not only in order to understand their own particular moments in time, and their understanding of times before their own, but also in order to illuminate the present. Trevor-Roper articulated this double-sidedness of classic thinkers in an unpublished paper he gave at Lancaster University to a conference on Max Weber and religion, held in July 1970:

> Any great thinker – & no one would deny Weber's claim to that title – needs to be considered historically two ways. First, his thought must be seen in the context of his own time, wh[ich] has conditioned it. Every thinking man, especially in political thought, reflects his own times, the particular circumstances to which his own thought, in part, is a response [...]. But equally, if a man's thought is worth remembering or reconstructing, it is by the extent to wh[ich] he transcends that context wh[ich] conditioned it and operates audibly to men whose own context is different.[6]

It is this union of past and present that constituted for Trevor-Roper the importance of History as a liberal education. This conviction is vividly expressed at the close of the preface to the Amreican edition of his collection of essays *Religion, the Reformation and Social Change*, published in 1967:

> History is a continuing and complex interaction of interests, experiments and ideas, as well as – in Gibbon's melancholy phrase – the register of the crimes, follies and misfortunes of mankind. A volume of essays cannot pretend to solve the problems of a crowded century. I shall be content if I have opened a few oblique slit-windows in the dividing wall between past and present through which some of these problems can be seen anew and provoke the thought, questions and dissent which are the life of historical study.[7]

Trevor-Roper devised a syllabus paper that led large numbers of Oxford undergraduate historians to read Gibbon and Macaulay early in their studies. He did not find room for Carlyle, though he sometimes encouraged pupils to read him privately, outside their formal studies. Trevor-Roper's commitments are much closer to the historical imagination of Gibbon than they are to any historian who wrote after him, with the notable exception of his beloved Burckhardt. By contrast he regarded Carlyle's historical perspective as all too deeply compromised by that concentration on the present which is so urgently displayed in his most powerful meditation on History, *Past and Present* (1843). Trevor-Roper's implicit repudiation of so much nineteenth-century historical writing is a matter of no small moment, and it says a great deal about both the art and the profession (in the deepest sense) of History, much of which ought to give historians, professional or otherwise, pause for reflection. Trevor-Roper's inaugural and valedictory lectures, 'History Professional and Lay' and 'History and Imagination', did much to confront historians with uncomfortable issues, and it is only fitting that reflection on his historical legacy should continue to do so. If he was very far from being as controversial a figure as Carlyle, Trevor-Roper nonetheless offered his own challenges to the Dryasdusts and the antiquarians whom Carlyle repeatedly satirised in his writings, and in this respect both men were indebted to the literary example of Sir Walter Scott.[8]

In contrast with that of Trevor-Roper, Carlyle's current reputation amongst practising historians is not high. Literary scholars, on the other hand, are fascinated by him, and after the Second World War some of the best work about him was produced by John Holloway and Basil Willey, prominent members of the English Faculty at Cambridge; likewise, Carlyle is a strong presence in the writings of the radical literary and social critic Raymond Williams, yet another Cambridge-educated Marxist convert of the 1930s.[9] The formidable scholarly enterprise of editing Carlyle's letters – the Duke-Edinburgh edition, decades in the making – was undertaken by a number of prominent literary scholars, and not by historians. Whatever Carlyle's authority might be with literary scholars, however, his stock is nothing like as high with historians. Despite his own relish for German thought and his epoch-making work on the French Revolution, he remains too apparently provincial a thinker for European intellectuals to consider, and aside from Hippolyte Taine's initial interest in him at the close of the nineteenth century, he has continued to be largely ignored on the continent, even though one can find in him a proto-Nietzschean contempt for sentimental morality of a kind that might well have attracted the interest of such stridently anti-humanist thinkers as Michel Foucault or any number of his acolytes. Whilst Nietzsche's praise for the supra-moral category of the Übermensch has survived its later associations with Nazism, as has his sublime contempt for Christianity, Carlyle's entirely accidental and blamelessly posthumous brush with fascist ideology, largely the result of his own supra-moral appeal to the heroic, has much more clearly blemished his reputation amongst historians.

Carlyle's commitments to a heroic past and an equally heroic future, both conceived in opposition to the corruptions, real and imagined, of a consistently loathed present, made him a singularly unattractive thinker to Trevor-Roper. Something of this, naturally, has to do with politics. 'Modernity' was never a problem for a sceptical conservative such as Trevor-Roper – a loyal member, after all, of the college that had produced Robert Peel, whose bracingly sceptical version of conservatism as a necessarily modern creed was hated both by Carlyle and by John Henry Newman, the apotheosis of the sort of Oxford-educated Roman Catholic convert of whom Trevor-Roper profoundly disapproved. And yet, even here, he found saving graces in the convert cardinal. Trevor-Roper's unpublished study of the Catholic Revival in nineteenth-century Britain is based around a contrast between a cisalpine, lay-minded, aristocratic, 'Gothic' Catholicism in England, of which Trevor-Roper generally approved, and an ultramontane, bigoted, clerical and predominantly plebeian Catholicism, the latter of which he associated with the Irish diaspora. Newman, whose egoism and bullying sensitivity Trevor-Roper abhorred, is nonetheless presented by him as an unlikely champion of the former tradition, as contrasted with the Italianate baroque strand of Catholicism promoted in England by cardinals Wiseman and Manning.[10]

His unfinished study of English Catholicism was a product of the late 1940s and early 1950s, when Trevor-Roper was increasingly distancing himself both from religion and from Marxism. Not for nothing did he refer to the religious developments of the mid-nineteenth century as the work of 'the generation of the converts'.[11] He knew what that meant, and he did not care for it. For Trevor-Roper, the problems of the present, especially as these affected the writing of history, were largely created by the prophets of progress and the apostles of reaction. An effective critic of the Marxist Christopher Hill, especially of Hill's comical attempt to locate the fastidious Milton amongst the hard-drinking revolutionaries of the Interregnum, and of Waugh, particularly when the latter was engaged in the pseudo-Recusant activity of piously scribbling about Thomas More, Trevor-Roper was always concerned to undo present-minded special pleading.[12] And Waugh was clearly in his sights when he observed that 'ancient, aristocratic, traditionally-minded families are seldom willing to see their cause publicly and vocally represented by jumped-up middle-class newcomers into the fold.'[13] Sociology and theology were inseparable in Trevor-Roper's thinking about religion, and the world invoked by *Brideshead Revisited* was not to his sceptical taste.

What Trevor-Roper most vehemently disliked was obscurantism, but his criticism of a failing also much condemned by Carlyle had the merit of always being couched in luminously clear prose, something which cannot be said of Carlyle's own peculiarly intoxicated, enraged and enraging style. Where Trevor-Roper valued the lucid economy of Latinity, Carlyle preferred to express his converse with the universe through a visionary Germanic idiolect. It is equivalent in prose terms to the contrast between Mozart and Wagner, embodying as it does that between the humanist inheritance of the Enlightenment and the spiritual yearnings of consciously post-Christian late romanticism. Carlyle was at least certain about exactly what it was he was repudiating. In a spirit reminiscent of all too many subsequent secretaries of state for education, Carlyle was to berate, in 1850, a system in which the young Trevor-Roper was himself to flourish, some 80 years later:

The State, once brought to its veracities by the thumbscrew in this manner, what *will* it think of these same seminaries and cathedrals! I foresee that our Etons and Oxfords with their nonsense-verses, college-logics, and broken crumbs of mere *speech*, – which is not even English, or Teutonic speech, but old Grecian and Italian speech, dead and buried and much lying out in our way these two thousand years past, – will be found a most astonishing seminary for the training of young English souls to take command in human Industries, and act a valiant part under the sun! The State does not want vocables, but manly wisdoms and virtues: the State, does it want parliamentary orators, first of all, and men capable of writing books? What a ragfair of extinct monkeries, high-piled here in the very shrine of our existence, fit to smite the generations with atrophy and beggarly paralysis, – as we see it do! The Minister of Education will not want for work, I think, in the New Downing Street![14]

Trevor-Roper's classical education had begun at Charterhouse and continued at Christ Church, where he enjoyed a very successful career as a classicist, and where he had allied himself with the young A.J. Ayer against the then still dominant clerical element in a college which, uniquely, is also a cathedral, and hence a citadel of the very worst sort for men of Carlyle's turn of mind.[15] Though he paid an enjoyable tribute, in his inaugural lecture as Regius Professor, to his former Christ Church tutor J.C. Masterman, as a historian Trevor-Roper was largely self-educated. More may have been gained from Keith Feiling, a historian of the Tory Party whose *Festschrift*

Trevor-Roper would edit; but again, it may have been independence of mind that he learned to appreciate from such instruction, rather than commitment to any one way of pursuing history. Indeed, he paid great tribute to Feiling's teaching in his memorial address given at Christ Church Cathedral in October 1977, by comparing his approach to teaching his subject with that described by Burckhardt.[16] He was more obviously indebted to another Christ Church don who would also serve in intelligence during the Second World War, and who also happened to be one of the greatest prose stylists of the twentieth century. As he acknowledged in his first book, *Archbishop Laud*, published in 1940, Gilbert Ryle, 'like Eve in Paradise, ranged through the whole wilderness, weeding out the solecisms, trimming the luxuriant phrases, and unmixing the metaphors'.[17] It was a philosophy tutor, then, rather than a historian who most aided him in acquiring a style.

One can, incidentally, easily draw parallels with the education of Gibbon, none of which is entirely fanciful. In his essay on Archbishop Ussher, Trevor-Roper recalls the hours he spent in church as a child avidly calculating the times of Easter from tables compiled by Ussher which were contained in prayer books; one is put in mind of Gibbon's image of his precocious antiquarian studies as constituting the bat and ball of his childhood.[18] As with Gibbon's time in the Hampshire militia proving not unprofitable to the historian of the Roman Empire, so it was rather more so with Trevor-Roper's time as a major in military intelligence, which provided him with a set of experiences that, along with a fertile capacity for critical observation, quickly proved enormously important in the development of his historical intelligence. (By contrast, the very thought of the brutally militaristic, but happily non-combatant, Carlyle ever having had the duty to bear arms is surely enough to prevent even Scottish republicans from defending the ideal of a citizen militia originally proposed by Andrew Fletcher of Saltoun in countering the implications of the Act of Union of 1707.)[19] Trevor-Roper's years in military intelligence deepened his sense of a living relationship between the past and the present: his sense of the divisions created by the Reformation was informed and accentuated by his experience of the political divisions of the 1930s, for both eras marked for him a crisis in the European conscience. The shadow of the 1930s, and his participation in the rhetoric of the Cold War in the 1950s and 1960s, informed his fascination with the European crisis of the seventeenth century.[20]

Carlyle was likewise fascinated, if not obsessed, by the seventeenth century, but more because he believed its heroic lessons were in danger of being lost by an unworthy nineteenth century than because of any belief that historical parallels with a troubled present might make a troubled past easier to understand. Consider his introductory observation to his edition of the *Letters and Speeches of Oliver Cromwell*:

> What and how great are the interests which connect themselves with the hope that England may yet attain to some practical belief and understanding of its History during the Seventeenth Century, need not be insisted on at present; such hope being still very distant, very uncertain. We have wandered far away from the ideas which had guided us in all preceding Centuries, but of which that Century was the ultimate manifestation: we have wandered very far; and must endeavour to return, and connect ourselves therewith again! It is with other feelings than those of poor peddling Dilettantism, other aims than the writing of successful Publications, that an earnest man occupies himself in those dreary provinces of the dead and buried. The last glimpse of the Godlike vanishing from this England; conviction and veracity giving place to hollow cant and formulism, – antique 'Reign of God,' which all true men in their several dialects and modes have always striven for, giving place to modern Reign of the No-God, whom men name Devil: this, in its multitudinous meanings and results, is a sight to create reflections in the earnest man! One wishes there were a History of English Puritanism, the last of all our Heroisms; but sees small prospect of such a thing at present.[21]

These sentiments mark out the very different perspectives on the seventeenth century voiced by Carlyle from those expressed by Trevor-Roper, and also the contrasting natures of their respective historical imaginations. It was the very fanaticism of Calvinist Puritanism to which Carlyle, the secularised legatee of Scotch Covenanting theology, devoted so much of the imaginative energy that Trevor-Roper detested in him, preferring, as Trevor-Roper did, what he identified as the Socinian Enlightenment pioneered in humanist culture by Erasmus and continued by the Arminians and by the sceptical adherents of the Great Tew Circle, and brought to a more sceptical philosophical conclusion by Bayle and such late proponents of a yet more heretical variant as Conyers Middleton, and supremely, Gibbon. Enlightenment may have had its origins in religion, as he argued, but it was a process of religious rationalisation in which the – to Trevor-Roper – meaninglessly metaphysical niceties of Trinitarian dogma and the nature of Christ were gradually discarded in favour of a form of religiously exalted humanism.[22] It was to these humanistic 'heretics' that he devoted so much of his scholarly labour, seeing in their civilised defences of learning and scepticism the solvent of the otherwise all-too-powerful orthodoxies of scholasticism and Calvinism. Enlightenment led to intellectual liberty, whereas orthodoxy killed thought.

Central to this profound disjunction between Trevor-Roper, the champion of Enlightenment, and Carlyle, its aggressive opponent, is the contrast between their reactions to German romanticism: the nineteenth-century German Renaissance was inspiration to Carlyle, and his historical philosophy is unthinkable without his exposure to it. It was readings of Goethe (whom Trevor-Roper greatly if selectively admired) and other German writers that distanced Carlyle from the late inheritance of the Scottish Enlightenment in which he had been reared at Edinburgh University. Although himself somewhat critical of the Scottish Enlightenment he did so much to define, Trevor-Roper was infinitely closer to it and its proto-sociological reading of the past than he ever was to the German historical schools that began to flourish in the nineteenth century. There is a caesura in his appreciation of historiography, in which the conservatism of Ranke and Tocqueville – though even their views had been compromised by the counter-linear, counter-progressive experience of the barbarities of the twentieth century – eventually gave way to Trevor-Roper's appreciation of the attractively pessimistic humanism promoted by Burckhardt, which had unpredictably and magnificently broken out in Nietzsche's Basle. (In common with his Christ Church friend and ally, Hugh Lloyd-Jones, the Regius Professor of Greek, he was also a critical admirer of Nietzsche.)[23]

And then there is Max Weber, whose work on the 'Puritan ethic' did so much to inform Trevor-Roper's own writings on Protestantism and capitalism in the 1940s and 1950s in the then-burgeoning field of socio-economic history.[24] But this was a decidedly critical relationship, as can be appreciated in the paper on Weber given in 1970. After detailing the achievements and the shortcomings of Weber's *The Protestant Ethic and the Spirit of Capitalism*, Trevor-Roper closed his paper by placing Weber's interest in charisma in politics in its full, post-Bismarckian context, and it is a reading that does not offer any comfort. Where Burckhardt predicted authoritarianism with regret, Trevor-Roper saw in Weber's post-First World War political writings a more sinister import. It is necessary to quote it in full, as it gives voice to the post-Second World War context in which Trevor-Roper expressed his disapprobation of so much German thought:

We must admit that out of its nineteenth-century German context, the 'catastrophic philosophy of history' which Weber among others accepted has found its recent justification. Both the Marxists and the Nazis drew their nourishment from that soil. They both believed in 'charisma', or the cult of personality; and they both believed that charismatic power could be institutionalised, 'routinized', and become permanent, creating a new type of man. Hitler believed that the problems of German history, which had perplexed Weber, could be solved by the emergence of a new prophet, and that when he had done his work, and fixed upon Germany the insti- tutionalised rule of a new status-group, a new mentality could be created, so that in a short time, it would be 'impossible to imagine any other form of society but our own.' And if in Germany, as usual, the hero failed, else- where the doctrine has been applied more successfully. However industrial capitalism may have gone in Europe, it is being implanted in Russia and China by the charismatic power of the prophet institutionalised to create a new ethic, and a new type of rational bureaucratic man. This, I suppose, can be seen as a posthumous vindication of Weber's general theory.[25]

For Trevor-Roper, the course of twentieth-century history had provided an all-too-extended commentary on Weber's pessimism.

German thought had no doubt proved a stimulating import into British intellectual life, but it was one about which Trevor-Roper was ambivalent. He was highly critical of the hero-worshipping Carlyle as a cultural broker in this regard. This criticism reached its highpoint in his intense repudiation of Carlyle in passing comments in *The Last Days of Hitler*. Midway through that thrillingly Tacitean account of a court run mad, Trevor-Roper describes Goebbels reading to Hitler in the bunker from his favourite book, Carlyle's *Life of Frederick the Great*. Trevor-Roper's distaste for the glimmers of hope this reading gave both auditor and reader modulates, in a glorious instance of literary craftsmanship, into an incredulous account of their superstitious faith in horoscopes; the unreal dynamic of Carlyle's brand of romanticism is accorded the same status as the patent nonsense of astrology. Yet more strikingly, it is Carlyle's cult of the hero, and not Nietzsche's of the Superman, that he denounces in the epilogue to the book as the sort of thinking that made possible the tyrannical sway of Hitler and his courtiers.[26]

Trevor-Roper only once wrote about Carlyle at any length: an expansive essay published in June 1981, in the *Times Literary Supplement*. It is an important essay, marking as it does his conscious distancing from so much that he repudiated: the darkness of Calvinist theology, the ignorance inherent in peasant cultures, the mythologising tendencies of German romanticism, the cult of power and a concomitant mortification of the critical intellect in the face of cruelty and bullying. Those elemental forces of unreason which Carlyle praised as the living nature of faith in a secularised world were the very things that Trevor-Roper despised, recognising, as he clearly did, at least to his own satisfaction, their repugnant residue in the dynamics of Nazism in the 1930s and 1940s. In his 1981 essay he chose to return to the moment he had elaborated in *The Last Days of Hitler*, with Goebbels reading Carlyle to the Führer. There he concluded regretfully that, 'In the intellectual pedigree of Nazism, Carlyle cannot be refused a place.'[27] Whether this is an entirely fair reading of Carlyle is an open question, but it is an understandable one on the part of someone who came of age in the 1930s. For Trevor-Roper there was little to celebrate in the German Renaissance if what it gave birth to in Britain was the dangerously anti-democratic, damningly authoritarian acerbity of Carlyle.

What is more, Carlyle had turned himself against the Scottish Enlighten-ment, in the study of which Trevor-Roper, along with Duncan Forbes at Cambridge, was a pioneer.[28] What Carlyle denounced, however, Trevor-Roper celebrated: much of his own inspiration as a historian came from the historians of the Enlightenment; sometimes, as with his Voltaire-like denunciation of the European witch-craze, it bordered dangerously on the unconsciously ironic. His claim, for example, that witchcraft flourished particularly in the thin, hallucinatory air of mountainous regions reads like a combined parody of Voltaire at his rationalist worst with the methods of the *Annaliste* historians, who partly saw themselves as Montesquieu's heirs in the promotion of sociological history. (The essay is stronger as an exercise in intellectual history; Trevor-Roper knew that physical explanations were not enough.)[29] Unsurprisingly, therefore, Trevor-Roper would begin to see that what was lacking in later Enlightenment historians was a quality that Carlyle possessed, his 'one great virtue': imagination. Carlyle's 'insistence on the power of the human will, on the necessary function of imagination, of "wonder", was a valuable corrective to the increasingly impersonal presentation and interpretation of the Scottish "philosophical historians" after Hume'. It was, above all, as a writer, however, rather than as a historian, that Carlyle triumphed: 'Perhaps it is the surest sign of Carlyle's genius that we read him still, although his ideas are totally discredited.'[30] That is, in every sense, no small qualification.

However positively assessed, the Enlightenment favoured by Trevor-Roper, a champion of historical reason, had been succeeded by the Counter-Enlightenment of Carlyle and like-minded German historians, and this had necessarily distanced politics and religion from the rationalism of which Trevor-Roper saw himself as a servant. As a consequence, Carlyle had to be listened to, since mid-twentieth-century European history was a sad, sorry spectacle of the triumph of unreason. The abhorrent world of Hitler's Germany and Stalin's Russia ultimately made Trevor-Roper question the pious faith in reason and progress of Macaulay, Carlyle's contemporary, who had failed to read the runes, and of whom Trevor-Roper was an ambivalent admirer.[31] (Trevor-Roper noted that the complaisant Whig theory of progress had become the property of Marxist historians; yet another of the ironies of History.)[32] But Carlyle had helped to make that world in which might made right, as the peroration of Trevor-Roper's powerful essay made clear. Consequently, Carlyle had had to be written against. From the carnage of so much around him, Trevor-Roper was to apply the tools of reason and tolerance he found in Erasmus and his heirs in a Socinian Enlightenment; he condemned the witch-craze of the seventeenth century and its Calvinist and Catholic promoters just as he condemned the anti-Semitism and the McCarthyism he associated with it.[33]

In Trevor-Roper's writings on the past, the present is thus ever discernible, just as in his writings on the present he finds the constant presence of the past. Whilst he could, for example, forgive Philby's initial attractions to Marxism in the 1930s, he could absolutely not forgive the intellectual and moral suicide that marked his loyalty to Stalin's Russia. This profound distaste affected his remarks on Graham Greene's admiring preface to Philby's attempt at self-exculpation; it was the combination of naive Marxism with obscurantist Catholicism that so enraged Trevor-Roper, marking as it did for him a union of contemporary and archaic delusions, of orthodoxies left dangerously unquestioned by intellectual independence.[34]

Trevor-Roper also relished the presence of the past in the present in more agreeably playful tones, never more clearly than in his knowing index entries, as in his entry for Peterhouse in *Catholics, Anglicans and Puritans*: 'high-table conversation not very agreeable [...] its new chapel [...] shocking goings-on there [...] four revolting Fellows of [...] main source of perverts'. Under Christ Church, by contrast, one reads: 'sound against Cambridge extremists [...] an open society [...] its characteristic solidarity'. It was, then, more than a purely local loyalty, and more of a sense of having had the good fortune to be a member of an institution which incarnated the very best of the independently minded, sceptically conservative past in an active and busy present, that Trevor-Roper recorded when he very knowingly cited Macaulay's acute observation that Christ Church men 'wherever dispersed, were as much attached to their college as a Scotchman to his country or a Jesuit to his order'.[35] Trevor-Roper was always amused by the varieties of Scottish national commitment, and ever critical of what Carlyle called 'Jesuitism', but he was forever loyal to the community in which he had learned to think historically, and to connect the past with the present through the firm exercise of the imagination in studying and writing history.

Trevor-Roper was very much a man of his Oxford generation, and, as a result, rather more than that. The uniquely fraught experience of the 1930s made many of the more thoughtful men and women of the era consider afresh the entire legacy of Western culture, and of its various mediators. Trevor-Roper repudiated those, such as Carlyle, who had all too readily denounced that inheritance; he celebrated instead those, such as Burckhardt, who critically appreciated it. Burckhardt, whose greatest work was *The Civilisation of the Renaissance in Italy*, was infinitely preferable to Carlyle, who never explored the visual arts. It was the inspiring example of Burckhardt, along with Trevor-Roper's friendship with the connoisseur Bernard Berenson, which led to his own explorations in art history, explorations that never forgot that art has its own fraught relationship with politics. For Trevor-Roper, the history of art was not a speciality to be encouraged, but was best considered as an aspect of History. As he put it in his study of *Princes and Artists*, first published in 1976: 'the great art historians, or at least those who have meant most to me – Jacob Burckhardt, Carl Justi, Emile Mâle – have been historians in the widest sense: historians not of art only, but of men and ideas.'[36]

Burckhardt was something of a cultural lodestar in Trevor-Roper's philosophy of history, a cicerone whose guidance helped him make subsequent sense of the 1930s and 1940s. Loathed by the Nazis, Burckhardt was to prove the antithesis of Carlyle in Trevor-Roper's historical pantheon. The Nazi assault on European culture affected many of Trevor-Roper's Oxford contemporaries, and not least Isaiah Berlin. It was in these postwar decades, reflecting on the frightening power of irrationalism in modern European history, that Berlin arrived at his definition of a Counter-Enlightenment, a movement of ideas which supposedly reacted against the secular imperatives of the Enlightenment, reinstating religion and metaphysics where before rationality and natural philosophy had been the preferred solvents of super-stition. In the Counter-Enlightenment, spearheaded, according to Berlin, by the likes of J.G. Hamann and J.G. Herder, lay the roots of nationalism and all that was to follow in the twentieth century. Historians now routinely dispute the reality of a Counter-Enlightenment and of the 'Romantic Reaction' which Berlin likewise diagnosed as informing it; whatever the rights or wrongs of such a revision, it is necessary, in doing justice to Berlin's particular historical vision, to understand the circumstances in which he had discerned the lineaments of Counter-Enlightenment.[37] It was in a Europe in which Enlightenment – as celebrated by such émigré scholars as Ernst Cassirer – had all too readily given way to the mystagogues of Nazism and fascism that Berlin saw the long-delayed triumph of the Counter-Enlightenment and the murderous irrationalism that it intermittently nourished.[38] And in this identification he was not alone; Trevor-Roper had also witnessed such a decline into savagery and a new barbarism; it was there when Goebbels read Carlyle to the Führer in the bunker, and tracing the genealogy of pitiless nationalism was to begin to preoccupy Trevor-Roper almost as much as it would increasingly preoccupy Berlin.

For Berlin, the exiled French philosopher Joseph de Maistre was to play an analogous role to that performed by Carlyle in Trevor-Roper's account of a nineteenth-century reaction against Enlightenment. In essay after essay, de Maistre was seen by Berlin as an approving prophet of fascism; however anachronistic, however teleological such a claim might have seemed to Berlin's many critics, he was himself convinced by it.[39] What de Maistre was to Berlin, Carlyle was to Trevor-Roper, for whom Carlyle was an antidote to the facile 'Whig interpretation of history' which Herbert Butterfield had originally denounced in 1931. But where Butterfield, secure in his Cambridge redoubt at Peterhouse, subsequently looked to Providence and a renewed sense of Christian urgency in reacting against the politics of the 1930s and 1940s, the secular Oxonians resorted to a more humanly tragic understanding of history.[40] As Trevor-Roper remarked in May 1949 – in a letter to Berenson – of the Cambridge reception of Butterfield's *Christianity and History*, 'their professor of history (a very undistinguished historian called Butterfield) has published a series of lectures of darkest mysticism [...] which has evoked a chorus of rapture from those melancholy fenlands.'[41]

The immediate postwar turn to religion, in which both Butterfield and C.S. Lewis were lionised as apostles – as pioneering public intellectuals in a new age of Christian commitment – was not at all to Berlin's or Trevor-

Roper's tastes. Religion, if anything, had been deeply compromised in the eyes of Berlin and Trevor-Roper by its more than merely occasional alliance with extremist politics, from Franco's Spain outwards and onwards. Both men had supported the Republican cause in the Spanish Civil War, and both had expressed vehement distaste for Waugh's pro-Italian account of the war in Abyssinia. In Trevor-Roper's eyes, Christianity had too often compromised itself politically in the 1930s. He expressed himself forcibly on such matters in the late 1950s in a review of a book on the iniquities of American Catholicism, a review which the *Times Literary Supplement* tactfully, perhaps, chose not to publish:

> The Church of Rome has never been, and has seldom claimed to be liberal: it is an authoritarian system, based on dogma, fundamentally opposed to toleration, free enquiry, and individual liberty, and justifying itself without reference to these liberal virtues. Its resistance to totalitarianism has always been rivalry, not opposition.[42]

And this criticism of Catholicism was subsequently extended by him to High Anglicanism and Dissent; his suspicions of the potentially dire political consequences of Christianity only strengthened as he grew older. Considering what he thought of as the long reactionary nature of Peterhouse, in a letter dated 15 July 1986, Trevor-Roper alluded to Butterfield, a predecessor of his as Master of the college, in decidedly unflattering terms: 'In the 1630s it was more Laudian than Laud. By the 1930s it seems to have been Methodist – Butterfield (a *guru* of cloudy reaction) preached from tubs all over the Fens; but Methodism was by then a form of abject reaction.'[43] Much of Trevor-Roper's dislike of the clericalism he associated with Peterhouse conservatism has to be understood in these terms: Butterfield's experience of, and reaction to, the 1930s, were not matters of which Trevor-Roper approved.[44]

Aside from producing such occasional calls to arms as *The Englishman and his History* in 1944, Butterfield was nothing like as politically *engagé* in the late 1930s and the 1940s as was the young Trevor-Roper. Butterfield continued to write approvingly of the German historical tradition in the 1950s and 1960s; his personal and cultural relations with Germany were stronger than Trevor-Roper's, and his patience with what Trevor-Roper considered to be its political declension was likewise more considerable.[45] And in common with all Trevor-Roper's historiographical loyalties, this was a deeply considered position, and one in which he followed the premier German historian of –

and erstwhile apologist for – historicism. Friedrich Meinecke (1862–1954) was a strong admirer of the historical tradition in which he had been reared, but, in 1946, following the collapse of Nazi Germany, he issued a civilised recantation of what he thought the culpability of Germany's historians in what he called *Die Deutsche Katastrophe*. Immediately translated as *The German Catastrophe*, Meinecke's slim but impressive tract had a measurable impact on Trevor-Roper and other contemporaries. When, in due course, Meinecke's classic assessment of German historicism eventually appeared in English translation, in 1972, as the curiously-entitled *Historism*, it was Isaiah Berlin who provided a critically admiring foreword.[46]

Trevor-Roper's own assessment of German historicism was critically consistent. Consider, for example, Meinecke's role in Trevor-Roper's portrayal of Burckhardt as the civilised insider-outsider within German historicism. Tracing the school from its origins in the German Enlightenment and its conclusion in Meinecke's studies of historicism in the late 1930s and 1940s, Trevor-Roper noted how it had been corrupted from the late nineteenth century onwards into a form of state-worshipping historico-political collusion – here very much following the itinerary later regretted by Meinecke himself – before its eventual and deserved defeat as a way of thinking about the past in immediately postwar Europe. Trevor-Roper, in a British Academy 'Master Mind' lecture delivered in 1984, expressed the argument far more succinctly than any paraphrase can hope to achieve:

> The rise of Hitler did indeed at first disturb Meinecke, as that of Bismarck had first disturbed Ranke; but like Ranke, he would come round, and by 1940 he was openly exalting in the military victories of Hitler as Ranke had done those of Bismarck [...]. All this time the dissenting voice of Burckhardt was heard in Germany only in whispers or silenced by official disapproval. He was regarded as defeatist, parochial, unable to rise to the great events of history.

But, as so often in Trevor-Roper, history was not on the side of the powerful: 'by 1943 the tide had turned.'

> As the impending defeat of Germany became clear, the established orthodoxy began at last to fail. In the last months of the war Meinecke himself turned to Burckhardt. 'Will Burckhardt triumph over Ranke?' he rhetorically asked; and when all was over, in 1948, at the age of

eighty-five, in a famous lecture on 'Ranke and Burckhardt', he declared
his conversion [...]. At that moment the historical philosophy of Ranke
(though not necessarily its scholarly deposit) may be said to have been
declared bankrupt, and Burckhardt, the outsider, so isolated in his own
time, to have been recognised as a 'master mind'.[47]

The generation of the 1930s had definitively turned against the 'German
Idea' which men such as Carlyle had so widely and effectively disseminated
in mid-nineteenth-century England.[48]

This is not to argue for a crude anti-German impetus in Trevor-Roper.
Rather his admiration for the products of German culture was far more
discriminating than had been that of Carlyle, that tireless enthusiast for
all things German, from History to authoritarianism. For Trevor-Roper
there was much to denounce in the past, but he was equally aware that an
indiscriminate denunciation was not enough: the tendency tendentiously to
denounce, after all, was one of the many problems which he identified in
Carlyle as a historian. History induced political pluralism in Trevor-Roper,
as philosophy had done for Berlin: concomitantly, liberalism was the natural
product of serious reflection on the complexity of human life. But it was
never a sentimental variant of liberalism; it paid attention to the particular,
and especially to what Trevor-Roper and Berlin characterised as individual
genius. The experience of the 1930s inspired in Trevor-Roper and Berlin an
awareness that judgements had to be made, but always in the round. For
understandable reasons, Berlin could not bear Wagner, but, as a letter of
1988 from Trevor-Roper to Alasdair Palmer made clear, Trevor-Roper could,
occasionally, bring himself to admire his genius:

> In a week's time we are going to Bayreuth. I have never been there and
> am not, in general, a lover of Wagner. But every five years I make the
> effort, recognising that, like Carlyle and Victor Hugo and others, though
> a monster, he was also a man of genius; and art and learning should not
> be judged by the personality of the author, nor (what with Wagner is
> particularly relevant) by the practical consequences later drawn from them
> or fathered on him.[49]

But the difference between Wagner and Carlyle was that, as a historian,
the latter ought to have been altogether less carefree with the truth, less
ready to abandon morality for the naked worship of power. Carlyle's genius,

unlike that of Wagner the composer, was measurable by the standards of History, and, for Trevor-Roper, it had been found wanting. The gravamen of Trevor-Roper's central charge against Carlyle was all too clear: Carlyle had mistaken History for Prophecy.

Unlike Carlyle, Trevor-Roper chose not to prophesy, but rather to clarify. By devoting himself to intellectual clarity he also chose to avoid the apparently profound and the semi-mystical in favour of the demands of an engaged and properly secular readership. His was a consistently humanist commitment to *this* world rather than to fond imaginings of another and better one, be it a Christian Heaven or a Marxist Utopia. In his taste for the ironies of human history, alongside his manifest hatred of cruelty and the lauding of power, Trevor-Roper was at one with Tacitus and Gibbon. It is these inclinations, along with a style worthy of being cited in such illustrious company, that affirm Trevor-Roper's claim to be one of the great historians, and also to be quietly and non-dogmatically a genuine and largely persuasive philosopher of history.

11

The Classicist[1]

S.J.V. Malloch

When the young Hugh Trevor-Roper expressed a preference for specialising in mathematics in the sixth form at Charterhouse, Frank Fletcher, the headmaster, told him curtly that 'clever boys read classics'.[2] The passion that he had already developed for Homer in the under sixth form spread to other Greek and Roman authors. In his final year at school he won two classical prizes and a scholarship that took him in 1932 to Christ Church, Oxford, to read Classics, *literae humaniores*, then the most prestigious honours degree in the university.[3] There he would win the Hertford and Craven Scholarships and earn a First in Honour Moderations in 1934. 'A glittering career as a classicist awaited' him, in the words of Blair Worden in his fine biographical essay.[4] Then a change took place: Trevor-Roper switched to Modern History (a title which then covered all periods later than Ancient History).

What had happened to drive him from classical studies? He reflected publicly on this question in his address as president-elect of the Joint Association of Classical Teachers in May 1973. This 'Apologia Transfugae' ('Apology of a Deserter') created a small sensation within the world of classical studies.[5] Trevor-Roper's tendentious view of the discipline was dramatically misconstrued by the *Times Educational Supplement* and provoked criticism from his old friend Hugh Lloyd-Jones, the Regius Professor of Greek at Oxford. The 'Apologia', which exposes tensions within classical studies about how scholarship should be conducted, also offers insights into Trevor-Roper's priorities as a historian. The picture is filled out by his other writings, published and unpublished, which supply contexts on both sides of his time as an undergraduate. For the earlier period, they reveal the origins of his love of ancient literature and the narrow limits of his schooling in Classics. For the later, they demonstrate an enduring classicism that was central to his intellectual life as he was crafting an identity as a historian. Peter Ghosh, in a stimulating essay on Trevor-Roper's engagement with the history of ideas, has written that 'the starting point for our understanding of the mind and achievement of Hugh Trevor-Roper must lie in the years between 1945 and 1957.'[6] A study of Trevor-Roper's classical interests reveals that the decisive formation came earlier. His classicism was characterised by a love of ancient language and literature that can be traced throughout his life. It was a distinctive classicism, since it rested on a repudiation of the narrow philological focus of classical scholarship that was conventional at the time. That reaction helps to explain Trevor-Roper's change of intellectual career. But it did not end his classicism. The attitude to Classics which he worked out for himself would be absorbed into his mature conception of the practice of historical studies.

English public schools flourished in the nineteenth century on the back of the social aspirations of an increasingly wealthy middle class. Education was regarded as a marker of social status, and the cultural authority of Classics ensured that it was considered the fundamental educational ingredient in the creation of the manners and style of a gentleman. From the later nineteenth century onwards, challenges to the permanency and universality of Classics from many directions undermined its cultural primacy, and gradually it became merely one of many competing 'disciplines'. But Classics, and in particular Latin, remained strongly embedded in the curriculum of the public schools, and a public school education remained appealing to middle-class parents with social aspirations.[7]

One such parent was Trevor-Roper's mother, Kathleen. She was determined to send her children to good schools, a 'social necessity', in Trevor-Roper's words, 'if one was to keep one's place in the social hierarchy', although she knew nothing of them.[8] At the first, Belhaven Hill, which Trevor-Roper entered in 1924 aged ten, he was thoroughly drilled in the classical languages by Wilfred Ingham, or Bungey as he was called because of his springing step.[9] One of the two founders of Belhaven, Bungey seemed a living embodiment of Victorian and Edwardian schoolmasterly eccentricity. He 'had some hobby horses which he would ride, with whip and spur', remembered Trevor-Roper in old age:

One of them was 'dative verbs'. Dative verbs are verbs which, in the Latin language, require the dative, not the accusative case in the nouns which they govern. They also have some other incidental eccentricities. Bungey could not mention dative verbs without making a human parallel and then launching into a diatribe against it. Dative verbs, he would declare, are tiresome, wayward, eccentric, unpredictable verbs which will not conform to the rational rules accepted by their verbal colleagues but insist on going their own way, just like certain persons who always try to be different, thus causing unnecessary difficulties in a well-ordered society … and then he would be off, unstoppable, far from the set course, denouncing human dative verbs, sometimes, I felt, with a staring eye on me.[10]

It was a measure of the narrowness of language-learning at Belhaven that when Trevor-Roper borrowed Mommsen's *History of Rome* from the school library, he was judged by Bungey to have taken his 'zeal for learning too far'.[11] But Bungey, staring eye or not, was fond of Trevor-Roper and held him up to his classmates as a model.[12] Trevor-Roper flourished at Belhaven, and in 1927, aged 13, he successfully sat for a scholarship to Charterhouse.[13]

With its strong classical tradition, Charterhouse established Trevor-Roper's love of classical literature by broadening his reading. In the under sixth form he specialised in Classics, which he was to read to 'learn the language and appreciate the style'.[14] Frank Fletcher introduced him to 'the three greatest of Greek poets – Homer, Aeschylus, and Pindar – and the greatest of the Roman historians, Tacitus'.[15] Homer and Aeschylus were the great revelations. Trevor-Roper's progress in reading Homer had been slow until his vocabulary 'broke in my hands' as he read the description of the Gardens of Alcinous in *Odyssey* 7, lines 112–32.[16] Thereafter he could read the poem 'freely and easily and enjoy it'.[17] In his wartime notebooks he reflected on the experience under a rubric that described the 'memorable moments' in his life up to around 1940. There he remarks that he had 'never wavered' in his 'passion' for Homer since,[18] and in a later memoir he confirmed that the experience had converted him into a 'passionate classicist'. All his life he knew long passages of Homer by heart. But the 'greatest discovery' of that period, as Trevor-Roper would remark in the 'Apologia', was 'the Aeschylus of the *Suppliant Women*, of the *Seven against Thebes*, and, above all, of the *Oresteia*, with his vivid, highly charged, complicated metaphors, swollen to bursting by the pressure of tormenting thought'.[19] Image and metaphor were central to Trevor-Roper's appreciation of classical literature and style.[20]

This expansion in Trevor-Roper's life of reading and study was counter-balanced by the narrow complacency of several of his Classics teachers at school and university. Their style would come to characterise conventional classical education in his mind. A.L. Irvine (1881–1967), a Wykehamist and scholar of Christ Church, had been teaching classical and English literature at Charterhouse since 1914.[21] He prided himself on being a 'full man':

> Irvine's ideal was 'the scholar and the gentleman' who had absorbed classical and English literature and some decorative learning and who derived pleasure from it, and he introduced his pupils to these pleasures, but any suggestion that there was a world – whether of literature or of thought – outside those limits was inadmissible to him. He did not encourage exploration beyond the frontiers of the fair domain which he had acquired, or doubt within it.[22]

The undeveloped taste of the schoolboy no doubt benefited from such instruction, which he could gradually shed as he acquired his own tastes and feelings; but the danger of Irvine's method, as Trevor-Roper reflected in a notebook in 1942, was that the finality of his pronouncements might discourage 'all further experiment'.[23]

Trevor-Roper's late memoirs confirm the claim of his 'Apologia' that the narrowness of classical studies drove him to study history. They demonstrate too that he made the change also with a mind to his career. Offers from relatives to take up positions in a solicitor's office in Manchester or in the family firm in South America appealed less than the prospect, which lay ahead of him if he pursued an academic career, of being a teacher. But he decided that teaching history would be more rewarding than 'teaching composition in the [ancient] languages and in tinkering with texts', pursuits which took up 'too much of the time and energy of classical teachers'.[24]

Trevor-Roper commenced his 'Apologia' with an account of humanism, a term he proposed to use in its 'correct and original sense: the study of *Literae humaniores*, human as distinct from divine texts, Homer and Virgil, not Scripture and the Fathers'.[25] Despite rejection of the doctrine by Enlightenment thinkers, humanism 'clung' to the centre of education in eighteenth- and nineteenth-century Britain and Germany.[26] Trevor-Roper marvelled at the contradiction that the Industrial Revolution was advanced by elites in Britain who were reared on the literature of a 'city-state and empire' whose slave-owning ruling classes regarded industry and commerce as essentially 'vulgar'. In Britain Classics could be recommended as the literature of liberty, of equality among free citizens. That was possible in the Germany of the early nineteenth century, but after 1850 humanism had to be adapted to a society that was industrialised and opposed to the doctrines of the Hellenism which it openly expressed. Yet the 'absurd' claim of continuity was upheld: German historians could see eighteenth-century Germany as the new Greece, the empire of Bismarck as the new Rome.[27] How could such a contradiction be maintained? Trevor-Roper argued that the 'figment' that modern society represented classical values could only be upheld through hypocrisy or by narrowing classical studies to language or literature and divorcing texts from their contexts. The Victorians were 'expert in the necessary hypocrisy':

> just as they could scientifically destroy the intellectual basis of Christianity
> and yet ceremoniously assert, and evidently believe, the truth of the same
> Christianity, so they were perfectly capable of looking at the literature of
> Antiquity and not seeing what was plainly there.[28]

In Germany scholars took refuge in technical expertise: they edited and emended texts that were divorced from their historical context, and claimed 'for this narrow field of erudition, a moral and intellectual superiority almost directly proportionate to its narrowness'.[29] This obsession with philology was embodied for him in 'two grim, frowning faces' that emerged from 'the semi-Freudian fog' hanging before his eyes: 'the remote, patrician visage of the Teutonic Knight Ulrich von Wilamowitz-Moellendorf; then, behind him, *longo intervallo*, the sour, crabbed face of the spent English poet, A.E. Housman.'[30]

Wilamowitz (1848–1931) symbolised for Trevor-Roper the 'barrenness of a purely literary and philological approach to the Classics'. Housman (1859–1936) offered the same warning, 'in even more minatory tones', on native soil.[31] Trevor-Roper witnessed this scholarly tradition in the flesh particularly in the person of Eduard Fraenkel (1888–1970), the refugee German professor who came to Oxford in 1934 and stayed at Christ Church in 1934–5.[32] Trevor-Roper did not like Fraenkel's ungrateful complaints to the Steward's Office in Christ Church on seeing his accommodation for the first time or his arrogant conduct in his famous seminars. He enjoyed the discomfiture there of senior Oxford classicists such as Maurice Bowra, whom Fraenkel treated as 'mere *Privatdozenten*', but Fraenkel's method confirmed his 'prejudices' by reminding him of Wilamowitz and Housman.[33]

A later experience confirmed Trevor-Roper's sceptical opinion of the 'ingenious reconstructions' of textual critics. When, as a don, he had his writings typed out by a copyist, he noticed that the most common error involved jumping from one word to an occurrence of the same word a line or so later (*saut du même au même*), 'omitting the intermediate text and thus making nonsense of the whole passage'. Trevor-Roper claimed that no amount of 'tinkering' could restore the original sense. Assuming that modern typists committed the same kinds of errors as medieval copyists of classical texts, he believed that 'such omissions are the cause of many corruptions in ancient manuscripts, and ingenuous conjecture is effort wasted'.[34]

Trevor-Roper claimed that it was 'refreshing' to turn from 'textual pedantry' to a consideration of the comparative methodologies which were 'recently' being imported into and reviving the discipline.[35] His prime example was Moses Finley and his 'exciting' – and now classic – book *The World of Odysseus* (1955).[36] Finley employed methodologies from outside classics, such as sociology and anthropology, to shed light on the world of the Homeric epics. Traditionalists, Trevor-Roper observed, would not have admitted such 'frivolities': when Eduard Fraenkel heard the word *Geistesgeschichte* ('cultural history') he declared summarily that *Geistesgeschichte* was merely a polysyllabical word for *Quatsch* ('nonsense').[37]

The 'Apologia' had its characteristic moments of provocative mischief, and the provocation succeeded. The *Times Educational Supplement* splashed its front cover of 25 May 1973 with a cartoon by Richard Willson depicting Trevor-Roper destroying the Acropolis with a benign smile on his face. The caption read 'Professor Trevor-Roper laying about the classicists'.

Trevor-Roper 'laying about the classicists' (*Times Educational Supplement*)[38]

John Gretton, the *Times Educational Supplement* reporter on the scene, praised the address, but misunderstood and misrepresented it. Trevor-Roper's 'brilliant' 'demolition job' of Classics, Gretton reported, could hardly have been performed with 'greater wit and panache' as he 'slaughter[ed] his private demons in public – and before the very high priests of the religion, to boot'.[39] Gretton missed Trevor-Roper's clear profession of love for ancient literature and his emphatic support of Classics in education.[40] Trevor-Roper was prompted by Gretton's 'grotesque caricature' of his 'Apologia' to widen the audience of his lecture by printing a 'slightly abbreviated' version in the *Spectator* of 14 July 1973. Meanwhile he had been corresponding with Hugh Lloyd-Jones, to whom he had sent a typescript of the lecture. The issues raised between the two men mattered deeply to Lloyd-Jones. He wrote a letter to the *Spectator* setting out his views, and republished it nine years later in *Classical Survivals*.[41] Three of his points deserve attention.

First, Lloyd-Jones objected to Trevor-Roper's praise of Finley's *World of Odysseus*, a book he thought good, but 'hardly as good' as Trevor-Roper implied, not least because of Finley's tendency to forget that Homer wrote fiction.[42] More fundamentally, he chafed at Finley's dismissive attitude to other approaches and to the value of the classical languages to the study of ancient history:[43] Finley's lack of formal language study made him a 'tailless fox who has had such success in persuading English classical scholars, who once got sound linguistic training, to cut off their own tails also'.[44] Lloyd-Jones and Finley came from very different scholarly trajectories. Educated at Westminster School, Lloyd-Jones went up to Oxford in 1940, when classical studies retained the character that Trevor-Roper remembered from his youth, and earned a First in Greats in 1948. The technical accomplishment that won him the Chancellor's Latin Prose Prize and the Ireland Scholarship in 1947 and made him *proxime accessit* for the Hertford[45] was displayed in editorial and textual work on Greek texts throughout his career. Although he ranged widely across fields and, like Finley, wrote with broad audiences in mind, his roots were very much in the philological tradition. Finley had come to the classical world quite late in his education, as a PhD student at Columbia, after taking a degree in Psychology from Syracuse University and an MA in Public Law from Columbia.[46] He taught ancient history at Rutgers University from 1948, but was dismissed in 1952 for political reasons (see below) and thereafter made his career in England.[47] As a historian he concentrated on analysing institutions and structures, which he illuminated with perspectives deriving from the social sciences. He deplored what he saw as the stranglehold of classical philology on the study of ancient history in England.[48]

Finley was Trevor-Roper's kind of historian. There are many signs of compatibility between the two men, beyond their rejection of the value of textual criticism. Trevor-Roper, who believed that disciplines needed to be refreshed by voices outside them, and who thought of himself as an outsider to historical studies, identified with Finley's origins as an outsider to classical ones.[49] He identified with Finley's pursuit of 'total history', which sought to combine the accounts of ancient historians with the evidence of fictional texts and material culture to shed light on historical problems.[50] He identified with Finley's popularising streak, which echoed his own.[51] But it was Finley's work on Homer that especially generated Trevor-Roper's interest in him. *The World of Odysseus* was his 'favourite'[52] among recent works of classical scholarship for its use of comparative methodologies.[53] He judged its approach sufficiently consistent with his own historical philosophy to include his review of the book in his *Historical Essays*,[54] which were concerned with historical problems and advocated a broad approach to history.[55] Shortly before publishing the review, Trevor-Roper wrote to Bernard Berenson that he thought the book 'wonderfully good; fresh and clear and illuminating: I have never read anything so fresh and exciting on the Homeric age, and so completely free from pedantry.' Such was his excitement at reading the book that in 1955 he had tried to recruit Finley to Christ Church, only to be pre-empted and outbid by an offer from Cambridge procured by Trevor-Roper's old tutor, D.L. Page, the Regius Professor of Greek.[56] Finley was then a guest lecturer in Britain after his dismissal from Rutgers in 1952 on the ground that he refused to respond to allegations that he had been a member of the Communist Party when called on to do so before a Senate sub-committee.[57] Although Trevor-Roper, the scourge of Marxist historiography,[58] would not have supported Finley as a paid-up member of the Communist Party, he was prepared to accept him merely as a 'fellow traveller'.[59] He took a more moderate line on Finley's politics in the mid-1950s than Lloyd-Jones did 20 years later, when they mattered less: Lloyd-Jones thought that Finley, the 'Communist interloper', was a 'dedicated Marxist of a rather grim and humourless kind'.[60] In reply Trevor-Roper was still not persuaded: 'As for Moses Finley [...] [*sic*] well, he may be a "communist interloper" and a "tailless fox", but I must admit that I found *The World of Odysseus* exciting nevertheless!'[61]

Secondly, Lloyd-Jones took exception to Trevor-Roper's treatment of Wilamowitz. Lloyd-Jones had a different perception of the specialisation that arose in German classical studies in the later part of the nineteenth century. It had arisen not, as Trevor-Roper maintained, from an attempt to 'mask the remoteness of classics from contemporary reality', but from an interest in studying antiquity in its totality (*Altertumswissenschaft*). The 'danger' of this approach, as Lloyd-Jones saw it, lay in the attempt to study every element of the civilisation in detail.[62] Wilamowitz, for Trevor-Roper the villain of the piece, was for Lloyd-Jones the scholar who had revitalised the broad approach when, around 1870, specialisation was at its worst. Lloyd-Jones similarly resuscitated Fraenkel. He pointed out that, although initially unpopular in Oxford, Fraenkel was eventually welcomed by the classical establishment there. Lloyd-Jones doubted whether Fraenkel's personal faults had reduced the worth of his scholarship.

Thirdly, Lloyd-Jones challenged Trevor-Roper's rejection of the value of textual criticism. He argued that 'we still have to have some people capable of judging a reading, in order to have proper texts of the main authors, and in order to make sure that their words are rightly understood.'[63] Similarly, he disliked the impression that Trevor-Roper had given that 'all emendation is fraud'. Trevor-Roper had claimed that the frequency of errors of omission was 'the cause of many corruptions in ancient manuscripts. With that assumption', he continued, 'all the "palmary emendations" from Scaliger to Housman disappear, like piffle before the wind.'[64] Lloyd-Jones regarded this deduction as 'ignorant and superficial' and hoped that Trevor-Roper would not print it.[65]

In response to Lloyd-Jones's letter, Trevor-Roper altered his text to allow for the flourishing of scholarship and culture in Germany in the first half of the nineteenth century, toned down his judgement on textual criticism and added a minor concession about Fraenkel (see below). But his portrait of Wilamowitz remained essentially the same, and in fact he sharpened its rhetorical colour.[66] Trevor-Roper's main line of defence lay in the subjectivity of his impressions: his aim had not been to offer an objective account of the state of classical studies, but an essay in autobiography. He claimed that he was not judging Wilamowitz's work or attempting to represent its true content, but seeking to convey 'juvenile' impressions which, he reminds Lloyd-Jones, he had stressed were 'no doubt erroneous' and 'irrational': 'the figures of Wilamowitz and Housman were to me stereotypes, not realities.'[67] His revisions emphasised these points still further: 'We all dramatise our past. No doubt my own juvenile judgment was faulty. No doubt I read the wrong works of Wilamowitz. Everyone agrees that Dr Fraenkel mellowed greatly in later years. But still ...'[68]

Trevor-Roper's claim in his 'Apologia' that he had not read a word of Greek for several years after transferring his studies to History was misleading.[69] In fact he had continued to study Classics, at a very high level, for two terms after 1934.[70] His first publication, produced at the end of his undergraduate career, was an essay entitled 'Homer Unmasked!', in which his love of classical literature is manifest.[71] But it also parodies traditional classical scholarship. Evaluating Homer's knowledge of horses and racing in the *Iliad*, Trevor-Roper declared that he had solved the 'Homeric Question': Homer was a bookie who 'saw life steadily and saw it from a collapsible stool on the racecourse', not with the outlook of 'the snobbish racing journalist, Pindar, who always wore spats and liked to be seen chatting to tyrants in the Club Enclosure'.[72] Trevor-Roper's couching of conventional argumentation in a jocular tone supplies a clever parody of classical scholarship. His eccentric solution was inspired by Samuel Butler, the author of *Erewhon*, in whom Trevor-Roper was then greatly interested. In *The Authoress of the Odyssey* (1897) Butler had proposed that the *Odyssey* was composed by a Sicilian woman from Trapani who wrote herself into the text as Nausicaa, princess of Scheria.[73] Butler, too, was critical of a narrow philological approach to the Classics. 'Homer Unmasked!' also looked forwards. Trevor-Roper's historical interest in Homer placed him on the same intellectual trajectory as Finley, who, 20 years later, would read Homer for historical purposes in *The World of Odysseus*.

Trevor-Roper was inspired by Butler's *Note-Books* to keep ones of his own during the war.[74] In their reflections on life, people and books, they bear witness to his determination to sustain his intellectual life during service in military intelligence that could be tedious and frustrating.[75] They offer rich testimony to Trevor-Roper's love of classical literature and appreciation of classical literary style. The title that he gave them advertises this intellectual interest at the start of the enterprise: πτερόεντα, 'winged (words, thoughts)', from Homer's ἔπεα πτερόεντα.[76] In an entry of 1942, Trevor-Roper records that since the start of the war he had reread 'all Homer, Pindar, Thucydides, Lucretius, [and] Horace'.[77] They are only some of the ancient writers who populate the notebooks. Later ones are Augustine and, from the sixth century, Procopius and Pseudo-Dionysius the Areopagite.

The notebooks drew on classical authors to characterise and elevate scenes in the countryside. Horace, for example, complemented an idyllic morning before a hunt at Ham Green:

> it was a mild morning, and I walked abroad, and the fields were still dewy and the bare woods black, dead black, against the white morning sky; and I sat on a gate, my senses dwelling on the scene, and read in my pocket Horace of the pastoral world of Calabria, and Liris, now Garigliano, the silent stream, and Galaesus, and the creaking oakwoods of Garganus.[78]

Horace came to mind, too, in delicious moments of pastoral solitude,[79] but it is perhaps the picturesque entry on Coldingham in Berwickshire which best captures the classicism of Trevor-Roper's appreciation of pastoral solitude:

> There I would take the dogs out, with or without a gun, and walk out of the wood and over the moor; or I would go to the top of the wood, and from the eminence there would overlook a vast distance bounded by the Cheviots on one hand and by the Lammermuirs on the other, and in front by the sea. In that clear air, all the autumn colours stood out, the colours of golden corn standing in the fields, or stubble-fields dotted with cornshocks, or green pasture, or moor in heather-flower; and there was a pastoral loneliness, that most exquisite loneliness, that Lucretius so happily describes [at 5.1387]
>
> > Per loca pastorum deserta atque otia dia
>
> that is emphasised rather than broken by the noise of rooks and pigeons and curlews.[80]

The countryside and its fauna produced some of Trevor-Roper's most beautiful writing, and they would endure in his stylistic repertoire as a source of metaphor and analogy.

Trevor-Roper was interested in classical language and literary forms as part of his quest to cultivate his own literary style under the inspiration of his mentor Logan Pearsall Smith.[81] His favourite Latin prose authors, he wrote in a notebook in March 1944, were Apuleius and Augustine, those 'baroque' authors who 'recreated their Latin language in its long sterility'.[82] After Smith had revealed to his young friend that adverbs were the secret of style, Trevor-Roper learnt that Apuleius had made the same discovery in the Latin tongue. When he wrote a Bodleian oration in 1946, he took Apuleius for his model and 'contrived to include no less than 73 adverbs'.[83] Influenced by such innovation and linguistic richness, Trevor-Roper advocated a more general use in English of Latin abstract neuter nouns ending in *-um* in preference to adjectives ending in -ousness,[84] and embellished his own classical style with baroque Latinate vocabulary. In a wartime notebook, for example, the prose style of John Henry Newman is characterised as 'majestic, but deliquescent, – an old eighteenth-century mansion in Ireland, derelict and forlorn among the silent superstitious bogs and hills'.[85] The *recherché* 'deliquescent' complements the pastoral, period metaphor which it introduces. It also points the contrast with Gibbon's style in the same passage: 'firm, spacious, and technically faultless; like a stately eighteenth-century house, the mansion of an English duke'.[86]

Trevor-Roper reflected on the problems of literary form in his wartime notebooks. It was a sign of greatness, he wrote, 'so to have perfected a form or technique that posterity can do no more with it'.[87] When Augustans such as Virgil and Horace took up and perfected in Latin the metres that the Greeks had mastered, 'their successors just went on churning them out – Statius, Lucan, Valerius Flaccus, Silius Italicus, Ausonius, Claudian, successive generations of dreary hacks'.[88] Trevor-Roper ruminated in the same passage on new prose forms.[89] He regarded Augustine's *Confessions* as a masterpiece, 'because, by toil and sweat, through lonely vigils and intellectual agony, he imposed a unity on his fierce, recalcitrant, tumultuary imaginings, and wrought a new vessel capable of holding them'.[90] Trevor-Roper's classical interests informed his thinking on problems which he would face in his own historical projects. One book that he was already planning was a 'History of the English Ruling Classes', from the Tudor period to the present, but he was baffled by the challenge of imposing form on 'so vast a subject'.[91] In the following decade he would struggle with the problem of marrying narrative and social analysis in writing a study of the English Puritan Revolution.[92] He would put both projects aside, defeated in part by the problem of form.

In so self-conscious an enterprise as the wartime notebooks – he even compiled an index to them – Trevor-Roper's classicism helped to elevate pleasurable moments in the country and to stimulate his cultivation of style.

Although he sustained his historical interests during the war, he had no opportunity for historical writing. After the war he resumed it. Henceforth his classicism, which in wartime had found mainly a literary expression, would work its way into his writings on modern subjects and supply formidable analogical and metaphorical weaponry.

Trevor-Roper returned to the deficiencies of contemporary classical scholarship in his inaugural lecture of November 1957 as Regius Professor of Modern History at Oxford. As in his later 'Apologia' he had Eduard Fraenkel in his sights. Arguing that the humanities owed 'their title to existence to the interest and comprehension of the laity',[93] Trevor-Roper advocated popularisation in preference to a specialisation that pursued perfect knowledge. In 'classical studies',

> what has happened is not that the subject has lost its value but that a humane subject has been treated as an exact science: professional classical scholars have assumed that they are teaching only other professional classical scholars; consequently they have killed the classics. When I see a Greek Tragedy, one of the greatest works of human literature, a tragedy no longer than a single book of *Paradise Lost*, put out into the world with a commentary of three large octavo volumes round its neck, weighing in all nearly half a stone, I fear the poor thing will not get far: it will languish and die, die of strangulation and neglect in some corner of a forgotten bookshelf.[94]

The work in question was Fraenkel's recent edition of Aeschylus' *Agamemnon*, 'the most detailed commentary ever devoted to a Greek book', as Lloyd-Jones would describe it.[95] Trevor-Roper warned historians to avoid the same pitfall and advocated rendering research accessible to lay audiences. Here they could take a more positive lesson from a different aspect of current classical publication:

> if an interest in the classics survives today, apart from subsidies they enjoy from the past, that may well be due to the enterprise of Sir Allen Lane and his Pelican books, where they appear, purged of otiose learning, reanimated by lay interest, than to the heavy cosseting of professional scholars.[96]

It was an elegant point of symmetry with the 'Apologia' that by 1973 Finley's *World of Odysseus* was appearing as a Pelican book.[97] In his inaugural, as well as in the 'Apologia', Trevor-Roper extolled the role of intellectual outsiders. They had stimulated historical studies since the eighteenth century, and could continue to do so now.

Few would now disagree with the demands that Trevor-Roper made of classical scholars: that they should have broad intellectual horizons; that they should be open to methodologies from outside the discipline; that they should study literature in its historical context; and that they should make the fruits of their research intelligible to lay audiences. Less convincing was his rejection of the value of textual criticism. Here Lloyd-Jones was right. A long tradition of philological scholarship underpinned the editions that allowed Trevor-Roper to enjoy classical authors and historians such as Finley to use literary texts to illuminate ancient societies, and philological methodologies are required to render useful new discoveries on vellum, papyrus, stone and bronze. Trevor-Roper's manoeuvre of celebrating the work of Dodds and Finley in opening up new vistas in the study of antiquity merely sidestepped the fate of classical philology by moving the emphasis to historical studies. He disparaged philologists and editors, and had no positive advice for them.

Trevor-Roper was, nonetheless, deeply indebted to the philological tradition that he mocked. It was an immersion in the language of the classical world, not in its history, that had brought him to love Greek and Latin literature. His schooling created habits and pleasures of reading that would never leave him. He read Sophocles' *Oedipus Coloneus* for the first time during the Christmas vacation of 1962–3 as part of a resolution to read and reread the Greek tragedians: 'I must go quietly through the whole canon, even if I fall behind in the latest historical periodicals.'[98] Homer, Virgil and Horace were his constant companions. As Master of Peterhouse he had a copy of Virgil bound as a prayer book for reading during chapel services.[99] In 1988, not long after retiring from Peterhouse, when asked on the BBC Radio 4 programme *Desert Island Discs* to name a book other than the Bible and Shakespeare that he would wish to have on his island, he replied, 'the works of Virgil' on the ground that they were infinitely rereadable. His choice led to an invitation to become president of the Virgil Society for 1989–90.[100] His presidential address demonstrated his commitment to reading texts in their historical and intellectual contexts. Above all it illustrated his sensitivity to literary style. In saluting Virgil as the high point of Latin poetry, he asked what quality had enabled him to assert his 'invincible superiority'. The answer was style: 'where else in world literature can we find such economy, such flexibility, of language, such supreme artistry in its manipulation, such musical sensitivity, such sustained elevation.'[101] For Trevor-Roper true appreciation of Virgil rested on knowledge of Latin. At the end of his address he offered Dryden's warning of 'the sacrilege of translating Virgil' as a clear lesson for 'lovers of literature': 'we must not allow the study and knowledge of the Latin language to die.'[102] With that, at least, Lloyd-Jones would have strongly agreed.

12

The Historian as Public Intellectual[1]

Rory Allan

Writing in 1981 in the 'Foreword' to the *Festschrift* marking Hugh Trevor-Roper's retirement from the Regius Chair of Modern History at Oxford, Hugh Lloyd-Jones noted that his friend and fellow Regius Professor wrote on

> a wide variety of subjects and problems not merely for his fellow-scholars but for the public reader [...]. Only narrow specialists could maintain that the time spent upon his many contributions to magazines and newspapers has been wasted; they have been of untold benefit to the general reader, and unlike most writings of this kind are well able to stand the test of time.[2]

Trevor-Roper's 'many contributions' were more than ephemeral journalism, capturing the incidental atmosphere of the moment; rather, they were expressions of a historical philosophy. It was a historical philosophy closely aligned to many of the premises of the eighteenth-century 'philosophic historians'. Like them, Trevor-Roper maintained that ideas and patterns of human behaviour are not locked in chronological cages, but spill over boundaries of time and place to speak of universal truths gleaned from the variety of human experience. Like them, he saw contemporary problems within historical contexts, saw that the lessons of history are of public use and saw the duty of the historian to be the eloquent broker of those lessons to a public readership. Because the patterns of the past were visible in the present, history was a participant in the contemporary world and historians could widen their readers' horizons. As he wrote in 1972, 'All great historians are to some extent contemporary historians [...]. History is asking questions [...] and the particular questions which men ask about the past must depend, to some extent, upon the problems which they face in the present.'[3] Such an approach challenged the normal assumptions of professional history. Most of its practitioners write for one another rather than for public instruction. They rarely venture beyond their periods or subjects to formulate and risk historical generalisations. Trevor-Roper's writings always speak of more than their subject matter, and do so in a prose that differs in its beauty from the ruck of most academic writing. His style enlivened and provoked the public mind. It was for that purpose that Trevor-Roper gave so much of his productive time to journalism, more time perhaps than to any other literary activity.

Trevor-Roper's credo was simple: history spoke with the wisdom of the ages; it illuminated contemporary concerns but was being choked by the dryness of academia. Of course, a great many of his writings rested on a foundation of rigorous historical research, which had to be tested before scholars in particular fields. Yet the more we see the general philosophy that traverses scholarly boundaries the more we can view the essays and the articles as expressions of the same rigorous mind, controlled by that same unifying philosophy. That philosophy was only rarely spelled out. He published no such abstract treatise as E.H. Carr's *What is History?* (a work which anyway affronted his own guiding principles).[4] Normally he was content, as he put it, to allow readers to 'discover' his 'philosophy' from its concrete illustrations.[5] We can best understand it by retracing the steps by which it was developed.

Like many of the most passionate evangelists, Hugh Trevor-Roper was a convert. Having come up to Christ Church, Oxford, as a Classics scholar in 1932, by Trinity term of 1934 he had decided to change to Modern History. This apostasy was not born solely out of intellectual considerations. History was also, for the undergraduate Trevor-Roper, about the future, and there was a practical purpose to the conversion. He had in mind a career in the diplomatic service, and he saw his historical education as the means to secure a Prize Fellowship at All Souls College, then considered the best training-ground for the foreign service examination. It was only after his failure to win a fellowship that he resigned himself to the lot of a research student, with a thesis to write. His entry into historical academic life had not, at least to his own mind, amounted to much: 'I cannot say that my study of history as an undergraduate was very profound';[6] indeed, 'I was trained as a classical scholar not as a historian.'[7] Having been an unorthodox undergraduate he became no less unorthodox a graduate, disdaining both academic earnestness and his allotted supervisor, Canon Claude Jenkins, Professor of Ecclesiastical History, or 'fluffy old Jenkins'.[8] The result of his academic individualism, as Peter Ghosh has noted, was that Trevor-Roper became an 'autodidact: he was unconventional, original, deeply receptive; but he was also uncertain of his path, receptive to conventional as well as unconventional thinking, and subject to false starts and hesitation'.[9]

One false start, and his repudiation of it, form a crucial episode in the intellectual development of the young historian. Recalling his first term as a student of History at Christ Church in 1934, Trevor-Roper told of the time when he was invited into the rooms of a young college tutor – Patrick Gordon Walker – and was convinced of the virtue of the Marxist philosophy of history: 'The vast pageant of history, hitherto so indeterminate, so formless, so mysterious, now had, as it seemed, a beautiful mechanic regularity.'[10] His acceptance of determinist ideas of class struggle was still evident in his contribution to a 1938 debate conducted in the letter pages of the *Spectator*, inaugurated by A.L. Rowse's review of A.L. Morton's *A People's History of England*. In it, Trevor-Roper argued that German Marxists had 'laid the foundations of a new historical system and so changed the basis of historical study'.[11]

Whilst Trevor-Roper and the Marxists both saw history as teaching general lessons, the lessons he learned and taught soon diverged from theirs. His insistence, which ran through his life, on the historical effects of pluralist exchange, freedom of will, and occasionally mere accident, can be traced to his early repudiation of Marxism and the determinism of its mechanistic philosophy.[12] The political circumstances of the late 1930s demonstrated to him, in dramatic form, the poverty of Marx's interpretation of history. For all their claims to predict the future, neither Marx nor his followers had allowed for the violent rise of fascist dictatorships in Europe, and as European war drew nearer, the 'beautiful mechanic regularity' of Marxist history was shattered by contemporary events. It was not enough to dismiss fascism as a doomed anomaly; Trevor-Roper recognised the scale of its threat and saw in the Marxists' failure to perceive it the blindness of their historical philosophy. It was a point to which he would repeatedly revert in the challenges to Marxist history that persisted throughout his career.[13]

Another youthful rejection, no less stark, of ideological dogma would have equally enduring consequences for his historical thinking. The 1930s were a time of religious revival and conversion; England alone saw some 12,000 Catholic converts each year.[14] In Oxford, Catholic proselytisers, with their newly built Oxford headquarters, Campion Hall, located just across the road from Christ Church, targeted its young representatives of the ruling classes, whom it hoped to make into leaders of the faith as well as of the nation. As an undergraduate, Trevor-Roper himself was courted by the new Master of Campion Hall, Father Martin D'Arcy. In retrospect, the anticlerical Christ Church trio of *enfants terribles*, Gilbert Ryle, A.J. Ayer and Trevor-Roper, may seem to have been blazing a rationalist trail through a somnolent ecclesiastical landscape. Yet Christ Church was at heart an insular clerical community, dominated by its chapter of dean and canons. In such a setting, the course of Trevor-Roper's intellectual development looks maverick. In his wartime notebooks, he recalled a moment walking around Christ Church Meadow when 'I suddenly realised the undoubted truth that metaphysics are metaphysical, and having no premises to connect them to this world, need not detain us while we are denizens of it.'[15] With this epiphany, he began to see the clergy as 'parasites on the credulity of the mob',[16] and to see in clerical authority what he had already witnessed in political fascism and would come to observe again in communism: the suppression of intellectual freedom and truth.[17] The 1930s had been an age of clashes between ideological blocs that echoed discordantly amongst the cloistered quadrangles of Oxford: 'in the ivory tower of British universities the epicurean hedonism and flamboyant aestheticism of the 1920s gave way to radical political agitation.'[18] Looking back on the late 1930s in his unpublished seven-chapter memoir, Trevor-Roper identified it as the period of his intellectual conditioning. Like many of his contemporaries he had been politically awakened. He had visited Germany in 1935, had stood among a braying crowd which he saw lapping up the demagoguery of a Nazi orator, and had been so horrified by what he saw that he vowed never again to visit the country and to cease his study of its language.[19] Yet whereas others of his generation were attracted to ideologies as the basis of political understanding, he found it in history:

> I confess, I am a Whig. I agree with Burke + de T[ocqueville] + Acton and all those other thinkers who, like them, have distrusted unitary doctrine and centralised authority and positive, universal political theories, whether 'right' or 'left'. I believe in organic societies, with plural organs, historically developed, conscious of their past.[20]

He brought that conviction to the study of past as well as present ideological confrontations. It was in writing on the closed doctrinal systems of the Reformation, and on the 'Erasmian tradition' that repudiated those mental prisons, that he argued that 'the idea of ideological blocs systematically opposed to one another in intellectual matters is a naïve idea such as can only occur in doctrinaires and bigots.'[21] Similarly, his disgust at the rank doctrinarism of the Congress for Cultural Freedom, organised by the Ford Foundation in 1950, at which he was a delegate, led him to conclude that 'it was simply Wroclaw [the 1948 'World Congress of Intellectuals in Defence of Peace'] in reverse.'[22] Whether it was the Catholic Inquisition's suppression of dissent or the Cold War's paranoid dogma, Trevor-Roper's stance was the same: he was a pluralist. This was a general philosophy that conditioned his subsequent philosophy of history.

Trevor-Roper's wartime journals show the development of his more mature reflections upon history to have taken place in the years of the Second World War. Indeed, 'it was only after my book on Laud was published [in 1940] that I really began to think about history.'[23] As Trevor-Roper himself acknowledges in his notebook of 1940–2, a great 'revolution' in his intellectual development occurred in 1940,

> when I became a friend of Logan Pearsall Smith, under whose influence I discovered that this solid, austere research [for the book on Laud] [...] was, after all, compatible with a faith in literary style, – a faith which, somewhat neglected during the period of research, took note again and blossomed in the cracks and interstices of the rocky experience of war.[24]

The first, and surely the most important, work of history Trevor-Roper consulted in 1940 was Edward Gibbon's *Decline and Fall*.[25] Reading it shaped Trevor-Roper the historian, for it bridged the gap between his general pluralist philosophy and the more specific philosophy of history he was to develop. In Gibbon he saw reflected his own values, for Gibbon demonstrated that 'only free competition, free interchange of goods and ideas, could ensure continuity of progress against the opposite tendency of centralisation which caused human ingenuity and wealth to be invested in mere power, propaganda, war or display.'[26]

But his enthusiasm for Gibbon was more than the thrill of discovering an ally; it was the thrill of discovering a teacher. For Gibbon showed him, in epic form, how he might achieve the ambition Pearsall Smith had instilled within him: 'to solve intellectual problems and present my solutions in satisfying aesthetic form'.[27] Trevor-Roper had first encountered Gibbon as part of his classical training,[28] before becoming a historian. He had responded to *Decline and Fall* as Gibbon's eighteenth-century readers, a pre-professional audience, had been invited to do: to the epic narrative, the pleasing literary style, the enlightened philosophy. Gibbon was engaged in disseminating ideas of mind to the general reading classes, and the Trevor-Roper who identified with him was the man who stated in his inaugural lecture as Regius Professor that 'the humane subjects [...] exist primarily not for the training of professionals, but for the education of laymen.'[29] Literary style was the instrument of that education. It was more than just ornament to Trevor-Roper; it was the means of conveying ideas to a general audience. Vivid metaphors and pictorial imagery were not only easy on the ear, but brought ideas more compellingly and strikingly before the mind; they blended beauty with lucidity, pleasure with purpose. As he wrote in 1942, 'I can't understand anything that I can't present to my imagination in pictorial form; and when I comprehend anything vividly, it's always in the terms of some visual image.'[30] The power of language to recreate the feelings and textures of past ages was the means by which past human experience was received and understood by the imagination. It was also the means by which the 'great gulf' between succeeding generations was bridged.[31]

Admirer of eighteenth-century 'philosophic historians' as he was, Trevor-Roper found some of them more sympathetic than others. He was repelled by the crudities of Voltaire's historical writing because Voltaire, in contrast to Gibbon, had a 'vicious method of separating the various aspects of history into distinct chapters when in fact they are causally connected'.[32] Besides, as Trevor-Roper's essay on 'The Romantic Movement and the Study of History'[33] reminds us, he saw that the early nineteenth-century Romantic reaction against Enlightenment history, and the imaginative reconstruction of the past by such figures as Sir Walter Scott, has added a new dimension to the study of the past. Trevor-Roper's own writing blends the two approaches, eliding the philosophical reflection of Enlightenment history with the gift of transporting the reader to particular eras and their particular textures. It is a rare if not unique combination. He addressed the imagination as well as the intellect of the reader, and always the engagement and education of a public rather than academic reader are in his mind. In his writing he *speaks* to us, in prose that profits from being read aloud, so that what we read on the page echoes in our ears as a chorus of written and oral harmony. Many of his most striking essays began their lives as public lectures, and in them the frequency of rhetorical devices is palpable. Open any of his essays and before long you find yourself being addressed with a rhetorical question.[34] The entitlements and pleasures of the reader are at the heart of his inaugural lecture as Regius Professor, which was both an argument for style's value as the means of rendering history appealing to the public, as well as a glittering demonstration of how to do so. His valedictory lecture would in turn remind us that effective language is 'the necessary vehicle and sole preservative, for us, both of history and of imagination'.[35] As he wrote to his friend and former tutor Sir John Masterman: 'if one looks at the admittedly great historians, one finds that they all had style as well. It goes with the character, as the bouquet goes with the wine, inseparable if the substance be good.'[36]

Trevor-Roper's lectures on Gibbon are perhaps the most revealing of his own historical philosophy that he ever gave; his reflections on a great historian tell us what Trevor-Roper thought constituted a great historian. 'The historical greats' write,

> not only for their own contemporaries, but for us. And they write not only about their chosen periods – Gibbon about the late Roman Empire and the Middle Ages, Macaulay about 17th century England – but, implicitly, about their periods, about all periods.[37]

So too did Trevor-Roper; his essay on Erasmus can be read as a plea for an end to warring Cold War ideologies,[38] just as his essay on seventeenth-century art sees Hitler invoked as a comparison.[39] Since the laws of history prevail in the present as much as in the past, the true historian is no less curious about it:

> However remote his subject, however erudite his sources, Gibbon never forgets he is a man of the world, and of the eighteenth-century world at that. He loved polite conversation, society [...] he is interested in everything around him; his information on all topics is up-to-date.[40]

Replace the eighteenth with the twentieth century, and this is Trevor-Roper.

Because 'philosophical historians' traced in their works trans-historical truths, their histories became timeless; they were permanent philosophies which are not invalidated by incidental errors of fact or temporary prejudices. History should be practised with a philosophical awareness of a historical continuum of ideas, for 'the interest of history lies not in its periods but in its problems,'[41] and consequently it abjures narrowness. As John Robertson has noted, Trevor-Roper's interests did vary over time, moving from the seventeenth century to Enlightenment historiography and back again.[42] These, however, are changes in the manifestations of a consistent historical philosophy. As his career progressed he discovered new fields which illuminated and confirmed it – Erasmus's pluralism and Burckhardt's *Ahnung* (the capacity 'to see the present lying in the past')[43] being obvious examples – but he saw in them not something new to him; rather he was giving new expression to a philosophy that derived from the Enlightenment and that he pursued throughout history. In the preface to the 1957 collection *Historical Essays*, Trevor-Roper set himself up as the heir to the 'philosophic historians', noting that 'Essays like these, various in time, depth and subject, can only bear republication if they receive an underlying unity from the philosophy of the writer.'[44] It was from Gibbon, the broker of his apostasy, that Trevor-Roper adopted the elements that constituted that philosophical unity: literary style, public edification, contemporary engagement, philosophic history. To a great extent, to understand Trevor-Roper's interpretation of Gibbon is to understand Trevor Roper's conception of history. Thomas Carlyle's comment on Gibbon could equally have been uttered by Trevor-Roper: 'Gibbon is a man whom one never forgets – unless oneself deserving to be forgotten; the perusal of his work forms an epoch in the history of one's mind.'[45]

As we have seen, Trevor-Roper was no ordinary historian. The university historian's ordinary arena, bound by the conventional quadrangle of the tutorial, the lecture theatre, the academic journal and the learned book, was only a part of the man. He demanded that history be made to live in the present, that history be used: 'History that is not useful, that has not some lay appeal, is mere antiquarianism.'[46] History was an active participant in contemporary life; if the internal struggle of Palestine, the 'mystical fanatics on the left struggling against the realist revolutionaries on the right after the initial military victory', was 'just like the development of revolutionary politics in Cromwell's time',[47] then a historian of the seventeenth century might yet become an insightful observer of the Middle Eastern scene. Even on so topical a subject as the 1977 Bill for Scottish devolution, Trevor-Roper's perspective reached back to the Scottish Enlightenment.[48] We know that Trevor-Roper believed in the power of philosophic history to articulate universal causal laws; we know too that, whilst never over-pressing examples, and sensitive to their imperfections and limitations, he believed 'in parallels in history – what happened in the fourth century B.C. can throw light on the twentieth century'.[49] Such thinking rendered the historian a contemporary commentator, but it should also render a contemporary commentator a historian, and Trevor-Roper was unforgiving of those who professed to understand the present without a historical awareness of its historical formation.[50] Such a calling was more than mere indulgence; it was the historian's duty. Yet again, as of Gibbon, so of Trevor-Roper:

> Gibbon believed [...] in *virtù*, in the public spirit, the spirit of freedom, of public service by the subjects or citizens of a state [...] only the republican virtues of active, responsible citizenship, only free competition, free interchange of goods and ideas, could ensure continuity of progress.[51]

If history had its use in contemporary affairs, the historian had his use in being the midwife of that possibility and it was his civic responsibility to do so. According to Trevor-Roper, it was this application of historical understanding to the demands of present-day statesmanship, together with the capacity to give it eloquent expression, that made Clarendon a great historian: 'he had an empirical insight into the working of contemporary politics; he had a profound historical philosophy, and he had a magnificent style.'[52]

Above Trevor-Roper's desk there hung a portrait of the man he called 'the Prince of the Humanists', Erasmus, whom he revered not only for his capacity for thought but for his capacity to address both the 'professional' and the 'lay' reader. Humane subjects 'owe their title to existence to the interest and comprehension of the laity'.[53] He wanted, as he said during his appearance on BBC Radio 4's *Desert Island Discs*, to eradicate the kind of history that was a 'boring private subject for the specialists themselves only, who forget altogether about the public'.[54] Trevor-Roper often played truant from his professional academic life, a burden of which he frequently despaired in his letters to Bernard Berenson.[55] The period of his amplest journalism was the Cold War, when the public looked to intellectuals as interpreters of an explicitly ideological conflict. As he recalled of the period in the manuscript of his memoir,

> These post-war years saw a great outpouring of vapours in the press about the new philosophy which was to revive our civilisation after the welcome defeat of Nazism and the less welcome advance of Russian communism in Eastern Europe. These events had heated something of an intellectual void which needed to be filled.[56]

It was in this context that Trevor-Roper published in a weekly magazine, the *New Statesman*, and republished within the hard covers of his *Historical Essays*, his essay 'A Case for Co-Existence: Christendom and the Turks', which sets the relationship between two warring yet interacting sixteenth-century powers against the ideological division of twentieth-century Europe.[57]

As Noël Annan has noted in his analysis of the intellectual world of postwar Britain, 'the years 1945–1975 were the golden age of the don. The boffins had captured the public imagination.'[58] Historical writing enjoyed a singularly high public profile in this period, with academics such as A.J.P Taylor, Isaiah Berlin and Trevor-Roper using the national and international media as their lecture halls. They were stars enough to claim the attention of the *New Yorker*, which in 1962 sent the Indian writer Ved Mehta to write a two-part piece on the renowned 'English Historians'.[59] Their profile was further raised by television; in May 1963 a BBC internal memorandum to the controller of programmes reported that Trevor-Roper had enthusiastically proposed giving a televised series of lectures on 'grand historical subjects': 'The Fall of Rome', 'The Reformation', 'The Renaissance' and so on. As the memorandum continued, 'no one is better than he at taking such huge subjects and making them absorbingly interesting.'[60] The lecture-series which emerged and appeared on television in late October 1963 was rather different but no less ambitious, a survey of a period of 1,100 years, which he went on to publish first in the *Listener* and then in 1965 as a book, *The Rise of Christian Europe*.[61] In the same year, Trevor-Roper gave the Trevelyan Lectures on 'Whig and Tory History', which again he eschewed publishing in academic form. Instead he broadcast abbreviated versions of them to a general audience on BBC Radio and published them in the *Listener*.[62] With the same instinct he joined the television programme *The Brains Trust*, a discussion panel with an audience of more than ten million that regularly featured such thinkers as A.J. Ayer, Noël Annan and Alan Bullock.[63] But the bulk of his work for a general audience was in newsprint. He became a regular contributor to the *New Statesman*, a publication that could boast a readership of 'nearly half-a-million thinking people',[64] from the late 1940s. From the mid-1950s he was held on retainer by the *Sunday Times* to write book reviews and 'special articles', for which he travelled across the world writing historically minded appraisals of overseas politics or such sensational events as the Eichmann Trial.[65] He also wrote for the *New York Review of Books* from the mid-1960s for the rest of his working life. Now that the historical essay has given way to the scholarly article, Trevor-Roper's attitude towards a professional historian's audience seems to belong to a past age.[66] His inaugural and valedictory lectures read, in retrospect, like laments for its passing. The inaugural bears resemblances, even in its metaphors, to G.M. Trevelyan's *Clio: A Muse*, itself a work of a receding generation. Like Trevor-Roper, Trevelyan insisted that 'if historians neglect to educate the public, if they fail to interest it intelligently in the past, then all their historical learning is valueless.'[67] Yet there was nothing backward-looking about Trevor-Roper's commitment to the public duties of a historian, or about his regret at the widening chasm between the public and academia. To him, the *raison d'être* of humane subjects was permanent.

Consequently, it is a mistake to ignore Trevor-Roper's journalistic output and a vulgar one to suggest, as Bruce McFarlane did, that there were two Trevor-Ropers: the historian and the journalist.[68] Trevor-Roper never divorced the two categories. Though he could be scornful of 'journalists' who lacked historical grounding or instincts, his own journalism takes its depth from his historical knowledge and reflection, just as his historical scholarship is informed by reflection on the present. Any division must surely be one of medium, not content. Remarkable powers of scholarship underlie his collections of essays. Yet in the first of them, *Historical Essays*, only one is taken from an academic journal. One apiece is taken respectively from the magazines *Encounter*, *Commentary*, the *Spectator* and the *Times Literary Supplement*, four from *History Today*, and the remaining 33 from the *New Statesman*.[69] Similarly, later volumes of essays, such as his 1985 *Renaissance Essays* and the 1992 collection *From Counter-Reformation to Glorious Revolution*, are taken from such diffuse sources as the *New York Review of Books, Horizon* and a radio broadcast.[70] As the Dacre Papers in the Christ Church Archive attest, his journalistic articles were not hastily written affairs. They were the product of a serious and erudite level of research and reading; the clippings of his newsprint casually rest atop folders erupting with notes from books read at the Bodleian, articles and scholarly references. Trevor-Roper was no enemy of exhaustive scholarship, for it was only through rigorous research that history was refreshed and transformed. He applauded the work of historians such as Frances Yates for deriving broad conclusions from closely detailed research.[71] He followed Gibbon in insisting that 'all historical writing must rest firmly on a base of genuine erudition [...] the exclusive cult of facts led to pedantry, but the neglect of them is fatal.'[72] But, like Gibbon, he demanded that such research expand horizons, not contract them; 'private expertise' may refine knowledge, but it could also suffocate it.[73] Professional theologians of the sixteenth century may well have derided Erasmus – 'today they would accuse him of journalism' – but one can readily understand

Trevor-Roper's identification with him: 'in fact he used professional methods – more professional than theirs – but directed by a lay spirit.'[74]

The marriage of scholarly investigation and public impact was most strikingly achieved in the most widely read of his writings, *The Last Days of Hitler* (1947), a work that in Peter Ghosh's words 'is not journalism, though it lies close to it',[75] and is a 'historiographical classic'.[76] Trevor-Roper constructed a book that would have sensational lay appeal – it had begun its public life as a briefing to the assembled journalists at the Hotel am Zoo in Berlin on 1 November 1945, entitled 'The Last Days of Hitler and Eva Braun' – yet was an impressive work of almost instant *history*. Even though the events he analysed were so recent, Trevor-Roper saw that he had the opportunity to produce an accurate historical account:

> The theatre [of events] in which the action took place was closed; the actors were few and known; there were no seats for the public or the press; no reviews; no bulletins. The primary documents were few, and these were in my hands. Theoretically therefore the story could be told without fear of later correction.[77]

The book he then wrote remains in print to this day and despite the profusion of subsequent studies of the time, the picture first drawn by Trevor-Roper remains significantly unaltered.[78] A.J.P. Taylor, in reviewing the volume, noted that it was 'a book sound in scholarship, brilliant in its presentation, a delight for historian and layman alike'.[79]

From Taylor, Trevor-Roper's closest rival, this was generous recognition. Yet Taylor's own writings for a lay audience suffer by comparison with Trevor-Roper's. He too was an academic historian who wrote in the popular press. But his popular writings earned him a degree of obloquy never visited on Trevor-Roper, and saw him pilloried by his critics as 'the motoring correspondent of the *Sunday Express*'.[80] Disapproval of Taylor's articles for the paper – his boyish pieces on the pleasures of speeding from which the sneer arose – is sometimes cited as the reason he was turned down for the Stevenson Chair in International History at the London School of Economics in 1952, and lost out on the Regius Professorship to Trevor-Roper in 1957.[81] Whilst both men certainly valued the financial income of their newspaper work, Taylor's articles lacked the moral and intellectual purposes of Trevor-Roper's. No consistent line is evident in Taylor's mischievous journalism, which he himself airily dismissed as 'rubbish'.[82] Taylor said it himself: 'As I once wrote about Bernard Shaw, I had a great gift of expression and nothing to say.'[83] His style sacrifices nuance to the thrill of epigrammatic embroidery. Whereas for Trevor-Roper the media represented an important tool of communication between scholars and the public, for Taylor it was a toy. The difference was that Taylor was an historian who also wrote for the public. To Trevor-Roper the roles were inseparable — it was, for him, part of the job.

13

The Prose Stylist

John Banville

'In literature we move through a blest world in which we know nothing except by style, but in which everything is saved by it.' That was Henry James, writing encouragement to himself in his notebooks. It is an assertion which Hugh Trevor-Roper would surely have agreed with and approved. Some historians consider that a scholar should not possess a fine writing style. If we notice the style in which history is written, they will say, then the prose may be admirable but the history will inevitably be bad. Trevor-Roper would have none of this. 'I find more pleasure in good literature,' he declared, 'than in dull (even if true!) history.'[1] Again, this will be a scandal to some.

As a prose stylist he most admired Francis Bacon, Donne, Hobbes, Sir Thomas Browne, Gibbon and, perhaps surprisingly, Flaubert, and, perhaps more surprisingly, George Moore. Stylistically, his nearest though laggardly competitor among his contemporaries would have been Evelyn Waugh, who loathed him personally – they both greatly admired Gibbon and sought to emulate his sonorous periods. Among historiographers he had few peers. A.J.P. Taylor, his friendly rival, once remarked that when he read one of Trevor-Roper's essays, tears of envy stood in his eyes.

Trevor-Roper made literature out of history, and what marvellous literature it is. Hard work was the engine that drove his success. By the time his education was finished – if education ever does finish – he had read all the Greek and Latin classics, and much else besides. In 1942, when he was 28, he noted in his journal: 'Since the war began, I have re-read a great deal of literature, including all Homer, Pindar, Thucydides, Lucretius, Horace, and much of Dante, Shakespeare, Milton and Tennyson.'[2] Not read, mind you, but *re*-read. Nor was it all pleasure: as he ruefully observed, a scholar must grind his way through many dusty, dull and even worthless books if his own work is to have the sparkle of mastery.

And sparkle it did, and does. He hated dullness, dry specialisation, the finicking picking-over of dusty trifles. Here he is writing in 1973 to one of his graduate students, Jeremy Cater:

> Above all, *enjoy* writing. It is not always easy to do so. One has to get over the flat somehow. But if one is excited by a subject, or a discovery, one should be able to communicate the excitement; and after all, we write to be read. Why should we expect 'the reader' to read us unless we make some effort to interest him in our wares?'[3]

We write to be read ... Wittgenstein once remarked of himself that he was before anything else a maker of metaphors. One might not go so far as to say the same thing of Trevor-Roper, but what splendid tropes he fashioned. Here is an example, from the Prologue to that curious book, his biography of the Sinologist, pornographer and fantasist, Edmund Backhouse. Backhouse, he wrote,

> was an institution – or rather, since that word implies a certain stability, a continuous furtive presence, like some shy night-animal which lives in a far corner of the park, and has lived there since time out of mind, but is seldom seen, although once or twice, in times of drought or dearth, to the astonishment of all, it has come to the house to be fed.[4]

Writing in 1986 to Alasdair Palmer, a young philosophy graduate whom he had befriended after a chance encounter on a train to Cambridge, Trevor-Roper makes the case against the narrow specialisation that was becoming more and more the norm in academe:

> A scholar, even for the sake of his scholarship, as well as for that of his life, *must* have other interests. Scholarship which is confined to one rut becomes antiquarianism: it needs a context, and the possibility of comparison, and the invigorating infusion of reality, and life.

Later on in the same letter, responding to Palmer's complaints about the narrowness of college affairs, he identifies

> that phenomenon which has come to obsess me: the death of the spirit which threatens every man unless he is conscious of the danger and has a

real purpose which can keep it alive and enable it to thrust its way through the choking weeds and thorns to the air and to the sun.[5]

Trevor-Roper was, like Evelyn Waugh, a master of that technique in which a run of high-flown rhetoric collapses, at the very last moment, into comic bathos. Here is one of his most splendidly sustained metaphors, from that delightful, early work *The Wartime Journals*. He is writing of the durability of the Christian Church, most of the doctrines of which he considered to be nonsense:

> the ease with which, when all the apparent props have been demolished beneath it, the Temple remains suspended in mid-air, while its priests run up alternative supports, of more modern material, suggests that these props, so far from being essential elements of the building, are mere external décor, added by the directors to appease the high-brows; like the architecture of suburban cinemas.[6]

Trevor-Roper revelled in his notion of himself, which not a few of his colleagues shared, as a cantankerous and dangerous, and not infrequently tipsy, wielder of the cudgels. Writing in 1951 to his brother-in-law Dawyck Haig, he declared that

> the physical circulation of the blood is kept going by furious battles on every front, — war against the clergy at home, war against impertinent adversaries abroad, controversies in the learned journals, battles in the university, and of course deep and regular potations of exhilarating champagne and stupefying port.[7]

Nor does he fear consequences, or being called on to deal with them; a little way on in the same letter he contemplates suing an American judge for libel:

> What luck! at once an exhilarating whiff of life has ruffled again the rapidly stagnating pool: the quiet well-feathered nests of lawyers in the discreet legal lanes of WC1 and EC2 are all astir; sharply-worded ultimata are flying hither and thither through those cosy boskages; and the air above Chancery Lane is already thick with the musty odour of horsehair wigs wagged this way and that in learned, sententious altercation.[8]

However, behind Trevor-Roper's carefully maintained pose as a clubbable good fellow, there flourished the soul of an artist, for whom style was 'the true elixir of life'[9] and who found in the world of the Ancient Greeks a 'perpetual intermingling of the human and the divine which makes poetry possible'.[10]

One of Trevor-Roper's earliest literary exemplars was Logan Pearsall Smith, the American essayist and critic. Smith was in his seventies when Trevor-Roper first met him in 1940, an encounter Trevor-Roper later described as a revolutionary event in his life. Smith's family were Philadelphia Quakers, but he had settled permanently in London, where he conducted a famously exclusive and high-toned salon in his apartment in St Leonard's Terrace, Chelsea. He was the author of two little books of ruminations, *aperçus* and witticisms, *Trivia* and *More Trivia*, which were masterpieces of style, and the influence of which is everywhere evident in Trevor-Roper's early writings.

Trevor-Roper had come to Smith's attention after the latter had read the young historian's first book, *Archbishop Laud*. Smith liked to have clever young people, mostly men, about him – his protégés included the critics Cyril Connolly and Raymond Mortimer, the diarist James Lees-Milne and the novelist Rose Macaulay – and in *Archbishop Laud*, despite its muted tones, he had spotted a stylist after his own heart. 'I liked you before I saw you,' Smith wrote to Trevor-Roper a year after they met.[11] Trevor-Roper, who was in his late twenties, also recognised a fellow spirit. The editor of *The Wartime Journals*, Richard Davenport-Hines, writes:

> Smith and his friends knew the corrupting force of slipshod or dishonest words: knew, too, the redemptive humanising power of scrupulous vocabulary. 'The great art of writing is the art of making people real to themselves with words,' he insisted.[12]

When Smith died in 1946, Trevor-Roper paid him a heartfelt tribute, saying that from his friend he had learned everything: 'My whole philosophy seems, now that I consider it retrospectively, to have come from him, and what I would have been without him I cannot envisage, cannot imagine.'[13]

Another eminence in Trevor-Roper's early adult life was the philosopher Gilbert Ryle, whom he had known at Oxford and who worked with him as a wartime code-breaker, greatly relieving the tedium and frustrations of life in the secret service. Ryle was a linguistic philosopher whose 'combination of dialectic tension and conversational magnanimity', Davenport-Hines writes, '– his brisk impatience tempered by occasional vast forbearance – especially attracted Trevor-Roper'.[14] On the acknowledgements page of *Archbishop Laud* Trevor-Roper gave warm thanks to his friend, who read the proofs of the book and 'who, like Eve in Paradise, ranged through the whole wilderness, weeding out the solecisms, trimming the luxuriant phrases, and unmixing the metaphors'.[15]

His attitude to religion was entirely dictated by his social sense. He was, he said, an Anglican, not a Christian, and approved of the Church of England because it supported civil liberty and had 'a certain constitutional relation to common sense'.[16] However, he regarded the fundamental doctrines of Christianity and the other religions as 'trash'.[17] Where Catholicism was concerned, he gave no quarter, seeing that faith and communism as two sides of the same coin, both equally repressive, delusionary and trashy.

It may seem surprising, therefore, that he loved Ireland – 'truly my spiritual home'[18] – though a particular version of the place: mist at morn on hunting fields, jorums of drink, sequestered country houses 'whose peeling walls and overgrown gardens yet preserve a pattern of antique stateliness and hospitality'[19] and in which survived the faded relicts of a finer age. The real Ireland of his day, an agrarian backwater run by priests, petty shopkeepers and small farmers – who, 'triply isolated by geography, neutrality and the censorship [...] live as remote as the dwellers in Tristan da Cunha or the Falkland Islands'[20] – he referred to as 'that floating monkey-house'[21] yet lavished upon it some of his finest rhetorical flourishes:

> Through all our history she clings to us, a poor, half-witted, gypsy relative, defying our improvement, spoiling our appearances, exposing our pretences, an irreclaimable, irrepressible slut, dirty when we are most clean, superstitious when we are most rational, protesting when we are most complacent, and when we are most prosaic, inspired.[22]

He appreciated too the worth of Irish writers such as Yeats and Joyce, who 'saved our language, when it was worn thin and colourless by the use of centuries'.[23] For all that, however, he was an Englishman to the bone, and a Northumbrian in particular – some of the loveliest passages in *The Wartime Journals* are devoted to his native county, which bears surely the most evocative name of all the shires. Yet he is no Little Englander and has only 'burning contempt' for heart-of-oak popular historians such as Arthur Bryant 'and all the others whose intellectual standards were not prized for themselves but as a means to shabby success'.[24]

He was a historian whose interests ranged over the world, and he was as much at ease writing about the Emperor Maximilian I or the doges of Venice as he was in his studies of the English Civil Wars. He had a strong commitment to the European ideal, and many present-day English politicians of the Eurosceptic strain would benefit from a reading of, for instance, Trevor-Roper's masterly study of Erasmus and Christian humanism in the volume *Renaissance Essays*.

In his later career, when he was Regius Professor of Modern History at Oxford, and then Master of Peterhouse, he was frequently criticised for not publishing the great, synthesising book of which all judged him capable. In *The Wartime Journals* he had confidently mapped out such a book. To be called 'A History of the English Ruling Classes', it would begin with 'the silent, patient, nibbling rat-faced country landlords and lawyers of early Tudor days'[25] and end with the faded aristocracy of the modern age, or merely with 'a bare recital of their great houses, now put to public uses, or pulled down, or peeling tenantless, those mausoleums, those cenotaphs, of a vanished race'.[26] What a glory it would have been, that book, and what a sore loss its absence is. It may be, however, that Trevor-Roper's greatness lay in his powers as an essayist, for certainly it was in the essay form that he achieved a breadth of vision and an acuity of insight which the drudgery of a full-length work might have dissipated. Blair Worden had noted that when Trevor-Roper was asked late in life why he had not published more long books, he recalled the remark by Jacob Burckhardt – on whom he wrote a magnificent essay – about the dreary tomes churned out by his contemporaries: 'They forget the shortness of life.'

Trevor-Roper was a snob, as he freely admitted. 'I believe in an élite (but not a static élite)', he wrote, 'for whom there must always be hewers of wood and drawers of water.'[27] All the same, he had no illusions about the aristocracy. Insisting that 'living and manners are an art' and that 'on the whole the upper classes have the best opportunities of perfecting it', he went on:

> Not that they do, – at least nowadays in their decay. When I live among them, and observe the lack of education and values amongst most of them, their dreary pleasures, and the sickening triviality of their lives, I despise them.[28]

Most of the passages quoted so far are from Trevor-Roper's private letters and journals. When he is writing 'in public', in the books, the essays and reviews, he is no less lively, though his professional prose displays a wonderfully steady, burnished sheen that is a constant joy to bask in. He believed absolutely in the power of the written word to capture the most elusive and evanescent of our thoughts and sensations. Writing to his stepson James Howard-Johnston in 1960, when the young man was experiencing the usual worries and insecurities of late adolescence, Trevor-Roper expresses both parental sympathy and his faith in language:

> Let my last words (for the time being) be these: don't be frightened. If in doubt, if in depression, if in anxiety, say so without fear. We have invented language, refined it so that it can express even the subtlest thought, even the obscurest sensations; why then should we not use it, and dissolve difficulties by articulating them?[29]

14

A Conversation

This interview, conducted by Charles Monaghan, appeared under the title 'Portrait of a Man Reading' in the Washington Post *'Book World' on 2 February 1969.*

What is the first book you remember reading?
I was taught to read at the age of four on a book called *Line by Line*, which was based on the Bible. It was broken up into syllables: 'In the be-ginn-ing.' I read whatever I could lay my hands on at home. I lived in the country and there wasn't much. I read everything I could about nature and natural history. I also read Kipling, *Jungle Book*, that sort of thing. An unthinking maiden aunt once gave me a book called *Songs of the Campaign*. I suppose she thought it was some inspiring martial thing. It turned out to be the most macabre poems about death in World War I – complete with illustrations of skeletons. And, of course, I read *Alice in Wonderland*. I know my Lewis Carroll very well.

And at school?
At school I think I read far too much too early. Things I couldn't appreciate. I read too much Dickens at an early age. It spoiled him for me. I first read Sir Walter Scott at school. I feel him to be a very great, neglected writer. *Old Mortality, The Heart of Midlothian* – I have recently read them aloud to my stepchildren. I think Victorian taste has ruined many people's appreciation of Scott. The Victorians liked *Ivanhoe* and *Kenilworth*, the medieval novels. His novels about the seventeenth and eighteenth centuries are much better.

Did you start on history then?
I read a lot of history, but just for pleasure. I remember reading Prescott, and Trevelyan on nineteenth-century England. I read some Spanish history – I learned Spanish at school – and also some Italian medieval history on my own. But I wasn't a historian then. I was a classical scholar. And I continued in classics when I came up to Christ Church, Oxford. I keep up with that. I recently read through the whole of Polybius. And I have been reading some non-classical Latin. Renaissance things. I read the whole of Virgil not long ago. And Homer – I read him often.

What other languages do you read?
French, German, Italian, Spanish, Portuguese. But I haven't a great deal of time for pleasurable reading in them. I seldom read German for pleasure, for instance. If I have to read German things I'd much prefer a translation if one was available. But in French, Italian, Spanish, I prefer the original.

What are your tastes in fiction?
I'm not a great reader of fiction. I read through all of Jane Austen with pleasure. I read through George Eliot at school, but I was too young to appreciate her then. But about a year ago I read *Middlemarch*. Most marvellous book. Best thing in nineteenth-century English fiction, I think. It's on the Russian level. I'm a great admirer of the Russian writers. Above all, Turgenev. I like writers to write well. I would put Turgenev at the top of all novelists. I've read a lot of George Moore and admire his style. And one writer, who is not a novelist but whom I revere, is Charles Doughty. I think his *Arabia Deserta* is a masterpiece. You see, I mind very much about language. I hate slovenly writing. I give my graduate students a very hard time about this. I insist that their theses must be readable. Of course, I don't always succeed.

What are your tastes in poetry?
I have slightly conservative tastes there. For instance, I'm afraid I'm against T.S. Eliot. I recognise his greatness, but I could never read him for pleasure. I dislike the ideas behind his writing. I find them devitalising. I think modern poets don't take enough trouble over words. Gerard Manley Hopkins must be the last one who troubled about words.

How about French poetry?

I don't think the French have ever produced a great poet – those dreadful alexandrine lines. The curious thing is that the Germans had some great poets – at a time when no one else was writing any great poetry. Stefan George and Rilke – I admire them both.

And historians. Who do you think are the great classical historians?

Herodotus, Thucydides, Polybius, Tacitus. I put them all in a little series that I edited for Washington Square Press. My taste runs to the great 'philosophical' historians. I mean they may not be up-to-date in mere scholarship, but their ideas are permanently valuable. Who – except a pedant – would exchange Thucydides for a completely accurate chronicle of the Peloponnesian War?

And after the classical age?

Between the end of the ancient world and the Renaissance, there is no European historian who interests me greatly. After the Renaissance, I'd put Machiavelli, Guicciardini and Sarpi on the list.

Among the English historians?

Clarendon seems to me a great historian – profound as well as vivid and contemporary, but I'd put Gibbon at the top. Then – but much lower – Macaulay.

Among contemporary historians?

Lewis Namier. Among all the historians I've known personally, he had the greatest influence on me. I didn't meet him until after the war. When I wrote *The Last Days of Hitler*, he sent me a letter about it and we corresponded and became great friends. He was at the University of Manchester then.

I greatly admire the present school of French historians. I mean the people who started the periodical *Annales*. Marc Bloch – he was killed by the Germans – Lucien Febvre, Fernand Braudel. They write sociological history and are aware that you can't break up history into little bits – constitutional history, political history and so forth. They avoided the narrow division between ideas and social structure. You know, history is more than the history of human actions. It must include ideas and social change.

How about those who are writing {...} history now?

I admire the work of John Elliott. He's a Cambridge Hispanist who's at London now. I have great respect for Dom David Knowles, the medievalist who just retired as Regius Professor at Cambridge, though we don't agree entirely in our outlook on history. Knowles has done great work, but he is a little ... perhaps conservative is the word. He hasn't made people change their ideas, as Namier did. Another historian for whom I had great friendship and respect, by the way, is Pieter Geyl, the Dutchman who died two years ago. And then, there are the historians of ideas, particularly Frances Yates. I venerate her. She has touched nothing that she has not illuminated – and changed. And she has touched so much.

Among living historians?
W.K. Jordan at Harvard. He's a historian of England in the sixteenth and seventeenth centuries. He's written nothing that isn't frightfully good – and original and exciting. His works on philanthropy open a new aspect of social history.

What kind of history do you like best?
I like historians who work on the frontier between history and literature, or between history and ideas. A classic example is Marcel Bataillon, a Frenchman who wrote *Erasme et L'Espagne*. I venerate that book. It's a great fat book, but I carried it with me all the time as I travelled around Spain. Another man like that is Joseph Needham, who's writing *Science and Civilization in China*. It's still in process. I think five volumes are out. He's no great stylist and I have no doubt that he may be wrong in some matters – certainly his views are highly controversial – but the work is exciting to read. Dullness is the great enemy. Of course, one should try to be right. I have no use for sloppy scholarship, but we all make mistakes, and they don't matter much. Time and the normal processes of scholarship will correct them. In the long run, the errors of great historians are more valuable than the correctitudes of minor historians. What I don't like is potboiler history. You know, a history of the twentieth century by multiple hands. Such books may be useful for reference, but not to read. Books to read should have a tincture of literature and philosophy.

Where is the writing of history going from here?
I think political history is done for the present. There's plenty of material available, but no fresh ideas to invigorate it. I think the immediate future lies in the history of scientific ideas – of ideas generally, including religion. It's frightfully easy to take received ideas for granted, to accept without

thought the temporary orthodoxies of today, which are often the Victorian heresies of yesterday. This may sound a bit vain, but when my latest book of essays, *The Crisis of the Seventeenth Century: Religion, The Reformation and Social Change*, came out, John Elliott wrote and said no one would be able to look at the seventeenth century in the same way again. That delighted me. It was a great compliment, but it's the sort of thing all historians should strive for – to look at something in a different way, not merely to reinterpret old categories. For instance, look at Macaulay. He argued that the Whigs were the party of progress. This became an accepted idea, and although it is now discredited, in the form in which he put it, it has been taken over by the Marxists in a new form which is just as questionable – that one political party is the repository of progress and the other the repository of all reaction. That's the sort of oversimplification that one generation takes from another and that impedes a sensible view of history.

What are you reading now?
Read? I spend my whole time in committees. But I have just finished a huge book on German religious thought in the seventeenth century, marvellously erudite and rather crotchety. And I am now reading my way through the entire correspondence of Hugo Grotius. That is a wonderful experience. That is what I really enjoy. To get inside a great mind working inside a historical context. Of course, I also read books for review, books to keep up with my subject, necessary books. But I prefer real literature, real thought.

Notes

SOC.Dacre is the general classmark of Trevor-Roper's papers in the Christ Church Archive, Oxford.

After their first citations in each chapter, works by Trevor-Roper are normally referred to only by their titles.

Introduction

1 See 'Posthumous Books', in 'The Writings', above.
2 *New York Review of Books*, 15 August 2013.
3 Hugh Trevor-Roper, *The Wartime Journals*, ed. Richard Davenport-Hines (London, 2010), p. 38.
4 Doughty: *Wartime Journals*, pp. 231–7; ballads: ibid., pp. 110–11; *Don Quixote: One Hundred Letters from Hugh Trevor-Roper*, ed. Richard Davenport-Hines and Adam Sisman (Oxford, 2014), pp. 358–9; Scott: SOC.Dacre 1/2/W: 1 October 1969.
5 *Wartime Journals*, p. 80.
6 SOC.Dacre 1/2/W: April 1977.
7 SOC.Dacre 1/1/Pearl: 5 December 1975.
8 SOC.Dacre 17/1: 3 September 1953; 1/2/W: 10 September 1979.
9 *One Hundred Letters*, p. 139. The quoted letter is a literary credo.
10 Harry Ransom Center, Austin, Texas, Gerald Brenan Collection, Correspondence (hereafter Brenan Correspondence): 11 March 1968.
11 *Letters from Oxford: Hugh Trevor-Roper to Bernard Berenson*, ed. Richard Davenport-Hines (London, 2006), p. 48.
12 Warburg Institute Archive, London, Yates Papers, Correspondence: 19 July 1973.
13 Adam Sisman, *Hugh Trevor-Roper: The Biography* (London, 2010), p. 203.
14 SOC.Dacre 1/2/9: 2 July 1965 (Phillips).
15 SOC.Dacre 17/1: 5, 9 April 1954.
16 Sisman, *Hugh Trevor-Roper*, p. 301.
17 *One Hundred Letters*, p. 406.
18 Hugh Trevor-Roper, *History and the Enlightenment*, ed. John Robertson (New Haven, CT, and London, 2010), p. 144.
19 *Wartime Journals*, p. 189.

20 Hugh Trevor-Roper, *Religion, the Reformation and Social Change, and Other Essays* (London, 1967), pp. 205, 216–17.
21 Brenan Correspondence: 11 March 1968.
22 Hugh Trevor-Roper, *Historical Essays* (London, 1957), p. vi.
23 Hugh Trevor-Roper, 'The Past and the Present', *Past and Present* 42 (1969), pp. 3–17, at p. 4.
24 *Wartime Journals*, pp. 50, 52; *Historical Essays*, p. 277.
25 *Wartime Journals*, p. 224.
26 Brenan Correspondence: 11 March 1968; *Historical Essays*, p. 15.
27 *Historical Essays*, pp. v–vi.
28 Ibid., p. 178.
29 Hugh Lloyd-Jones, Valerie Pearl and Blair Worden (eds), *History and Imagination: Essays in Honour of H.R. Trevor-Roper* (London, 1981), p. 367.
30 Hugh Trevor-Roper, *The Rise of Christian Europe* (London, 1965), p. 7.
31 *Historical Essays*, pp. v–vi.
32 *History and the Enlightenment*, p. 246; *Rise of Christian Europe*, p. 10.
33 *Letters from Oxford*, pp. 141–2.
34 *Historical Essays*, p. 268.
35 *Letters from Oxford*, p. 142.
36 Brenan Correspondence: 11 March 1968.
37 *Historical Essays*, p. 268.
38 'The Past and the Present', p. 12.
39 *Rise of Christian Europe*, p. 184.
40 *Historical Essays*, p. 275; SOC.Dacre 9/5/1, p. 465.
41 *Historical Essays*, p. 286.
42 SOC.Dacre 1/2/9: 16 April 1955 (Bowra).
43 *Letters from Oxford*, p. 174.
44 Hugh Trevor-Roper, 'History Professional and Lay', in Lloyd-Jones et al., *History and Imagination*, p. 12.
45 *Letters from Oxford*, p. 251; *Historical Essays*, p. 277.
46 See particularly *Historical Essays*, p. 298.
47 *Historical Essays*, pp. 285, 298.
48 'The Past and the Present', p. 12.
49 SOC.Dacre 2/8/4.
50 Hugh Trevor-Roper, *Renaissance Essays* (London, 1985), p. vi.
51 Hugh Trevor-Roper, *Catholics, Anglicans and Puritans: Seventeenth-Century Essays* (London, 1987), p. vii.
52 SOC.Dacre 1/2/29: 3 March 1985 (Lloyd-Jones).
53 *Catholics, Anglicans and Puritans*, p. vii; Hugh Trevor-Roper, *From Counter-Reformation to Glorious Revolution* (London, 1992), pp. xiii–xiv.
54 Most strikingly, perhaps, in *From Counter-Reformation to Glorious Revolution*, chs 4, 5.
55 *History and the Enlightenment*, pp. 147–51.
56 *Renaissance Essays*, p. 284.

57 Especially ibid., ch. 3.

58 SOC.Dacre 1/1/S.

59 SOC.Dacre 1/1/M (Medawar); *Oxford University Gazette*, 1969–70, p. 846.

60 SOC.Dacre 1/1/Mc (McNair).

61 *History and the Enlightenment*, p. 180.

62 Cf. Chapter 14.

63 *One Hundred Letters*, p. 172; Robert Evans, *The World of Rudolf II* (Oxford, 1973).

64 *Historical Essays*, p. 163.

65 *Letters from Oxford*, p. 174; cf. Hugh Trevor-Roper, *Princes and Artists: Patronage and Ideology at Four Habsburg Courts, 1517–1633* (London, 1976), p. vii; for Trevor-Roper and art history see too his *The Plunder of the Arts in the Seventeenth Century* (London, 1970), reproduced in *From Counter-Reformation to Glorious Revolution*, ch. 6.

66 *Wartime Journals*, p. 217; *Rise of Christian Europe*, p. 194.

67 *Princes and Artists*, pp. vii, 96, 98, 101.

68 *Listener*, 18 January 1973.

69 SOC.Dacre 1/1/13: 22 February 1969.

70 Lloyd-Jones et al., *History and Imagination*, p. 356.

71 Ibid., p. 2.

72 *History and the Enlightenment*, pp. 137, 246.

73 Lloyd-Jones et al., *History and Imagination*, p. 358.

74 Hugh Trevor-Roper, *The Philby Affair* (1968; republished in Hugh Trevor-Roper, *The Secret World: Behind the Curtain of British Intelligence in World War II and the Cold War*, ed. E.D.R. Harrison (London, 2014)).

75 Sisman, *Hugh Trevor-Roper*, pp. 442–4.

76 Hugh Trevor-Roper, *The Invention of Scotland: Myth and History*, ed. Jeremy J. Cater (New Haven, CT, and London, 2008), p. xvii.

77 Kidd's discussion, reproduced from an article of 2005, has proved controversial too: see the attack on it by William Ferguson, and Kidd's reply, in *Scottish Historical Review* 221 (2007), pp. 96–112.

78 Said in conversation.

79 Hugh Trevor-Roper, *The Last Days of Hitler*, 7th edn (London, 1995), p. 205; cf. p. 206. References to *The Last Days* in this chapter are to this edition.

80 *Last Days of Hitler*, pp. xlvi, xlvii.

81 Ibid., p. 207; *Letters from Oxford*, p. 74.

82 Ian Kershaw, *To Hell and Back: Europe 1914–1949* (London, 2015), p. 448.

83 *Historical Essays*, p. 286.

84 SOC.Dacre 2/1/11.

85 *Rise of Christian Europe*, pp. 9–10.

86 *Religion, the Reformation and Social Change*, p. 1.

87 Ibid., pp. 100, 176.

88 *Historical Essays*, p. 286.

89 Ibid., p. 12. There is a similarity here between Trevor-Roper and another historian, albeit one with a different outlook, Owen Chadwick, who like

Trevor-Roper owed his youthful political awakening to Nazism. Chadwick's thought, too, was shaped by the parallel between the crisis of civilisation in the time of the Third Reich and the fall of the Roman Empire (see the obituary of Chadwick in *The Times*, 20 July 2015).

90 *Religion, the Reformation and Social Change*, p. xi.

91 Ibid., pp. 100, 176.

92 Ibid., p. 128.

93 *Last Days of Hitler*, p. 205; SOC.Dacre 1/1/T: Todd.

94 *Wartime Journals*, p. 52.

95 *Invention of Scotland*, p. xxii.

96 Hugh Trevor-Roper, *A Hidden Life: The Enigma of Sir Edmund Backhouse* (London, 1976), p. 267; SOC.Dacre 1/2/W: 30 September 1976.

97 SOC.Dacre 13/29 ('Autopsy'); cf. *One Hundred Letters*, pp. 321–2.

98 *Historical Essays*, p. 35.

99 *Religion, the Reformation and Social Change*, p. 24.

100 *Historical Essays*, p. 59.

101 'A Case for Co-Existence: Christendom and the Turks', in *Historical Essays*, ch. 26.

102 *Historical Essays*, pp. 59, 177.

103 Ibid., p. 59.

104 Lloyd-Jones et al., *History and Imagination*, p. 11.

105 *Historical Essays*, p. 59.

106 *Renaissance Essays*, p. 73; *One Hundred Letters*, p. 406.

107 *Renaissance Essays*, p. 65.

108 *Religion, the Reformation and Social Change*, p. 215; cf. *Historical Essays*, p. 52.

109 *One Hundred Letters*, p. 409.

110 *Catholics, Anglicans and Puritans*, pp. xii–xiii.

111 Christopher Hill, *The World Turned Upside Down* (London, 1972), p. 29.

112 *Religion, the Reformation and Social Change*, p. 215.

113 Lloyd-Jones et al., *History and Imagination*, p. 360.

114 *Encounter*, June 1957, pp. 27, 28.

115 SOC.Dacre 13/29 ('Autopsy').

116 *Last Days of Hitler*, pp. 68, 214–15.

117 Ibid, p. 208.

118 *Religion, The Reformation and Social Change*, p. 89.

119 *Historical Essays*, pp. 131, 207; SOC.Dacre 9/5/1, pp. 370, 686.

120 *Historical Essays*, p. 131.

121 *Letters from Oxford*, p. 250.

122 *History and the Enlightenment*, p. 221.

123 *Encounter*, July 1961.

124 *Renaissance Essays*, ch. 13; cf. SOC.Dacre 1/2/5: Michael Howard to Trevor-Roper, 25 June 1961.

125 SOC.Dacre 1/2/W: 30 January 1988.

126 SOC.Dacre 13/29 ('Autopsy'); and see *Wartime Journals*, p. 53.

127 SOC.Dacre 1/3/18: 10 October 1944. The term Whig has acquired a looser historiographical meaning, one invoked, in quotation marks, by Noel Malcolm in Chapter 4 to characterise Trevor-Roper's treatment of Erasmianism. In Chapter 5 John Robertson uses the term in a comparable way but, in contrast to Malcolm, finds 'a strongly anti-Whiggish streak' to Trevor-Roper's approach to the history of ideas. In Chapter 6, on the other hand, Colin Kidd calls Trevor-Roper a 'decidedly Whiggish' historian.

128 *One Hundred Letters*, p. 293.

129 In conversation.

130 *From Counter-Reformation to Glorious Revolution*, p. 215.

131 *Historical Essays*, p. 257.

132 *Letters from Oxford*, pp. 209, 213.

133 Sisman, *Hugh Trevor-Roper*, p. 367.

134 SOC.Dacre 9/5/1, pp. 178–9; cf. p. 298.

135 *Historical Essays*, p. 48.

136 *Renaissance Essays*, pp. 67, 135.

137 SOC.Dacre 9/5/1, p. 104.

138 *History and the Enlightenment*, p. 151.

139 SOC.Dacre 13/29 ('Autopsy'); *Wartime Journals*, pp. 51, 53.

140 On that subject as on the sixteenth-century aristocracy, his thought was influenced by the sociological generalisations of the Belgian historian Henri Pirenne, a key discovery in his reading: Sisman, *Hugh Trevor-Roper*, p. 184; Hugh Trevor-Roper, 'The Bishopric of Durham and the Capitalist Reformation', *Durham Research Review* 18 (1967), pp. 103–17, at p. 106 (reproduced from the *Durham University Journal*, 1946); *Wartime Journals*, p. 217; SOC.Dacre 6/37/1, pp. 3, 12, 17; and told in conversation.

141 SOC.Dacre 1/2/1: 11 November {1947] (Blake).

142 SOC.Dacre 1/2/W: 27 April 1983; cf. SOC.Dacre 13/12/2.

143 *Wartime Journals*, p. 53.

144 SOC.Dacre 13/29 ('Autopsy').

145 Brenan Correspondence: 11 March 1968.

146 SOC.Dacre 1/1/M (Medawar).

147 SOC.Dacre 1/1/E (Max Elton).

148 Sisman, *Hugh Trevor-Roper*, p. 400.

149 In conversation.

150 Sisman, *Hugh Trevor-Roper*, p. 400.

151 *Rise of Christian Europe*, p. 184.

152 SOC.Dacre 9/5/1, p. 465.

153 *Rise of Christian Europe*, p. 152.

154 SOC.Dacre 1/1/P (Martin Pares).

155 Lloyd-Jones et al., *History and Imagination*, p. 2.

156 *Renaissance Essays*, p. 149.

157 *Historical Essays*, p. 26; SOC.Dacre 9/7/1, folder 2.

158 See Chapter 2.

159 *Religion, the Reformation and Social Change*, p. 243; cf. SOC.Dacre 5/1/1, p. 158.
160 *Letters from Oxford*, p. 307.
161 Hugh Trevor-Roper, *Archbishop Laud* (London, 1962 edn), pp. vii–x.
162 *From Counter-Reformation to Glorious Revolution*, p. 148.
163 Sisman, *Hugh Trevor-Roper*, p. 299; cf. SOC.Dacre 9/7/2: to J.H. Hexter, 23 September 1957.
164 *Letters from Oxford*, p. 244.
165 SOC.Dacre 1/2/3: 25 January 1957.
166 SOC.Dacre 2/1/7.
167 SOC.Dacre 1/2/12: 7 August 1968.
168 Sisman, *Hugh Trevor-Roper*, p. 375.
169 Ibid.
170 *Times Literary Supplement*, 14 February 2007.
171 SOC.Dacre 1/2/1: 25 September 1948 (Sylvia Sprigge).
172 SOC.Dacre 1/2/12: 8 March 1968.
173 SOC.Dacre 17/2: 7 September 1953.
174 SOC.Dacre 17/2: 12 February, 5 March 1954.
175 SOC.Dacre 17/1: 17 March, 1 May 1954.
176 Sisman, *Hugh Trevor-Roper*, pp. 347–8, 373.
177 SOC.Dacre 13/29 ('Autopsy').
178 SOC.Dacre 17/1: 8 June 1953.
179 The alertness is well illustrated in the A.D. Peters Correspondence at the Harry Ransom Center, Austin, Texas.
180 Sisman, *Hugh Trevor-Roper*, p. 190.
181 SOC.Dacre 9/8.
182 *Wartime Journals*, p. 50.
183 *One Hundred Letters*, p. 159. The complaint was often repeated in conversation.
184 For the publications listed here see the bibliography at www.hughtrevorroper.co.uk or www.history.ox.ac.uk/research/project/hugh-trevor-roper/bibliography.htm.
185 SOC.Dacre 2/1/20–1.
186 Sisman, *Hugh Trevor-Roper*, p. 330.
187 SOC.Dacre 1/1/C (Crombie); 1/1/M (Meyer-Abich); *New Statesman*, 25 January 1963.
188 SOC.Dacre 2/1/11.
189 SOC.Dacre 1/2/5: 25 November 1961 (Daynes).
190 SOC.Dacre 1/1/6: 28 April 1962.
191 Brenan Correspondence: 11 March 1968.
192 *Letters from Oxford*, p. 159.
193 SOC.Dacre 17/1: 3 March 1954.
194 Harry Ransom Center, A.D. Peters Correspondence: 27 April 1956.
195 SOC.Dacre 17/1: 12, 17 August 1953.
196 SOC.Dacre 1/2/W: 5 October 1978; Sisman, *Hugh Trevor-Roper*, p. 427.
197 SOC.Dacre 17/1: 12, 29 August 1953.

198 *One Hundred Letters*, p. 84.

199 SOC.Dacre 17/1: 26 December 1953.

200 SOC.Dacre 17/1: 29 August; 21/12/53: 3 January 1954.

201 SOC.Dacre 17/1: 1, 21, 26 December 1953, 5 January, 5 March, 3, 6 April 1954.

202 *Wartime Journals*, p. 197; SOC.Dacre 17/1: 26 August 1953.

203 *Wartime Journals*, pp. 165–6.

204 Peter Ghosh, 'Hugh Trevor-Roper and the History of Ideas', *History of European Ideas* 378 (2011), pp. 483–505, at p. 488.

205 *Historical Essays*, p. vi.

206 SOC.Dacre 1/2/37: 26 January 1994 (Havran).

207 *Invention of Scotland*, pp. xvii–xviii.

208 SOC.Dacre 17/1: 1 January 1954; cf. *One Hundred Letters*, p. xv.

209 *Wartime Journals*, p. 122.

210 *One Hundred Letters*, pp. 73–4.

211 *Catholics, Anglicans and Puritans*, p. 302; *From Counter-Reformation to Glorious Revolution*, p. 320.

212 SOC.Dacre 1/2/W: 5 October 1978.

213 *One Hundred Letters*, pp. 324–5.

214 *Historical Essays*, p. vi.

215 *American Scholar*, March 1990.

216 SOC.Dacre 1/1/G (Gabor).

217 SOC.Dacre 9/8/1.

218 *Wartime Journals*, p. 150.

219 SOC.Dacre 6/37/1.

220 *One Hundred Letters*, pp. 308–9.

221 SOC.Dacre 1/2/2: 7 July 1951. The publisher was Richard Ollard.

222 Lloyd-Jones et al., *History and Imagination*, p. 11.

223 SOC.Dacre 1/2/W.

224 In conversation.

225 SOC.Dacre 1/2/29: 19 October 1986 (Cannadine).

226 University College London, Special Collections, Neale MSS (uncatalogued): Trevor-Roper to Sir John Neale, 31 July 1951 (I am grateful to Professor Nicholas Tyacke for showing me a copy of this letter).

227 SOC.Dacre 1/2/W: 26 November 1973.

228 SOC.Dacre 1/2/17: 25 December 1973.

229 *Historical Essays*, p. 285; Lloyd-Jones et al., *History and Imagination*, pp. 4–5.

230 Sisman, *Hugh Trevor-Roper*, p. 373.

231 *Catholics, Anglicans and Puritans*, p. 41; cf. *From Counter-Reformation to Glorious Revolution*, pp. xiii–xiv, 216.

1. The 'General Crisis of the Seventeenth Century'

1 Hugh Trevor-Roper, 'The General Crisis of the Seventeenth Century', *Past and Present* 16 (1959), pp. 31–64.

2 For indications of the revival of interest in 'the general crisis of the seventeenth century' see *American Historical Review* Forum, 'The General Crisis of the Seventeenth-Century Revisited', *American Historical Review* 113 (2008) pp. 1029–99; *Journal of Interdisciplinary History* 11/2 (2009), a number devoted entirely to the question; and, most recently, Geoffrey Parker, *Global Crisis: War, Climate Change and Catastrophe in the Seventeenth Century* (New Haven, CT, and London, 2013).

3 Eric Hobsbawm, 'The General Crisis of the European Economy in the Seventeenth Century', *Past and Present* 5 (1954) pp. 33–53 and 6 (1954), pp. 44–65.

4 Trevor Aston (ed.), *Crisis in Europe 1560–1660: Essays from 'Past and Present'* (London, 1965), pp. 5–58.

5 Ibid., p. 14.

6 Ibid., p. 29.

7 Ibid., p. 52.

8 Roger B. Merriman, *Six Contemporaneous Revolutions* (Oxford, 1938).

9 Blair Worden, 'Hugh Redwald Trevor-Roper, 1914–2003', *Proceedings of the British Academy: Biographical Memoirs of Fellows,* VI (Oxford, 2008), pp. 247–84, at p. 257.

10 Adam Sisman, *Hugh Trevor-Roper: The Biography* (London, 2010), p. 70.

11 First published in the *Times Literary Supplement*, and reprinted in Hugh Trevor-Roper, *Historical Essays* (London, 1957), ch. 42.

12 Fernand Braudel, *La Méditerranée et le monde méditerranéen à l'époque de Philippe II* (Paris, 1949).

13 *One Hundred Letters from Hugh Trevor-Roper*, ed. Richard Davenport-Hines and Adam Sisman (Oxford, 2014), p. 41.

14 I am grateful to Blair Worden for putting these notes at my disposal.

15 Reprinted in *Historical Essays*, ch. 27.

16 The conference proceedings were published in *Past and Present* 13 (1958), pp. 63–72.

17 *Historical Essays,* pp. 294–5.

18 A. Ballersteros y Berreta (ed.), *Correspondencia oficial de Don Diego Sarmiento de Acuña, conde de Gondomar* (*Documentos inéditos para la historia de España*), 4 vols (Madrid, 1936–45). Trevor-Roper studied these volumes closely and drafted two pages of corrections, identifying English names which the editor had either failed to identify or had identified wrongly.

19 Citations will be taken from the 1959 *Past and Present* article as reprinted in Aston, *Crisis in Europe*. See ibid., p. 61.

20 Ibid., p. 62.

21 Ibid.

22 Roland Mousnier, *Les XVIe et XVIIe Siècles* (Paris, 1953).

23 Aston, *Crisis in Europe*, p. 68.

24 Ibid., p. 69.

25 Ibid., pp. 72–3.

26 Ibid., p. 77.

27 Ibid., p. 83.

28 Ibid., p. 95.

29 *Past and Present* 18 (1960), pp. 8–42.

30 Hugh Trevor-Roper, *Religion, the Reformation and Social Change, and Other Essays* (London, 1967), ch. 2.

31 Ibid., p. 64.

32 Ibid., pp. 66–7.

33 Ibid., p. 74.

34 See J.H. Elliott, *Spain, Europe and the Wider World, 1500–1800* (New Haven, CT, and London, 2009), 'The General Crisis in Retrospect: A Debate without End', p. 58.

35 Aston, *Crisis in Europe*, p. 115.

2. The Puritan Revolution

1 *Letters from Oxford: Hugh Trevor-Roper to Bernard Berenson*, ed. Richard Davenport-Hines (London, 2006), pp. 9, 10.

2 Harry Ransom Center, Austin, Texas, A.D. Peters Papers: 10 August 1956.

3 Hugh Trevor-Roper, *Historical Essays* (London, 1957), p. 236.

4 SOC.Dacre 1/3/18: 31 March 1943.

5 Hugh Trevor-Roper, *The Wartime Journals*, ed. Richard Davenport-Hines (London, 2010), p. 53.

6 See Chapter 14.

7 SOC.Dacre 9/5/1, pp. 13, 35–8.

8 *Letters from Oxford*, p. 250.

9 See Trevor-Roper's memorial address in *Christ Church Magazine*, 1977.

10 Adam Sisman, *Hugh Trevor-Roper: The Biography* (London, 2010), pp. 36–8, conflates the two.

11 SOC.Dacre 13/57.

12 *Oxford University Gazette*, 1936–7, p. 631.

13 Hugh Trevor-Roper, *The Rise of Christian Europe* (London, 1965), p. 136.

14 *Wartime Journals*, pp. 40–1. Trevor-Roper surely misdated the walk to 1936. Cf. ibid., p. 33; see too SOC.Dacre 13/29 ('Autopsy').

15 *Letters from Oxford*, p. 47.

16 Hugh Trevor-Roper, *Archbishop Laud* (London, 1940), pp. 12, 15.

17 R.H. Tawney, 'Rise of the Gentry', *Economic History Review* 11 (1941), pp. 1–38, at p. 12.

18 Blair Worden, *Roundhead Reputations: The English Civil Wars and the Passions of Posterity* (London, 2001), ch. 9.

19 Sisman, *Hugh Trevor-Roper*, p. 183; *Archbishop Laud*, p. 50.

20 SOC.Dacre 6/33, p. 90.

21 Thomas Wilson, *A Discourse upon Usury*, ed. R.H. Tawney (London, 1925), pp. 50–4, 91.

22 Hugh Trevor-Roper, 'The Bishopric of Durham and the Capitalist Reformation', *Durham Research Review*, 18 (1967), pp. 103–17 (reprinted with stylistic corrections from the text of 1946), at p. 111; cf. SOC.Dacre 6/37/1, p. 2.

23 *Wartime Journals*, p. 150; SOC.Dacre 1/3/18: 5 October 1944.

24 The succour offered to Marxism by Trevor-Roper's essay on the bishopric of Durham is suggested by the presence of a rare copy of the text of 1946 in the library of Christopher Hill's Oxford college, Balliol.

25 Hugh Trevor-Roper, 'Archbishop Laud', *History*, September 1945, pp. 183–6; SOC.Dacre 1/3/18: 5 October 1944; Trevor-Roper's review of Karl Popper's *The Open Society*, in *Polemic*, May 1946.

26 SOC.Dacre 6/37/1.

27 Sisman, *Hugh Trevor-Roper*, p. 190.

28 SOC.Dacre 1/3/28: 3 August 1948 (to Charles Stuart); Sisman, *Hugh Trevor-Roper*, p. 188.

29 Sisman, *Hugh Trevor-Roper*, p. 191.

30 See Introduction.

31 Sisman, *Hugh Trevor-Roper*, p. 193.

32 SOC.Dacre 9/6/1.

33 *New Statesman*, 13 January 1951; cf. Hugh Trevor-Roper, 'The Gentry 1540–1640', *Economic History Review*, supplement (1953), p. 1.

34 *Letters from Oxford*, p. 287; cf. SOC.Dacre 9/6/1: Trevor-Roper to J.C. Aveling, 7 January 1954. Trevor-Roper's mind would change. By 1954, as he then told a correspondent in an intemperate moment, he thought that Tawney had used a 'dishonest method', and that 'the whole science of history is being vitiated' by 'such methods, whereby theories are [...] stated as facts on the basis of illustrations arbitrarily selected' (Sisman, *Hugh Trevor-Roper*, p. 206). For Trevor-Roper's disenchantment see too *Letters from Oxford*, p. 130; SOC. Dacre 9/6/1: letter to *Times Literary Supplement* 1955.

35 Sisman, *Hugh Trevor-Roper*, p. 206.

36 In the attack on Trevor-Roper for which he finds room in his *The Life of R.H. Tawney* (London, 2013), pp. 236ff., Lawrence Goldman declares the article not only guilty of 'vituperation' but 'highly personalized', a charge that appears to rest on the frequency with which the words 'Prof. Tawney' appear in it – as if it would be practicable to conduct a detailed criticism of an article without recurrently using the noun of its author's name. The extent of Goldman's acquaintance with Trevor-Roper's article can be gauged by his statement that Trevor-Roper ignores Tawney's essay 'Harrington's Interpretation of his Age'.

Goldman imagines that Trevor-Roper used Tawney's essay as a 'proxy' for an attack on Marxism.

37 *Encounter*, July 1958, p. 74.
38 SOC.Dacre 2/7.
39 In a conversation later in life Trevor-Roper, his memory of that time perhaps distorted by his subsequent views, attributed the change to Hill, but it is inconceivable that Trevor-Roper was not involved himself. It looks as if his senior colleague at Christ Church, Keith Feiling, acted as intermediary between Trevor-Roper and the Faculty Board: Oxford University Archives, FA4/11/1/6, fo. 36.
40 SOC.Dacre 2/7: lecture 1, 1949.
41 Hugh Trevor-Roper, *The Last Days of Hitler*, 7th edn (London, 1995), p. 45.
42 I owe this information to the late Owen Chadwick.
43 *Historical Essays*, p. 230.
44 Sisman, *Hugh Trevor-Roper*, p. 190.
45 R.C. Richardson, 'Cromwell and the Inter-War European Dictators', in R.C. Richardson (ed.), *Images of Oliver Cromwell* (Manchester, 1993), ch. 7.
46 *The Last Days of Hitler*, pp. 209, 212.
47 *New Statesman*, 29 May 1948.
48 *Letters from Oxford*, p. 23; see too Sisman, *Hugh Trevor-Roper*, p. 67.
49 *Historical Essays*, pp. 206–7.
50 *Letters from Oxford*, pp. 18, 21.
51 In *Essays Presented to Sir Lewis Namier*, ed. Richard Pares and A.J.P. Taylor (London, 1956).
52 The story of the composition of the book is told in Sisman, *Hugh Trevor-Roper*, pp. 291–2, 298–9, 301–2, 324–7, 347–8, 373–6; and in Blair Worden, 'Hugh Redwald Trevor-Roper 1914–2003', *Proceedings of the British Academy: Biographical Memoirs of Fellows*, VI (Oxford, 2008), pp. 262–7.
53 See e.g. *Last Days of Hitler*, ch. 1; *Archbishop Laud*, p. 98.
54 SOC.Dacre 7/2: lecture 7.
55 Tawney, 'Rise of the Gentry', p. 91; SOC.Dacre 6/7/1, pp. 99, 103.
56 'Trevor-Roper's "General Crisis": Symposium', *Past and Present* 18 (1960), pp. 114–15; Hugh Trevor-Roper, *Religion, the Reformation and Social Change, and Other Essays* (London, 1967), p. 74.
57 *New Statesman*, 4 March 1950.
58 SOC.Dacre, 6/33, p. 146.
59 Reprinted in *Historical Essays*, chs 27, 29.
60 Ibid., ch. 28.
61 *Religion, the Reformation and Social Change*, p. 100.
62 *New Statesman*, 8 September 1956; cf. SOC.Dacre 1/5/1, p. 223.
63 SOC.Dacre 9/5/1, p. 210.
64 See Introduction.
65 SOC.Dacre 9/6/1: Hexter to Trevor-Roper, 6 February 1954; Trevor-Roper to Hexter, 22 February 1954.
66 *Historical Essays*, p. 247.

67 *Letters from Oxford*, p. 248; SOC.Dacre 9/5/1, p. 118.

68 SOC.Dacre 9/5/1, p. 122.

69 *Historical Essays*, p. 193; *Letters from Oxford*, p. 250.

70 SOC.Dacre 9/4/2; *Letters from Oxford*, p. 250.

71 *Wartime Journals*, p. 308; for his difficulties with formlessness cf. ibid., p. 91.

72 *Wartime Journals*, p. 218.

73 *Letters from Oxford*, p. 3.

74 Ibid., p. 250.

75 SOC.Dacre 9/5/1, p. 102.

76 *Historical Essays*, p. 131.

77 *Religion, the Reformation and Social Change*, p. 72.

78 SOC.Dacre 9/5/1, pp. 111–12, 122, 124, 126.

79 SOC.Dacre 9/4/2; 1/5/1, p. 122.

80 SOC.Dacre 9/4/2.

81 SOC.Dacre 9/5/1, p. 230.

82 Ibid., p. 464.

83 Ibid., p. 11.

84 Ibid., p. 228.

85 SOC.Dacre 9/7: Trevor-Roper to Joel Hurstfield, 12 September 1957.

86 SOC.Dacre 9/5/1, p. 33.

87 Ibid., p. 94.

88 Ibid., p. 218.

89 *Polemic*, May 1946, pp. 59–60; *Historical Essays*, p. 223.

90 SOC.Dacre 9/5/1, p. 171.

91 Ibid., p. 284.

92 Ibid., p. 293.

93 Ibid., pp. 17, 23, 276; cf. *Historical Essays*, p. 193. His view of Bedford had changed since his portrayals of him as a 'great capitalist': *New Statesman,* 9 April 1949; SOC.Dacre 7/2, lecture 2: 1950.

94 SOC.Dacre 9/5/1, p. 275.

95 Ibid., p. 347.

96 Ibid., pp. 61, 419, 456.

97 Ibid., pp. 375, 470–1, 494.

98 SOC.Dacre 9/4/2.

99 SOC.Dacre 1/2/9: 21 July 1965 (Lloyd-Jones).

100 Michael Howard, *Captain Professor* (London, 2006), p. 135.

101 Valerie Pearl, *London and the Outbreak of the Puritan Revolution* (Oxford, 1961).

102 SOC.Dacre 1/2/18: Pearl to Trevor-Roper, 3 February 1966.

103 SOC.Dacre 1/2/3: 31 May 1956.

104 SOC.Dacre 9/5/10b.

105 SOC.Dacre 9/5/10a.

106 Sisman, *Hugh Trevor-Roper*, p. 348.

107 I have tried to reconstruct the stages of the composition of the manuscript in SOC.Dacre 9/5/1 (pt).

292 • Notes to Pages 76–83

108 At one point he seems to have considered concluding in 1653: SOC.Dacre 9/5/10D.
109 See Introduction; SOC.Dacre 9/5/1, pp. 493, 551.
110 See Introduction.
111 SOC.Dacre 13/35. The volume contains material on his visit to China in the early autumn of 1965.
112 SOC.Dacre 2/7; 2/8.
113 SOC.Dacre 9/5/1, p. 210.
114 Ibid., p. 129; cf. *Religion, The Reformation and Social Change*, pp. 71, 85.
115 Ibid., p 102.
116 Ibid., pp. 178ff.
117 'The Gentry', p. 44; cf. *Historical Essays*, p. 244.
118 SOC.Dacre 9/5/1, pp. 78, 208, 210.
119 *Historical Essays*, p. 53; cf. SOC.Dacre 9/5/1, pp. 158, 208, 210, and Introduction.
120 SOC.Dacre 9/5/1, pp. 65, 69, 112.
121 *Religion, the Reformation and Social Change*, chs 8, 9.
122 See Introduction.
123 SOC.Dacre 9/5/1, p. 7.
124 *Letters from Oxford*, p. 244.
125 SOC.Dacre 9/5/1, p. 493.
126 Ibid., p. 473.
127 *Religion, the Reformation and Social Change*, p. 259.
128 SOC.Dacre 9/5/5, p. 85.
129 SOC.Dacre 9/5/1, p. 64.
130 SOC.Dacre 9/5/10a.
131 *Historical Essays*, p. 244.
132 SOC.Dacre 9/5/10.
133 SOC.Dacre 1/1/J (Jacob).
134 Perez Zagorin, *The Court and the Country* (London, 1969); P.W. Thomas, 'Court and Country', in Conrad Russell (ed.), *The Origins of the English Civil War* (London, 1973).
135 John Morrill, *The Revolt of the Provinces* (London, 1976), pp. 19–21.
136 *Religion, the Reformation and Social Change*, p. 349; *Historical Essays*, p. 204.
137 On the other hand, Trevor-Roper, though he had used a regional case-study to illustrate national developments in his article on Sutton in 1946, did not really explore the localist dimension of parliamentarian sentiment, which became a leading scholarly preoccupation with the appearance of Alan Everitt's *The Community of Kent and the Great Rebellion* (Leicester, 1966).
138 Trevor-Roper knew Brian Manning's Oxford doctoral thesis of 1957, 'Neutrals and Neutralism in the English Civil War', but was not impressed by it and did not cite it. SOC.Dacre 9/5/1, pp. 83, 371, 445, 454.
139 SOC.Dacre 9/5/1, p. 371.

140 SOC.Dacre 9/7/1, ch. 8, p. 29. The classic statement is Clive Holmes, *The Eastern Association in the English Civil War* (Cambridge, 1974).

141 Ibid., pp. 13, 275.

142 Ibid., p. 13. Another unpublished argument, this one in the unfinished book on Thomas Sutton, foreshadows the account of the following of the late Elizabethan Earl of Essex to be found in Mervyn James, *Society, Politics and Culture* (Cambridge, 1986), ch. 9.

143 Worden, 'Hugh Redwald Trevor-Roper', pp. 265–70.

144 Especially in Hugh Trevor-Roper, *Catholics, Anglicans and Puritans: Seventeenth-Century Essays* (London, 1987).

145 John Morrill, *The Nature of the English Revolution* (London, 1993), part 1.

146 *Catholics, Anglicans and Puritans*, ch. 2.

147 Hugh Trevor-Roper, *From Counter-Reformation to Glorious Revolution* (London, 1992), pp. xiii–xiv. He has in his eye J.C.D. Clark, *Revolution and Rebellion* (Cambridge, 1986).

148 *From Counter-Reformation to Glorious Revolution*, pp. xiii–xiv and ch. 11. For the persistence of his interest in the messianic strain see his *Renaissance Essays*, pp. 183–6; and his *Europe's Physician: The Various Life of Sir Theodore de Mayerne* (New Haven, CT, and London, 2006), p. 338.

3. Three Foreigners: The Philosophers of the Puritan Revolution

1 Hugh Trevor-Roper, 'Three Foreigners and the Philosophy of the English Revolution', *Encounter*, February 1960, pp. 3–20.

2 The modern edition of Comenius's works only began to appear in Prague in 1969 (*Johannis Amos Comenii Opera omnia* (Prague, 1969–), 15 vols, in progress (60 vols projected). J. Minton Batten, *John Dury, Advocate of Christian Reunion* (Chicago, 1944), began the recension of Dury's published works but hardly touched the vast amounts of Dury's extant manuscripts, scattered throughout European archives. The extent of these materials has been recently revealed in Pierre-Olivier Léchot, *Un christianisme 'sans partialité': Irénisme et méthode chez John Dury (c.1600–1680)* (Geneva, 2011). The reconstruction of Samuel Hartlib's role is inextricably related to the rediscovery of his own archives.

3 G.H. Turnbull, *Hartlib, Dury and Comenius: Gleanings from Hartlib's Papers* (London, 1947), pp. 362–4.

4 *One Hundred Letters from Hugh Trevor-Roper*, ed. Richard Davenport-Hines and Adam Sisman (Oxford, 2014), pp. 130–1: letter to Valerie Pearl, 12 September 1965.

5 Hugh Trevor-Roper, *Religion, the Reformation, and Social Change, and Other Essays* (London, 1967), p. 249, n. (Hereafter the *Encounter* version of the essay will be referred to as 1960, and the *Religion, the Reformation and Social Change* version as 1967.)

6   I am grateful to Charles Webster for a photocopy of this letter. Trevor-Roper had evidently ascribed to Bishop Williams the 'academy' with which Hartlib was briefly associated on his return from Chichester to London in 1631. Turnbull laid out the evidence for its having been sponsored by Robert Greville, Lord Brooke. Turnbull also doubted whether 'we owe Evelyn's Sylva to H', and Trevor-Roper's published text weakens that link. Turnbull finally pointed out that the 'oriental professor' to whom the draft referred was not Comenius but Johan Rittangel, and Trevor-Roper seems to have filleted in a paragraph to accommodate the point. The letter also refers to 'the relationship of [John] Gauden to H. which we discussed when you were here', and Turnbull was probably the source for the footnote (1967, p. 262, n. 1) in which Trevor-Roper acknowledges that there was no evidence of any link between Gauden, the preacher of a sermon before the Long Parliament on which Trevor-Roper's text lays some stress, and the 'three foreigners'. Turnbull was not convinced that John Dury's treatise, published by Hartlib as *England's Thankfulness or an Humble Remonstrance presented to the Committee for Religion in the High Court of Parliament* in 1642, substantiated Trevor-Roper's account of the relationship of the 'three foreigners' to the Long Parliament at all. Turnbull had published an account of the document in G.R. Turnbull, 'The Visit of Comenius to England', *Notes and Queries*, 31 March 1951, pp. 137–40.

7   Trevor-Roper's version of 1967 alluded only scantily to the archive (e.g. 1967, p. 257, n. 2).

8   Thus the delicious description of John Dury 'clambering up that laborious and rugged way after St Paul' (1960, p. 8; 1967, p. 252) comes from Sheffield University Library, Hartlib Papers MS 34/2/1B (William Waller to [? John Dury], 27 February 1639). The passage about John Pym in *Ephemerides* (1634) is readily located in the archives (Hartlib Papers MS 29/2/7B). Trevor-Roper shared his notes on John Pym with Christopher Hill, who cited them with acknowledgement in *The Intellectual Origins of the English Revolution* (Oxford, 1965), p. 98. The undated citation of Cheney Culpeper (1960, p. 10; 1967, p. 257), however, is not in the archive. It is almost certainly one of several items which have unaccountably been lost since Trevor-Roper consulted them. It therefore does not figure in M.J. Braddick and M. Greengrass (eds), *The Letters of Sir Cheney Culpeper, 1641–1657*, Royal Historical Society Camden Series, Vol. VII (London, 1999), pp. 122–400. The 1967 recension of the essay includes a reference (p. 281, n. 3) to material furnished by Charles Webster relating to Henry Cromwell's attempts to found a college in Ireland.

9   'I hope that Hartlib's papers will be deposited in the British Museum but, so far as I know at present, no decision on the matter has yet been made by their owner' (Turnbull to John Beach Whitmore, 18 April 1945, Sheffield University Library, Turnbull Papers 70/31/5. I am grateful to Leigh T.I. Penman for letting me see an advance copy of his paper: '*Omnium exposita rapinae*: A Biography of the Papers of Samuel Hartlib (ca. 1600–1662)', a

major investigation of the fate of Hartlib's papers across the centuries, from where I derive this reference.

10 For a brief résumé of the early connections between Hartlib and Comenius, see Donald R. Dickson, *The Tessera of Antilia: Utopian Brotherhoods and Secret Societies in the Early Seventeenth Century* (Leiden, Boston, Cologne, 1998), p. 159.

11 Mark Greengrass, 'Archive Refractions: Hartlib's Papers and the Working of an Intelligencer', in M. Hunter (ed.), *The Archives of the Scientific Revolution* (Woodbridge, 1998), pp. 35–48; cited p. 36.

12 Hartlib Papers MS 7/26/1A (cited from www.hrionline.ac.uk/hartlib).

13 Richard Yeo, *Notebooks, English Virtuosi and Early Modern Science* (Chicago, 2014), p. 102.

14 That process is brilliantly reconstructed by Leigh Penman in '*Omnium exposita rapinae*: A Biography of the Papers of Samuel Hartlib', which supersedes everything hitherto written on the subject of the archive's subsequent history.

15 Attracted, perhaps, to the 'magus' that he imagined Hartlib to be, Dircks was best known in his own day as the populariser of the theatrical illusion known as Pepper's Ghost, an effect first conceived by the sixteenth-century Neapolitan Giambattista della Porta. Henry Dircks, *A Biographical Memoir of Samuel Hartlib, Milton's Familiar Friend* (London, 1865).

16 See the account of his travels in Ján Kvačala, 'Kurzer Bericht über meine Forschungsreisen', *Acta et commentationes Imperialis Universitatis jurievensis olim dorpatensisz* 3 (1895), pp. 1–48. Cf. his detailed account of Comenius's life, *Johann Amos Comenius. Sein Leben und seine Schriften* (Berlin and Leipzig, 1892).

17 A. Patera, *Jana Amosa Kosmenského Korrespondence* (Prague, 1892).

18 G.H. Turnbull, *Samuel Hartlib: A Sketch of his Life and his Relations to J.A. Comenius* (Oxford, 1920).

19 Letter cited in n. 4 above.

20 *Religion, the Reformation and Social Change*, p. 249.

21 *Letters from Oxford: Hugh Trevor-Roper to Bernard Berenson*, ed. Richard Davenport-Hines (London, 2006), p. 10.

22 W.A.L. Vincent, *The State and School Education, 1640–1660, in England and Wales: A Survey Based on Printed Sources* (London, 1950).

23 *New Statesman*, 11 February 1951. I am very grateful to Judith Curthoys, archivist at Christ Church, for providing me with a copy of this review at short notice. Vincent shows no signs of familiarity with George Turnbull's 1920 study of Hartlib, which was based on published sources (Turnbull, *Samuel Hartlib*), or with his 1947 book.

24 Adam Sisman, *Hugh Trevor-Roper: The Biography* (London, 2010), p. 299.

25 Hugh Trevor-Roper, 'The General Crisis of the Seventeenth Century', *Past and Present*, 16 (1959), pp. 31–64.

26 1960, pp. 6–7; 1967, pp. 245–6.

27 1960, p. 20; 1967, p. 293.

28 C.P. Snow, 'Afterthoughts on the "Two-Cultures" Controversy', *Encounter*, February 1960, pp. 64–8. Interestingly, Snow quotes Comenius on the ways

of arriving at a common understanding across the supposed divide of the two cultures.

29 Bernard Levin, *The Pendulum Years: Britain in the 1960s* (London, 1970). The theme of the book is the antagonism between the forces pulling Britain into the future, and those taking it back to the past.

30 Harold Hartley (ed.), *The Royal Society: Origins and Founders* (London, 1960).

31 *Notes and Records of the Royal Society* 15 (1960).

32 Among other publications from that year, reflecting these views, see Trevor Williams, *The Royal Society: A Tercentenary Portrait* (London, 1960); [Sir] Geoffrey Keynes, D.H. Wilkinson and M. Hoskin, 'The Tercentenary of the Royal Society', *Listener,* 21 July 1960 – part of nine special programmes broadcast by the BBC in the second half of the month to celebrate the event. The tercentenary ceremony in the Royal Albert Hall on 19 July 1960 was also televised by the BBC and, later that same evening, a special programme of talks by Fellows of the Royal Society was introduced by HRH the Duke of Edinburgh – see *Notes and Records of the Royal Society* 16 (1961), p. 101. Cf. 'The Formation of the Royal Society: A Tercentenary', *History Today*, August 1960.

33 M. Purver, 'A Consideration of Problems Concerning the Origin and Background of the Royal Society', examined 9 June 1959. The examiners were Dr E.A.O. Whiteman (internal) and Professor Douglas McKie (external).

34 Thomas Sprat, *The History of the Royal Society of London* (London, 1667), p. 53.

35 M. Purver and E.J. Bowen, *The Origins of the Royal Society* (Oxford, 1960), pp. 6, 8.

36 SOC.Dacre 1/1/P (Purver): Cyril Hinshelwood to Trevor-Roper, 9 May 1962: 'Some people thought that the argument exaggerated the importance of what had gone on in Oxford, and underestimated the contribution that Gresham College had at a somewhat earlier date. Harold Hartley told me he felt this, and I believe various other people thought the Oxford brochure a little *pro domo*'. I am, once more, very grateful to Judith Curthoys for her kindness in making this – and the subsequent material cited from the archive – available to me at short notice.

37 SOC.Dacre 1/1/P: Trevor-Roper to Margery Purver, 9 February 1962; Margery Purver to Trevor-Roper, 23 March 1962; Trevor-Roper to Margery Purver, 1 May 1962. He wrote to the syndics of Oxford University Press on 9 May 1962, saying that it was 'an important contribution to a complex and interesting subject [...] impressed by the scholarship and method behind it'.

38 Robert K. Merton, *Science, Technology and Society in Seventeenth-Century England* (Bruges, 1938).

39 See the passages highlighted by Hill in 1997 as indicative of the book's purpose: e.g. Christopher Hill, *Intellectual Origins of the English Revolution Revisited* (Oxford, 1997), p. 6: 'Leaving Puritanism aside, I propose to discuss some of the other ideas [...] that motivated seventeenth-century revolutionaries.'

40 Ibid., original preface, p. xi (dated June 1963); '[in the lectures] I therefore picked out evidence which seemed to me to support my case [...] I was

advancing a thesis, not attempting to sketch the intellectual history of England.'

41 SOC.Dacre 1/1/P: Margery Purver to Trevor-Roper, 4 May 1965.

42 SOC.Dacre 1/1/P: Trevor-Roper to Margery Purver, 30 June 1962 (written after he had sent her a revised draft, 22 September 1964).

43 Margery Purver, *The Royal Society: Concept and Creation* (London, 1967), p. xi. I think Trevor-Roper suspected Hinshelwood, one of the delegates at the press, of having been behind its rejection.

44 Hugh Trevor-Roper, 'Intellectual Origins of the English Revolution: Review', *History and Theory* 5/1 (1966), pp. 61–82.

45 *One Hundred Letters*, p. 132.

46 Sisman, *Hugh Trevor-Roper*, pp. 339–40.

47 C. Webster, *The Great Instauration: Science, Medicine and Reform, 1626–1660* (London, 1975).

48 Charles Webster, 'New Light on the Invisible College: The Social Relations of English Science in the Mid-Seventeenth Century', *Transactions of the Royal Historical Society* 24 (1974), pp. 19–42.

49 Michael Hunter, *The Royal Society and its Fellows, 1660–1700: The Morphology of an Early Scientific Institution* (Chalfont St Giles, 1982); Michael Hunter, *Science and Society in Restoration England* (Cambridge, 1981); Michael Hunter, *Establishing the New Science: The Experience of the Early Royal Society* (Woodbridge, 1989).

50 Trevor-Roper to Robert Blake, 1 August 1977; cited in *One Hundred Letters*, Introduction, p. xxviii.

51 Howard Hotson, *Johann Heinrich Alsted 1588–1638: Between Renaissance, Reformation, and Universal Reform* (Oxford, 2000).

52 Glyn Grammar School, Epsom, 1967–8; teacher – R. ('Gus') Dorling.

4. Ecumenism and Erasmianism: The Wiles Lectures, 1975

1 SOC.Dacre 2/5 (Wiles Lectures 1975). I am very grateful to both the archivist, Judith Curtoys, and Professor Blair Worden for their help in facilitating my study of this text and related materials; I thank Blair Worden also for his thoughtful comments on a draft of this essay.

2 All of these were published by Cambridge University Press except Colley's book (issued by Jonathan Cape, London). A fuller listing is given on the Queen's University website at www.qub.ac.uk/schools/Schoolof History and Anthropology/News/WilesLectureSeries/PastLectures and www.qub.ac.uk/schools/SchoolofHistoryandAnthropology/News/WilesLectureSeries/Past Lectures/WilesLectures1954–88 (accessed 20 September 2015).

3 I use the figure provided by the 'inflation calculator' at www.bankofengland.co.uk/education/Pages/resources/inflationtools/calculator/flash/default.aspx# (accessed 20 September 2015).

4   The correspondence (including the rules of the Trust, and details of the 1974 postponement) is in SOC.Dacre 2/5 (Wiles Lectures 1975).

5   Anne Whiteman, Fellow and Vice-Principal of Lady Margaret Hall, Oxford, was an expert on the religious history of Restoration England; Margaret Aston, who had completed her doctorate at Oxford in 1962, was developing a distinguished career as a historian of late medieval religion.

6   The only ones who had produced any substantial work on European history were Aston, who had published *The Fifteenth Century: The Prospect of Europe* (London, 1968), and Elton, author of *Reformation Europe, 1517–1559* (London, 1963). In his later thank-you letter to Trevor-Roper Elton wrote: 'you've opened up all sorts of things – ideas, ambitions, especially inter-connections – that I had absolutely no notion of' (SOC.Dacre 2/5 (Wiles Lectures 1975): letter of 24 May 1975).

7   The Northern Irish historian J.C. (Jim) Beckett, who was about to retire from the History Faculty, worked mainly on later periods, but did subsequently publish a biography of the seventeenth-century Duke of Ormond.

8   Toby Barnard, personal communication.

9   Lord Lexden, personal communication.

10   Blair Worden and Toby Barnard, personal communications.

11   Lord Lexden, personal communication.

12   It also did not help that, as Blair Worden recalls, 'he had a cold, and was run down and exhausted' (personal communication).

13   SOC.Dacre 2/5 (Wiles Lectures 1975): Lecture I typescript, pp. 1–2 (hereafter these lecture typescripts will be referred to simply as 'Lecture I', 'Lecture II', etc.).

14   Lecture I, p. 4.

15   Ibid., pp. 8, 9–10. Trevor-Roper develops here a point about the relationship between Erasmianism and Calvinism first made in his major early essay on Erasmus: Hugh Trevor-Roper, *Historical Essays* (London, 1957), p. 54.

16   Lecture I, p. 11.

17   Lecture II, p. 5.

18   Ibid., pp. 5–7.

19   Ibid., pp. 14 (quotation), 18 (General Council).

20   Lecture III, p. 8.

21   Ibid., pp. 21–3.

22   Lecture IV, p. 6.

23   Ibid., p. 12.

24   Ibid., p. 18.

25   Ibid., p. 21.

26   SOC.Dacre 2/5 (Wiles Lectures 1975): letter of 29 May 1975.

27   SOC.Dacre 2/5 (Wiles Lectures 1975): Trevor-Roper, letter of 2 June 1975; and Warren, letter of 7 July 1975).

28   SOC.Dacre 2/5 (Wiles Lectures 1975): Trevor-Roper, letter of 14 July 1975; and Warren, letter of 23 February 1976.

29 SOC.Dacre 2/5 (Wiles Lectures 1975): Williams, letters of 1 and 20 April 1976.

30 SOC.Dacre 2/5 (Wiles Lectures 1975): letter of 8 November 1978.

31 SOC.Dacre 2/5, not filed: notebook with 'ὕλη β ['material, 2'] Wiles' on cover, pp. 1, 3, 25.

32 On this period of his life see Adam Sisman, *Hugh Trevor-Roper: The Biography* (London, 2010), pp. 430–53.

33 'The Good and Great Works of Richard Hooker', *New York Review of Books*, 24 November 1977.

34 Derek Baker (ed.), *Studies in Church History, Vol. 15: Religious Motivations and Social Problems for the Church Historian* (Oxford, 1978), pp. 213–40.

35 See Hugh Trevor-Roper, *Europe's Physician: The Various Life of Sir Theodore de Mayerne* (New Haven, CT, and London, 2006), pp. 117–39.

36 Noel Malcolm, *De Dominis (1560–1624): Venetian, Anglican, Ecumenist and Relapsed Heretic* (London, 1984). This book was reviewed by Trevor-Roper in the *Journal of Theological Studies* 37 (1986), pp. 645–7.

37 Theodore K. Rabb, *Jacobean Gentleman: Sir Edwin Sandys, 1561–1629* (Princeton, NJ, 1998), p. 38.

38 Patterson had previously published an article on the Synod: 'James I and the Huguenot Synod of Tonneins of 1614', *Harvard Theological Review* 65 (1972), pp. 241–70.

39 W.B. Patterson, *King James VI and I and the Reunion of Christendom* (Cambridge, 1997), pp. 31–74 (interest in Church reunion), 141 (Grotius and Casaubon), 153 (quotation).

40 Lecture I, pp. 6–7.

41 Lecture III, p. 9.

42 'Ecumenism' usually involves an attempt to agree on some substantive common ground; 'irenicism' may involve no more than an agreement to disagree peacefully.

5. Intellectual History: 'The Religious Origins of the Enlightenment'

1 This contribution is a revised and slightly abbreviated version of an article published under the same title in *English Historical Review* 124/511 (2009). I am grateful to the literary executors of Lord Dacre of Glanton and Dame Frances Yates for permission to cite and quote from their correspondence, and to Dr Dorothea McEwan, then archivist at the Warburg Institute, and Judith Curthoys, archivist of Christ Church, for their assistance in consulting the papers. I renew my thanks to Peter Ghosh, Sarah Hutton, Colin Kidd and Adam Sisman for their comments on the original article; more particularly I continue to be grateful to Blair Worden, both for his comments on this chapter and its earlier version, and for invaluable guidance on the Trevor-Roper archive.

2 Hugh Trevor-Roper, *Religion, the Reformation and Social Change, and Other Essays* (London, 1967).

3 Hugh Trevor-Roper, *Archbishop Laud* (London, 1940) and 2nd edn (London, 1962).

4 Particularly influential in supporting this thesis was the work of Ira O. Wade, *The Clandestine Organisation and Diffusion of Philosophic Ideas in France from 1700 to 1750* (Princeton, NJ, 1938).

5 Peter Gay, *The Enlightenment: An Interpretation, Vol. I: The Rise of Modern Paganism* (New York, 1966).

6 Thus Michael Bentley, *Modernizing England's Past: English Historiography in the Age of Modernism 1870–1970* (Cambridge, 2005), pp. 61–4; also p. 136, where Trevor-Roper is described as an 'icon' of 'post-war modernism'. On Bentley's idiosyncratic construction of 'modernism', see the review by Peter Ghosh in *English Historical Review* 121 (2006), pp. 1509–12.

7 Blair Worden's evocative, penetrating biographical memoir outlines the ground such a study will need to cover: 'Hugh Redwald Trevor-Roper 1914–2003', *Proceedings of the British Academy: Biographical Memoirs of Fellows*, VI (Oxford, 2008), pp. 247–84. Irene Gaddo's monograph, *Il piacere della controversia: Hugh Trevor-Roper storico e uomo pubblico* (Naples, 2007) balances the main themes of his public career against an overview of his interests as a historian; she does not directly address the question of the development of those interests. Adam Sisman's *Hugh Trevor-Roper: The Biography* (London, 2010) provides the student of historiography with the essential personal dimension, setting his intellectual interests alongside his institutional, publishing and journalistic commitments.

8 I cite the essay as printed in the second edition of *Religion, the Reformation and Social Change* (London, 1972), pp. 193–236. Hereafter 'Religious Origins'.

9 'Religious Origins', p. 194, n. 1. The review was in *History and Theory* 5/1 (1966), pp. 61–82.

10 'Religious Origins', pp. 204–14.

11 Ibid., pp. 215–26.

12 Ibid., pp. 226–32.

13 Ibid., pp. 232–6.

14 'Preface to the First Edition', in *Religion, the Reformation and Social Change*, pp. xiv–xv.

15 'Religion, the Reformation and Social Change', in *Religion, the Reformation and Social Change*, pp. 1–45.

16 'The General Crisis of the Seventeenth Century', in *Religion, the Reformation and Social Change*, pp. 46–89.

17 'The European Witch-Craze of the Sixteenth and Seventeenth Centuries', in *Religion, the Reformation and Social Change*, pp. 90–192; on Erasmus, pp. 129–30, esp. n. 3; on Weyer, pp. 146–7; on Grotius, p. 181; on 'the final victory', p. 183.

18 Hugh Trevor-Roper, *Protestantesimo e trasformazione sociale* (Rome and Bari, 1969; repr. 1975), p. 5. The review of *Religion, the Reformation and Social Change* appeared in the *Times Literary Supplement*, 19 October 1967, pp. 973–4.

19 Hugh Trevor-Roper, 'Desiderius Erasmus', in *Historical Essays* (London, 1957), pp. 35–60.

20 He owned a first edition of the English translation of 1930, though there is no indication when he acquired it: Max Weber, *The Protestant Ethic and the Spirit of Calvinism*, trans. Talcott C. Parsons, with a foreword by R.H. Tawney (London, 1930). For his admission that he initially accepted Weber's thesis, see the preface to the second edition of *Archbishop Laud* (1962), p. viii.

21 *Letters from Oxford: Hugh Trevor-Roper to Bernard Berenson*, ed. Richard Davenport-Hines (London, 2006), pp. 199, 200–1, letters to Berenson of 10 June, 18 August 1956.

22 SOC.Dacre 9/7/1, box organised in files entitled 'Weber' (notes on the nineteenth-century antecedents of the controversy, on Weber, his contemporary and subsequent critics), 'Miscellaneous' (notes), 'Economic Diaspora: written chapters' (contains drafts of the book) and 'Bibliography-Queries' (including letters to and from Kathleen Wood, Dept. of Printed Books, Bodleian Library, 1951–6).

23 SOC.Dacre 9/7/2, file entitled 'Prices': Hugh Trevor-Roper to J.H. Hexter, 23 September 1957: 'I am writing what I hope will be a magnum opus (at any rate, it looks like being magnum in size) on the Puritan Revolution.'

24 SOC.Dacre 1/2/3: correspondence involving Herman Kellenbenz, J.H. Elliott and Peter Matthias, concerning a visit by Kellenbenz to Oxford, January to June 1957; and SOC.Dacre 9/7/1, file headed 'Economic Diaspora: Written Chapters': 'Questions for Kellenbenz'.

25 SOC.Dacre 9/7/2, 'Prices': Eric Kerridge to Hugh Trevor-Roper, 14 September 1958, Hugh Trevor-Roper to Henry Phelps-Brown, 11 August 1958, to which Phelps-Brown responded on 12 August with three hand-drawn graphs of prices and wages in England 1581–1665 and a typed commentary, as well as sending offprints of articles written with Sheila Hopkins.

26 SOC.Dacre 18/1, file 'RRSC C17 Crisis': Lawrence Stone to Hugh Trevor-Roper, 6 February, 18 July 1959: 'I think the issue of Marxism is dead and that the periodical is now genuinely free from ideological control.'

27 SOC.Dacre 9/7/2, file containing the announcement and an abstract of the lecture given in Paris, 15 March 1960; and SOC.Dacre 18/1, file 'RRSC C17 Crisis': announcement and text of the lecture delivered at Rome, 17 March 1960.

28 Published in G.A. Hayes-McCoy (ed.), *Historical Studies, Vol. IV: Papers Read Before the Fifth Irish Conference of Historians* (Dublin, 1963); for the comment on its reception, *Religion, the Reformation and Social Change*, p. xii. But see F.S.L. Lyons's indignant rebuttal of Trevor-Roper's memory, in his review of the volume for the *Irish Times*, 3 February 1968 (cutting in SOC.Dacre 18/1: 'RRSC Reviews'): 'the local religious reinforcement was neither powerful nor

articulate nor even particularly relevant [...] My own impression was that most of his hearers had a stunned feeling of having been struck by something rapid, forceful and quite outside their experience – rather as if a jaunting car had been hit at a level-crossing by a main-line express.'

29 'Religion, the Reformation and Social Change', pp. 3–4 and notes.

30 Ibid., pp. 4–5 and n., pp. 18–23, notes on pp. 20, 22. German scholarship is cited in the German originals. But Trevor-Roper also knew that Weber's 'arguments are drawn almost exclusively from English Puritan writers' (p. 20, n. 1). The comparative scope of his own essay was explicitly intended to distinguish it from the work of both Weber and R.H. Tawney, 'Weber's most distinguished successor', who had confined himself to English examples (p. 7). On Weber's debt to British scholarship on Puritanism, see Peter Ghosh, 'Max Weber's Idea of "Puritanism": A Case Study in the Empirical Construction of the Protestant Ethic', *History of European Ideas* 29 (2003), pp. 183–221, now reprinted in Peter Ghosh, *A Historian Reads Max Weber: Essays on the Protestant Ethic* (Wiesbaden, 2008).

31 'Religion, the Reformation and Social Change', pp. 7–13 and notes.

32 Weber, *Protestant Ethic*, pp. 98–128, reinforced by the discussion in the notes, pp. 218–40, nn. 5–107 of ch. IV.

33 'Religion, the Reformation and Social Change', p. 25. Although 'the idea occurs constantly in the works of Erasmus', no references are provided.

34 Hugh Trevor-Roper to Peter Miller, 18 March 1999. I am grateful to Professor Miller for permission to cite this letter, and for a transcript. The original is now in SOC.Dacre 1/1/M. Miller himself has quoted extracts of the letter in his review of *Europe's Physician: The Various Life of Sir Theodore de Mayerne*, by Hugh Trevor-Roper, *New Republic*, 13 November 2006. The work by Pintard referred to is: René Pintard, *Le Libertinage erudit dans la première moitié du XVII siècle*, 2 vols (Paris, 1943).

35 Hugh Trevor-Roper to Peter Miller, 18 March 1999: 'Of one thing I can be certain. However my interest in Erasmianism may have developed, it was not a direct result of my work on Laud. I do not think highly of that book, which I wrote, under no supervision, before I had really given any thought to history, historical philosophy, or the history of ideas [...] It was only after my book on Laud was published that I really began to think about history and the history of ideas.'

36 Marjorie Hope Nicolson (ed.), *Conway Letters: The Correspondence of Anne, Viscountess Conway, Henry More, and their Friends, 1642–1684* (London, 1930); revised edition, with an introduction and new material (but not detracting from the original) by Sarah Hutton, (Oxford, 1992). Trevor-Roper returned to the book often, and was still urging it on others in *Europe's Physician: The Various Life of Sir Theodore de Mayerne* (New Haven, CT, and London, 2006), p. 419, n. 30: 'Read – for it is the mirror of a whole society, and deserves to be read in full – Marjorie Hope Nicholson's perfectly edited *Conway Letters*.'

37 Marcel Bataillon, *Érasme et l'Espagne, recherches sur l'histoire spirituelle du xvie siècle* (Paris, 1937). In September 1951 Trevor-Roper informed Berenson that he was reading 'at last that great work, Bataillon's *Erasme en Espagne*': *Letters from Oxford*, p. 74, 25 September 1951.

38 Delio Cantimori, *Eretici italiani del cinquecento* (1939), ed. Adriano Prosperi (Turin, 2002); cited in Trevor-Roper, 'Erasmus', in *Historical Essays*, p. 53, n. 2, p. 54, n. 1; Trevor-Roper, *Protestantesimo e trasformazione sociale*, p. 11.

39 H. John McLachlan, *Socinianism in Seventeenth-Century England* (Oxford, 1951); Trevor-Roper inscribed his copy with the date 1951, and the marginal markings are evidently his. This copy is now in the Dacre Archive.

40 'Erasmus', in *Historical Essays*, p. 54, n. 1, p. 55, n. 2; 'Religious Origins', p. 217, n. 1, in which Trevor-Roper supplemented the reference with the complaints of Bishop Goodman and Sir Edward Peyton that Laud befriended Socinians. These further instances of Laud's favour to Socinians were added in manuscript by Trevor-Roper to his copy of McLachlan's *Socinianism*, pp. 97–9. Goodman's accusation is also quoted in the 'Preface to the Second Edition' of *Archbishop Laud* (1962), p. x, to illustrate Trevor-Roper's altered and expanded understanding of Laud's intellectual liberalism.

41 McLachlan, *Socinianism*, pp. 1–24, 'The Origins and Character of Socinianism'.

42 McLachlan, *Socinianism*: this argument is developed through Chapters 3–8.

43 Ibid., pp. 320–33. The title of the final chapter, 'English Socinianism Becomes Unitarianism', is belied by the chapter's content, which does not support the announced teleology.

44 'Religion, the Reformation and Social Change', pp. 42–3 n., referring to the work of R.K. Merton, R.F. Jones, R. Hooykaas and Christopher Hill.

45 SOC.Dacre 1/2/7: John Cooper to Hugh Trevor-Roper, 28 May 1963.

46 SOC.Dacre 1/2/7: Helli Koenigsberger to Trevor-Roper, 21 September 1963, referring to his own article 'Decadence or Shift? Changes in the Civilisation of Italy and Europe in the Sixteenth and Seventeenth Centuries', *Transactions of the Royal Historical Society* 5/10 (1960).

47 The chronology of the attempt to write the book on the Civil War is reconstructed, with an acute analysis of the difficulties which may have frustrated its completion, by Blair Worden in his memoir, 'Hugh Redwald Trevor-Roper', pp. 262–7.

48 SOC.Dacre 13/29. The notebook is a soft-bound quarto, with lined pages. Printed on the cover is the trade title 'Students Notes', with 'No. 18' below. On the cover (in pencil), and the first lined page (in ink) is the date '1963', in Trevor-Roper's hand. The first 35 pages were paginated by him (but even pages un-numbered before p. 18); six more follow unpaginated. The 'resolutions' are on p. 3. He used the notebook again in 1999, filling five further pages, beginning with the date '1999': this time, however, the entries are simply short notes from books he was reading. (Among these was René Pintard, *Le Libertinage erudit*, in a 1983 re-edition; he may have gone back

to this at Miller's prompting.) I am grateful to Blair Worden for drawing the notebook to my attention. Hereafter, 'Notebook'.

49 'Notebook', pp. 7–9; the paper was published as 'The Historical Philosophy of the Enlightenment', *Studies on Voltaire and the Eighteenth Century (SVEC)* 27 (1963), pp. 1667–87. Now in Hugh Trevor-Roper, *History and the Enlightenment*, ed. John Robertson (New Haven, CT, and London, 2010).

50 'Notebook', p. 9.

51 Ibid., pp. 10–16. 'Altogether,' he concluded, 'Wesley has little use for anything this side of death.'

52 Ibid., pp. 27–34; for his earlier expression of interest, *Letters from Oxford*, pp. 250–1, Trevor-Roper to Berenson, early January 1958.

53 'The Scottish Enlightenment', *SVEC* 58 (1967), pp. 1635–58. It was given as a lecture to the Second International Enlightenment Congress, held at St Andrews, but meeting for the purpose of the lecture in Edinburgh in the same year. Now in *History and the Enlightenment*.

54 Originally published in the *Scottish Historical Review* 84/2/218 (2005), pp. 202–20, and followed by a splendid exchange with William Ferguson: William Ferguson, 'A Reply to Professor Colin Kidd on Lord Dacre's Contribution to the Study of Scottish History and the Scottish Enlightenment', and Colin Kidd, 'On Heroes, Hero-Worship, and Demonology in Scottish Historiography: A Reply to Dr Ferguson', *Scottish Historical Review* 86/1/221 (2007), pp. 96–112.

55 'The Historical Philosophy of the Enlightenment', p. 1672.

56 'The Scottish Enlightenment', pp. 1652–4. The identity of Ogilvie and his associates continued to fascinate Trevor-Roper, who returned to the problem in his late article, 'Pietro Giannone and Great Britain', *Historical Journal*, 39 (1996), pp. 657–75; republished in *History and the Enlightenment*.

57 'Religious Origins', p. 230. The importance of Giannone, alongside Gibbon, to Trevor-Roper was noticed by Bentley, *Modernizing England's Past*, p. 63, n. 73.

58 *Archbishop Laud* (1962), p. ix.

59 Hugh Trevor-Roper, 'Review of Christopher Hill, *Intellectual Origins of the English Revolution* (Oxford, 1965)', *History and Theory* 5 (1966), pp. 61–82. See p. 80, n. 33 for the observation that Hill's determination to identify Puritanism with intellectual progress reproduced similar arguments by American social scientists, notably R.K. Merton, disciple of Weber and author of *Science, Technology and Society in Seventeenth-Century England* (1938; repr. New York, 1970).

60 Warburg Institute Archive, London, Yates Papers, Correspondence: Trevor-Roper to Frances Yates, 15, 22 June 1964; Frances Yates to Trevor-Roper, 19 June 1964.

61 Yates Papers, Correspondence: Trevor-Roper to Frances Yates, 1 June 1966; SOC.Dacre 1/2/10: Trevor-Roper to Robert Silvers (editor of the *NYRB*), 26 May 1966. The letter juxtaposed this eulogy of Yates with a further

instalment of a long-running spoof at the expense of Lawrence Stone. Trevor-Roper informed Silvers of his latest encounter with Agnes Trollope, the redoubtable breeder of basset hounds from 'The Quern, Buttocks, Ambleside, Westmoreland', who was afraid that Lawrence Stone was not going to answer her letter, published in the *NYRB*, about the prevalence of *coitus interruptus* in Puritan England.

62 Hugh Trevor-Roper, 'Frances Yates, Historian', *Listener*, 18 January 1973, pp. 87–8. The essay was by way of a review of Yates's recent book, *The Rosicrucian Enlightenment* (London, 1973). Besides paying tribute to the work of Yates's predecessors at the Warburg Institute, Trevor-Roper acknowledged that his own interest in a different, non-linear approach to the Renaissance was first aroused 'by a now forgotten German philosopher, Moritz Carrière', who wrote in the 1840s.

63 For Yates's self-description to Bataillon (and much else of interest about her), see Patrizia Delpiano, '"Il teatro del mondo": Per un profilo de Frances Amelia Yates', *Rivista Storica Italiana* 105 (1993), pp. 180–245, esp. 230–1 and nn. 159, 238. Yates so described herself to Bataillon in November 1967, having received from Trevor-Roper a copy of his book (almost certainly *Religion, the Reformation and Social Change*) and read it earlier in the summer: SOC.Dacre 1/2/11: Francis Yates to Professor Trevor-Roper, 8 September 1967. It may therefore have been Trevor-Roper who inspired her to think of herself as Erasmus's disciple.

64 'The European Witch-Craze', pp. 132–3, n. 1, and p. 147, n. 2, citing Yates, *The Valois Tapestries*, Studies of the Warburg Institute (London, 1959).

65 Yates Papers, Correspondence: Hugh Trevor-Roper to Frances Yates, 16 December 1969. 'Calvinism and the Enlightenment' was also the title given to 'The Religious Origins' by Theodore Rabb, on receiving from Trevor-Roper a copy of the book which contained it: SOC.Dacre 1/2/11: Theodore Rabb to Trevor-Roper, 26 October 1967. His comment, 'the article on Calvinism and the Enlightenment I have always admired. On re-reading it, I find I am still convinced', suggests that he had heard or read it before its publication in *Religion, the Reformation and Social Change*.

66 Yates Papers, Correspondence: Hugh Trevor-Roper to Frances Yates, 13 January 1970. In between he had written another long letter to her on 28 December 1969. Melville was a Scots Presbyterian.

67 Hugh Trevor-Roper, 'The Paracelsian Movement', in *Renaissance Essays* (London, 1985), pp. 149–99; 'Medicine at the Early Stuart Court', in *From Counter-Reformation to Glorious Revolution* (London, 1992), pp. 27–46.

68 Hugh Trevor-Roper, *Europe's Physician: The Various Life of Sir Theodore de Mayerne* (New Haven, CT, and London, 2006).

69 Yates Papers, Correspondence: Hugh Trevor-Roper to Frances Yates, 8 May 1971: two undated letters, apparently from 1971–2, 21 July 1972, 9 February, 19 July 1973. In one of the undated letters (probably of 1972, since it encloses notes he had made on the manuscript of *The Rosicrucian Enlightenment*), Trevor-

Roper repeats the admission that in 'The Religious Origins' he had missed the stage in the cracking of Calvinism which had occurred at Heidelberg, though there it had 'a different solvent' from that applied by the Arminian/Socinian heretics in Holland, Switzerland and Scotland.

70 Hugh Trevor-Roper, 'The Great Tew Circle', in *Catholics, Anglicans and Puritans: Seventeenth-Century Essays* (London, 1987), pp. 166–230; 'Hugo Grotius and England', in *From Counter-Reformation to Glorious Revolution*, pp. 47–82. The latter was subsequently published in the volume of the conference to which it was originally delivered, in 1991: S. Groenveld and M. Wintle (eds), *The Exchange of Ideas: Religion, Scholarship and Art in Anglo-Dutch Relations in the Seventeenth Century (Britain and the Netherlands)* (Zutphen, 1994).

71 'The Great Tew Circle', quotation on p. 189.

72 'Gibbon and the Publication of *The Decline and Fall of the Roman Empire* 1776–1976', *Journal of Law and Economics* 19/3 (1976), pp. 489–505; 'Dimitrie Cantemir's *Ottoman History* and its Reception in England', *Revue Roumaine d'histoire* 24 (1985), pp. 51–66; 'Introduction' to Lord Macaulay, *The History of England* (Harmondsworth, 1979); 'Thomas Carlyle's Historical Philosophy', *Times Literary Supplement*, 26 June 1981, pp. 731–4; 'Jacob Burckhardt', *Proceedings of the British Academy* 70 (1984), pp. 359–78; 'Pietro Giannone and Great Britain', *Historical Journal* 39 (1996), pp. 657–75; 'Gibbon's Last Project', in David Womersley (ed.), *Edward Gibbon: Bicentenary Essays, SVEC* special issue 355 (1997), pp. 405–19. 'From Deism to History: Conyers Middleton' was originally given as the Leslie Stephen Lecture in Cambridge in 1982, and subsequently revised and enlarged. All these, together with earlier essays on the Scottish Enlightenment, Hume, Gibbon and the Romantic movement and the study of History, are republished in *History and the Enlightenment*. For the chronology of Trevor-Roper's interest in historiography, see the Introduction to that volume.

73 'Historian of Crisis', *Times Literary Supplement*, 19 October 1967, pp. 973–4. The reviewer is not identified in the *TLS* online archive.

74 Gaddo, *Il piacere della controversia*, pp. 200–1.

75 Trevor-Roper would distinguish his own from Berlin's concept of *Ideengeschichte* on these grounds in a letter to Hugh Lloyd-Jones, SOC.Dacre 1/3/30: 5 November 1981. I am grateful to Adam Sisman for the reference.

76 Frances Stonor Saunders, *Who Paid the Piper? The CIA and the Cultural Cold War* (London, 2000), pp. 76–84. Given that the Congress funded *Encounter* (ibid., pp. 165–89), the subsequent publication there of Trevor-Roper's essay on Erasmus was even more pointed.

77 'Historian of Crisis', p. 974.

78 'Wandering Scholar in England', *Sunday Times*, 11 April 1976; I owe this reference to Adam Sisman.

79 For example, Roberto Vivarelli, *I caratteri dell'età contemporanea* (Bologna, 2005), where Trevor-Roper's essays on Erasmus and the religious origins of the Enlightenment are repeatedly cited as 'fundamental' to an appreciation

of Erasmus and his legacy to the modern world: pp. 26 n., 223–4 n., 226 n., 242–3 n. Facile by comparison is the portrayal of selected opponents of totalitarianism during the Cold War as 'Erasmians' by Ralf Dahrendorf, *Erasmiani: Gli intellettuali alla prova del totalitarismo* (Rome and Bari, 2007) (Italian translation of *Versuchungen der Unfreiheit: Die Intellektuellen in Zeiten der Prüfung* (Munich, 2006)). Ironically, Dahrendorf ranks Isaiah Berlin as the leading Erasmian in Cold War England, and makes no mention of Trevor-Roper. (Berlin was, however, awarded the Erasmus Prize in 1983.)

80   As in Natalie Zemon Davis, *Society and Culture in Early Modern France* (Stanford and London, 1975), and Lisa Jardine, *Erasmus, Man of Letters* (Princeton, 1993).

81   Marcel Bataillon, 'A propos de l'influence d'Érasme' (first published in 1970), and 'Vers une définition de l'Érasmisme' (first published in 1972), both reprinted in Marcel Bataillon, *Érasme et l'Espagne*, ed. Daniel Devoto and Charles Amiel, new edn, 3 vols (Geneva, 1991), vol. 3, Annexes, pp. 305–12, 141–54. For Dutch scepticism, M.E.H.N. Mout, 'Erasmianism in Modern Dutch Historiography', in M.E.H.N. Mout, H.H. Smolinsky and J. Trapman (eds), *Erasmianism: Idea and Reality* (Amsterdam, 1997), pp. 189–198; recently reinforced by Judith Pollmann, 'The Bonds of Christian Piety: The Individual Practice of Tolerance and Intolerance in the Dutch Republic', in R. Po-Chia Hsia and H.F.K. Van Nierop (eds), *Calvinism and Religious Toleration in the Dutch Golden Age* (Cambridge, 2002), pp. 53–71.

82   It is here, in the enthusiasm for Frances Yates, that Bentley's charge (*Modernizing England's Past*, pp. 61–4) that Trevor-Roper remained wedded to a reductive 'modernism' most obviously breaks down.

83   Richard Davenport-Hines, 'Introduction', in *Letters from Oxford*, p. xx, quoting the 'Autopsy'; also the intelligent discussion by Gaddo, *Il piacere della contreversia*, pp. 170–7.

84   G.A. Wells, *The Jesus of the Early Christians: A Study in Christian Origins* (London, 1971); and G.A. Wells, *Did Jesus Exist?* (London, 1975). These were items 82 and 83 in the catalogue of 'The Working Library of Lord Dacre', issued by Toby English in 2005. Wells had sent Trevor-Roper the typescript of the first in 1966, seeking advice and help with its publication; in reply, Trevor-Roper commented that 'the argument almost convinces me', SOC.Dacre 1/4/W: Hugh Trevor-Roper to G.A. Wells, 23 May 1966.

85   SOC.Dacre 1/1/W: draft letter of Hugh Trevor-Roper to G.A. Wells, 13 December 1993, thanking Wells for another book, and asking him, rhetorically, why it is so important for Christians to believe the doctrine of the Trinity. 'Perhaps I ought to put the question to Prof. Wiles or Prof. McQuarrie. But I would despair of an intelligible answer from them.' Maurice Wiles and John Macquarrie were professors of theology at Oxford and students of Christ Church: Wiles was an authority on Arianism, author of *Archetypal Heresy: Arianism through the Centuries* (Oxford, 1996).

86   John G.A. Pocock, *Barbarism and Religion, Vol. 1: The Enlightenments of Edward Gibbon* (Cambridge, 1999), esp. pp. 53–4, 59–61; and Sarah Mortimer, *Reason*

and Religion in the English Revolution: The Challenge of Socinianism (Cambridge, 2010).

87   Sarah Hutton, in her new edition of the *Conway Letters*.

88   David Wootton, 'Locke, Socinian or Natural Law theorist?', in J. Crimmins (ed.), *Religion, Secularization and Political Thought* (London, 1989); John Marshall, 'Locke, Socinianism, "Socinianism", and Unitarianism', in M.A. Stewart (ed.), *English Philosophy in the Age of Locke* (Oxford, 2000).

89   Giuseppe Giarrizzo, *Edward Gibbon e la cultura europea del settecento* (Naples, 1954); 'Fra Protestantesimo e deismo: le origini della moderna storiografia inglese sul cristianesimo primitivo [...] C. Middleton (1683–1750)', *Ricerche di Storia Religiosa* 1/1 (Rome, 1954), pp. 151–99; *David Hume politico e storico* (Turin, 1962). Franco Venturi, *Illuministi italiani III riformatori lombardi,piemontesi e toscani, V Riformatori napoletani* (Milan and Naples, 1958, 1962); 'L'illuminismo nel Settecento europeo', in *XIe Congrès International des Sciences Historiques, Stockholm 1960, Rapports IV* (Uppsala, 1960), pp. 106–35, translated as 'The European Enlightenment', in Stuart Woolf (ed.), *Italy and the Enlightenment: Studies in a Cosmopolitan Century* (London, 1972). Venturi had met Trevor-Roper on a visit to Oxford in 1955.

90   See the essays collected in *History and the Enlightenment*.

91   Daniel Roche, *Le siècle des lumières en province: Académies et académiciens provinciaux 1680–1789*, 2 vols (Paris and The Hague, 1978); Robert Darnton, 'In Search of the Enlightenment: Recent Attempts to Create a Social History of Ideas', *Journal of Modern History* 43 (1971), pp. 113–32; N.T. Phillipson, 'Culture and Society in the Eighteenth-Century Province: The Case of Edinburgh and the Scottish Enlightenment', in Lawrence Stone (ed.), *The University in Society*, 2 vols (Princeton, 1974), vol. 2.

92   Franco Venturi, *Utopia and Reform in the Enlightenment* (Cambridge, 1971), pp. 1–5. The lectures were delivered in 1969.

93   'Religious Origins', pp. 200, 213.

94   But see now B.W. Young, 'Conyers Middleton: The Historical Consequences of Heterodoxy', in S. Mortimer and J. Robertson (eds), *The Intellectual Consequences of Religious Heterodoxy 1600–1750* (Leiden, 2012), esp. p. 244, for an argument that Middleton was, after all, an Erasmian.

6. The Politics of the Scottish Enlightenment

1   *The Times*, 27 January 2003.

2   Hugh Trevor-Roper, 'George Buchanan and the Ancient Scottish Constitution', *English Historical Review*, Supplement, 3 (1966); Hugh Trevor-Roper, 'The Highland Tradition of Scotland', in E. Hobsbawm and T. Ranger (eds), *The Invention of Tradition* (Cambridge, 1983).

3   See e.g. D. Stevenson, 'Professor Trevor-Roper and the Scottish Revolution', *History Today* (February 1980), pp. 34–40.

4   For a detached – if somewhat appalled – American perspective on the nationalist hostility aroused by Trevor-Roper's work on the Scottish Enlightenment, see R. Sher, 'Storm over the Literati', *Cencrastus* 28 (1987–8), pp. 42–4.

5   T. Nairn, *The Break-Up of Britain* (London, 1981; first published 1977), p. 120.

6   Hugh Trevor-Roper, 'Scotching the Myths of Devolution', *The Times*, 28 April 1976, p. 14.

7   For an excellent overview of the debate, see C. Berry, *Social Theory of the Scottish Enlightenment* (Edinburgh, 1997), ch. 8. Our understanding of this topic has also been immeasurably enhanced by E. Rothschild, *Economic Sentiments* (Cambridge, MA, 2001).

8   Nairn, *Break-Up of Britain*, p. 112.

9   C. Beveridge and R. Turnbull, *The Eclipse of Scottish Culture* (Edinburgh, 1989); A. Broadie, *The Tradition of Scottish Philosophy: A New Perspective on the Enlightenment* (Edinburgh, 1990).

10 One wonders how far Trevor-Roper's hostility towards religious extremism (not only of the 'Scotch' variety) was shaped during his childhood in Glanton, Northumberland, by local memories of the 'Glanton dispute' which convulsed the Exclusive Brethren: see B.R. Wilson, 'The Exclusive Brethren: A Case Study in the Evolution of a Sectarian Ideology', in B.R. Wilson (ed.), *Patterns of Sectarianism: Organisation and Ideology in Social and Religious Movements* (London, 1967), pp. 306–7.

11 See e.g. Hugh Trevor-Roper, *A Hidden Life: The Enigma of Sir Edmund Backhouse* (London, 1976).

12 Hugh Trevor-Roper, 'The Ossian Forgeries: Wrong but Romantic', *Spectator*, 16 March 1985, pp. 14–15.

13 A. Calder, 'The Enlightenment', in I. Donnachie and C. Whatley (eds), *The Manufacture of Scottish History* (Edinburgh, 1992), p. 48.

14 Beveridge and Turnbull, *Eclipse*.

15 D. Withrington, 'What Was Distinctive about the Scottish Enlightenment?', in J. Carter and J. Pittock (eds), *Aberdeen and the Enlightenment* (Aberdeen, 1987).

16 Hugh Trevor-Roper, 'The Scottish Enlightenment', *SVEC* 58 (1967), pp. 1635–58.

17 Hugh Trevor-Roper, 'Hume as a Historian', in D.F. Pears (ed.), *David Hume: A Symposium* (London, 1963); Hugh Trevor-Roper, 'The Religious Origins of the Enlightenment', in *Religion, the Reformation and Social Change, and Other Essays* (London, 1967); Hugh Trevor-Roper, 'The Romantic Movement and the Study of History', John Coffin Memorial Lecture, University of London, 1969; Hugh Trevor-Roper, *Tyninghame Library* (pamphlet, n.p., 1977); Hugh Trevor-Roper, 'The Scottish Enlightenment', *Blackwood's Magazine* 322 (November 1977), pp. 371–88 (henceforth the two pieces of the same title will be distinguished as 'Scottish Enlightenment', *SVEC*, and 'Scottish Enlightenment', *Blackwood's*); Hugh Trevor-Roper, 'Pietro Giannone and Great Britain', *Historical Journal* 39 (1996), pp. 657–75.

18 'Scottish Enlightenment', *SVEC*, p. 1636.

19 Ibid., p. 1635.

20 Ibid., p. 1637.

21 Ibid., p. 1644.

22 Max Weber, *The Protestant Ethic and the Spirit of Capitalism*, trans. Talcott Parsons (London, 1930). For Trevor-Roper's views of Weber see the title essay 'Religion, the Reformation and Social Change', in *Religion, the Reformation and Social Change*, esp. p. 42, n.

23 Trevor-Roper, 'Religious Origins'.

24 G.D. Henderson, *Mystics of the North-East* (Aberdeen, 1934).

25 C. Hill, 'Protestantism and the Rise of Capitalism', in F.J. Fisher (ed.), *Essays in the Economic and Social History of Tudor and Stuart England in Honour of R.H. Tawney* (Cambridge, 1961). Hill preferred a Tawneyite reformulation of the Weber thesis, though without quite abandoning Weber: C. Hill, 'Daniel Defoe (1660–1731) and Robinson Crusoe', in *The Collected Essays of Christopher Hill, Vol. 1* (Brighton, 1985), p. 110; C. Hill, 'William Perkins and the Poor', in *Puritanism and Revolution* (London, 1958), p. 230, n.

26 H.T. Buckle, *On Scotland and the Scotch Intellect* [from *The History of Civilisation in England* (1857–61)], ed. H.J. Hanham (Chicago, 1970); W.E.H. Lecky, *History of the Rise and Influence of the Spirit of Rationalism in Europe, Vol. 1* (London, 1865), pp. 137–47; J.M. Robertson, *A Short History of Freethought, Vol. 2* (London, 1915), pp. 181–2.

27 Trevor-Roper, 'Hume as a Historian'.

28 D. Forbes, *Hume's Philosophical Politics* (Cambridge, 1975).

29 'Hume as a Historian', p. 94.

30 Ibid. Nevertheless, for an acknowledgement of the wider Scottish contribution to the English Whig tradition in historiography, see Hugh Trevor-Roper, 'Introduction', to T. Macaulay, *History of England* (Harmondsworth, 1979).

31 'Giannone', p. 666.

32 Ibid., p. 667.

33 C. Kidd, 'Scotland's Invisible Enlightenment: Subscription and Heterodoxy in the Eighteenth-Century Kirk', *Records of the Scottish Church History Society* 30 (2000), pp. 28–59; C. Kidd, 'Subscription, the Scottish Enlightenment and the Moderate Interpretation of History', *Journal of Ecclesiastical History* 55 (2004), pp. 502–19.

34 Trevor-Roper, *Tyninghame Library*.

35 C. Jackson, *Restoration Scotland 1660–1690: Royalist Politics, Religion and Ideas* (Woodbridge, 2003); C. Kidd, 'Religious Realignment between the Restoration and Union', in J. Robertson (ed.), *A Union for Empire* (Cambridge, 1995), pp. 147–8, 151–3.

36 'Scottish Enlightenment', *SVEC*, p. 1658.

37 Trevor-Roper, 'Romantic Movement', p. 4. Cf. Trevor-Roper, 'Sir Walter Scott and History', *Listener*, 19 August 1971, pp. 225–32.

38 Trevor-Roper, 'Romantic Movement', p. 4.

39 Ibid., p. 5.
40 Hugh Trevor-Roper, *The Philby Affair* (London, 1968), p. 29.
41 F. Stonor Saunders, *Who Paid the Piper? The CIA and the Cultural Cold War* (London, 2000; first published 1999), pp. 78–80, 84.
42 *Philby Affair*, p. 31.
43 Hugh Trevor-Roper, 'Karl Marx and the Study of History', in *Historical Essays* (London, 1957), p. 289.
44 Hugh Trevor-Roper, *The Past and the Present: History and Sociology* (London, 1969), p. 16.
45 Hugh Trevor-Roper, 'The Moral Minority', *New York Review of Books*, 13 March 1986, pp. 7–10. In 'The Lost Moments of History', *New York Review of Books*, 27 October 1988, pp. 61–7, Trevor-Roper warned against the fallacy of historical inevitability, but also had sharp words for those neo-Tory, or more properly, neo-Jacobite historians who believed that the past could be preserved 'in pickle'.
46 Hugh Trevor-Roper, 'The Gentry 1540–1640', *Economic History Review*, supplement (1953); Hugh Trevor-Roper, 'The General Crisis of the Seventeenth Century', in *Religion, the Reformation and Social Change, and Other Essays* (London, 1967); Hugh Trevor-Roper, *The European Witch-Craze of the Sixteenth and Seventeenth Centuries* (Harmondsworth, 1990; first published 1969).
47 'Scotching the Myths'.
48 *The Times*, 23 September 1976, p. 14; *The Times*, 15 October 1976, p. 15.
49 Hugh Trevor-Roper, 'Foreword', in T. Dalyell, *Devolution: The End of Britain?* (London, 1977).
50 G. Rosie, 'Historian Fights for his Castle', *Sunday Times,* 30 October 1977, p. 4.
51 'Highland Tradition'.
52 See e.g. the contributions of J. Hunter, P.H. Scott, L. Paterson and A. Noble to the symposium 'Ossian and After: The Politics of Tartanry', *Bulletin of Scottish Politics* 2 (1981), pp. 55–81.
53 G.E. Davie, 'The Scottish Enlightenment', in G.E. Davie, *The Scottish Enlightenment and Other Essays* (Edinburgh, 1991); G.E. Davie, *The Democratic Intellect* (Edinburgh, 1964).
54 'Scottish Enlightenment', *Blackwood's*, p. 381.
55 Ibid., p. 374.
56 Ibid., p. 373.
57 Ibid., p. 372.
58 Ibid.
59 H.F. Klemme, 'Scepticism and Common Sense', in A. Broadie (ed.), *The Cambridge Companion to the Scottish Enlightenment* (Cambridge, 2003).
60 See e.g. 'The Hume–Reid Exchange', in Thomas Reid, *An Inquiry into the Human Mind on the Principles of Common Sense*, ed. D.R. Brookes (Edinburgh, 2000), pp. 255–65.

61 J.F. McMillan, 'Scottish Catholics and the Jansenist Controversy: The Case Re-Opened', *Innes Review* 32 (1981), pp. 22–33; J.F. McMillan, 'Thomas Innes and the Bull Unigenitus', *Innes Review* 33 (1982), pp. 23–30; M. Goldie, 'The Scottish Catholic Enlightenment', *Journal of British Studies* 30 (1991), pp. 20–62.

62 'Giannone'.

63 W. Ferguson, *Scotland's Relations with England* (Edinburgh, 1977), p. 243. For his hostile, penetrating and substantial review of Ferguson's *Scotland's Relations*, see Hugh Trevor-Roper, 'The Ideal of the Covenant', *Times Literary Supplement*, 9 September 1977, pp. 1066–7.

64 W. Ferguson, *The Identity of the Scottish Nation* (Edinburgh, 1998), pp. 206–7.

65 Ibid.

66 For Ferguson's view of Donaldson, see his obituary of Donaldson, *Proceedings of the British Academy* 84 (1994), pp. 265–79, and his review of Jim Kirk's biography of Donaldson, *Edinburgh University History Graduates Association Newsletter* 29 (March 1998), pp. 15–17.

67 G. Donaldson, 'Stair's Scotland: The Intellectual Inheritance', *Juridical Review* new ser. 26 (1981), pp. 128–45.

68 'Scottish Enlightenment', *SVEC*, p. 1644.

69 J. Kirk, *Her Majesty's Historiographer: Gordon Donaldson 1913–1993* (Edinburgh, 1996), p. 65.

70 G. Donaldson, 'The Enlightenment and the Illusion', *Scotsman*, 22 April 1988, p. 13. For Rifkind's speech, see *Scotsman*, 16 April 1988, p. 5.

71 Information from Dr Nicholas Phillipson.

72 W. Ferguson, 'The Making of the Treaty of Union of 1707', *Scottish Historical Review* 43 (1964), pp. 89–110.

73 'Scotching the Myths'.

74 L. Colley, *Lewis Namier* (London, 1989).

75 Beveridge and Turnbull, *Eclipse*; C. Beveridge and R. Turnbull, 'Calvinist Enlightenment', in C. Beveridge and R. Turnbull, *Scotland after Enlightenment* (Edinburgh, 1997). See also the brief overview of the problem in N. Ascherson, *Stone Voices: The Search for Scotland* (London, 2002), pp. 38–40.

76 Ouston did not complete his DPhil thesis but he made a marked contribution to the historiography of the pre-Union era. See H. Ouston, 'James VII and the Patronage of Learning in Scotland, 1679–1688', in J. Dwyer, R. Mason and A. Murdoch (eds), *New Perspectives on the Politics and Culture of Early Modern Scotland* (Edinburgh, 1982); H. Ouston, 'Cultural Life from the Restoration to the Union', in A. Hook (ed.), *The History of Scottish Literature, Vol. 2: 1660–1800* (Aberdeen, 1987).

77 J. Robertson, 'The Improving Citizen: Militia Debates and Political Thought in the Scottish Enlightenment', DPhil thesis, Oxford University, 1981, published in a revised version as J. Robertson, *The Scottish Enlightenment and the Militia Issue* (Edinburgh, 1985).

78 Robertson, *A Union for Empire*.

7. Special Service in Germany and *The Last Days of Hitler*

1 This essay was first published in *Vierteljahrshefte fuer Zeitgeschichte* 57/1 (January 2009). I would like to thank Renate Bihl, Judith Curthoys, Richard Davenport-Hines, Roy Hughes, Elizabeth James, Jeremy Noakes, Alysoun Sanders, Adam Sisman, Nathan Winter and Blair Worden for their assistance with the original article. Blair Worden also made many helpful suggestions for the English version.
2 Hugh Trevor-Roper, *The Last Days of Hitler* (London, 1947).
3 SOC.Dacre 10/29: L.B. Namier to H.R. Trevor-Roper, 28 April 1947.
4 Joachim Fest, *Inside Hitler's Bunker: The Last Days of the Third Reich* (London 2005), p. 177; A.J.P. Taylor, 'The Bunker Revisited', *New Statesman and Nation*, 8 July 1950. Taylor described the French translation of *The Last Days* as a book which developed its story with all the brilliance of symphony conducted by a great master: Chris Wrigley, *A.J.P. Taylor: A Complete Annotated Bibliography and Guide to his Historical and Other Writings* (Brighton, 1980), p. 308.
5 SOC.Dacre 6/34.
6 Hugh Trevor-Roper, 'Recherchen der ersten Stunde: Hugh Trevor-Roper ueber "Hitlers Letzte Tage"', in Henning Ritter (ed.), *Werksbesichtigung Geisteswissenschaften: Fuenfundzwanzig Buecher von ihren Autoren gelesen* (Frankfurt am Main, 1990), p. 45; Hugh Trevor-Roper, 'Hitlers Kriegsziele', *Vierteljahrshefte fuer Zeitgeschichte* 8/2 (April 1960), p. 124.
7 SOC.Dacre 13/29, pp. 167–75.
8 SOC.Dacre 10/20: Dick White to Lord Dacre, [June 1985].
9 Henrik Eberle and Mathias Uhl (eds), *The Hitler Book: The Secret Dossier Prepared for Stalin* (London, 2005), pp. 2890–2; V.K. Vinogradov, J.F. Pogonyi and N.V. Teprzov, *Hitler's Death: Russia's Last Great Secret from the Files of the KGB* (London, 2005). Vinogradov's book is based on documents provided by the Russian Federal Security Service and includes interrogations from bunker inmates captured by the Soviets. Often these are very informative and appear authentic, though Hans Rattenhuber's comment (purportedly in May 1945) that the defences of Hitler's headquarters 'were the equal of the fortifications of the Berlin Wall' does not inspire confidence: ibid., p. 186.
10 Antony Beevor, *Berlin: The Downfall* (London, 2003), p. 399; Hugh Trevor-Roper, 'Introduction to the Third Edition', in *The Last Days of Hitler* (London, 2002) (hereafter 'Introduction'), p. xx; SOC.Dacre 10/20, p. 12: A.G. Interrogation Report of Friedrich Olmes of 19 May 1945; SOC.Dacre 20/29: excerpt from the *Evening Standard* of Saturday 9 June 1945 and 'Public Statements by the Russians on Hitler's death'; The National Archives, Kew (TNA) WO 208/3787: CX CF/IV/73, 17 September 1945.
11 TNA KV 4/217: A.D.B.1. [White] to D.B. [Liddell], 14 March 1943; Hugh Trevor-Roper, *The Wartime Journals*, ed. Richard Davenport-Hines (London, 2012), p. 263.

12 TNA KV 4/100: Major General K.W.D. Strong to Sir David Petrie, 10 November 1944, 'Role of the Special Agencies in Combatting Underground Activities in Germany, Note of a meeting held in the Director-General's Room at 5 p.m. on 23rd November, 1944, to consider the SHAEF Proposals for the Creation of a German War Room in London for the Servicing of the C.I. Staffs in Germany'.

13 TNA WO 208/2701: 'History of the Counter Intelligence War Room'. As well as the history itself, this file also contains all the appendices. Not all the appendices survive in the version preserved in KV 4/100, but this file does have the names of the French intelligence officers deleted from WO 208/2701.

14 TNA WO 208/4701: 'History of the Counter Intelligence War Room'.

15 TNA WO 208/3787: C.I.B. [Dick White] to Lt. Col. T.A. Robertson, 10 September 1945.

16 TNA WO 208/3787: Counter Intelligence War Room [T.A. Robertson] to Brigadier D.G. White, 14 and 19 September 1945.

17 TNA WO 208/4701: 'History of the Counter Intelligence War Room'.

18 SOC.Dacre 13/29: pp. 338–9; 'Introduction', pp. xxvii, xxxvi.

19 TNA WO 208/3787: GSI (b), HQ, BAOR [Peter Ramsbotham] to GSI 1 Corps District etc., 18 September 1945.

20 'Introduction', pp. xxvi–xxvii.

21 SOC.Dacre 10/20, Trevor-Roper to Randall, 6 February 1946.

22 SOC.Dacre 10/28: 'The Death of Hitler' and 'The Death of Hitler' Revision note, 11 February 1946.

23 Trevor-Roper, 'Recherchen', p. 43.

24 SOC.Dacre 10/20: 'The Enquiry into Hitler's End'; 10/7, R.W. Leon to Lord Dacre, 23 May 1995.

25 SOC.Dacre 10/7, 'Willi Johannmeier HRT-R', 17 Dec. 1945; Ronald Smelser and Enrico Syring (eds), *Die Militaerelite des Dritten Reiches. 27 biographischen Skizzen* (Frankfurt/M 1997), p. 505.

26 SOC.Dacre 13/58: entries in Trevor-Roper's pocket diaries for December 1945 and January 1946.

27 SOC.Dacre 10/7: 'Willi Johannmeier HRT-R', 17 December 1945.

28 SOC.Dacre 10/7: CSDIC (WEA) to IB, 21 December 1945.

29 SOC.Dacre 10/7: 'Wilhelm Zander', H.R. Trevor-Roper, Major. Int. Corps, 1 January 1946.

30 Ibid.

31 SOC.Dacre 13/29, p. 358.

32 SOC.Dacre 10/7: 'Wilhelm Zander', H.R. Trevor-Roper Major Int Corps, 1 January 1946.

33 SOC.Dacre 10/20: 'The Enquiry into Hitler's End'; 10/7, 'Fortnightly Notes: The Discovery of Hitler's Wills' and 'Third Interrogation of Willi Johannmeier'.

34 SOC.Dacre 10/7: Maj. P.E. Ramsbotham to Maj. Trevor-Roper, 7 January 1945; Trevor-Roper to Brian Melland, Cabinet Office, Historical Section, 8 April 1966; Vinogradov et al., *Hitler's Death*, p. 163.

35 SOC.Dacre 10/7: Trevor-Roper to Brian Melland, Cabinet Office, Historical Section, 8 April 1966.

36 SOC.Dacre 13/29, pp. 367–8.

37 Ibid.

38 Trevor-Roper, 'Recherchen der ersten Stunde', p. 44.

39 SOC.Dacre 10/31; 13/29, pp. 368–69; 10/30: Trevor-Roper to Macmillan, 22 May 1946.

40 SOC.Dacre 10/30: White to Trevor-Roper, 18 March and 17 May 1946.

41 SOC.Dacre 10/30: 'Extract from Minutes of the Meeting Held on 14th June 1946', White to Trevor-Roper, 19 June 1946. As an undergraduate at Christ Church 'Tim' Milne had lived on the same staircase as Trevor-Roper. In later life he was much amused when his old friend was elevated to the House of Lords.

42 SOC.Dacre 10/30: Trevor-Roper to White, 19 June 1946.

43 SOC.Dacre 10/30: Trevor-Roper to Solly Zuckerman, 19 June 1946, 'Extract from JIC (46) 38th Meeting held on 29th June 1946 3. Publication of "The Last Days of Hitler" by Mr Trevor Roper', Zuckerman to Trevor-Roper, 4 July 1946; Hugh Trevor-Roper, *The Last Days of Hitler* (London, 1947), Foreword by [...] Deputy Supreme Commander Allied Expeditionary Force, 1943–45. Tedder's ponderous foreword is omitted from later English paperback editions and from the German paperback edition, *Hitlers letzte Tage* (Frankfurt am Main, 1965).

44 SOC.Dacre 10/30: White to Trevor-Roper, 4 July 1946, Trevor-Roper to White, 6 July 1946, Caccia to White, 17 July 1946, 'Memorandum' [by Hugh Trevor-Roper].

45 SOC.Dacre 10/30: Trevor-Roper to Dick White, 10 May 1946, Trevor-Roper to Hamish Hamilton, 21 May 1946; British Library, Macmillan Archive (BLMA), letters from Dickson to Trevor-Roper, Letter Book 490/420 14 June, Letter Book 491/95 8 July 1946, Letter Book 491/415 8 August 1946. The *Oxford English Dictionary* defines a mugwump as a great man or one who sits on the fence.

46 BLMA Letter Book 492/273, Lovat Dickson to Trevor-Roper, 17 September 1946.

47 BLMA, letters from Dickson to Trevor-Roper, Letter Book 493/119 17 October 1946, Letter Book 494/339 18 December 1946; BLMA, New Books and New Editions 23 November 2/43–September 11/47.

48 SOC.Dacre 10/29: David Thomson, review of *The Last Days of Hitler*, *Cambridge Review*, May 1947.

49 *The Last Days of Hitler* (1947), pp. 1–2, 255.

50 Franz Neumann, *Behemoth: The Structure and Practice of National Socialism* (New York, 1944), pp. 396, 469; Martin Broszat, *Der Staat Hitlers* (Lausanne, 1969).

51 Dieter Schenk, *Hitlers Mann in Danzig* (Bonn, 2000), p. 195; Wolfgang Haenel, *Hermann Rauschnings 'Gespraeche mit Hitler' – Eine Geschichtsfaelschung* (Ingolstadt, 1984), pp. 4–6; Elke Froehlich (ed.), *Die Tagebuecher von Joseph*

316 • Notes to Pages 181–5

Goebbels: Saemtliche Fragmente Teil I Aufzeichnungen 1924–1941 Band 4 (Munich, 1987), pp. 41, 73.

52 SOC.Dacre 10/29: L.B. Namier to H.R. Trevor-Roper, 28 April 1947.

53 Norman H. Baynes, *A Short List of Books on National Socialism*, Historical Association Pamphlet 125 (London, 1943).

54 *The Last Days of Hitler* (1947), p. 4; Hugh Trevor-Roper, 'The Mind of Adolf Hitler', introduction to *Hitler's Table-Talk 1941–1944* (London, 1953), p. x; SOC.Dacre 10/29: Trevor-Roper to Namier, 30 April 1947; Alan Bullock, *Hitler: A Study in Tyranny* (London, 1952); Hermann Graml and Klaus-Dietmar Henke (eds), *Nach Hitler: Der schwierige Umgang mit unserer Geschichte: Beitraege von Martin Broszat* (Munich, 1987), p. 249.

55 Haenel, *Geschichtsfaelschung*, pp. 25–7, 31–42; Hermann Rauschning, *Hitler m'a dit* (Paris, 1939); Trevor-Roper, 'Recherchen der ersten Stunde', p. 49; Ian Kershaw, *The Nazi Dictatorship: Problems and Perspectives of Interpretation*, 4th edn (London, 2000), p. 83.

56 Hermann Rauschning, *Germany's Revolution of Destruction* (London, 1939), pp. 16, 21, 34.

57 Ibid., p. 196.

58 *The Last Days of Hitler* (1947), pp. 4–5; Fest, *Inside Hitler's Bunker*, p. 125. Trevor-Roper neatly summed up his emphasis on the centrality of Russia in Hitler's world view in 'Hitlers Kriegsziele': 'mit dem Russlandkrieg stand oder fiel der Nationalsozialismus', *Vierteljahrshefte fuer Zeitgeschichte* 8/2, p. 129.

59 *The Last Days of Hitler* (1947), p. 84.

60 Ibid., p. 263. See also Hugh Trevor-Roper, 'Portraet des wirklichen Nazi-verbrechers' (1949), in Adelbert Reif (ed.), *Albert Speer: Kontroversen um ein deutsches Phaenomen* (Munich, 1978).

61 SOC.Dacre 10/29: J.K. Galbraith to Trevor-Roper, 15 July 1947.

62 Matthias Schmidt, *Albert Speer: Das Ende eines Mythos: Speers wahre Rolle im Dritten Reich* (Bern, 1982). Trevor-Roper's personal copy of Schmidt's book shows that he worked through it in his usual method, which was to mark significant passages and construct his own list of contents on the endpapers or inserts. He concluded: 'I cannot go as far as Matthias Schmidt' (in revising his view of Speer), 'Recherchen der ersten Stunde', p. 49.

63 Heinrich Schwendemann, 'Drastic Measures to Defend the Reich at the Oder and the Rhine: A Forgotten Memorandum of Albert Speer of 18 March 1945', *Journal of Contemporary History* 38/4 (October 2003), pp. 600–7.

64 Trevor-Roper, 'Recherchen der ersten Stunde', p. 49.

65 *The Last Days of Hitler* (1947), pp. 22–7, 40–2; Hans Mommsen, 'The Indian Summer and the Collapse of the Third Reich: The Last Act', in Hans Mommsen, *The Third Reich between Vision and Reality: New Perspectives on German History 1918–1945* (Oxford, 2001), pp. 109–10.

66 *The Last Days of Hitler* (1947), p. 8; SOC.Dacre 10/29: Dr Johann Neuhaeusler, Weihbischof to Herrn H.R. Trevor-Roper, 7 January 1950.

67 SOC.Dacre 10/29: Trevor-Roper to Herrn Weihbischof Dr Johann Neu-haeusler, 18 January 1950.

68 *The Last Days of Hitler* (1947), pp. 18–19.

69 J. Brodrick, SJ, 'Jesuits and Nazis', *The Tablet*, 21 June 1947.

70 *The Last Days of Hitler* (1947), pp. 21–2.

71 Brodrick, 'Jesuits and Nazis'.

72 SOC.Dacre 6/5: letter from Evelyn Waugh, 12 April 1947.

73 *The Last Days of Hitler*, 2nd edn (London, 1950), pp. lvi, 18–19, and footnote to pp. 22–3; SOC.Dacre 10/29: Bernard Bassett SJ to Trevor-Roper, 30 May 1947; F.W. Pick to H.R. Trevor-Roper, 26 May 1948; Trevor-Roper, *Hitlers letzte Tage*, pp. 52–3. It is unlikely Trevor-Roper had advance sight of the 1965 German edition, which reproduced the Swiss edition of 1948 published by Amstutz and Herdeg.

74 TNA FO 938/196: Francis Graham-Harrison to C.M. Anderson, 13 July 1947.

75 Ibid., Hugh Trevor-Roper to Robert Birley, 15 May 1947; Michael Balfour to D. Whyte, [PMD] Section, Foreign Office, 27 May 1947; BLMA Letter Book 497/606, Lovat Dickson to Trevor-Roper, 11 June 1947.

76 TNA FO 938/196, PMD Section (Whyte) to R.F. Allen, Macmillan & Co., 29 August 1947.

77 TNA FO 938/196, Michael Balfour, Control Commission for Germany (British Element) to David Whyte, G.I. (PDM) Section, Foreign Office, 27 May 1947; Foreign Office PMD Section to M. Balfour CCG (BE) Berlin, 6 June 1947; Trevor-Roper, *Hitlers letzte Tage* (n.p., Spiegel Verlag, 1947).

78 TNA FO 938/196: Foreign Office PMD Section to Verlag Amstutz, 6 September 1947; Amstutz to D.H. Whyte, PMD Section, 17 September 1947 and 5 February 1948; D.H. Whyte to P.S. to Chancellor, 3 December 1947; BLMA Letter Book 526/501, R.F. Allen to Dr Amstutz, 25 April 1952.

79 TNA FO 938/196: Information Centres Section Kiel to HQ Information Centres Section, March 1948; Land N. Rhine Westphalia, 'Reader's [*sic*] Reactions to the book "The Last Days of Hitler"; PRISC Branch to Information Centres Control Branch, CCG (BE) ZEO, 4 March 1948.

80 TNA FO 938/196: D.H. Whyte to Mrs Redlich, German and Austrian Service Desk, Norfolk House, 24 May 1948.

81 Anton Joachimsthaler, *The Last Days of Hitler: The Legends, the Evidence, the Truth* (London, 1999); A.J.P. Taylor, 'Funeral in Berlin', *Observer*, 29 September 1968.

8. 'The Chap with the Closest Tabs': Trevor-Roper and the Hunt for Hitler

1 The National Archives, Kew (TNA) WO 208/3787: Brigadier Dick White (Counter Intelligence War Room) to Main HQ, British Army of the Rhine (BAOR), 10 September 1945.

2 Hugh Trevor-Roper, *The Wartime Journals*, ed. Richard Davenport-Hines (London, 2012), p. 263. See too the story repeated in *One Hundred Letters from Hugh Trevor-Roper*, ed. Richard Davenport-Hines and Adam Sisman (Oxford, 2014), pp. xxii–xxiii.

3 TNA WO 208/3787: CI War Room to White, 14 September 1945; Robertson to White, 19 September 1945.

4 TNA KV4/100: 'History of the Counter-Intelligence War Room, March 1-November 1 1945', 17 January 1946, pp. 1–3.

5 Ibid., pp. 7–14, Appendix A.

6 Hugh Trevor-Roper, *The Last Days of Hitler*, 3rd edn (London, 1956), pp. 11–13, 22–6.

7 TNA FO 371/46748: telegram from British Embassy, Moscow, to Foreign Office, 2 May 1945; telegram from British Embassy to Foreign Office, 6 May 1945. Frank Roberts in the Moscow Embassy observed that the suicide of Joseph Goebbels and his family had been formally announced by the Russians, but that the Russians believed Hitler, Himmler and Göring had all gone to earth somewhere.

8 TNA FO 371/46914: British Embassy, Moscow, to Foreign Office, 22 May 1945; Foreign Office minute, 22 May 1945.

9 The most recent account of the Soviet investigation based on Soviet sources can be found in the editors' afterword in Henrik Eberle and Matthias Uhl (eds), *The Hitler Book: The Secret Dossier Prepared for Stalin* (London, 2005), pp. 280–3. See too Anton Joachimsthaler, *Hitlers Ende: Legenden und Dokumente* (Berlin, 2004) and Joachim Fest, *Inside Hitler's Bunker: The Last Days of the Third Reich* (London, 2005).

10 TNA FO 317/46748: G. Harrison (German Desk, Foreign Office) minute, 'Some Thoughts on Hitler's Death', 2 May 1945: 'There is every indication that the German propaganda will play up the manner of Hitler's death with a view to establishing a Hitler legend. We must do all in our power to play it down.'

11 TNA FO 371/46748: telegram from Joint Staff Mission, Washington, to Moscow mission, 2 May 1945; report from *The Times*, 24 May 1945; TNA FO 371/46747: British Embassy, Stockholm, to Foreign Office, 13 April 1945. The latter report included Bernadotte's claim that everyone he talked to in Germany who had seen Hitler thought he had become 'quite insane'.

12 TNA FO 1049/288: 'Ashcan Report' for the Control Commission for Germany, Political Division (n.d.), pp. 16, 20.

13 TNA WO 204/2349: statement taken by US First Army from Walter Hirsch, 28 May 1945.

14 For this story and others, see TNA WO 288/4475: BBC monitoring service, 'Hitler in Ireland', 16 June 1945; Donald M. McKale, *Hitler: The Survival Myth* (New York, 1981), pp. 44–6.

15 TNA FO 371/46748: article from *The Times*, 7 June 1945; WO 208/4475: MI6 minute, 'Reported Finding of Hitler's Body' [n.d. but 7 June 1945?];

'Jawbones Identified as Hitler's', *The Times*, 9 July 1945. Geoffrey Roberts, *Stalin's General: The Life of Georgy Zhukov* (London, 2012), p. 230, who confirms that Zhukov shared Stalin's suspicion that Hitler had not died in the bunker.

16 TNA FO 371/46748: question from Maj. Anstruther-Gray for Churchill, June 1945; FO 371/48749: question from Sir Waldron Smithers to Ernest Bevin, October 1945.

17 TNA PREM 4/100/13: UK delegation at San Francisco to Antony Eden (Foreign Office), May 1945; WO 32/11728: Army Council Secretariat, extract from conclusions of War Cabinet, 3 May 1945. The Foreign Office view was that the death of Hitler and Mussolini made trials of the lesser criminals 'inexpedient'.

18 Richard Overy, *Interrogations: The Nazi Elite in Allied Hands* (London, 2001), pp. 47–8, 96–8.

19 National Archives and Records Administration (NARA), College Park, MD, McCloy Papers, RG107, Box 1: Henry Morgenthau to John McCloy, 19 January 1945, 'Memorandum Re. the War Department Memorandum Concerning the Punishment of War Criminals', pp. 3–4; Box 2: Memorandum for the Lord Chancellor (John Simon) from Judge Samuel Rosenman, 21 April 1945.

20 TNA FO 371/46749, memorandum from the Joint Intelligence Committee, SHAEF, 30 July 1945, 'Hitler's Last Days', pp. 3–4; WO 219/1700, SHAEF, JIC Political Intelligence Report, Annex A 'Hitler's Last Days', 2 July 1945, pp. 3–4.

21 TNA WO 208/3287: HQ 30 Corps District to GS1b, Headquarters, British Army of the Rhine, 6 October 1945, encl. 'Interrogation Report of Hilco Poppen in Rotenburg Hospital, 30 Sept 1945'.

22 NARA RG338, Box 81: 21 Army Group Interrogation Centre, 'Interim Report in the Case of Werner Grothmann', 25 June 1945, pp. 10–11.

23 NARA, Jackson Main Files, Box 1: William Donovan (OSS) to Justice Robert Jackson, 25 September 1945; Box 39: memorandum from Colonel Street for Judge Advocate General's Office, 11 August 1945, 'Whereabouts of Major German War Criminals as of 11 August 1945'; TNA WO 311/576: War Office to Attorney General, 'List of Names of Major War Criminals', 31 July 1945.

24 TNA FO 371/46749: intelligence report for the Foreign Office, 8 October 1945, reporting a sighting of Bormann and Hitler in Norway.

25 TNA LCO 2/2980: 'Rough Notes, Meeting with Russians', 29 June 1945.

26 NARA, Jackson Files, Box 34: 'Indictment – 1st Draft', n.d., p. 1.

27 TNA FO 1019/98: Jackson to Maxwell-Fyfe, 22 September 1945; memorandum for Jackson from Maxwell-Fyfe, 23 September 1945, p. 2.

28 TNA WO 311/39: 'Report of Meeting of the British War Crimes Executive', 26 September 1945, p. 5.

29 TNA LCO 2/2982: IMT papers, '30.4.45', n.d. but October 1945. The Indictment was formally served on the prisoners on 19 October.

30 TNA FO 371/46749: 'Last Days of the Third Reich', newspaper cuttings; British Embassy Moscow to Foreign Office, 12 September 1945.

31 *Wartime Journals*, p. 263.

32 Sara Douglas, 'The Search for Hitler: Hugh Trevor-Roper, Humphrey Searle, and the Last Days of Adolf Hitler', *Journal of Military History* 78 (2014), pp. 165–92; E.D.R. Harrison, 'Hugh Trevor-Roper und "Hitlers letzte Tage"', *Vierteljahreshefte für Zeitgeschichte* 57 (2009), pp. 33–60.

33 *Wartime Journals*, p. 264.

34 TNA WO 208/3787, Trevor-Roper to Ramsbotham, encl. 'Present position of enquiry and recommendation for further action' [n.d. but October 1945], pp. 1–2.

35 TNA WO 208/3787: 'The Death of Hitler', Annexe.

36 TNA FO 1005/1735: Intelligence Group Office, CCG, Intelligence Directive No. 6, 11 August 1945.

37 TNA WO 208/3787: Air Division HQ, US Forces in Austria, 'The Last Days in Hitler's Air Raid Shelter', 8 October 1945, pp. 12–13.

38 TNA FO 1005/1706: HQ Berlin Area, Intelligence Bureau, Intelligence Summary No. 11, 15 September 1945, pp. 2–4.

39 TNA WO 208/3787: Trevor-Roper to Ramsbotham, n.d. but late October 1945.

40 TNA WO 208/3781: General Bishop to Advanced HQ, Control Commission for Germany, 26 October 1945.

41 TNA WO 208/3787: 'The Death of Hitler', pp. 3–4. The whole report is reproduced in Douglas, 'The Search for Hitler', pp. 195–200.

42 *Wartime Journals*, p. 264.

43 TNA WO 208/3781: cutting from *Paris-Matin*, 12 December 1945.

44 TNA WO 208/3790: Confidential, Censorship, Civil Communications, 10 January 1946.

45 TNA WO 208/3791: Censorship, Civil Communications, 30 October 1947, letter from Jonny J. to Alfried K., 25 October 1947.

46 See, for example, TNA FO 1005/1706: HQ Berlin Area, Intelligence Summary No. 3, 21 July 1945, p. 2: 'The hatred of Nazism is so genuine and universal that it needs no illustration.'

47 TNA WO 208/3791: Brig. C.E. Hirsch (Deputy Director of Military Intelligence) to Maj. Gen. J. Lethbridge, Control Commission for Germany, BAOR (n.d.).

48 For details of the relationship between Trevor-Roper and the subsequent investigation see Douglas, 'The Search for Hitler', pp. 178–88.

49 TNA WO 208/3790: Trevor-Roper to Searle, Intelligence Bureau, BAOR, 7 March 1945; 'Time Table of Events in Hitler's Bunker' (n.d.); Searle memorandum, 'The Hitler Case: Position as at 9 March 1945', pp. 1–3.

50 TNA WO 208/4428: Trevor-Roper to Searle, 6 February 1946.

51 TNA WO 208/4428: Maj. H. March (G2 SHAEF) to Intelligence Bureau HQ, BAOR, 5 March 1946; WO 208/3790: Searle to Trevor-Roper, 28 February 1946.
52 TNA WO 208/3791: HQ Intelligence Division, BAOR, to Regional Intelligence Staff, 3 December 1947. Trevor-Roper's account was still only defined as 'almost certain'.
53 Among the best is Ada Petrova and Peter Watson, *The Death of Hitler: The Final Words from Russia's Secret Archive* (London, 1995), which not only examined the testimony with a shrewd critical eye but also, thanks to access to Soviet archives and Hitler's jawbone, was able to unravel the confusing and at times mendacious course of Soviet analysis of Hitler's death.
54 Eberle and Uhl, *The Hitler Book*, pp. 284–8. On the possibility of a shot and a cyanide capsule see, for example, Hans-Joachim Neumann and Henrik Eberle, *Was Hitler Ill? A Final Diagnosis* (Cambridge, 2013), pp. 183–4; Petrova and Watson, *The Death of Hitler*, pp. 117–19.
55 Eberle and Uhl, *The Hitler Book*, pp. xxiv–xxv.
56 Petrova and Watson, *The Death of Hitler*, pp. 112–13.
57 TNA WO 208/3791: Federal Foreign Office to Secretary General, Allied High Commission, 24 February 1953; British Intelligence Organization (Germany) to Federal Foreign Office, 13 March 1953.
58 TNA WO 208/3787: newspaper article from *Der Mittag*, 17 May 1956; WO 208/3791: article from *Schleswig-Holsteinische Volkszeitung*, 31 December 1956.

9. Himmler's Masseur

1 Kersten's application for Swedish citizenship was the subject of a parliamentary debate on 29 April 1954; the Swedish Ministry for Foreign Affairs issued a communiqué on 2 February 1953 refuting the claim that Bernadotte had refused to take any Jews in the Swedish buses and that he had merely acted as a transport officer, as Trevor-Roper had alleged in his article, 'Kersten, Himmler, and Count Bernadotte', *Atlantic Monthly*, February 1953, pp. 43–5; the White Book was published by the Swedish Foreign Office on 26 April 1956. Trevor-Roper responded to the criticism of his account of the Swedish rescue expedition and of his 'consistent tendency to belittle Count Bernadotte's work' in an article for the Swedish newspaper *Dagens Nyheter*, 27 April 1956. He concluded that, 'while a few points of detail in my incidental summary of the Relief Expedition may be judged controversial in the light of new documents, my thesis itself – the sole cause and justification of the White Book – has triumphed by default.'
2 *Manchester Guardian*, 26 April 1956.
3 SOC.Dacre 10/52/1–3.
4 'So great was Himmler's faith in Kersten's ability that he submitted every one in the Third Reich whom he regarded as important to a sort of test,

which consisted of a physical examination by Kersten; for Kersten claimed that through his manipulations he could feel the nature of the nervous energy of an individual, and thereby judge his mental and intellectual capacities.' W. Schellenberg, *The Schellenberg Memoirs*, ed. and trans. Louis Hagan, with an introduction by Alan Bullock (London, 1956), p. 348.

5 Trevor-Roper was wary of Schellenberg's evidence, finding it 'always strongly tinged by self-interest'. This, he wrote, 'is particularly so in his relations with Bernadotte, since he believed that Bernadotte, if judiciously handled, might be able to influence his fate. I had personally a great deal to do with Schellenberg during and after the war and was closely concerned with his arrest and later interrogation; and consequently I have had plenty of opportunity of studying him. For these reasons I always treat his evidence with reserve, except when it can be shown that he had no personal interest in its representation.' SOC.Dacre 10/52/8: letter to Nobert Masur, 9 June 1954.

6 F. Kersten, *The Kersten Memoirs, 1940–45* (London, 1956). An earlier English version, from which Kersten tried to dissociate himself, had been published in America in 1947 before Trevor-Roper's involvement in the convoluted affair. Trevor-Roper also wrote an introduction to Joseph Kessel's novelistic biography of Kersten, first published in French, *Les Mains du Miracle* (Paris, 1960), and later in English as *The Magic Touch* (London, 1961).

7 SOC.Dacre 10/52/6. The handwriting suggests that the note was written towards the end of Trevor-Roper's life.

8 SOC.Dacre 10/52/1–3: undated fax from 1995.

9 Werner Neuß, *Menschenfreund und Mörder* (Halle, 2010).

10 SOC.Dacre 10/52/4: letter to Jan Wellmann, 15 October 1997.

11 Louis de Jong, 'Hat Felix Kersten das niederländische Volk gerettet?', in Hans Rothfels and Theodor Eschenburg (eds), *Zwei Legenden aus dem Dritten Reich* (Stuttgart, 1974).

12 Again, accounts vary. The introduction may have been made by August Rostberg, another industrialist, who, like Diehn, was a member of the 'Circle of Friends of the Reichsführer SS', a select group of German businessmen who helped finance Hitler.

13 Masur denied that Himmler had thus greeted him. SOC.Dacre 10/52/8: letter to Trevor-Roper, 2 June 1954.

14 Trevor-Roper pointed out that Schellenberg's draft for Bernadotte's memoirs had credited Kersten and Masur but that their names had been removed from the final version. 'The Strange Case of Himmler's Doctor', *Commentary*, 1 April 1957. In his memoirs, first published in 1956 and reissued in 2006, Schellenberg also acknowledges Kersten's role.

15 In the report presented to the Foreign Minister on 12 January 1950 the Commission found that Kersten had 'prevented, or at any rate largely contributed to preventing the plan to deport a large number of Dutch to the East'. The findings of the Enquêtecommissie Regeringsbeleid 1940–1945 were eventually published on 2 October 1952. Trevor-Roper later came to

think that Posthumus had been naive and that the Enquêtecommissie reflected that naiveté.

16 De Jong had approached Trevor-Roper on 27 October 1947 after reading *The Last Days of Hitler* and suggested that he get in touch with Kersten. 'You have dealt with him here and there in your book, mostly, I presume, on information supplied to you by Schellenberg. I am, however, convinced, that Kersten would be able to give you much more interesting information.' De Jong had met Kersten a number of times. At that time he regarded him as 'a great friend of Holland' who had helped to forestall 'many sinister nazi-plans regarding Holland.' SOC.Dacre 10/52/1. Trevor-Roper wrote to Kersten on 9 December 1947 and sent him a copy of the Swedish translation of *The Last Days of Hitler*, inviting him to make comments, so that he could correct possible errors in the next edition (SOC.Dacre 10/52/7). By 1957 De Jong suspected that Kersten was not to be trusted. He reminded Trevor-Roper of this when in 1972 he sent him his study of Kersten and the supposed rescue of the Dutch nation: 'I have come to the conclusion, not only that the story as told by Kersten, is a pure fabrication, but that he has also faked his so-called documentary proofs.' SOC. Dacre 10/52/3: De Jong to Trevor-Roper, 25 July 1972.

17 SOC.Dacre 10/52/2.

18 Hugh Trevor-Roper, *The Last Days of Hitler*, 1st edn (March 1947), p. 267. In an earlier footnote, on p. 146, Trevor-Roper reproved Bernadotte for 'a slip of memory' in connection with a meeting with Himmler and Schellenberg late on 23 April 1945 in the Swedish Consulate in Lübeck. Bernadotte had ascribed 'both to Himmler and (before Himmler's arrival) to Schellenberg the statement that Hitler could only last a few days and that Himmler was prepared to offer surrender'. Trevor-Roper pointed out that Schellenberg had 'no means of knowing, and says himself that he first heard the words from Himmler in Bernadotte's presence'. Trevor-Roper corrected the misquotation in the reprint of *The Last Days* published in April 1947.

19 On 12 July 1975 Trevor-Roper wrote to the historian Gerald Fleming, who bombarded him with letters in the course of his meticulous research into the authenticity of Kersten's documents that he had been drawn into the Kersten affair 'because Bernadotte involved me in correspondence and then took steps, which I somewhat resented, to get the correspondence published in Sweden. This showed that he had had an ulterior motive in writing an apparently personal letter to me.' SOC.Dacre 1/1/F.

20 SOC.Dacre 10/52/2.

21 Ibid.

22 The rules, a copy of which is in Trevor-Roper's files on Kersten (SOC.Dacre 10/52/9), stipulate that only 'the following persons are held to be duly qualified to present candidates for the Nobel Peace Prize:

> Members and late members of the Nobel Committee of the Norwegian Parliament, as well as the advisors appointed at the Norwegian Nobel Institute.

Members of Parliament and Members of Government of the different
states, as well as Members of the Interparliamentary Union.

Members of the International Arbitration Court at The Hague.

Members of the Commission of the Permanent International Peace
Bureau.

Members and Associates of the Institute of International Law.

University professors of Political Science and of Law, of History and
Philosophy.

Persons who have received the Nobel Peace Prize.

Trevor-Roper, then a lecturer in Modern History, did not fit any of these
categories.

23 SOC.Dacre 10/52/2: 'Note for my Own Memory', undated.

24 *Letters from Oxford*, ed. Richard Davenport-Hines (London, 2006), pp. 59ff.

25 Dacre Papers 10/52/1–3.

26 'Die Herkunft des "Bernadotte-Briefes" an Himmler vom 10. März 1945',
Vierteljahreshefte für Zeitgeschichte 26/4 (October 1978), pp. 571–600.

27 White, then director-general of MI5, replied on 1 October 1953 that to the
best of his knowledge British intelligence had not sent deception material to
the Germans via Bernadotte. SOC.Dacre 10/52/2.

28 SOC.Dacre 10/52/7: letter from Crossmann to Trevor-Roper, 24 April 1956.
Speculation that Bernadotte's assassination by Jewish extremists may have
been connected to the Swedish rescue mission has been a matter of some
dispute.

29 SOC.Dacre 10/52/4: letter to Harry J. Trimborn, an American journalist, who
asked Trevor-Roper whether his views on Bernadotte had changed, 4 August
1986.

30 *One Hundred Letters from Hugh Trevor-Roper*, ed. Richard Davenport-Hines and
Adam Sisman (Oxford, 2014), p. 412.

31 SOC.Dacre 10/23.

32 SOC.Dacre 10/25.

33 N. Masur, *En Jude talar med Himmler* (Stockholm, 1945). Kersten and Masur
also bickered about Masur's contribution to the rescue mission. Kersten
maintained that he had already secured the release of Jewish and other prisoners
from Himmler prior to the meeting on 21 April 1945. Whilst recognising
Kersten's achievement, Masur vigorously protested at the minimisation of his
own role in the negotiations of that night.

34 'First by telephone, then in person, first Masur then Storch descended upon
me, each denouncing the other. Already battered by the rival champions of
Bernadotte and Kersten, I was in no mood to take sides in this secondary
battle and contented myself with listening. But my sympathies were with
Masur. Even with the shield of the Swedish passport, it required no small
courage for a Jew to enter Nazi Germany in its last savage convulsions
and face, in person, the terrible exterminator of his people.' SOC.Dacre
10/52/1–3.

35 *The Last Days of Hitler*, p. 212.
36 Ibid., p. 29.
37 SOC.Dacre 10/52/5.
38 Trevor-Roper in 'Hitler Revisited: A Retrospective', *Encounter*, December 1988.

10. Trevor-Roper and Thomas Carlyle: History and Sensibility

1 I am deeply indebted to Blair Worden, Noël Sugimura, Mishtooni Bose, Ksenia Levina, Rory Allan, Joshua Bennett and Timothy Pleydell-Bouverie for their invariably helpful comments.
2 Hugh Trevor-Roper, 'The Faustian Historian: Jacob Burckhardt', in Hugh Trevor-Roper, *Historical Essays* (London, 1957), and 'Jacob Burckhardt', in Hugh Trevor-Roper, *History and the Enlightenment*, ed. John Robertson (New Haven, CT, and London, 2010), pp. 246–65.
3 For a sympathetic study of which development, see Harvey J. Kaye, *The British Marxist Historians: An Introductory Analysis* (Cambridge, 1984).
4 But see now J.G.A. Pocock, *Barbarism and Religion*, 6 vols (Cambridge, 1999–2015).
5 Isaiah Berlin, 'The Originality of Machiavelli', in *Against the Current: Essays in the History of Ideas* (London, 1979), pp. 25–79.
6 SOC.Dacre 9/101, fo. 2r.
7 Hugh Trevor-Roper, *The Crisis of the Seventeenth Century: Religion, The Reformation and Social Change* (Indianapolis, 1967), p. xiv.
8 See Hugh Trevor-Roper, 'The Romantic Movement and the Study of History', in *History and the Enlightenment*, pp. 176–91.
9 John Holloway, *The Victorian Sage: Studies in Argument* (London, 1953), pp. 21–85; Basil Willey, *Nineteenth-Century Studies: Coleridge to Matthew Arnold* (London, 1949), pp. 102–31; Raymond Williams, *Culture and Society 1780–1850* (London, 1958), pp. 85–98.
10 SOC.Dacre 9/8/1: typescript, pp. 45–136.
11 SOC.Dacre 9/8/1, p. 46.
12 Hugh Trevor-Roper, 'Milton in Politics', in Hugh Trevor-Roper, *Catholics, Anglicans, and Puritans: Seventeenth-Century Essays* (London, 1987), pp. 231–82. For the Trevor-Roper and Waugh correspondence see the *New Statesman*, 12 and 26 December 1953. For a more considered critique of Hill's approach to seventeenth-century intellectual history, see Trevor-Roper's review of Hill's *The Intellectual Origins of the English Revolution*, in *History and Theory* 5 (1966), pp. 61–82.
13 SOC.Dacre 9/8/1, p. 123.
14 Thomas Carlyle, 'The New Downing Street', in Thomas Carlyle, *Latter-Day Pamphlets* (London, 1850), at pp. 49–50.

15 A.J. Ayer, *Part of my Life* (London, 1977), pp. 75–114, 191–3. The present essay is naturally indebted biographically to Adam Sisman, *Hugh Trevor-Roper: The Biography* (London, 2010).

16 Hugh Trevor-Roper, 'Sir Keith Feiling', *Christ Church Annual Report* (1977), pp. 29–34, at p. 34. This encomium stands in sharp contrast with his younger views: see Hugh Trevor-Roper, *The Wartime Journals*, ed. Richard Davenport-Hines (London, 2012), pp. 26, 31, 189, 271–2. Such modulations are not uncommon in attitudes and memory.

17 Hugh Trevor-Roper, *Archbishop Laud* (London, 1940), 'Acknowledgements'.

18 Hugh Trevor-Roper, 'James Ussher, Archbishop of Armagh', in Hugh Trevor-Roper, *Catholics, Anglicans and Puritans: Seventeenth-Century Essays* (London, 1987), pp. 120–65, at p. 159.

19 See Andrew Fletcher, *The Political Works*, ed. John Robertson (Cambridge, 1997).

20 Hugh Trevor-Roper, 'The General Crisis of the Seventeenth Century', in *Religion, the Reformation and Social Change*, pp. 43–81.

21 Thomas Carlyle, *Oliver Cromwell's Letters and Speeches: With Elucidations*, 3rd edn, 4 vols (London, 1850), vol. 1, pp. 3–4. For invaluable discussion, see Blair Worden, 'Thomas Carlyle and Oliver Cromwell', *Proceedings of the British Academy* 105 (1999), pp. 131–70, and Blair Worden, *Roundhead Reputations: The English Civil Wars and the Passions of Posterity* (London, 2001), pp. 264–95.

22 John Robertson, 'Hugh Trevor-Roper, Intellectual History, and "The Religious Origins of the Enlightenment"', *English Historical Review* 124 (2009), pp. 1389–421; republished in Chapter 5 of this volume.

23 See especially Hugh Lloyd-Jones, 'Nietzsche', in Hugh Lloyd-Jones, *Blood for the Ghosts: Classical Influences in the Nineteenth and Twentieth Centuries* (London, 1982), pp. 165–81. In a letter to Blair Worden, Trevor-Roper wrote: 'I regard Nietzsche as among the greater German writers since Goethe.' Burckhardt, of course, was born Swiss – as Nietzsche became.

24 See the title essay in *Religion, the Reformation and Social Change*, pp. 1–42. For an acute discussion of the relationship between economic and intellectual history in Trevor-Roper's work, see Peter Ghosh, 'Hugh Trevor-Roper and the History of Ideas', *History of European Ideas* 37 (2011), pp. 483–505.

25 SOC.Dacre 9/10/1, fos 16r–17r. Earlier in this passage, he pointed to an unhappy parallel with the thinking of the despised Arnold Toynbee.

26 Hugh Trevor-Roper, *The Last Days of Hitler* (London, 1947), pp. 87–8, 205–15.

27 Hugh Trevor-Roper, 'The Historical Philosophy of Thomas Carlyle', in *History and the Enlightenment*, pp. 223–45, quotation at p. 242.

28 Hugh Trevor-Roper, 'The Scottish Enlightenment', in *History and the Enlightenment*, pp. 17–33; John Robertson, *The Case for the Enlightenment: Scotland and Naples 1680–1760* (Cambridge, 2005), pp. 24–6.

29 Hugh Trevor-Roper, 'The European Witch-Craze of the Sixteenth and Seventeenth Centuries', in *Religion, the Reformation and Social Change*, pp. 83–177, at pp. 96–7.

30 'The Historical Philosophy of Thomas Carlyle', p. 245.

31 Hugh Trevor-Roper, 'Lord Macaulay: *The History of England*', in *History and the Enlightenment*, pp. 192–222.

32 Hugh Trevor-Roper, 'The Religious Origins of the Enlightenment', in *Religion, the Reformation and Social Change*, pp. 179–80.

33 'The European Witch-Craze', pp. 100–5, 117–18.

34 Hugh Trevor-Roper, 'The Philby Affair', *Encounter*, April 1968, pp. 3–26.

35 Cited in Hugh Trevor-Roper, 'Laudianism and Political Power', in *Catholics, Anglicans and Puritans*, pp. 40–119, at p. 72.

36 Hugh Trevor-Roper, *Princes and Artists: Patronage and Ideology at Four Habsburg Courts, 1517–1633* (London, 1976), p. 10.

37 Isaiah Berlin, 'The Counter-Enlightenment', in *Against the Currents*, pp. 1–24; 'The Apotheosis of the Romantic Will: The Revolt Against the Myth of an Ideal World', in *The Crooked Timber of Humanity: Chapters in the History of Ideas* (London, 1990), pp. 207–37; 'The Romantic Revolution: A Crisis in the History of Modern Thought', in *The Sense of Reality: Studies in Ideas and their History* (London, 1996), pp. 168–93; *The Roots of Romanticism* (London, 1990); *Three Critics of the Enlightenment: Vico, Hamann, Herder* (London, 2000).

38 Ernst Cassirer, *The Philosophy of the Enlightenment*, trans. Fritz C.A. Koelln and James P. Pettegrove (Princeton, NJ, 1951).

39 I. Berlin, 'Joseph de Maistre and the Origins of Fascism', in *The Crooked Timber of Humanity*, pp. 91–174.

40 Herbert Butterfield, *Christianity and History* (London, 1949).

41 *Letters from Oxford: Hugh Trevor-Roper to Bernard Berenson*, ed. Richard Davenport-Hines (London, 2006), pp. 35–6.

42 SOC.Dacre 4/9/1, fo. 1r.

43 *One Hundred Letters*, p. 298.

44 For a positive appraisal, see Michael Bentley, *Herbert Butterfield: History, Science and God* (Cambridge, 2011).

45 Herbert Butterfield, *Man On his Past: The Study of the History of Historical Scholarship* (Cambridge, 1955).

46 Republished as 'Meinecke and Historicism' in Isaiah Berlin, *The Power of Ideas*, ed. Henry Hardy (London, 2000), pp. 205–13.

47 Trevor-Roper, 'Jacob Burckhardt', p. 265. For criticism of this interpretation of Meinecke, see Lionel Gossman, *Basel in the Age of Burckhardt* (Chicago, 2000), pp. 439–53.

48 See Rosemary Ashton, *The German Idea: Four English Writers and the Reception of German Thought, 1800–1860* (Cambridge, 1980), pp. 67–104.

49 *One Hundred Letters*, pp. 351–2.

11. The Classicist

1 This chapter is based on my essay 'The Classicism of Hugh Trevor-Roper', *Cambridge Classical Journal* (2015). Full acknowledgements are given there. Here I should like to thank Cambridge University Press for permission to reprint a shortened version of the essay.

2 SOC.Dacre 6/34/2 'Memoirs chs 1–7', '[Ch.] 5 Charterhouse', p. λ.

3 C. Stray, *Classics Transformed: Schools, Universities, and Society in England, 1830–1960* (Oxford, 1998), p. 282.

4 Blair Worden, 'Hugh Redwald Trevor-Roper (1914–2003)', *Proceedings of the British Academy: Biographical Memoirs of Fellows*, VI (Oxford, 2008), pp. 247–84, at p. 249.

5 'Apologia Transfugae' was first published in the *Spectator* in July 1973 (see below), and in *Didaskalos* 4 (1974), pp. 392–412 (subsequent references are to the latter version). The typescript is at SOC.Dacre 2/1/36.

6 Peter Ghosh, 'Hugh Trevor-Roper and the History of Ideas', *History of European Ideas* 37 (2011), pp. 483–505, at p. 502. Ghosh, it should be said, was reacting against an emphasis on a transition in Trevor-Roper's thinking in a still later period, the 1960s (p. 489). Ghosh uses the term 'classicism' of Trevor-Roper at p. 494, n. 133. He chastises Sisman for ignoring Trevor-Roper's classicism but largely ignores it himself (cf. p. 504).

7 Stray, *Classics Transformed*, pp. 180, 183–7, 200, 231, 259–60.

8 SOC.Dacre 6/34/2: 'Memoirs chs 1–7', quotation: '[Ch.] 3 Glanton to Alnwick/ Stancliffe', p. G; mother's lack of knowledge: '[Ch.] 4 Belhaven Hill', p. ζ.

9 Adam Sisman, *Hugh Trevor-Roper: The Biography* (London, 2010), p. 13.

10 SOC.Dacre 6/34/2: 'Memoirs chs 1–7', '[Ch.] 4 Belhaven Hill', p. γ.

11 Sisman, *Hugh Trevor-Roper*, p. 15.

12 Ibid., p. 13.

13 Ibid., p. 15.

14 SOC.Dacre 6/34/2: 'Memoirs chs 1–7', '[Ch.] 6 Christ Church', p. 9.

15 SOC.Dacre 6/34/2: 'Memoirs chs 1–7', '[Ch.] 5 Charterhouse', pp. μ–ν.

16 He described the moment at 'Apologia', p. 402.

17 Hugh Trevor-Roper, *The Wartime Journals*, ed. R. Davenport-Hines (London, 2012), p. 40, where the book and scene of the *Odyssey* are specified.

18 Ibid.

19 'Apologia', p. 402.

20 See further below.

21 On Irvine see R.B. Todd, *The Dictionary of British Classicists* (Bristol, 2004), vol. 2, pp. 498–9.

22 SOC.Dacre 6/34/2: 'Memoirs chs 1–7', '[Ch.] 5 Charterhouse', pp. ν–ο; *Wartime Journals*, p. 30.

23 *Wartime Journals*, p. 40.

24 SOC.Dacre 6/34/2: 'Memoirs chs 1–7', '[Ch.] 6 Christ Church', p. 10.

25 'Apologia', p. 393.

26 Ibid., p. 394.

27 Ibid., pp. 397–8.

28 Ibid., p. 398.

29 Ibid., p. 399.

30 Ibid., p. 400, a revision of the original version, which is in SOC.Dacre 2/1/36: 'Apologia' typescript, p. 9, which has: 'out of the haze there emerge two hostile, glowering faces: first, the grim, Prussian visage of Ulrich v. Wilamowitz-Moellendorf; then, behind him, *longo intervallo*, the sour, crabbed figure of A. E. Housman.' On Wilamowitz see W.W. Briggs and W.M. Calder (eds), *Classical Scholarship: A Biographical Encyclopedia* (New York and London, 1990), pp. 489–522. On Housman see ibid., pp. 192–204; Todd, *Dictionary of British Classicists*, vol. 2, pp. 477–80; D. Butterfield and C. Stray (eds), *A.E. Housman: Classical Scholar* (London, 2009).

31 'Apologia', p. 401.

32 In Killcanon Building, room 1. On Fraenkel see Briggs and Calder (1990), pp. 61–7; Todd, *Dictionary of British Classicists*, vol. 1, pp. 334–7; C. Stray, 'Eduard Fraenkel: An Exploration', *Syllecta Classica* 25 (2015), pp. 33–73.

33 'Apologia', p. 406.

34 Ibid., p. 409.

35 Ibid.

36 'The World of Odysseus can still be read for profit and for the reliable understanding of the "world" of the best two poems in the world's literature', S. Hornblower, 'Introduction', in M.I. Finley, *The World of Odysseus*, Folio Society edn (London, 2002), pp. xx–xxii (quotation at p. xxii).

37 'Apologia', p. 410. The declaration ascribed to Fraenkel is itself a variation on the claim of Housman that 'Überlieferungsgeschichte', the study of the transmission of texts, is a 'longer and nobler name than fudge': see A.E. Housman, *M. Annaei Lucani belli ciuilis libri decem* (Oxford, 1926), p. xiii.

38 Willson's cartoon is reprinted here by permission of the British Cartoon Archive at the University of Kent. I am grateful to Mark Bryant for his help in tracing the copyright of Willson's work.

39 J. Gretton, 'Classics Teachers "Fighting for our Lives"', *Times Educational Supplement,* 25 May 1973, p. 8.

40 'Apologia', pp. 410–12.

41 H. Lloyd-Jones, 'The Classics in Britain Today', in H. Lloyd-Jones, *Classical Survivals: The Classics in the Modern World* (London, 1982), pp. 52–5.

42 SOC.Dacre 1/2/21: Hugh Lloyd-Jones to Hugh Trevor-Roper, 4 June 1973.

43 M. Finley and K. Hopkins, 'Keith Hopkins Interviews Sir Moses Finley: October 1985 Transcript', *American Journal of Philology* 135 (2014), pp. 179–201, at pp. 179–81.

44 SOC.Dacre 2/1/36: Hugh Lloyd-Jones to Hugh Trevor-Roper, 4 June 1973.

45 N.G. Wilson, 'Peter Hugh Jefferd Lloyd-Jones (1922–2009)', *Proceedings of the British Academy* 172 (2011), pp. 215–29, at p. 220.
46 C.R. Whittaker, 'Moses Finley 1912–1986', *Proceedings of the British Academy* 94 (1997), pp. 459–72, at p. 460.
47 Ibid., pp. 462–4.
48 See M.I. Finley, 'Unfreezing the Classics', *Times Literary Supplement*, 7 April 1966, pp. 289–90. Cf. Whittaker, 'Moses Finley', pp. 466–7; Finley and Hopkins, 'Keith Hopkins Interviews Sir Moses Finley', p. 180.
49 'Apologia', p. 409. For Finley's status as an outsider cf. Finley and Hopkins, 'Keith Hopkins Interviews Sir Moses Finley', pp. 179–80. On Trevor-Roper's 'unorthodox intellectual formation' see Ghosh, 'Hugh Trevor-Roper', p. 485.
50 Cf. Whittaker, 'Moses Finley', p. 471.
51 See e.g. Finley, 'Unfreezing the Classics', p. 290; Hornblower, 'Introduction', p. xvi; F.S. Naiden and R. Talbert, 'Introduction', *American Journal of Philology* 135 (Special Issue: 'Moses Finley in America: The Making of an Ancient Historian') (2014), pp. 167–78, at pp. 172–3.
52 SOC.Dacre 2/1/36: 'Apologia' typescript, p. 20; 'Apologia', p. 409. In the published version Trevor-Roper opted for the more neutral 'more recently there is [...]'.
53 See *One Hundred Letters from Hugh Trevor-Roper*, ed. Richard Davenport-Hines and Adam Sisman (Oxford, 2014), p. 52, Trevor-Roper to Isaiah Berlin, 18 February 1955. For Finley's method see Hornblower, 'Introduction', pp. xvi–xx.
54 H. Trevor-Roper, 'The World of Homer', *New Statesman*, 14 July 1956, pp. 45–6, republished in *Historical Essays* (London, 1957), pp. 6–11.
55 *Historical Essays*, p. vi.
56 *Letters from Oxford*, pp. 98–9, Hugh Trevor-Roper to Bernard Berenson, 10 June 1956.
57 Whittaker, 'Moses Finley', p. 464; Hornblower, 'Introduction', pp. xi–xii, at p. xii.
58 Having once sympathised with its materialist explanation: Worden, 'Hugh Redwald Trevor-Roper', p. 247; Ghosh, 'Hugh Trevor-Roper', p. 492.
59 See *One Hundred Letters*, pp. 51–2, Hugh Trevor-Roper to Isaiah Berlin, 18 February 1955.
60 SOC.Dacre 2/1/36: Hugh Lloyd-Jones to Hugh Trevor-Roper, 4 June 1973.
61 SOC.Dacre 2/1/36: Hugh Trevor-Roper to Hugh Lloyd-Jones, 7 June 1973.
62 SOC.Dacre 2/1/36: Hugh Lloyd-Jones to Hugh Trevor-Roper, 4 June 1973.
63 Ibid.
64 'Apologia' typescript, pp. 19–20. For the expression 'piffle before the wind' cf. Daisy Ashford, *The Young Visiters* (London, 1919), ch. 5: 'Oh I see said the earl but my own idear [*sic*] is that these things are as piffle before the wind.'
65 SOC.Dacre 2/1/36: Hugh Lloyd-Jones to Hugh Trevor-Roper, 4 June 1973.
66 See above, n. 30.
67 SOC.Dacre 2/1/36: Hugh Trevor-Roper to Hugh Lloyd-Jones, 7 June 1973.

68 'Apologia' typescript, pp. 19–20; 'Apologia', p. 406 (see also pp. 399, 400).

69 'Apologia', p. 399.

70 Sisman, *Hugh Trevor-Roper*, p. 36.

71 H. Trevor-Roper, 'Homer Unmasked!', *Oxford Magazine*, 30 April 1936, pp. 514–17.

72 Ibid., p. 517.

73 S. Butler, *The Authoress of the Odyssey* (Bristol, 2003; first published 1897), pp. 8, 105–6; Trapani: pp. 162, 200; Nausicca: pp. 206–7.

74 R. Davenport-Hines in *Wartime Journals*, pp. 1–2, 11.

75 Ibid., p. 11.

76 See the four wartime notebooks at SOC.Dacre 13/29/1–4. The Homeric title does not occur in the edition of Davenport-Hines.

77 'Apologia', p. 396.

78 *Wartime Journals*, p. 121.

79 E.g. ibid., pp. 155, 284.

80 Ibid., pp. 100–1.

81 For Smith see *Wartime Journals*, pp. 280–1; Worden, 'Hugh Redwald Trevor-Roper', pp. 254–5. Among English-language models, Trevor-Roper was inspired by Gibbon, not least in his ornamentation, but in the smoothness of his prose he resembles Macaulay most. Both of course were classical stylists.

82 Favourite: see notebook SOC.Dacre 13/29/3 (not in *Wartime Journals*); baroque: *Wartime Journals*, pp. 62, 115, 119; sterility: ibid., p. 191.

83 Ibid., p. 289. The Bodleian oration is preserved at SOC.Dacre 2/1/37. An ink inscription in Trevor-Roper's hand calls it 'The "Apuleian oration"'. Some of the adverbs occur only in Apuleius.

84 *Wartime Journals*, p. 61; SOC.Dacre 1/3/18: Trevor-Roper to Logan Pearsall Smith, 21 October 1944. In the wartime notebook he urged use of 'meticulum, obsequium, fastidium, supercilium, bogum, impecunium'; the later letter added ridiculum.

85 *Wartime Journals*, p. 189; cf. p. 91, deliquescence.

86 Note, in both descriptions, Trevor-Roper's characterisation of literary style in visual and pastoral terms. For other Latinate vocabulary in the *Wartime Journals* see e.g. 'servitor' (p. 74); 'percolating up steep, winding lanes, and over the moors' (p. 215).

87 *Wartime Journals*, p. 54.

88 Ibid., p. 212; cf. p. 54.

89 Cf. too ibid., p. 132.

90 Ibid., p. 213.

91 Ibid., p. 218; cf. pp. 150–3. For this project see also Worden, 'Hugh Redwald Trevor-Roper', pp. 255–6; Ghosh, 'Hugh Trevor-Roper', p. 485.

92 In a letter asking J.H. Elliott to read an unfinished draft of the book, Trevor-Roper exclaimed, 'I cannot find a satisfactory form or ending for it': SOC.Dacre 1/3/144, February 1961. See also *Letters from Oxford*, pp. 249–50, 262–3; Worden, 'Hugh Redwald Trevor-Roper', pp. 263–7.

93 H. Trevor-Roper, *History: Professional and Lay* (Oxford, 1957), p. 14, reprinted in H. Lloyd-Jones, V. Pearl and B. Worden (eds), *History and Imagination: Essays in Honour of H.R. Trevor-Roper* (London, 1981), p. 8.

94 *History: Professional and Lay*, p. 15, in Lloyd-Jones et al., *History and Imagination*, pp. 8–9.

95 H. Lloyd-Jones, 'Eduard Fraenkel', in *Blood for the Ghosts*, p. 255. See also *Letters from Oxford*, p. 246.

96 *History: Professional and Lay*, p. 15, in Lloyd-Jones et al., *History and Imagination*, p. 9.

97 *The World of Odysseus* was published as a Pelican book in 1962. Other works by Finley followed suit: e.g. *Aspects of Antiquity*; *The Ancient Greeks*; *Ancient Slavery and Modern Ideology*.

98 SOC.Dacre 13/29: notebook entitled '1963' that commences 'Xmas Vacation 1962–3', 'Resolutions', p. 3. For this notebook cf. Robertson, 'Hugh Trevor-Roper', pp. 1402–3; Robertson in Trevor-Roper, *History and the Enlightenment*, p. x; Ghosh, 'Hugh Trevor-Roper', p. 489, n. 78.

99 Worden, 'Hugh Redwald Trevor-Roper', p. 249.

100 SOC.Dacre 2/1/63: M.M. Willcock to Trevor-Roper, 19 April 1989.

101 H. Trevor-Roper, 'Why Virgil?', *Proceedings of the Virgil Society* 20 (1991), pp. 60–75, at p. 66.

102 Ibid., p. 74.

12. The Historian as Public Intellectual

1 I am indebted to Blair Worden, Trevor-Roper's literary executor, for permission to consult and use the Dacre Papers; to Judith Curthoys, archivist at Christ Church, for her assistance in locating documents; to Jane Garnett, Felix Hale, Richard Davenport-Hines and, above all, Blair Worden and Brian Young for their invaluable comments on drafts.

2 Hugh Lloyd-Jones, 'Foreword', in Hugh Lloyd-Jones, Valerie Pearl and Blair Worden (eds), *History and Imagination: Essays in Honour of H.R. Trevor-Roper* (London, 1981).

3 SOC.Dacre 2/13/8: 'Gibbon + Macaulay' [1972], 'Gibbon I'.

4 Lloyd-Jones et al., *History and Imagination*, pp. 362–3.

5 'If these essays are united by any such philosophy, the reader will discover it.' Hugh Trevor-Roper, *Historical Essays* (London, 1957), p. vi.

6 SOC.Dacre 6/34: memoir in three chapters (untitled), c. 2. [unpaginated].

7 SOC.Dacre 1/1/11: letter to Peter Miller, 18 March 1999.

8 British Library, Macmillan Archive: letter to John Field, 16 May 1939.

9 Peter Ghosh, 'Hugh Trevor-Roper and the History of Ideas', *History of European Ideas* 37 (2011), p. 485.

10 Lloyd-Jones et al., *History and Imagination*, p. 358.

11 Quoted in Adam Sisman, *Hugh Trevor-Roper: The Biography* (London, 2010), p. 72.
12 Lloyd-Jones et al., *History and Imagination*, p. 359.
13 See, for example, 'Karl Marx and the Study of History' in *Historical Essays*, pp. 285–98.
14 S. Hastings, *Evelyn Waugh* (London, 1995), p. 227.
15 SOC.Dacre 13/29: wartime notebooks, I, pp. 15–16. Whilst Trevor-Roper dates this realisation to 'the summer of 1936' in this notebook of 1940–1, his diary of 1937 suggests that his memory is at fault, and that this epiphany took place a year later. SOC.Dacre 13/29.
16 SOC.Dacre 13/29: Diary of 1937, 8 December.
17 *Historical Essays*, pp. 16–17.
18 SOC.Dacre 6/34: memoir in seven chapters [unpaginated].
19 Sisman, *Hugh Trevor-Roper*, pp. 40–2.
20 SOC.Dacre 6/34: memoir in seven chapters [unpaginated].
21 'Desiderius Erasmus', in *Historical Essays*, p. 52.
22 Sisman, *Hugh Trevor-Roper*, p. 200. In August 1948, the Soviets organised the World Congress of Intellectuals in Defence of Peace in Wroclaw to denounce 'American Imperialism'. The 1950 Congress for Cultural Freedom was later revealed by the *New York Times* to have been part-funded by the CIA.
23 SOC.Dacre 1/1/11: letter to Peter Miller, 18 March 1999.
24 SOC.Dacre 13/29/1: notebook 1940–2, Πτερεντα, p. 16.
25 J. Robertson, 'Introduction', in Hugh Trevor-Roper, *History and the Enlightenment*, ed. John Robertson (London, 2010), p. vii.
26 SOC.Dacre 2/13/8: 'Gibbon + Macaulay' [1972], 'Gibbon III'.
27 SOC.Dacre 13/29/203: 'Autopsy'.
28 'Apologia Transfugae', *Spectator*, 14 July 1973, p. 45.
29 Lloyd-Jones et al., *History and Imagination*, p. 8.
30 Hugh Trevor-Roper, *The Wartime Journals*, ed. R. Davenport-Hines (London, 2012), p. 113.
31 Quoted in Blair Worden, 'Hugh Redwald Trevor-Roper, 1914–2003', *Proceedings of the British Academy: Biographical Memoirs of Fellows,* VI (Oxford, 2008), pp. 247–84, at p. 278.
32 *History and the Enlightenment*, p. 7.
33 Hugh Trevor-Roper, 'The Romantic Movement and the Study of History', in *History and the Enlightenment*, pp. 176–91.
34 See 'Karl Marx and the Study of History', in *Historical Essays*, pp. 285–98, for a typical example of a work where the argumentative flow is propelled by rhetorical questions.
35 Lloyd-Jones et al., *History and Imagination*, p. 369.
36 *One Hundred Letters from Hugh Trevor-Roper*, ed. Richard Davenport-Hines and Adam Sisman (Oxford, 2014), pp. 61–2, letter to Sir John Masterman, 13 December 1956.
37 SOC.Dacre 2/13/8: 'Gibbon + Macaulay' [1972], 'Gibbon I'.

38 *Historical Essays*, pp. 35–60.

39 Hugh Trevor-Roper, *From Counter-Reformation to Glorious Revolution* (London, 1992), p. 114.

40 SOC.Dacre 2/13/8: 'Gibbon + Macaulay' [1972], 'Gibbon II'.

41 *Historical Essays*, p.vi.

42 J. Robertson, 'Hugh Trevor-Roper, Intellectual History and the "Religious Origins of the Enlightenment"', *English Historical Review* 124 (2009), pp. 1389–421; republished as Chapter 5 of this volume.

43 Lloyd-Jones et al., *History and Imagination*, p. 368.

44 *Historical Essays*, p. vi.

45 C.R. Sanders and K.J. Fielding (eds), *The Collected Letters of Thomas and Jane Welsh Carlyle* (Durham, NC, 1970), vol. 2, p. 314, T. Carlyle to Jane Baillie Welsh, 26 March 1832.

46 Lloyd-Jones et al., *History and Imagination*, p. 2.

47 *Letters from Oxford*, p. 23, letter to Bernard Berenson, 18 September 1948.

48 Hugh Trevor-Roper, 'The Scottish Enlightenment', *Blackwood's Magazine*, November 1977; Sisman, *Hugh Trevor-Roper*, p. 442.

49 V. Mehta, 'Onward and Upward with the Arts: The Flight of Crook-Taloned Birds (I)', *New Yorker*, 8 December 1962.

50 Hugh Trevor-Roper, 'The Past and the Present: History and Sociology', *Past and Present* 42 (1969), pp. 3–17.

51 SOC.Dacre 2/13/8: 'Gibbon + Macaulay' [1972], 'Gibbon III'.

52 'Clarendon the Great', *Sunday Times*, 13 March 1955.

53 Lloyd-Jones et al., *History and Imagination*, p. 8.

54 Hugh Trevor-Roper, *Desert Island Discs*, BBC Radio 4, 21 August 1988.

55 A typical example may be found in *Letters from Oxford: Hugh Trevor-Roper to Bernard Berenson*, ed. Richard Davenport-Hines (London, 2006), p. 9.

56 SOC.Dacre 6/34: memoir in seven chapters (untitled).

57 *New Statesman*, 14 May 1955, reprinted in *Historical Essays*, pp. 173–8.

58 N. Annan, *Our Age* (London, 1990), p. 509. Isaiah Berlin argues that this 'golden age' had in fact started during the war: 'This has been very much a don's war,' and the methodical efficiency of Oxbridge dons in official wartime service destroyed their 'reputation for starry-eyed incompetence once and for all'. The experience of the war had instilled in many the notion of using their minds for the good of the nation. I. Berlin, *Flourishing: Letters 1928–1946* (London, 2004), p. 502.

59 *New Yorker*, 8 December 1962. Despite the attention it brought him, Trevor-Roper felt he had been made 'the villain of the piece' by Mehta: as he privately recorded 'From the start he was aggressive […] He accused my room – it was my room in the Faculty Library – of being drab and grey, as if that was an indication of my character. I disliked that, and wondered what sense he relied on, if he were really, as he said, "totally blind".' SOC.Dacre 13/29: notebook, 1963.

60 BBC Written Archives, TV Art 3: memorandum from D. Baverstock to C.P.Tel (S. Hood), 16 May 1963.

61 Hugh Trevor-Roper, 'The Stages of Progress', *Listener*, 28 November 1963; 'The End of Antiquity', *Listener*, 4 December 1963; 'The Dark Ages', *Listener*, 11 December 1963; 'The Crusades', *Listener*, 18 December 1963; 'The Medieval Renaissance', *Listener*, 25 December 1963; 'Europe Turns West', *Listener*, January 1964; Hugh Trevor-Roper, *The Rise of Christian Europe* (London, 1965).

62 Hugh Trevor-Roper, 'Three Historians: I – The Earl of Clarendon', *Listener*, 30 September 1965; 'II – David Hume', *Listener*, 7 October 1965; 'III – Lord Macaulay', *Listener*, 14 October 1965.

63 Sisman, *Hugh Trevor-Roper*, p. 295.

64 Ibid., pp. 210–11, 371.

65 For an example of his foreign political reporting see his 'Revolution on a Switchback – Modern Mexico in the Making', *Sunday Times*, 24 June 1958. From Jerusalem he wrote a trio of articles for the *Sunday Times* on the Eichmann Trial: 'Behind the Eichmann Trial', 9 April 1961; 'The Nuremburg of the Jewish People', 16 April 1961; 'What the Eichmann Trial Means to World Jewry', 23 April 1961.

66 Worden, 'Hugh Redwald Trevor-Roper', p. 279.

67 G.M. Trevelyan, 'Clio: A Muse', in *Clio: A Muse* (London, 1931), p. 152. Just as Trevelyan judges of professional historians that 'there is no "flow" in their events, which stand like ponds instead of running like streams', so Trevor-Roper argues that 'it is the essence of humane studies, since their central object is the study of man, that they all flow down towards the centre, even though the professionals in each of them have a natural tendency to move upstream in search of distant sources and sometimes get lost on the way.' *Clio: A Muse*, pp. 148–9; Lloyd-Jones et al., *History and Imagination*, p. 12.

68 B. McFarlane, 'Turning-Points', *New Statesman*, 18 February 1966.

69 *Historical Essays*, p. v.

70 Hugh Trevor-Roper, *Renaissance Essays* (London, 1985), pp. vi–viii; *From Counter-Reformation to Glorious Revolution*, pp. vii–viii.

71 *Listener*, 18 January 1983.

72 SOC.Dacre 2/13/8: 'Gibbon + Macaulay' [1972], 'Gibbon II'.

73 Lloyd-Jones et al., *History and Imagination*, p. 11.

74 Ibid.

75 Ghosh, 'Hugh Trevor-Roper and the History of Ideas', p. 484.

76 Ibid., p. 495.

77 Hugh Trevor-Roper, 'Preface to the Seventh Edition' (1955) in Hugh Trevor-Roper, *The Last Days of Hitler* 7th edn (London, 2012), p. xvi.

78 Sisman, *Hugh Trevor-Roper*, p. 155.

79 A.J.P. Taylor, 'The Bunker Revisited', *New Statesman*, 8 July 1950.

80 Quoted in S. Collini, *Absent Minds: Intellectuals in Britain* (Oxford, 2006), p. 377.

81 K. Burk, *Troublemaker: The Life and History of A.J.P. Taylor* (London, 2000), p. 206.

82 Quoted in Collini, *Absent Minds*, p. 379.

83 A.J.P. Taylor, *A Personal History* (London, 1983), p. 205.

13. The Prose Stylist

1 *One Hundred Letters from Hugh Trevor-Roper*, ed. Richard Davenport-Hines and Adam Sisman (Oxford, 2014), p. 145.

2 Hugh Trevor-Roper, *The Wartime Journals*, ed. Richard Davenport-Hines (London, 2012), p. 71.

3 *One Hundred Letters*, p. 212.

4 Hugh Trevor-Roper, *Hermit of Peking: The Hidden Life of Sir Edmund Backhouse* (New York, 1977; published in Britain as *A Hidden Life: The Enigma of Sir Edmund Backhouse*), p. 7.

5 *One Hundred Letters*, pp. 308, 311.

6 *Wartime Journals*, p. 203.

7 *One Hundred Letters*, pp. 21–2.

8 Ibid., p. 22.

9 *Wartime Journals*, p. 62.

10 Ibid., p. 96.

11 Ibid., p. 13.

12 Ibid., p. 18.

13 Ibid., p. 281.

14 Ibid., p. 7.

15 Ibid.

16 Ibid., p. 205.

17 Ibid., p. 203.

18 Ibid., p. 74.

19 Ibid.

20 Ibid., p. 58.

21 Ibid., p. 57.

22 Ibid., p. 190.

23 Ibid., p. 191.

24 Ibid., p. 31.

25 Ibid., p. 150.

26 Ibid., p. 153.

27 Ibid., p. 53.

28 Ibid., p. 51.

29 *One Hundred Letters*, p. 79.

Index

Abbot, George, Archbishop of Canterbury 35–6, 106–7, 108, 109–10
Aberdeen Doctors 159
Abyssinian War (1935–36) 236
Acontius, Jacobus 119, 122, 125, 126, 133, 134; *Stratagematum Satanae* 126
Act of Union (1707) 118, 146, 149, 159, 160–1, 228
Acton, John Dalberg-Acton, 1st Baron 30, 36, 258
adverbs, capacities of 3, 251
Aeschylus 242, 252
African history 17
All Souls College, Oxford 256
Allan, Rory ix, 30, 255–67
Allied Counter-Intelligence War Room 168–70, 192, 193, 197, 201
Amiel, Barbara (*later* Baroness Black of Crossharbour) 209
Amsterdam: Arminianism in 139; Calvinism in 133
Amstutz and Herdeg (publishers) 189–90
Andrewes, Lancelot, Bishop of Winchester 106, 110
Anjou, François, Duke of 133
Annales school 9, 48, 232, 277
Annan, Noël, Baron 92, 264
anticlericalism 57, 116, 152, 257–8
anti-Semitism 215, 233
'Apologia Transfugae' (lecture/essay) 240, 242, 243–9, 252–3
appeasement 21
Apuleius 250–1
arbitristas 49
Archbishop Laud xiii, 26–7, 67, 116, 117, 127, 131, 228, 271, 302n35; research for and influences on 2, 56–9, 122, 125, 259, 272
Aristophanes 35
Arminians and Arminianism 20, 74, 83; and ecumenism 106–7, 109–10, 113; Erasmian origins 119, 122, 125, 126, 127–8, 141–2; and origins of Enlightenment 118–19, 121, 131, 143, 150, 229; and Scottish Enlightenment 151

Arminius, Jacob 118
Armytage, W.H.G. (Harry) 87, 95
art history 12–13, 133, 140, 234, 282n65
Aston, Margaret 103, 297n5, 298n5–6
Aston, Trevor (ed.), *Crisis in Europe* 45
Atlantic Monthly 214, 321n1
Attlee, Clement, 1st Earl, reads *The Last Days of Hitler* 188
Aubrey, John 54
Augustine, St 7, 55, 250–1; *Confessions* 251
Augustus, Roman Emperor 24
Auld Licht movement 157
Ausonius 251
Austen, Jane 276
Axmann, Artur 175
Ayer, Sir Alfred Jules (Freddie) 227, 258, 264; *Language, Truth and Logic* 57

Backhouse, Sir Edmund 18, 136, 217, 269; see also *Hidden Life, A*
Bacon, Francis, Viscount St Alban 121, 136, 268; Baconianism 74, 91, 93, 94, 96, 136
Bad Oeynhausen 168, 193
Balfour, Michael 189
ballad literature 3, 12
Balliol College, Oxford 35, 109, 289n24
Banville, John ix, 2, 268–74
Barbeyrac, Jean 118
Barnard, Toby 103, 104
Bartlett, Robert, *The Natural and the Supernatural in the Middle Ages* 102
Bassett, Bernard 188
Bataillon, Marcel 133; *Érasme et l'Espagne* 125, 126, 127, 128, 138, 140, 278, 303n37
Bauer, Hans 201, 205
Baxter, Richard 135
Bayle, Pierre 229
Baynes, Norman H., *A Short List of Books on National Socialism* 181
Beattie, James 156–7
Beckett, J.C. (Jim) 298n7
Bedford, William Russell, 5th Earl of 72–3, 79, 84, 291n93
Belhaven Hill (school), Dunbar 32, 241–2